Hope for Justice and Power

Broad-based Community Organizing in the Texas Industrial Areas Foundation

Kathleen Staudt

University of North Texas Press
Denton, Texas

Printed in the United States of America.

10 9 8 7 6 5 4 3 2 1

Permissions:
University of North Texas Press
1155 Union Circle #311336
Denton, TX 76203-5017

The paper used in this book meets the minimum requirements
of the American National Standard for Permanence of Paper
for Printed Library Materials, z39.48.1984. Binding materials
have been chosen for durability.

Library of Congress Cataloging-in-Publication Data

Hope for justice and power : broad-based community organizing in the
Texas Industrial Areas Foundation / Kathleen Staudt.
    First edition.
    p. cm.
  Includes bibliographical references and index.
  ISBN 978-1-57441-794-4 (cloth)
  ISBN 978-1-57441-805-7 (ebook)
1. Industrial Areas Foundation—Case studies. 2. Community
organization—Texas—Case studies. 3. Political participation—Texas—
Case studies. 4. Social justice—Texas—Case studies. 5. Community
and school—Texas—Case studies. 6. Community and college—
Texas—Case studies. 7. Texas—Social conditions—20th century.
  HN79.T4 S83 2020
  306.209764—dc23

                        2019047769

The electronic edition of this book was made possible by the support
of the Vick Family Foundation. Typeset by vPrompt eServices.

Dedicated To

Grassroots organizers and leaders
in the IAF affiliates

and

Sr. Christine Stephens: July 18, 2018 (RIP)

"As an organizer and mentor, Stephens
was tough but reasonable. In negotiations,
she was politically astute and open to
compromise, but never surrender."
—John MacCormack,
San Antonio Express-News
July 25, 2019

Contents

Acknowledgments

Than book is a labor of love shared with a wide variety of audiences. These audiences include those with an interest:

- in learning what might be called civic education in Texas: a painless way to gain insights about our major institutions and public policies in the state; how those institutions and policies vary by region, era, and place; and strategies for change via community organizing;
- in acquiring practical skills and concepts—organizing tools—about what has been called "public work" in the oldest and most successful social justice model—the Industrial Areas Foundation (IAF) along with its varying practices in different regions of Texas, from the borderlands to cities;
- in acquiring in-depth knowledge about education, from elementary to secondary, post-secondary, and higher education: a fragmented and complex system with many stakeholders;
- in insisting that attention to educational politics and policies be included in analyses of Texas local and state politics;
- in also insisting that there is more to Texas politics than its three branches of government; and
- in forging common ground, with civility, in politics without shrill, polarizing, and partisan language among diverse Texans, especially Mexican Americans.

Perhaps I can also build some consensus around identities beyond the tired labels of liberal and conservative. As someone who has long studied and taught international politics, the word "liberal" in its classical sense, outside the US in the other 95 percent of the world's population, has clear meanings: limited government in market economies (rather than proactive government, as used in the US). Adding to the confusion is the global economy, its "neoliberal" label worldwide, and critics of neoliberalism who draw from all parts of a left-right ideological spectrum. To be sure, trade is good, but it requires accountability to employees and citizens.

I want to give thanks to many people for the long-term preparation that went into this book, including a wide variety of people: teachers, colleagues, friends, and students. To Industrial Areas Foundation (IAF) leaders, organizers, and supporters in the borderlands, too many to name, I especially want to extend thanks to Adriana García, Eddie

Chew, Dolores and Eloiso de Avila, Alicia Franco, Kevin Courtney, Rev. John Nelsen, and Fr. Pablo Matta. If I earn any royalties from this book, they will go to the local IAF affiliate in El Paso, EPISO/Border Interfaith. And to Sr. Maribeth Larkin, whose wisdom sometimes feels inspired, thank you for strengthening El Paso over several decades in ways that respect borderlands culture. El Paso surely could use more organized civic capacity. I also thank IAF organizers and leaders in other parts of Texas who gave me quality time in lengthy interviews, among them organizers Josephine López-Paul, Emilee Bounds, and Doug Greco. It was heartening to speak with volunteer leaders and paid organizers to realize how many former teachers and persons of faith invest enormous quantities of valuable time into work with and for their communities. As Organizer Greco said in an interview (Chapter 5), work in schools gives us a lens through which to see the world. The University of Texas at El Paso (UTEP) Library is a gem, with caring librarians and high-technology access to journals and books.

I thank the University of Texas at San Antonio (UTSA) Special Collections at the John Pearce Library whose archives surely contain the best and most comprehensive holdings not only on the San Antonio IAF affiliate, C.O.P.S./Metro Alliance, but also on statewide IAF activity, including the remarkable near-twenty-year experience with serious parental engagement and leadership work to improve students' successes and pathways to higher education. UTSA's IAF collection consists of 145 boxes that include everything from press releases, annual reports, and Texas Education Agency reports to internal memos and sign-in sheets for Get-Out-the-Vote efforts. C.O.P.S./Metro must be applauded for its transparency in sharing material that documents important history on activism. The librarian said the collection is one of the most used, with a scholar from Japan among recent users. At the University of Texas archives, one finds IAF Founder Saul Alinsky's letters from the 1950s and 1960s.

To colleagues and compatriots, I thank Irasema Coronado, Gregory Rocha, Beatriz Vera, Oscar Martínez, Gregorio Casar, Arturo Pacheco, Susana Navarro, Azuri González, Carla Cardoza, Gina Nuñez, José Villalobos, and numerous other professors and local activists, many of whom focus on their teaching and expertise alone or on single-issue community, social justice, and feminist work. Conversations over many years have given me new insights for teaching and learning.

I especially want to thank my now-grown children, Mosi and Asha Dane'el. My days would be incomplete without love and insights to keep me energized.

Over the years, thousands of students have shared insights with me about the U.S.-Mexico borderlands. Among those whose knowledge about the community, the region, and its schools helped me for this book, I thank Drs. Pauline Dow, Lizely Madrigal, Sergio García, Timothy Quezada, Leslie Gonzales, Alicia Parra, and Pilar Herrera along with Leticia Ibarra and Joanne Bogart.

And when I think back to my professors in political science graduate school at the University of Wisconsin, the one who stands out for this book is the late Murray Edelman. His seminar on organizational theory, albeit an off-putting course title, opened my eyes to political institutions, bureaucracies, and political rhetoric. Edelman never put boundaries around the discipline, but encouraged us to think beyond and draw ideas from sociologists and economics. Who could have imagined that Philip Selznick's book *TVA and the Grass Roots* or Anthony Downs, *Inside Bureaucracy*, would forever shape my thinking in the sub-discipline fields of Comparative Politics and Public Administration and Policy, even in my field research for the PhD dissertation in Kenya. I admire the courage of political scientists who dare to teach and write in inter-disciplinary ways, to insist that field research in the real world advances knowledge so much more than the office-bound number crunching. I am a great believer in eclectic and mixed methods that join people-centered field research with validation and data bases when available.

Let me, finally, say a few words on the writing format. In Chapter 1, I outline the IAF lingo and put its language in bold type. I capitalize the words Leader and Organizer before an IAF person's name because the titles have a special meaning in IAF's work. For civic knowledge and those who wish to explore further, I have listed websites and videos at the end of some chapters called "For further reflection."

Finally, the external reviewers for the manuscript provided a thorough and comprehensive set of suggestions. I owe them a great debt for strengthening the content in this book.

Enjoy!

List of Acronyms

AP	Advanced Placement
CCHD	Catholic Campaign for Human Development
CEO	Chief Executive Officer
C.O.P.S.	Communities Organized for Public Service
CREEED	Council on Regional Economic Expansion and Economic Development
DAI	Dallas Area Interfaith
EDAP	Economically Distressed Areas Program
EPCAE	El Paso Collaborative for Academic Excellence
EPISO	El Paso Interreligious Sponsoring Organization
GOTV	Get Out The Vote
ICE	Immigration and Customs Enforcement
ISD	Independent School District
IAF	Industrial Areas Foundation
IEF	Interfaith Education Fund
IRS	Internal Revenue Service
LGBTQ	Lesbian, Gay, Bisexual, Trans, Queer
LULAC	League of United Latin American Citizens
MALDEF	Mexican American Legal Defense and Education Fund
NGO	Non-Governmental Organization
PTA	Parent Teacher Association
SBOE	State Board of Education
TEA	Texas Education Agency
TEKS	Texas Essential Knowledge and Skills
TNO	Texas Network of Organizations
TMO	The Metropolitan Organization
WTOS	West Texas Organizing Strategy

Chapter 1

An Introduction to Hope
for Justice and Power

"Hope is a powerful weapon."

Nelson Mandela[1]

"We can't allow the politics of despair to corrode our spirits."

Ernesto Cortés, Jr[2]

"The electoral process, when not invigorated by a culture of account-ability, often becomes a vehicle for domination, rather than a corrective for it."

Jeffrey Stout, Princeton theology professor[3]

I hope readers share the quest to deepen democracy beyond voting in Texas and U.S. political institutions. Yes, a competitive two- or multi-political party system can be effective for democratic accountability, but strong people's non-government organizations (NGOs) must also operate in between elections to surpass the power of money in a country and state riddled with inequalities, reaching all the way from the national level, embedded in a global economy, into households.

Since my student days and beyond, participating in both social movements and NGOs, I have seen some fruits from those struggles, from growing up in an industrial Midwest city and union family to involvement in civil rights and feminist groups, serving on a dozen nonprofit boards, and petitioning neighbors to oust an overpaid school superintendent who barely worked in my kids' school district. As a professor, I taught political science for forty years, so my life was immersed in public affairs. But my unique experience involved twenty years of participation in broad-based organizing with people of many backgrounds in multiple institutions that work for social justice at local levels, from 1998 onwards.

By organizing for social justice, I mean working with others to build capacity to achieve public goals that go beyond the time-consuming and expensive criminal justice system to address fair wages acquired in an equal-opportunity employment system, accessible and affordable health care, environmental sustainability, infrastructure, and equitable voices

1

in political processes at all levels of governance—that is, twenty-first century progressive ideas and actions.[4] To organize at the grassroots necessarily involves organizing from place-based actions that reflect local people's voices, optimally from a strong base. Among my various compartmentalized community commitments, I have been an unpaid leader for twenty years in the local Industrial Areas Foundation (IAF) affiliates, EPISO (El Paso Interreligious Sponsoring Organization), the largest community organization in the sixth largest city of Texas, along with Border Interfaith, EPISO's newer sister IAF affiliate in this spread-out borderlands with Mexico. Both organizations joined together in late 2018. In those twenty years, I worked with eight different IAF trained and paid organizers, plus met many more at trainings and distant meetings.

Existing books about the IAF, many of them written by IAF senior organizers and directors, do not take us far into the twenty-first century. Some books offer moving analyses, with a focus on their founders, organizers, leaders, and supervisors in the earlier years of IAF organizing. *Cold Anger*, a book by Mary Beth Rogers published in 1990, centered on the early years of IAF in the Southwest, its successful strategies, and particularly the famous Texas IAF founder Ernesto (Ernie) Cortés, Jr., still energetic after forty-five years of organizing. The late Saul Alinsky founded the Industrial Areas Foundation in 1940 and wrote *Reveille for Radicals* (1946) and *Rules for Radicals* (1971); the late Edward Chambers succeeded him as national IAF head for forty-seven years and wrote *Roots for Radicals* in 2003 without a focus on Texas. Amazingly, only a few independent books have been written about the Texas IAF affiliates, the oldest and largest community organizing effort in the state, giving greater coverage to San Antonio, Houston, and South Texas.[5] Here I cover a broad swath of Texas, but especially Dallas, Austin, El Paso, and Lubbock.

Paradoxically, too few mainstream books about Texas politics cover community organizing, processes, and achievements, even in Latino, Latina (Latinx) political studies, or in Texas, Mexican American political studies.[6] In twenty-first-century Texas, Mexican American volunteer leaders comprise the largest group within the IAF grassroots base.[7] Several scholars have documented the importance of organizational pathways to participation, including in voting and electoral politics.[8] Organizations like the IAF offer pathways to multiple forms of participation. Although many Latino politics studies focus on opinion surveys, elections, and officials, in the recent volume, *The Roots of Latino Urban Agency*, Armbruster-Sandoval calls for us to "shift our understanding of

Chicano/Latino politics from one based on a presumed need for *unity* based on ethnic and/or racial homogeneity to one built on the ongoing construction of *solidarity* among diverse people in common causes that resist all forms of subordination."[9] As we see in Chapter 6, using state parlance, "Hispanic" students represent the majority of Texas public school students and thus the future of the Texas political economy.

To understand the twenty-first-century IAF, we must know something about the IAF's eighty-year history and its founder, covered briefly below in the first part of this introductory chapter. Next, we go on to the driving questions for this book, along with some of the sub-questions posed around contradictions between principles (IAF "rules") and practice— contradictions that can produce some tension in local organizing efforts. Following that, I stress the importance of putting people into organizational analysis, particularly bottom-up, everyday perspectives. And finally, I offer definitions of broad-based community organizing in local contexts, followed with IAF language, bolded and discussed with a preview of what is to come in the rest of the book.

Saul Alinsky, founder of twentieth-century community organizing

The Texas Industrial Areas Foundation (IAF) has been shaped by the late (1972) Saul Alinsky who founded the Industrial Areas Foundation in 1940 and wrote several books about the principles and precepts of the IAF organizing model. Born in Chicago of Russian immigrants in 1902, he was raised in a faith tradition, but turned away from organized religion in his teens. He was well educated at the University of Chicago and worked with unions in the 1930s (the Congress of Industrial Organizations [CIO]), but turned to community organizing in southwest Chicago neighborhoods. For decades, Chicago had been ruled by a political machine which distributed patronage for votes, but did not empower people to hold the political machine accountable for good governance. The same is true in many U.S. cities. Alinsky went on to organize and to recruit organizers all around the U.S. in diverse communities, from African American to White ethnics and Mexican Americans.

Many people are familiar with Alinsky's 1971 book, *Rules for Radicals*, a pragmatic narrative or described better yet, a type of toolkit for uniting people of different backgrounds to focus on goals important to them. The Public Broadcasting Service (PBS) provided an excellent series with original film footage of Alinsky's organizing feats, as listed at the close of this chapter (if people don't mind watching black and white footage!). I will be citing material from his rules book in several chapters of this book. However, it would be important to summarize key ideas from his first book *Reveille for Radicals*, published by the University of Chicago Press. Readers should not be deterred by the book's 1946 publication date, for it contains the kernel of ideas still relevant in the twenty-first-century IAF.

Alinsky emphasized the importance of human beings interacting in relationships, listening to and learning with one another with respect and dignity, which is a key part of the organizing model (with its lingo found in the final section of this chapter). Consider some of Alinsky's remarks about what it means to be a "radical" in his inspiring first chapter. A radical is "that unique person who actually believes what he says. He is that person to whom the common good is the greatest personal value."[10] "The Radical refuses to be diverted by superficial problems. He is completely concerned with fundamental causes rather than current manifestations." The word "radical" is both off-putting and celebrated in the twenty-first-century U.S., but Alinsky's conception of radical falls squarely within the American political traditions.

Alinsky's 1971 *Rules for Radicals* book began by addressing young self-described "radicals" of the late 1960s, many of them social movement activists, whose tactics differed from the IAF model. As I discuss in Chapter 4, the meaning of the word radical, as practiced in twenty-first-century Texas IAF activities, stands distinct from the radicals of the 1960s and 1970 for those of us who lived in those times, such as anti-war protesters, who hardly knew much about the machinery of government back then.

Subsequent chapters in Alinsky's book proceed to outline, with examples, what he describes as a "people's organization." "Native leaders" listen to the people, and organizers understand "community traditions," including segregated congregations of that era whose parishioners attended the Polish Catholic, the Bohemian Catholic, and Slovenian Catholic churches, among others. Note that Alinsky does not describe the IAF model as faith-based organizing, even though his examples show how congregants and clergy engage with people to stand up to powerful institutions. In Alinsky's Chapter 8 on tactics, and with some drama and grim humor, he thickly describes confrontational organizing that challenged the "Tycoon" Department Store and its owner, Mr. "Snoot." Drama and humor remain important in Texas IAF affiliates, as Chapter 2 describes with a San Antonio department store, though this sort of dramatic confrontation is less prominent in the twenty-first-century IAF.

Alinsky has been called a socialist, communist, and atheist. He is hated by anti-Semitic people. Alinsky is a critic himself. He criticizes "liberals" in Chapter 1 of the 1946 book for their "paralysis," "hesitancy to act" amid equivocations, and "discomfort with power." To remind readers from my Acknowledgements to this book (and in Chapter 2), I too take issue with the way U.S. politics characterizes the word "liberal" as proactive government—apart from the classical meaning of this centuries-old term for limited government in market economies—and their political reluctance to criticize the global neoliberal economy.

More criticism of Alinsky emerged before the 2016 presidential elections, bizarrely connecting him with those who opposed Hillary Clinton whose senior thesis focused on Alinsky, to include unflattering pictures of both in Facebook memes. In preparation for this book, I found that the faculty Lyceum committee invited Alinsky to speak at the University of Texas at El Paso (UTEP) campus in October 1970. Alinsky was pictured on the front-page of the student newspaper *The Prospector.*[11] Long-term EPISO leaders, the El Paso-based IAF affiliate that began in 1982 (see Chapter 2 on its origins) had no idea he had spoken in El Paso.

Nowadays, in the twenty-first-century Texas IAF, people rarely evoke Alinsky's name or pay lengthy homage to him. I doubt that all the paid IAF staff at local levels have read his books or treat his rules or everything he said as mandates with which to comply. Some but hardly all those IAF rules still evoke meaning, as the late Edward Chambers articulated, reprinted near the end of this chapter (and revisited in the concluding chapter of this book).

Saul Alinsky probably never realized that the IAF would become not only an organization with scores of affiliates all over the United States, but also an organizing model in Canada, the UK, Germany, New Zealand, and Australia. While I bring up the internationalization of the IAF model again in my concluding chapter, it is beyond the scope of this book to cover the IAF everywhere. My attention is devoted to Texas IAF affiliates and their twenty-first-century community organizing model with a strong local base in multiple regions of a state with democratic and economic impediments both to a fuller democracy and to greater equality between the haves and have-nots (as Alinsky referred to income or class and occupational groups). The Texas IAF is part of the national IAF subdivision that operates under the West/Southwest IAF region. Below readers will find my driving questions for the focus of this book.

Questions that drive this analysis

I aim to answer three main questions in this book: (1) How does the Texas IAF operate, especially in the twenty-first-century, with what kinds of leaders and organizers at grassroots levels? (2) How do voluntary organizations like local IAF affiliates govern and maintain themselves? (3) How do IAF affiliates deal with or resolve contradictions and tensions between the rules/principles and practices? To this book, and true to my discipline of political science, I bring institutional approaches to the study of governance and non-governmental organizations. IAF affiliates are formal nonprofit organizations with tax-exempt status; they are not social movements that come and go, protesting, chanting, and marching in the street to call attention to issues and problems. As Rufus Browning and coauthors titled their 1984 book, *Protest Is Not Enough: The Struggles of Blacks and Hispanics for Equality in Urban Politics.*[12]

What do scholars say about the differences between social movements and formal community organizations? While both share an overlapping "collective agenda of change" and use stories and occasionally religion, Greg Martin provides a helpful distinction between those social movements that practice non-conventional tactics outside of mainstream politics versus those that mobilize resources and practice contentious politics in normal politics.[13] In my experience, IAF affiliates fall within the category of resource mobilization in normal politics like other participatory groups in U.S. politics. However, one cannot simply call IAF affiliates interest groups that rely on support from individual dues to lobby for change. IAF agendas, while not nearly as ambitious as the global and transformation agendas of many social movements, achieve realistic goals in targeted local and state political institutions; they also identify and develop leaders. I lean toward the use of formal organizations in this analysis rather than of movements.

To sustain formal institutions is a challenging effort. The challenges involve recruiting participants, building consensus around goals, actually achieving goals, and generating revenue to support an office, utilities, and limited paid organizer staff. After all, most people who participate from merely occasionally to intensely in organizations like IAF affiliates do so voluntarily; they are not compelled to join or comply as is true of governments with authoritative laws that require or forbid behavior. In the IAF, participants become active to achieve their material interests (and later, I discuss the importance of "self-interest" in the IAF model), their social interests, and their ideological, policy, and faith-based interests. In Chapter 4, I examine these interests in greater depth, with a special focus on religious faith. Why? Most IAF participants belong to member institutions such as faith-based congregations; volunteer leaders do not join as individuals (as we find in the vast bulk of NGOs, like the former social justice organization called ACORN or traditional organizations like the League of Women Voters and the LULAC [League of United Latin American Citizens]). Indeed, IAF member institutions pay dues to their local IAF affiliate in order to maintain their independence, autonomy, and self-sufficiency from government organizations that grant money with strings attached. Unpaid volunteers (referred to as one of three tiers of "leaders" in IAF terms, covered later in this chapter) form the large powerful people base for IAF community organizations. Yet as we also see in Chapter 5 and in studies by Benjamin Márquez, past IAF affiliates were dependent on particular denominational sources of funding which might call into question the IAF's principled (an IAF Iron Rule) emphasis on self-sufficiency. (Again, I make reference to the list of rules in the appendix of this chapter, revisited once again in the concluding chapter.)[14]

Few formal NGOs articulate their principles and organizing model to their local base volunteers as well as the Industrial Areas Foundation. In an organization which devotes considerable time and attention to volunteer leadership training, IAF staff have written articles and performed in videos; promoted readings about philosophy, the Greek Peloponnesian War, and contemporary politics; and produced what it calls "trainings" that aim to put such principles into action, as shown in its national website, www.industrialareasfoundation.org, and covered in the body of this book.

Contradictions exist in organized life, whether governmental and non-governmental organizations. Formal organizations only imperfectly practice what they preach, whether in government agencies from top to bottom with policies that selectively diffuse into the mid- and lower levels of bureaucracy, or in selectively transmitted information upward from bottom to top of those bureaucracies.[15] The same is true in non-governmental organizations, though NGOs' hierarchical levels tend to be flatter (i.e. two or three hierarchical levels) than those in government or in public universities (the latter typically five or six levels) or in the outlier extreme of skewed hierarchy, military organizations.[16] Even Alinsky remarked that "practically all people live in a world of contradictions."[17] We take up six contradictions below, in the form of framing questions, with a brief discussion of the tensions they produce to be covered in the body of this book.

Six contradictions, tensions and/or resolutions

Whether in government or NGOs, formal organizations and people who work and volunteer within them experience contradictions between what is said and what is done. In popular parlance, we might refer to talking the talk but not walking the talk. Such contradictions produce tensions, reassessments, departures, and rebuilding in formal organizations. For evolving and changing organizations, it is important to understand why. In this study, my focus on institutions and organizational theories provided a lens to understand contradictions and the ensuing tensions in staff recruitment, rules, procedures, incentives, penalties, and decision-making processes to develop strategies and accomplish goals.

Institutional insights can clarify democratic accountability in the larger political system and in the organizations with which people affiliate for two reasons. First, once people know who makes which decisions in what government/public institutions at what levels of government, they can better target strategies for reform. This book contains an enormous amount of material on public policies and how they play out in Texas state and local governments for what people can and cannot change. Besides policies about health, environment, wages, and infrastructure, the chapters also include attention to public policies that, when listening to people in small-group meetings, matter in their everyday lives, such as public policies related to housing, wage theft, predatory lending, and public safety along with the often-problematic implementation of those policies.

Second, once people know institutional dynamics within NGOs like the IAF, participants can work to assure accountability within their own organizations. Alas, little practical civic education exists in the state of Texas, even in required high school social studies and public higher education introductory American government classes. Furthermore, courses in public policy tend to focus more on getting issues onto political agendas and passing bills into laws, rather than on policy details and implementation. As subsequent chapters show, constant vigilance is necessary to assure that local ordinances that IAF helps to pass, or laws at the state level, do not get ignored or starved of budgetary resources.

To address IAF affiliates as organizations within which accountability issues emerge, I analyze six contradictions listed below in the body of this book. These contradictions can produce tensions within the organization and its ability to achieve the goals that volunteer leaders articulate. Tension is not suppressed in IAF organizations. In fact, IAF organizations embrace the concept of "tensions," (the word is located in "rules" later in this chapter), especially in the dramatic actions to make them more engaging and enlightening, as I hope readers find in this book as well. Some are easier to resolve than others, an issue I revisit in the concluding chapter. The following contradictions, posed as questions, have been threaded through one or more subsequent chapters with examples of the tensions they produce.

1. *Are IAF affiliates faith-based or broad-based organizations?* We see in subsequent chapters that IAF affiliates bring both reasoned and moral dimensions to policy criticism and reform, but not a religious agenda into public policy. However, most volunteers (called "leaders," as developed below) participate as a result of their faith-based member institution, a church or synagogue. In a country that emphasizes the separation of church and state, what can emerge in an IAF affiliate is a tension between the sacred and secular, in the emphasis (or not) on religious faith in social justice action versus people's self-interests.

   This contradiction is important for several reasons. For one, the IAF's association with faith may bode ill in an era of people's declining commitment to religion. The U.S., like many western countries, is experiencing a decline in religious affiliation, (see chapter 2), especially among youth. For another, faith-based affiliations can unduly frame IAF agendas and therefore the recruitment of new volunteer leaders and paid organizers particularly among youth whose commitment to such issues as reproductive health and LGBTQI equality may be stronger than their commitment to other forms of social justice.[18] In the body of this book we consider various issues such as prayers before and after meetings, sacred funding with strings attached, and clergy visibility in leadership. How the IAF affiliates address these tensions will have consequences for their ability to thrive in future decades.

2. *To what extent do IAF affiliates collaborate with other social justice organizations and universities in formal or informal coalitions?* IAF affiliates themselves are internal coalitions among member institutions, mostly congregations and a minority of nonprofit health, education, and labor/professional organizations in the bigger IAF affiliates located in Dallas, Houston, Austin, and San Antonio. The broad swath of member institutions gives IAF affiliates power in numbers, dues, and potential new volunteers who

may find their public voices, learn new skills, and perhaps even become prospective recruits as paid organizer staff. Yet collaborations always take extra time and labor to assure that democratic accountability exists to all members and member institutions in coalitions. In later chapters, we see the mixed blessings of collaborations, sometimes enormously successful as in the workforce training organizations that partner with community colleges like Project Quest (San Antonio), Project Arriba (El Paso), Capital Idea (Austin) and others in Houston, Dallas, and South Texas, but in other alliances reaping limited success such as the laborious multi-year effort like the El Paso Lift Up Alliance against wage theft and the Education Summit, all twenty-first-century efforts, as analyzed in chapter 7.

This collaboration contradiction is important because the expansion of organizations and people beyond the IAF member institution coalition complicates IAF agendas and increases labor demands on its volunteer leaders. As we see in subsequent chapters, once consensus is achieved in decision-making, volunteer leaders generally provide a unified front in their public actions. Non-IAF volunteers have not been part of such process or training. While new coalition partners and allies could generate a wider and stronger numerical base of support, civil society's growing number of NGOs has become a crowded field in which competition may occur.

3. *What is the mix of top-down and bottom-up decision-making in a dispersed, but relatively flat hierarchical organization like the IAF affiliates vis a vis IAF statewide staff and the West-Southwest IAF (what I call the "superstructure")?* The IAF model claims that priority agendas and issues emerge from local small-group meetings (called "house meetings," discussed later in the chapter), though considerable influence is exercised from above, that is, from the statewide and regional staff as they interact with carefully recruited, trained, and rotated paid organizers.

This sort of question addresses the symbiosis between top and bottom amid the extent to which organizing models flexibly change over time. The historic IAF model draws from 1940 and experiences thereafter, yet the IAF also features and celebrates the constancy of building and rebuilding its organized base. In studies about other NGOs, contrasts have been drawn between a Blueprint and a Learning-Process approach.[19] Blueprint models tend to be imposed by sometimes-inflexible foundation funders or government agencies (the latter, money from which the IAF does not directly accept), though some funders trust local leaders to adapt flexibly to local contexts and change. Here, my question refers more to the model imposed within the formal organization, the IAF, and its flexibility to local contexts around Texas.

This contradiction is crucial for IAF's ability to realize internal democratic accountability. If local volunteer leaders doubt that their house-meeting derived local agenda reflects interests imposed from above, cynicism could set in, coupled with stop-out or drop-out by participants in the local base. To the extent that the IAF reflects a more hierarchical organization, such as its dominant Catholic member institutional base in Texas (see Chapter 2), the tension could be yet another reflection of the sacred-secular contradiction discussed above.

4. *Has the IAF moved toward a more gender-balanced model of paid staff and its unpaid volunteer base, called "leaders," as well as toward an agenda that responds to women and special gender-based discrimination in wages, violence, and health?* Some critics of the IAF call attention to the leadership styles that characterize traditional men's behavior, such as aggressiveness, but do women's ways of organizing[20] (such as listening and conversing) vary from that traditional model? Paid IAF staff have become more gender-balanced over time, as we see from the interviews in the body of this book. However, there is more to gender balance than the demographics of paid leaders—namely gendered policy issues. As such, does the IAF mute coverage of so-called "women's issues," related to women's bodies like reproductive health and sexual assault? People generally, perhaps women as well, may be reluctant to vocalize body issues in small-group house meetings for the potential stigma or protection of personal privacy in what is usually a faith-based setting. Such issues may never emerge in IAF agendas. I appreciated the way Dallas Area Interfaith leaders found ways to weave some of these issues like violence against women in a public safety agenda within an IAF paradigm (covered in Chapter 3).

This contradiction is important because the IAF may alienate women volunteer leaders and potential organizers who migrate toward other NGOs that respond to their self-interests and/or a feminist public agenda. The exclusion of reproductive choice issues may reinforce another concern about over-influence from the dominant Catholic member institutions and funding from the Catholic Campaign for Human Development.

5. *How do IAF affiliates deal with the constant drive to generate revenue not only to support local paid staff and office expenses, but also to pay fees to the statewide and regional operations?* IAF affiliates clearly benefit from technical assistance, for which they pay dues: to the IAF, to the Industrial Education Fund, and to the Network of Texas Organizations. They achieve access to trainings, to constant professional development for their paid organizers, and to the visibility that comes from social media and press releases issued by the broader operations. However, the challenge of paying dues is particularly acute in poverty-stricken counties of Texas, such as the three borderlands affiliates in the South Texas valley, Del Rio, and El Paso.

Of course, fundraising is a common struggle to support and expand operations in nonprofit tax-exempt nonprofit 50lc3 and 50lc4 organizations[21] such as IAF affiliates and many other non-governmental organizations. Local IAF affiliates collect minimal dues (1-2 percent) from member institutions, but some congregations cannot or do not pay and thereby lose their membership. IAF also conducts money campaigns, develops "Ad Books" (see chapter 5), and reaches out to local businesses and banks and to foundations that award grants based on their agendas and potentially overlapping agendas which may or may not coincide with the IAF affiliate.

This contradiction is important because if and when local volunteer leaders believe themselves to be beleaguered by tripartite dues structures, they may become cynical and stop out or drop out of participation, particularly if they have no voice in the amount of dues or the use to which that money is put. To the extent that IAF affiliates depend on CCHD or business sources of funding, the need for money may compromise their autonomous agenda and create possible dependencies rather than self-sufficiency as articulated in IAF principles.

6. *How does the word "radical," self-proclaimed in IAF books and perceived both positively and negatively in the wider public, operate in the twenty-first-century?* As already addressed earlier in this chapter, Alinsky himself unpacked the term for how it resonates with old-fashioned ideals about the way U.S. democracy is supposed to work. In subsequent chapters, readers see the sorts of strategies,

policy issues, and tactics used in the twenty-first-century Texas IAF.[22] I question whether the "radical" term for this reformist, pragmatic NGO project, grounded in community institutions, accurately portrays the reality of organized efforts, particularly given the way IAF works with business leaders, nudging policy reforms to reduce the worst of exploitation in only incremental ways. Perhaps this indicates a mature phase in IAF work.

This is an important contradiction because it affects the public perceptions of local affiliates. The rhetoric of "radical" may resonate with some but horrify others. Better that the IAF accurately project its twenty-first-century self! Moreover, if the local IAF agenda is compromised, whether from dependency on particular religious sources of funding or from wealthy donors, the Alinsky-style "radical" adjective would not be an accurate description of IAF's politics.

These six questions about contradictions and the tensions that ensue—all of them interconnected—are not unique to the IAF. Many NGOs and nonprofit organizations face similar challenges. Besides these six concerns, unique challenges emerge because of the overarching conservatism of the state (Texas) and the variations in the places where IAF organizes: Austin, Dallas, El Paso, Houston, Del Rio, Lubbock, San Antonio, and South Texas. In this book, we "travel" around the state and hear stories from their paid organizers and volunteer leaders, the grassroots of everyday life who form the base of political participation.

Putting people into organizing for social justice

The everyday labors of active political participants have long fascinated me. Political science departments once offered courses on political socialization that focused on how, why, and what children and adults learn about politics. So in this book I dig deeper with sub-questions like the following. For those energetic IAF paid organizers and participants at the grassroots level: what makes them tick? What have they accomplished? What keeps them going (and why do some drop out or stop out)? What will the IAF's next challenges involve and how can it meet those challenges?

In particular, I wonder about the extent to which the Texas IAF will thrive in post-2030 society with declining numbers of people who attend church and respect church hierarchy, thus reducing the pool from which many IAF paid staff and unpaid participants come, especially in a non-competitive state government that increasingly puts challenges in front of efforts to achieve social justice victories. Among these challenges, covered in Chapter 2, I include the exploding growth of money in electoral campaigns and appointments along with the conservative philosophy which authorizes state interference over local control in city ordinances, called pre-emption, and undermines progressive social justice achievements at city council levels in the name of protecting business-friendly public policies, covered in subsequent chapters. Additionally, the twenty-first-century contains a crowded field of community organizations, some of them fleeting social media operations, but none in Texas as big or with as long a history as the IAF. None exercises the discipline and focus that constructive IAF principles and strategies, what some call "cold anger,"[23] that is, constructive channeled anger, bring to bear on achieving goals. The more we put people and places into broad-organizing analysis, the better our understanding of organizational effectiveness and resilience over the decades.

The Industrial Areas Foundation (IAF), born in 1940 in the Midwest as noted earlier, developed a strong presence in the bigger and smaller cities of Texas since the early 1970s, during the last and first quarters of the twentieth and twenty-first-centuries. IAF affiliates and their paid organizer staff members identify and train volunteer leaders to participate in local and state political institutions, a tough row to hoe in an only weakly democratic state which has increasingly become a "pay-to-play" system with enormous amounts of money donated for campaign, political access, and appointments as Chapter 2 discusses. Still we see growing voices of people like IAF volunteer leaders that heretofore lacked a public voice or presence, buoyed with hope after successfully changing policies. With tried and tested principles and practices, selectively changing as IAF "rebuilds" over nearly fifty years, IAF leaders organize for secular social justice goals politically at the local and state levels, from a broad base but mostly from faith-based member institutions and some nonprofit associations. Social justice involves more than legal rights in a system with expensive, time-consuming, and opaque processes. Once again, the broader notion of social justice includes fair and equitable wages, inclusiveness, access to affordable housing and health, and environmental stewardship to sustain life, issues that IAF affiliates have addressed as chapters in the body of this book analyze.

Like all organizations, the IAF changes, but also reveals a familiar continuity across decades, cities, and IAF affiliates. To what extent does continuity exist? Well before the IAF pronounced its "iron rule" principles about organizing (see Box 1.2 at the close of the chapter), Robert Michels warned about the "iron law of oligarchy" in organizations[24] though his focus was on European political parties, so hardly generalizable as a law-like principle. However, his book signaled a warning to organizations working in democracies to practice internal democratic accountability. The voices of younger and more diverse leaders, who perhaps question more than the founding generation, offer one step toward accountability. My pictures for the front cover of this book show the faces of IAF organizers and leaders in the twenty-first-century across the grassroots of Texas.

Although Texas moved from its one-party Democratic dominance to one-party Republican dominance in recent decades, whatever the party in power, IAF affiliates meet with representatives and officials, persist and achieve their multiple victories in many policy areas, as I cover in subsequent chapters: workforce training, wider access to affordable health care, decent wages linked to local governments and their contractors, and education.[25] With its former Alliance School networks, the Texas IAF created lasting legacies around raising expectations in schools through teamwork among parents, principals, and teachers. Nevertheless, one-party domination in state government has made it difficult to develop relationships with all representatives, especially in rural counties outside the IAF urban areas, despite democratic expectations that all representatives should to be accountable to people in their whole districts. Since 2016, IAF affiliates have begun building efforts to develop leadership in semi-rural parts of the state, outside the big cities.

Organizations evolve over stages, from founding to maintenance, survival, revival, and/or demise. In the study of NGOs, we know that in the creation stage, a founder-leader-entrepreneur understood and continues to understand political opportunity structures to seize new initiatives. NGOs with a purpose survive and thrive when they carve spaces and new places to generate more leaders.[26] Dallas Area Interfaith (DAI) Leader Brenda Shell, whose story begins in Chapter 3, said this was "like a domino effect." She was one among many people interviewed for this book.

Methods and sources for the analysis

The methods I used to answer questions in this book are eclectic. They consisted of interviews, observations, case studies, participation, descriptive data bases, and reviews of archival, primary, and secondary documents in various Texas cities, big and small, with cross-referencing to other sources to validate findings. Most chapters start with interviewees' stories (for a story-driven organization) and include boxes that highlight dramatic activity (all of that in italicized format). I hope that readers share my appreciation for endnotes, for that is where I elaborate more on the conceptual perspectives for analysis. The book is based partly on my own stories and experiences (called "auto-ethnography"[27]), given my two decades (1998-current) on the inside of grassroots IAF organizing in which I have invested 2,000 hours or more. At the most basic level, I analyze a "bottom-up," on-the-ground perspective on the Texas IAF.

This analysis is meant to be complete, fair, and balanced. As noted, I cover and compare a wide swath of Texas, focusing especially on those IAF places with little visibility beyond their websites: Dallas, Austin, Lubbock, and the borderlands, plus referencing to other IAF affiliates in San Antonio, the Rio Grande Valley, and Houston. Trained as a political scientist, but listening and observing like an anthropologist, I have spent a professional lifetime as scholar-activist living, teaching, researching, and writing in Texas, specifically in the U.S.-Mexico borderlands.

I agree with one of my favorite writers, El Pasoan and *fronterizo* (borderlander) Benjamin Sáenz, who said publicly at the University of Texas at El Paso event titled Narrating the Borderlands on June 15, 2018: "I'm not here to make the border look good or bad. I'm here to make it real." I could say the same about this and other books I have written. I write to make Texas IAF affiliates real, rather than look good or bad. With an emphasis on contradictions, tensions, and resolutions, I believe advances can be made in NGO principles and practices and generally in civil society activism in a state like Texas.

For the last twenty years, I have been an unpaid (volunteer) leader in Border Interfaith through my church, which is a paid member institution. That activity enabled me to learn lots about pragmatic local and state politics, similar to the learning I gained at the national level decades ago when I worked in Washington, D.C., with President Carter's political appointee Arvonne Fraser, who died in 2018 while I was writing this book. She Rests in Power. I learned as much or more about pragmatic politics from community and national leaders like Fraser as I did in graduate school at the University of Wisconsin where I earned the PhD. Let me share a somber note to budding leaders: one does not learn as much in coursework about practicing pragmatic politics as in and through actual experience. So for this project, I am indebted to IAF organizers and leaders over the years, especially those who took the time for interviews. I have worked closely with eight organizers over twenty years. Sometimes I wonder if there's some informal, pay-it-forward type reciprocity for my countless interviews with visiting journalists, scholars, and student groups seeking insights about the US-Mexico borderlands.

Broad-based community organizing and its language(s)

Before moving toward a primer on IAF language, let me provide some boundaries around the term community organizations and the IAF in particular. First we start by defining broad-based community organizing.

In his twenty-first century compendium devoted to community organizing in cities, with which I had the pleasure of participation in multiple conferences to plan the volume, Brown University political scientist Marion Orr defined community organizing as "the process that engages people, organizations, and communities toward the goals of increased individual and community control, political efficacy, improved quality of life, and social justice."[28] His own field research focused on BUILD, an IAF organization in Baltimore. Many community organizations exist like those Orr defined, as covered in the closing chapter of this book, but the IAF is the oldest and most coherent among them. Orr's edited volume, from which the definition comes, contains detailed chapters on the early years of Alinsky, the IAF in various locales, the now-defunct ACORN, and the PICO National Network (now named Faith in Action) a softer version of the IAF model.

From Alinsky onwards, the IAF has been an organization that identifies and trains leaders, builds organized power, and pursues an agenda for social justice policy reforms, in line with what Marion Orr defined above. The IAF seeks systemic change in laws, policies, and budgets. While the IAF is not an episodic protest-oriented social movement that relies primarily on street marches, I saw some early sign-waving pictures in archival files at UTSA's Special Collections library. Movements tend to be less hierarchical than organizations, even leaderless, perhaps without the need for fundraising and the laborious process of acquiring tax-exempt status from the IRS (Internal Revenue Service), given their zeal and creativity in arts, music, and social media,[29] but often lacking in long-term relationships of trust among participants. Still valuable, protests can galvanize people, issues, and problems to push them onto the public agenda from a relatively stable and visibly powerful base of people. Neither is the IAF a service or charitable organization where people donate time, talent, and money to help others in need as chapter 4 analyzes in the secular-sacred discussions. Some people, particularly in sacred institutions like churches, seem more comfortable with helping people through direct service such as feeding the hungry, clothing the poor, and sheltering the homeless rather than what the IAF does: working with people together on a systemic basis to change policies in order to reduce the need for these helpful services. The IAF proclaims its over-all emphasis on policy changes that allow people to support themselves through fairly compensated work ("self-sufficiency," an IAF rule with many applications for its practices and goals) rather than dependence on charity and social assistance.

Moreover, IAF affiliates acquire their own resources, such as member institutional dues, grants, and what it calls "investments" from friends of the organizations, such as local businesses, rather than from government agencies, as is common in many nonprofit organizations. IAF affiliates with a website have a "donate" button, like so many nonprofit organizations. IAF participants speak for themselves, rather than rely—like nonprofit organizational staff—on advocacy for their clients, as in a traditional social-work paradigm. In IAF organizations, (voluntary) leaders acquire the tools and training to speak for themselves and, together, use skills and show power in public settings.

My political anthropology tag means I pay close attention to what Norton Long once called "urban ecology" and its sector stakeholders, such as environmental, human rights, and union or professional associations.[30] Chapter 2 briefly examines the Texas cities in which IAF affiliates organize. The ecology consists of shifting sands and muddy grounds, given the changing casts of characters after each of the many elections in fragmented Texas government: state, county, city, and school boards in both the primaries and regular partisan and nonpartisan elections.

Key to IAF affiliates' power is their capacity for a "seat at the table" in decision-making processes. By a seat at the table, I mean IAF capacities to work with officials (elected, appointed, and bureaucratic); their ability to achieve policy victories; and their production of an appearance from almost all candidates in public high-attendance Accountability Sessions, who then respond publicly—with yes or no and why—to questions about the IAF agenda. I elaborate on this in Chapters 2 and 3. This seat at the table comes from the power of numbers and of people in relationships with others over time.

Sociologists have used the term "social capital" for the relationships of trust people build with one another in order to get things done (note 5); the few scholarly books on the IAF emphasize social capital building in conceptual frameworks. In the twenty-first century, for others to know about the IAF beyond those historic relationships, a seat at the table also requires a website, communication strategy, and/or a Facebook page which, alas, is not part of all IAF affiliates, which tend to stress face-to-face relationships. However, political sociologists argue the importance of both "strong and weak ties" in relational networks.[31] A seat at the table requires both types of ties, including the weak ties in social media for visibility in local contexts.

As the IAF shifted its statewide strategy in 2016 to build relationships with officials in the suburbs and semi-rural or rural counties surrounding IAF-affiliate cities, represented in huge media-covered accountability sessions and get-out-the-vote campaigns, Texans bore fruit in 2018 with a more competitive process, though the state has not yet returned to a two-party state. However, when the majority party loses seats, as happened in the 2018 state legislative elections with twelve seats picked up by Democrats in north and central Texas,[32] a message is sent to the dominant party that can result in somewhat greater responsiveness and/ or a willingness to work in bipartisan ways—i.e. across party lines. I take this issue up again in subsequent chapters, but see the endnote reference to the six-minute video of the Dallas Area Interfaith (DAI) Accountability Session, with its 2,000 attendees, leaders, and the powerful voices of clerical leaders from multiple denominations, to understand the flavor and drama of such events as discussed below.[33] (I offer a primer on IAF language in the section below.)

I have planned and participated in many of these Accountability Sessions, usually once every year or two, sometimes twice a year in the many elections of Texas, but the thrill and excitement are always there, even watching these six minutes on the DAI video. Participants arrive in large numbers, an opening non-denominational prayer is offered, co-moderators manage the already-rehearsed event carefully with a script, participants tell short, one-minute stories, IAF volunteer leaders ask candidates questions from the local IAF agenda, and candidates respond with yes or no answers, plus a short explanation on their answers, beamed to the wall and/or written on a large poster. The candidates' answers represent a public commitment, about which the local IAF follows up after the election for policy or budgetary reform. Media coverage of these IAF events tend to be larger than other local electoral

Accountability "yes-no questions," EPISO/Border Interfaith, 2018. Photograph by Kathleen Staudt.

forums and debates. Candidates are not surprised with questions, for they have been briefed ahead of time and sent the exact questions twenty-four hours ahead of the event. No campaign literature is allowed; the event is nonpartisan.

Besides the elected officials, in the book I also emphasize the business communities and what Harvey Molotch called "growth machines" that tend to dominate urban politics in less-transparent ways, both in the United States and certainly in Texas in historic and contemporary eras.[34] The money and leadership behind growth machines might expand the labor market and jobs, perhaps even create decent-paying jobs. However, that expansion does not necessarily lift all people's wages or diminish internal inequalities. Indeed, in a less regulated market economy like the U.S., inequalities will likely increase unless organized power intervenes, whether that organized power be unions (now representing only a tenth of the U.S. labor force), identity and civil rights groups, or social justice organizations like the IAF. At the same time, the businesses that dominate urban politics need to be unpacked analytically; they are not all alike, for some act on their interests in expanding quality workforce training programs in partnership with the IAF placing graduates in living-wage, middle-class jobs as outlined in chapters from Section III of the book.

Other businesses do not. Readers can determine whether such partnerships diminish or enhance the IAF edge in progressive reform.

Economic inequality is certainly a priority problem issue for most social justice NGOs, and the IAF focuses on economic class more than ethnic identity. However, to reduce economic inequalities in Texas means one must deal with the ways gender, race, language, and ethnicity intersect, especially in education, residential location (including historic segregation), and workforce training. When the IAF organizers and trainers offer workshops about "Pressures on our Families," they speak about "family agendas" but frame issues in wage and opportunity terms rather than specifically tackling racism and sexism. No doubt this resonates with the voices that bubble up from the small-group "house meeting" format discussed below. IAF addresses injustices in more subtle ways than leaders in or scholars of ethnic, racial, and feminist politics might like.[35] Newer social justice organizations embrace identity politics and work toward goals not always immediately achievable, sometimes spreading awareness. As civil society grows, participants can choose from a wide menu of community organizations.

Understanding IAF lingo

For readers curious about how people pursue change and social justice in these trying, polarized political times, I offer insights on how IAF affiliates speak about and do their "public work,"[36] now going into their fifth decade of presence in Texas. To do this, I need to convey the IAF language used in training and interaction as I have experienced that language over twenty years.

While the IAF uses moral arguments, holds meetings in churches and synagogues, and even uses Biblical stories in its training, IAF is not about religion, proselytizing, or prayer in schools. Such practices could prove awkward or ineffective in twenty-first-century America, always anxious about the "separation of church and state" (the Constitution's First Amendment, and its non-establishment of a religion clause). IAF does not promote religious agendas, but clergy members exercise leadership and often speak in public events or during relational meetings for the moral authority they may bring. After all, how could an alliance of faith-based institutions, from Protestantism to Judaism and Catholicism, possibly agree about religious matters?! However, meetings with public officials illustrate their mistaken assumptions about presumed IAF-affiliated religious agendas, as Box 1.1 illustrates.

Box 1.1 Mistaken Assumptions

As an IAF leader, I remember some semi-humorous experiences when public officials made assumptions about Border Interfaith delegations based on the organization's name. A school super-intendent, when asked about how his board of school trustees evaluates his work, responded that he answered to a higher power, to God, to our delegation's surprise. Well, our interest was more mundane: the performance incentives under which he managed the district. We wanted to understand his self-interests and behaviors.

In another experience, a City Council representative, with his M.D. occupational background, immediately presented himself as one who never performs abortions. IAF leaders always prepare for relational meetings with an agenda and roles assigned for each agenda item, clarified in a "pre-meeting." As we quickly made clear, we were not there to talk about abortion or reproductive justice. Besides, the city council does not address those issues.

At an organizational anniversary fundraising dinner, gradu-ate students sat at a table that a public official had generously donated. They observed, ate dinner, and listened to a former IAF co-chair, now retired clergy, speak about social justice. We talked about the event later in connection with readings on participation in the judgment-free flow of seminar discussion. About half of the students bemoaned the "sermon-like speech," while the other half said that they left "inspired" and "committed to action." But they invested their actions in other organizations and finished their degrees, half of them leaving El Paso for better wages and oppor-tunities elsewhere.

The IAF has its own lingo—common concepts—which I highlight in bold type. This discourse is introduced, spread, and deepened in train-ing, both for paid organizers and unpaid leaders. **Power**, a core concept, is analyzed, unpacked, and its acquisition, celebrated; power is not treated as an awkward or dirty word even though newcomers to IAF might cringe at the word or believe it contradicts the humility fostered in some faith traditions. The acquisition of power is viewed as fundamental to altering power relations, that is, the typical grip that a political-economic elite and money hold in local and state politics or the reliance on individual experts to change policies.

IAF training topics typically include "Power Analysis," in lengthy trainings and even short versions in steering committee meetings. The organizer or trainer asks questions like the following, with magic marker and poster paper at hand. What is power? Who has it? How do mediating institutions like IAF affiliates counter the overwhelming power of money and elite influence?[37] For newcomers to IAF training, or with a similar exercise in my courses in political science, people typically give responses like elected officials, like the Mayor or County Judge (CEO for Texas counties), but rarely respond with wealthy people who donate money to elect officials and gain access and influence in public decisions about budgets, who head institutions, and/or have power to stay open for business or close shop in a community. And as trainers always remind those who participate in IAF Leadership Academies in the Southwest, the word *poder* in Spanish better captures the constructive meaning of power: to be able to (get things done). See Box 1.2 for a brief summary of the long-term fascination among social scientists with the concept of power.

The IAF seeks to change power relations through exercising the power of numbers. IAF also works to develop **relational power** as a key to success. And IAF affiliates use moral power in the language or rhetoric used in rationales for reform (see Chapter 4). IAF participants develop relationships of mutual respect both with one another and with those in government, business, and education and nonprofit walks of life. On the in-IAF group relationships in El Paso, for example, monthly local steering meetings begin with one-on-one conversations. "Pick someone you don't know very well," say the steering committee co-chairs: invariably the two people converse from different congregations, occupations, and language groups. At local training events, the "one-on-ones" get more time over meals, even with prompt questions posted on the tables to get conversations going: why are you here? What are your hopes and dreams for your family, for your work in the organization? At distant trainings with overnight stays, participants are assigned a roommate, generally from a different city and probably different faith affiliation.

IAF also develops relationships with powerful leaders in their communities. Various types of relational meetings occur. In one type of meeting, IAF does practical "research": what are you hearing about immigration (one among many issues)? What do you think ought to be done in our community? IAF learns about the "interests" that people have

---

Box 1.2 Conceptualizing Power in the Academic Disciplines

Political science and sociology scholars, affiliated in fields long fascinated with power, have produced lengthy tomes on the concept, only some of which I briefly summarize here. Traditionally, power was viewed as power "over" others, i.e. domination and control through using power resources such as money, land, force, official authority, and expertise. Those somewhat negative connotations gave way to more positive ways to view power, such as the ability to get things done as so many feminist theorists have analyzed, as power "to" do things.[38] These differences gave way to two perspectives on power: whether it is centralized in a power elite, tending to come out of sociology, or diffused and varied based on particular policy issues—a pluralist approach.

In a classic article from political science, an even more nuanced perspective comes with the perspective that power may be unseen, particularly in the ability to keep issues and procedures off of the public agenda in so-called "non-decisions." The powerful benefit from, in a famous phrase, the "mobilization of bias": exploiting conflict and/or suppressing it.[39]

Given the contradictions and tensions outlined earlier and the analysis to come in subsequent chapters, we can see where IAF affiliates might fit in these perspectives. In the interest of revenue generation, IAF affiliates might avoid putting the "pay to play" system on local or state agendas to the extent that businesses which support them would be affected. And from Alinsky onward, IAF affiliates push (non-decision) issues onto public agendas in pluralist fashion, for example in anti-wage-theft ordinances or local regulations that put checks on payday lenders.

---

in the business, nonprofit, educational, and elected official worlds. IAF always meets with new officials after they have been sworn into office to develop a working relationship with them and to gain insights about possibilities for success on the issues that bubble up from its small-group meetings, known as **house meetings**. At relational meetings, particular formats are followed. First, participants introduce themselves: "My name is _____, a leader in _____ (IAF affiliate) and

---

Box 1.3 House Meeting Report Form

_Date_____   _Time_____
Name of Congregation [member institution]: _____
Name of leader conducting the meeting: _____
Context (parent, congregants, neighborhood, etc.): _____
How many house meetings were conducted? _____
Interesting Stories and Issues:

_____

_____

_____

Interesting People:
   Name   _Phone_   _E-Mail_

_____

_____

_____

Next Steps:

_____

---

a member of _____ (name of congregation)." See the typical type of form in Box 1.3 which documents the multiple house meetings (adapted from Border Interfaith, 2019) which either the facilitator or a notetaker complete and then report out to the large group.

In El Paso, with my IAF hat on, we have met with many officials in relational meetings. For example, we met with the mayor many times—in his current role, in his previous and no doubt future role as a businessman, and in his past role as Republican state legislator and thus with ties to the dominant party leadership—so much so that he knows the introduction: "yea, yea, I know your routine" he kiddingly says.[40]

At all meetings, internal or with officials and community-wide leaders, IAF brings a printed agenda, showing the affiliate logo, and outlines a focus or framework for the meeting; each of the three to five participants know what issue they will bring up from their pre-meeting and who closes the meeting with a query about reactions or next steps. Usually a commitment comes at the end of the thirty- to sixty-minute meeting: for information and insights from their perspectives and contacts, for support on an upcoming vote, and for another introduction, among other items. In El Paso, we do not hold signs outside City Hall and chant for change in ordinances (for example, to regulate payday lenders or to reduce wage theft). Rather, we meet with council representatives in relationships of mutual respect to figure out how a constructive action could be done: the language, the timing, its optimal champion on council, and the subsequent cultivation of a majority of votes. Perhaps not surprisingly, virtually all people viewed the payday lending industry with disgust, given its usurious interest rates and fees. Of course the payday lenders also visit with city council representations to protect their self-interests. With wage theft, too: Good employers did not want to be associated with employer wage thieves (who undercut competition with businesses that follow the laws!).

Leaders and prospective leaders stress and practice **relationality** in one-on-one meetings. Large events also matter. The larger the number of attendees at IAF actions—the power of numbers—the greater the impression made on IAF leaders, attendees, media, and officials explaining or promising policy change, especially when attendees promise to vote and to encourage five to ten of their friends to vote (a typical question at the end of an Accountability Session). At planning meetings, healthy **turnout** by member institutions is a constant push. Again, the Dallas Area Interfaith video noted above (endnote 33) shows strength in the power of numbers.

Insiders quickly learn the language, but it may be puzzling to outsiders or to readers. Who are IAF participants? Here I just describe the terms, but in Chapter 5 I illustrate participants' pathways through interviews and analysis.

Volunteers, called **leaders,** emerge from the IAF **member institutions,** usually congregations and in Texas, mostly Catholic parishes, but in big cities, some nonprofit organizations as well. Leaders are not paid, but they contribute voluntary time and talent to organizing efforts and meetings. Several types of leaders exist: primary or **core leaders** with a following and an understanding of the big picture of IAF in their communities and states and networks that they may bring to IAF work. **Secondary leaders** have a following in their institutions: they participate in IAF affiliate committees, planning, and relationship meetings. **Tertiary leaders** attend public events, assist in follow-up activities, and provide other generic support. Existing leaders are always prospecting for new leaders to be cultivated through experiences in organizing events, developing agendas or facilitating meetings, speaking at dramatic public events, and sharing the sometimes tedious and laborious workload. A simple "ask" can produce positive responses: How about participating in our event? Let's meet and I'll tell you more about how things work. Leaders consist of a cross-section of women and men from multiple income, ethnic/racial, religious, and occupation groups that tend to match the demographics of their communities. Once again, IAF is not about identity politics, but rather about issue-based politics that cut cross identity, ethnic, and racial groups. However, the predominant population in the member institutions will influence the distribution of demographic groups. IAF affiliates in the borderlands and San Antonio consist largely of Mexican Americans.[41]

Leaders facilitate small-group meetings, called **house meetings,** in their institutions where they share **stories**—some of them tragic—about problems which are in their **self-interest** to solve. *Colonia* residents may lack water, sewer, roads, and or natural gas lines (they pay larger amounts for butane cans). City dwellers tell stories about poorly maintained roads, problematic interaction with their children's school teachers, and few parks among other issues. IAF puts great stock into the identification of self-interests as motivating factors for participation, whether leaders in member institutions or business people in health fields who have self-interests in quality training for nurses, provided in IAF-nurtured, but stand-alone training programs like Project Arriba, Project Quest, and Capital Idea (covered in Chapter 8). Other house meeting stories emerge like the following: adult children leave the city for lack of good-paying jobs; health costs and lack of insurance prolong sickness or bankrupt people; the fear of deportation; the criminalization of trivial offenses that turn completed jail sentences into life sentences instead. At committee and steering committee meetings, leaders and the organizer discuss strategies to achieve some of these goals, given their power base and relationships. They cannot do everything, so they recognize the limits of their power.

In Texas, thousands of people live in unplanned communities outside the city limits, called *colonias*, without access to full, conventional public services such as water and sewer systems taken for granted elsewhere. The number of *colonia* residents without infrastructure was ten times what it once was in Texas before IAF affiliates got engaged. Continuing into 2018–19, El Paso-area borderland *colonia* residents with broken septic systems became leaders working with the

IAF affiliate, specifically with former organizer and long-term core leader Alicia Franco, to get the multiple, fragmented water authorities to agree to meet, work on the problem, figure out solutions, and apply for grants to fund solutions. The process of bringing together those with interests and responsibilities is more complicated than many people would imagine. This multi-year process also involves coordination with state representatives who tap state EDAP (Economically Distressed Areas Program) funding and seek more of it each legislative session.[42] Because Texas IAF operates statewide, non-borderland IAF leaders can also push to support such funding from their representatives, whether Republican or Democrat, not only those from the borderlands. IAF power operates at local and state levels, and affiliate delegate leaders discuss statewide strategy at meetings in the central part of the state (Austin, San Antonio) to call attention to priority issues on which they might work with the current legislative session.

IAF paid **organizers** work with leaders (and **core leaders** in institutions) to meet regularly with steering committees and subcommittees and to develop public **actions,** designed to produce **reactions,** leverage, and **relational meetings** with public officials to pursue strategies to achieve pragmatic goals. These are not pie-in-the-sky visions, but **winnable goals** that are politically possible in a particular place and era. Organizers, who are employees who earn middle-class salaries comparable to high school principals, work for both their local leaders and the larger IAF structure. Their salaries constitute a major item in local budgets for which funds must be generated from member dues, donors, and non-government grants in local 501c3 and 501c4 tax-exempt organizations with budgets that range from approximately $100,000 to $400,000 annually and involve technical assistance fees paid to the IAF, Texas Network of Organizations (TNO), and Interfaith Education Fund (IEF) who, together, provide trainings and support for organizers and leaders. After each activity, participants meet to reflect and **evaluate** events in a constant effort to improve processes. How did we do on turnout? People respond: B+. What about our floor team (leaders who register attendees or quiet any in the audience who shout out for their candidate, for example). Response: perhaps graded a C. How well did the co-moderators do (response: A− say some). What could they have done better? And so on.

The ideal organizers work in the background; only occasionally do they speak for the organizations in public or to the press. Their centralized training and experience in successful approaches is passed on from one affiliate to another through rotation and continuous socialization (more on this in Chapter 5).

In public **actions,** leaders engage with public officials to secure public commitments from them about their issue-oriented agendas. As noted earlier, one common action is the dramatic high-attendance (in the hundreds or thousands) **Accountability Sessions,** sometimes called candidate forums, carefully planned, dramatic, and scripted events complete with rehearsals. In those events, leaders tell stories that drive candidates to publicly promise with their responses to yes-no questions on IAF's winnable policy goals and are allotted brief explanation time to explain their responses, including the final question of whether candidates will meet with leaders if elected. No personal attacks are allowed, as is stressed in pre-event briefings with candidates, written rules, and by co-moderators at the events themselves.

As registered nonprofit organizations, IAF affiliates behave in **nonpartisan** ways; they do not endorse parties or candidates, but seek to develop relationships with whomever is elected, regardless of party affiliation. Candidates, briefed in advance complete with the exact IAF affiliate's questions twenty-four hours in advance—regardless of whether they publicly answer "yes" or "no" to the issue-oriented questions—often comment that these sessions are the best-organized and best-attended they experienced during their campaigns. However, those politicians who resent their inability to control public-event agendas become alienated, sometimes hindering relational work with the IAF affiliate thereafter. In El Paso, the large EPISO/Border Interfaith events generate around 600 attendees. In the bigger cities of Texas, such as Dallas, event attendee numbers reach into the thousands. Houston is so spread out that regional Accountability Sessions have been held. The presence of the print and TV media press magnifies exposure to wider audiences, although websites only exist in the stronger IAF affiliates. Another organized action involves a public, parent, or **civic academy** with an educational theme to discuss issues, generally attracting a hundred people.

Local IAF goals reflect participants' expressed struggles in house meetings. When IAF affiliates achieve goals, the achievement boosts leaders' hopes and spurs them toward other goals. IAF family agendas do not involve hand-outs or subsidies. Indeed, IAF promotes what it calls the **Iron Rule of Self-Sufficiency.** As organizers repeat and repeat again to unpaid leaders, "Our main rule is never, ever do for others what they can do for themselves," said former EPISO organizer Arturo Aguila in

Accountability Session "rules," EPISO/Border Interfaith, 2018. Photograph by Kathleen Staudt.

the press.[43] IAF goals are hardly utopian, but rather practical goals that can be achieved in the current context (i.e. winnable) and that remind me of Voltaire's supposed remark translated to: "Perfect is the enemy of good." Yet one might ask whether such goals are strong or "radical" enough to challenge power relations and result in enforceable, substantive change.

IAF rules, taught in trainings and repeated training sessions, consist of principles that evolved over the years. Box 1.4 lists the more recent ones, though nearly two decades old, quoted from the late national IAF Director Edward Chambers.[44] I am going to **bold** those that I heard and witnessed over many years. In the concluding chapter, I offer categories for the rules based on analyses in the body of this book that range from common sense and homilies to rules practiced more in the last quarter of the twentieth-century or those that produced contradictions.

Many rules make good common sense. Some contain humor. Some may reflect underlying dialectical reasoning. Yet other rules and principles sound radical, conflictual, and didactic in an organization that has changed as IAF builds and re-builds over time, some might argue, even mellowed or matured as readers may conclude after reading further.

Box 1.4 IAF "Universals of Organizing"

* *The iron rule: Never, never do for others what they can do for themselves.*
* *All action is in the inevitable reaction.*
* *All changes come about as a result of threat or pressure.*
* *Every positive has a negative, and every negative a positive.*
* *Action is to organization as oxygen is to the body.*
* *Never go to power for a decision, but only with a decision.*
* *The law of change: Change means movement; movement means friction; friction means heat; heat means controversy, conflict.*
* *Power precedes program.*
* *The opposition is your best ally in radicalizing your people.*
* *Anything that drags along for too long becomes a drag.*
* *Power without love is tyranny; love without power is sentimental mush.*
* *Your own dues money is almost sacred; other people's money starts controlling you.*
* *Power can never be conferred; it must be taken.*
* *The haves will never give you anything of value.*
* *Have-nots should not be romanticized; they cheat, lie, steal, double cross and play victim just like the haves do.*
* *Peace and justice are rarely realized in the world as it is; the pursuit, not possession, of happiness takes place amid struggle, conflict, and tension.*
* *Avoid cynics and ideologues; they have nothing to offer.*
* *Right things are done for wrong reasons, and bad things are often done for right reasons.*
* *Given the opportunity, people tend to do the right thing.*
* *Life force is about natality, plurality, and mortality.*

In the concluding chapter, I revisit the rules with insights applied from the analysis in the body of the book. Chambers's rules, mixed with philosophical musings, sound like the earlier 1971 language of Alinsky who wrote in an era of youthful radical rebellion and social movement protests without youth necessarily practicing sound organizing principles.

In particular, Alinsky wrote a chapter on tactics (reprinted as a short Vintage book and re-issued in 2018) which leaned even more in a confrontational and conflictual direction; for example, he wrote about "the enemy" and "the target," or the use of "ridicule," "polarization," and "threat," even as the concepts of relationality and compromise taint such practices.[45] Such language is not the twenty-first-century IAF, in my experience and through interviews, but rather founding lore from fifty years ago, albeit which continues to affect public perceptions of the IAF. If anything, current practices resemble more Alinsky's 1946 book quoted in the beginning of this chapter emphasizing practical, "people organizing," and relying on instrumental strategies for realizing the goals that people have articulated.

Let me now outline the chapters along with the way they develop the frame set forth in this introduction.

Outline of chapters

This book, threaded with IAF stories and institutional concepts, is divided into several sections with one or more chapters. Conceptual material is touched upon in the text, but developed further in appendices and endnotes for readability. Underneath the concluding reflections of some chapters, resources for further reading or viewing are found. Chapter 2, in particular, has a lengthy list on Texas government, balanced news sources, and local cities in which IAF operates.

After this introductory chapter in Section I, Section II contains content on historic and contemporary Texas and the state and local political economies, situating IAF affiliates therein and Dallas Area Interfaith (DAI) in the Dallas-Fort Worth (DFW) region.

Chapter 2 starts with tough challenges and resistance to IAF organizing and how the IAF overcame them in with the growth of affiliated organizations around the state. The chapter begins with a brief history of impediments to Texas democracy, its changing political process and institutions, IAF coverage in the state and IAF county/city contexts, including population, economic, and demographic data on each county. The rise of state-level one-party rule amid the power of wealth and pay-to-play politics makes it increasingly difficult for IAF to proactively move its agenda. However, the mostly nonpartisan representation at the local level offers better opportunities for IAF to move local agendas to achieve accountability in governance.

Chapter 3 begins with stories from a Dallas Area Interfaith leader, then focuses entirely on Dallas and DAI strategies and achievements in this remarkable issue-based multi-racial coalition, complete with a timeline of achievements. DAI leaders discuss their most important recent achievements in far-ranging areas, from housing to hospital bonds and Catholic parish picture IDs in interactions with police around public safety.

Section III, Organizing with a Purpose, contains two chapters. Chapter 4, beginning with the eloquent words of a rabbinical leader about people's search for meaning in the twenty-first-century, examines the language of broad-based and faith-based community organizing in a state (and country) of extreme religious fissure and declining interest in faith-based institutions, especially among younger people. In Chapter 5, we look at the stories of unpaid leaders and paid organizers, along with their different roles in the IAF. I discuss the interaction of the IAF superstructure and local affiliates.

Section IV is devoted to education and the extent to which partnerships and pipelines exist between schools and community organizing, the potential lifeblood of future IAF strength. Starting with the story of an inspirational teacher-leader, Chapter 6 contrasts the achievements of the statewide IAF Alliance School model and its legacies in the current era, focusing on Austin Interfaith, EPISO, and Valley Interfaith in South Texas, including the institutionalization of some but not all Alliance School practices. In Chapter 7, the focus is on IAF collaboration and partnership with other organizations, specifically with the seeming growth in civic capacity between educators and business people to pursue educational reform in an Education Summit. Over twenty years, both groups still do not see eye to eye on basic demand-supply principles about an educated populace and brain drain from areas with low wages. El Paso's Education Summit in 2000 forms the case study around which the chapter is organized, but the chapter closes with another collaboration in good faith, which resulted in a weakly implemented ordinance on wage theft. Chapter 8 examines the tenuous relationship between higher education and IAF affiliates, calling attention to clashing organizational cultures and the institutional incentives that shape people's work. On a brighter note, the chapter also analyzes the six IAF-facilitated but independent workforce training centers that moved thousands of impoverished people toward middle-class salaries in a successful partnership with community colleges.

Section V, Closing Perspectives, brings together the analytic issues of the book and the prospects of a strong IAF future in the twenty-first-century field of multiple community organizations in Texas with more or less opportunity for social justice work. In that chapter, I address the six contradictions, the tensions thereby produced, and their possible resolutions. The Appendix to this section, drawing on senior organizer Elizabeth Valdez's idea, is a Letter to Texans, modeled on her training for leaders that asks them to write about their communities based on Paul's Letter to the Corinthians.

In closing, let me reiterate that IAF work is relational, time consuming, and persistent, sometimes requiring years to accomplish specific goals. As such, it is difficult to produce a year-by-year timeline of outcomes and accomplishments, for some IAF work involves training, applied research, and re-building processes in between the production of outcomes like changed policies. Perhaps IAF work, while being effective, seems less exciting or immediate than the episodic protest marches in which people participate to call attention to the separation of children from migrant families or police killings in African American communities. Protests, social media outrage, and social movements galvanize people around horrific problems and thereby push those problems onto policy agendas.

Alone, however, without a base of organized power and detailed experience-driven solutions, movements can do little to answer the classic question, "what is to be done?" given the fragmented complexities and less-than-transparent budgeting process in the US political system at all levels in the federal system of government. However, IAF and other social justice organizations cannot "do it all," certainly not at national levels,[46] but increasingly less so at state and local levels during a time when the Texas legislative and executive branches undermine local democracies with the principle of "pre-emption" that undermines city ordinances deemed anti-business, like living wages and anti-fracking efforts. To state history and political institutions we now turn in the next chapter.

For further reflection

See Texas IAF Founder Ernesto Cortés, Jr. videos:
Power: https://www.youtube.com/watch?v=C9pKOrAi97c
Relational Meetings: https://www.youtube.com/watch?v=g42mLGATG-c
Community organizing: https://www.youtube.com/watch?v=mbUuhsy
    HODw
See the national website along with articles by IAF organizers: http://www.
    industrialareasfoundation.org/

Search You Tube for many videos, positive and negative, about the late Saul Alinsky. The PBS (now ITVS) documentary "The Democratic Promise: Saul Alinsky and his Legacy" is particularly useful—available in online rentals or reasonably priced purchases.

Notes

1. From his *Prison Letters*, featured in the *New York Times*, "Hope Is a Powerful Weapon: Unpublished Mandela Prison Letters," the *NYT* editors, June 6, 2018.

2. He is quoted in Michael King, "Point Austin: Welcome to Hard Times," *Austin Chronicle*, February 13, 2009. https://www.austinchronicle.com/news/2009-02-13/740124/ Accessed Feb. 9, 2019.

3. Jeffrey Stout, *Blessed Are the Organized* 2010 (Princeton: Princeton University Press, 2010), 70.

4. I distinguished progressiveness in this era from the "progressive era" a century ago. See Chapter 2.

5. Besides Mary Beth Rogers, *Cold Anger: A Story of Faith and Power Politics* (Denton: University of North Texas Press, 1990) and IAF director Edward Chambers, *Roots for Radicals: Organizing for Power, Action, and Justice* (New York: Continuum Press, 2003), the academic books about the IAF include Mark Warren, *Dry Bones Rattling: Community Building to Revitalize Democracy* (Princeton: Princeton University Press, 2001) and Dennis Shirley, *Community Organizing for Urban School Reform* (1997) and *Valley Interfaith and School Reform: Organizing for Power in South Texas* (2002) (both Austin: University of Texas Press), and Stout (2010).

6. Among them, I include textbooks assigned in the state-mandated introduction to American and Texas Government courses, such as the otherwise fine Anthony Champagne and Edward Harpham (with Jason Casellas in the 2017 edition), *Governing Texas* textbooks (New York: W. W. Norton, 2015, 2017) and the more analytic *Lone Star Tarnished*, by Cal Jillson, now in its third edition (New York: Routledge, 2012, 2015). I know, because I taught political science in higher education for forty years in Texas and used Texas politics books plus perused other studies for this research.

7. Given the fluidity in the unpaid volunteer leadership base (see Chapter 5), I cannot offer precise percentages. In Texas, nine of ten people that the Census classifies as "Hispanic" share Mexican heritage.

8. Readers will find cited various scholarly books on Latinx politics (a gender-neutral term, pronounced Latin-ex) throughout the book, but one is particularly important here for its analysis of pathways into participation based on the Latino National Political Survey by Lisa J. Montoya, "Gender and Citizenship in Latino Political Participation," in *Latinos Remaking America*, edited by Marcelo M. Suárez-Orozco and Mariela M. Páez (Berkeley: University of California Press, 2008). She says, "The most consistent predictor of Latino participation has been the mobilization role of membership in organizations," p. 424. IAF affiliates resemble such organizations. School participation is another predictor, statistically significant at the .001 level. See also Biliana C. S. Ambrecht, *Politicizing the Poor: The Legacy of the War on Poverty in a Mexican-American Community* (New York: Praeger, 1976). See also the rich comparison of two women's organizations in the Los Angeles area: Mary S. Pardo, *Mexican American Women Activists: Identity and Resistance in Two Los Angeles Communities* (Philadelphia: Temple University Press, 1998). Among the few Latino scholars to focus on Mexican American political organizations, see Benjamin Márquez who has written about LULAC, MALDEF (a legal organization), and La Mujer Obrera. See reference list.

9. Ralph Armbruster-Sandoval, "Latino Political Agency in Los Angeles Past and Present," in Sharon Navarro and Rodolfo Rosales, eds. *The Roots of Latino Urban Agency* (Denton: University of North Texas Press), 29–30. Nevertheless, the index to this volume shows only one reference to the IAF, namely, in the late 1940s connection between Edward Roybal, Alinsky, and the CSO (Community Service Organization) in Los Angeles. In the Texas IAF, once a leader is elected to office, the official is no longer part of this non-governmental organization (NGO). Some of the women-mother activists Pardo interviewed got their start in the CSO and the IAF, specifically UNO (United Neighborhood Organization).

10. Saul Alinsky, *Reveille for Radicals* (Chicago: University of Chicago Press, 1946). See Chapter 1 (quotes through page 20). Subsequent chapter 1 paragraphs come from this book as well. The University of Texas Library archives contains Alinsky's correspondence from the 1950s and 1960s.

11. Little did I know that Saul Alinsky spoke at the University of Texas at El Paso (where I taught for forty years), about ten years before the IAF affiliate EPISO was founded: https://theprospector.newspaperarchive.com/tags/alinsky/

12. Rufus Browning, Dale Rogers Marshall, and David H. Tabb, *Protest Is Not Enough: The Struggle of Blacks and Hispanics for Equality in Urban Politics* (Berkeley: University of California Press, 1984) on ten places in California. Among fine scholarly works on urban politics, I would include Clarence Stone whose *Regime Politics* of the postwar era through the 1980s in Atlanta is classic, along with studies of civic capacity in reforming urban education (the latter of which are cited in later chapters).

13. Greg Martin, *Understanding Social Movements* (London and NY: Routledge, 2015). See Ch 1 generally, and pages 5 and 8 specifically. Social movements use stories and religion, but may be global and transformative in scope, and thus unlikely to achieve sweeping goals except to advance awareness and provide an edge behind which formal organizations can work. In one chapter, Martin asks how organized should a social movement be? IAF affiliates are very well organized; they achieve goals in targeted strategies. In an El Paso-based comparison of the anti-*feminicidio* binational movement and the organized IAF affiliate, EPISO, we see no overlap in Kathleen Staudt and Clarence Stone, "Division and Fragmentation: The El Paso Experience in Global-Local Perspective," in *Transforming the City: Community Organizing the Challenge of Political Change*, Marion Orr, ed. (Lawrence: University Press of Kansas, 2007), 84–108. More discussion of social movements can be found in Kathleen Staudt, *Violence and Activism at the Border: Gender, Fear, and Everyday Life in Ciudad Juárez* (Austin: University of Texas Press, 2008). See Chapters 1 and 4 on social movement mobilization in the Coalition Against Violence toward Women and Families at the Border and in other social movements.

14. Benjamin Márquez, "Mexican-American Political Organizations and Philanthropy: Bankrolling a Social Movement," *Social Science Review* 77, no. 3 (September, 2003): 329–46. His evidence-based analysis from IRS 990 forms that larger nonprofit organizations must complete focuses on the 1990s. As will be discussed in later chapters, dependence on the Catholic Campaign for Human Development (CCHD) can shape agendas. El Paso's Border Interfaith currently counts a third of its budget from the CCHD—budgets for which are circulated among steering committee members at monthly meetings.

15. Anthony Downs, *Inside Bureaucracy*, remains one of the best expositions of laws and propositions on this topic (Boston: Little Brown, 1967). See also my *Managing Development: State, Society, and International Contexts* (Sage, 1991) Chapter 5 on the warped ways "news" is

condensed for a president as it makes its way from competing agencies and organizational mindsets to the White House.

16. Sociologist Rosabeth Kanter wrote about flat and skewed hierarchies in *Men and Women of the Corporation*, (New York: Basic Books, 1977, second edition 1992).

17. Alinsky, 1946, p. 116.

18. LGBTQI stands for Lesbian, Gay, Bisexual, Transgender, Queer, and Intersex.

19. An influential article analyzing projects and organizations in many parts of the world is David Korten, "Community Organization and Rural Development: A Learning-Process Approach," *Public Administration Review* 40, no. 5 (1980): 480-511. Korten faults technical assistance and donor agencies (like USAID and the World Bank) for their "Blueprint" models in which planners decide features in advance, often at a distance from the locale in which the efforts will be carried out, rather than an ongoing evaluation and modification of efforts ("Learning Process").

20. Gender studies examine the socially constructed expectations of women, men, and people.

21. These numbers refer to tax-exempt designations, reviewed and authorized by the Internal Revenue Service (IRS). Unlike the 501c3, the 501c4 designation permits organizations that promote the common good to involve themselves in activities related to legislation, though they cannot operate in partisan ways or endorse candidates. https://www.irs.gov/charities-non-profits/other-non-profits/social-welfare-organizations

22. IAF founder Saul Alinsky peppered the titles of his books with the word "radical," as did Edward Chambers.

23. Mary Beth Rogers eloquently defines anger "which, for the working poor, arises most often from being ignored, invisible, left out, overlooked, dismissed, and burdened by the small frustrations and daily humiliations of a constant struggle to get by.... rooted in direct experience and held in collective memory." IAF organizing cools down the "hot anger" (which can be self- or other destructive) and turns it into a tool for hopeful and constructive change (1990: 9–10).

24. Robert Michels, *Political Parties: A Sociological Study of the Oligarchical Tendencies of Modern Democracy* (New York Press, 1911, reprinted in 1962, 1968), a classic that is often cited as a warning to organizations working in democracies to practice internal democracies.

25. See Rogers, 1990; Dennis Shirley's books, *Community Organizing for Urban School Reform* and *Valley Interfaith and School Reform:*

Organizing for Power in South Texas (Austin: University of Texas Press, 1997 and 2002, respectively); Robert H. Wilson, *Public Policy and Community: Activism and Governance in Texas* (Austin: University of Texas Press, 1997); and Mark Warren, *Dry Bones Rattling: Community Building to Revitalize American Democracy* (Princeton: Princeton University Press, 2001).

26. Sidney Tarrow used the phrase political opportunity structures in *Power in Movement: Social Movements and Contentious Politics* (New York: Cambridge University Press, 1998, second edition); James Q. Wilson, in *Political Organizations,* talks about the creation stage in Chapter 10 (New York: Basic Books, 1973, 1995, second edition).

27. In "Autoethnography: An Overview," *Forum: Qualitative Social Research* 12, no. 1 (2011), Carolyn Ellis, Tony E. Adams and Arthur P. Bochner define autoethnography as an "approach to research and writing that seeks to describe and systematically analyze (graphy) personal experience (auto) in order to understand cultural experience (ethno)," p. 1. Like ethnographers, they take extensive field notes, interview cultural members, "and examine members' ways of speaking and relating" with theoretical tools and research literature, p. 3. And like the anthropologist interviewed in *The Chronicle of Higher Education*, April 23, 2017, "Scholars Talk Writing: Ruth Behar," it is "ethically necessary that we write in the first person" in accessible, vivid, and clear language, p. 3. I used Voluntary Consent Forms in my formal interviews, which people signed agreeing to whether they could be quoted (or if they wanted to check the quotes ahead of time, about which I duly complied).

28. Marion Orr, "The Changing Ecology of Civic Engagement," in his edited volume *Transforming the City: Community Organizing and the Challenge of Political Change* (Lawrence: University Press of Kansas 2007), 2. Thanks for Orr and others, I attended two working seminars at Brown University to prepare my co-authored chapter for Orr's volume.

29. A voluminous literature on social movements exists, starting from anti-war protests to Black Power and Chicano movements and the feminist movement. Jo Freeman did a superb analysis of the energy yet "tyranny of leaderlessness" in movement groups compared with established women's organizations, in *The Politics of Women's Liberation* (New York: McKay, 1975).

30. Norton Long, "The Local Community as an Ecology of Games," *American Journal of Sociology* 64, no. 3 (1958): 251–61. Orr frames his analysis from many of Long's concepts. Clarence Stone wrote extensively about civic capacity in different urban regimes. See his

edited volume, *Changing Urban Education*, 1998, and Stone, Jeffrey Henig, Bryan Jones, and Carol Pierannunzi, *Building Civic Capacity: The Politics of Reforming Urban Schools* (Lawrence: University Press of Kansas, 2001).

31. Mark Granovetter, "The Strength of Weak Ties," *American Journal of Sociology* 78 (1974): 1360–80. Strong ties involve multiple and dense relationships, while weak ones are episodic, like networks.

32. Cassandra Pollock, et.al., "Democratic Women Lead Biggest Shift in Texas House since 2010 Midterm Elections," *Texas Tribune,* November 6, 2018. https://www.texastribune.org/2018/11/06/texas-midterm-election-results-texas-house-races/

33. See the video at https://www.youtube.com/watch?v=KXjj67AG 1UI&feature=youtu.be (Accessed Nov. 10, 2018). Incumbents refused to attend the huge event, missing the opportunity to demonstrate accountability to all people and groups in their districts. See Jonathan Malesic in *Rewire*'s religious news, "Why Republicans Skipped an Interfaith Forum," https://rewire.news/religion-dispatches/2018/10/16/why-dallas-republicans-skipped-an-interfaith-forum/. Accessed Nov. 10, 2018.

34. Harvey Molotch, "The City as a Growth Machine: Toward a Political Economy of Place," *American Journal of Sociology* 82, no. 4 (1976): 309–332.

35. An example of critical-race studies that dismiss the IAF would include Rodolfo Rosales, *The Illusion of Inclusion: The Untold Story of San Antonio* (Austin: University of Texas Press, 2000). Most ignore the IAF, despite the predominance of Latinx organizers and leaders in Texas.

36. "Public work" is a phrase coined by Harry Boyte and Nancy Karl, *Building America: The Democratic Promise of Public Work* (Philadelphia: Temple University Press, 2005).

37. Irasema Coronado and I addressed these kinds of *questions* among cross-border NGOs in our book *Fronteras no Más: Toward Social Justice at the US-Mexico Border*, (New York: Palgrave USA, 2002).

38. One of the first was Rosabeth Kanter, *Men and Women of the Corporation* (New York: Basic Books, 1977), but see others in, for example, Jane Parpart, Shirin Rai, and Kathleen Staudt, *Rethinking Empowerment: Gender and Development in a Global/Local World* (New York: Routledge, 2002).

39. Peter Bachrach and Morton Baratz, "Two Faces of Power," *American Political Science Review* 56, no. 4 (1962): 947–52. The phrase comes from E. E. Schattsneider in *The Semi-Sovereign People* (1960) who discusses how political organization mobilizes bias in exploiting

some conflicts and suppressing others. On nuance in the pluralist perspective, see Rodney Hero, *Latinos and the U.S. Political System: Two-Tiered Pluralism* (Philadelphia: Temple University Press, 1992).

40. Mayor Dee Margo, August 18, 2018. He knows us all.

41. Readers may note that I alter the names for people with Mexican heritage: government agencies use the word Hispanic; social scientists, Latino, Latina, and gender-neutral Latinx; Mexican Americans, as frequently used by people themselves in Texas.

42. With my IAF hat, I have attended numerous relational meetings with officials in which Alicia Franco takes the lead in explaining issues in *colonias* and funding for utilities, which have been a constant, unending part of the EPISO agenda. Readers should disabuse themselves of the notion that all U.S. residents have access to safe water and sewer systems.

43. Aguila was quoted in Marty Schladen, "Mark Success, Shape Future: Religious Organizations Gather on 40th Anniversary," *El Paso Times*, April 30, 2016, pp. 1-2B. I attended the anniversary event in San Antonio that day with hundreds of others, hearing keynote addresses from the San Antonio mayor, Bexar County judge, and IAF leaders.

44. From *Roots for Radicals*, Edward Chambers, 2003, pp. 103–4.

45. Saul Alinsky, *Rules for Radicals: A Pragmatic Primer for Realistic Radicals* (New York: Vintage, 1971), 127–36.

46. The IAF does not work at a national level. See Richard Wood's analysis of PICO National Network (now called Faith in Action), "Higher Power: Strategic Capacity for State and National Organizing," in Orr, 2007, pp. 162–192, and its costly efforts to bring local federation leaders to Washington, D.C.

Chapter 2
"Texas Historical Perspectives:
A Flawed Democracy"

L et me begin with a story, an "origins story" as anthropologists might call it, of El Paso's IAF affiliate El Paso Interreligious Sponsoring Organization (EPISO), born in a hostile and resistant context. I based the following on documents and clippings from EPISO office files.

In the early 1980s, thirty men—all Catholic priests except for one Scottish Presbyterian pastor, Rev. Gordon Bowie of University Presbyterian Church—signed a document supporting the creation of EPISO. Fr. William "Bill" Ryan, the priest at St. Matthew Catholic Parish, signed, and with a vote, congregants decided to become a member institution. I relished the opportunity to examine paper documents, typewritten materials, and carbon copies of letters which can hardly be found any more in this electronic day and age except in formal archives, such as the outstanding University of Texas at San Antonio (UTSA) collection on the Industrial Areas Foundation.[1]

Soon thereafter, Catholic conservatives, in particular a couple at St. Matthew Parish, began a crusade to revoke their congregation's vote to become a member institution and to persuade other parishes in El Paso and throughout Catholic conservative media elsewhere to shun IAF organizations. In this, the height of the patriotic Cold War with Russians (the former Soviet Union), in Op Eds and media articles, they used hyperbolic language to call the IAF organizer Robert Rivera an "outside agitator" and "communist" who "used Marxist tactics."

The local media fanned this fire, as did David Crowder's headline "Religious leaders quietly hire troublemaker to better city." At first glance, I wondered why the journalist used the word "troublemaker" in the headline. Then I saw that Crowder's phone interview with national IAF organizer Edward Chambers made that clear. Chambers said, "We're troublemakers. We go in and ask questions about politics and finance you're not supposed to ask." And in the article, opponent David Escobar warned of something he thought was more ominous: "They use a script." Yes, IAF affiliates plan, organize, and script complicated public events! So do professors, students, managers, preachers, and many others.

The couple at the Catholic parish, devoted to the Reverence for Life ministry of the parish and Diocese, pursued a life-long crusade against the right to abortion—what other people in this still-contentious debate call reproductive justice. The husband took that ministry to his grave (as I found later, reading his obituary). EPISO refused to participate in the anti-abortion ministry because the IAF is a social justice organization which strategizes around consensus issues from its base and member institutions rather than a Catholic agenda. Besides, in an IAF organization like EPISO with mostly Catholic member institutions, few reproductive choice issues would likely bubble up in house meetings (recall the lingo from chapter 1). Then and now, IAF affiliates do not align themselves with one or another side of this complex health issue that affects women's lives more than men's. Rather, IAF affiliates' priorities focus on decent wages, water and sewer public service, immigration, education, and workforce training. Moreover, funding from the Catholic Campaign for Human Development forbids attention to family planning and abortion, and some IAF organizations have come to depend on these grant funds.

EPISO survived and eventually thrived, but not without its controversial legacy as a radical "confrontational" organization. IAF Accountability Sessions, with their "yes or no" format plus short explanation for candidates more accustomed to saying "maybe" in public settings, seemed uncomfortable to some. EPISO began to acquire a seat at the public table, for example, on the advisory committee of the El Paso Collaborative for Academic Excellence from 1992 through 2011 (see Chapter 7). Candidates began to look forward to the best-planned and attended forums (the accountability sessions) in the region, for candidates would always know and understand the questions in advance at events with the IAF base, hundreds of issue-oriented voters in attendance, all promising in unison toward the end of the session to encourage five or ten of their friends to vote.

As in any IAF affiliates, member institutions come and go, depending on the clergy and core leaders' sentiments within the church. Organizers also come and go, assigned by the state IAF senior organizers and rotated periodically; the way organizers work affects whether leaders come in, stay in, or drop out, but local leaders have little hand in selecting them even as organizers meet monthly with leaders, their steering committee members (see Chapter 5).

Because EPISO's member institutions came largely from Catholic parishes located on the east side and lower valley of the huge El Paso

County—over 1,000 square miles, only slightly smaller than the state of Rhode Island—Judeo-Christian clergy on El Paso's west side began meeting and discussing the possibility of building a second, sister organization of different faiths that eventually formed as the Westside Interfaith Alliance with a slightly different organizational culture, i.e. less "confrontational."

To accommodate growth in member institutions in the center, north-east, and colonias off the I-10 corridor, the new sister IAF organization named itself Border Interfaith, with member institutions that included a synagogue, Protestant and Catholic churches, and for some years, a small Buddhist community and teacher association. Border Interfaith leaders engaged with the Imam and El Paso's Islamic Center leaders in relational meetings on multiple occasions, but the Imam was deported and its leaders in the low-profile mosque passed on the opportunity to become a member institution.

Both El Paso IAF affiliates use different colors and logos (on pins, shirts, and signs). The round bilingual EPISO logo is red, white, and blue, with the words "Standing for Families" at the top half of the circle, and "En Defensa de Nuestras Familias" on the bottom half. The square Border Interfaith logo is green and white, with multiple religious symbols, such as the cross, the six-pointed star, the Buddhist yin-yang, and the Islamic crescent moon. Whatever the public perception, over time, neither IAF affiliate behaved in confrontational ways as the Alinsky-Chambers language suggested (recall Chapter 1). Like both of San Antonio's once stand-alone affiliates, COPS and Metro Alliance, EPISO and Border Interfaith consolidated themselves into a single organization in late 2018 with the hopes to blend once distinctive organizational cultures and rebranding in a new name.

Chapter framing

Since 1845, when Texas entered the U.S. as a slave state, it had had a long history of depressed political and public participation. Faith-based and broad-based community organizations have the potential to turn around that history with greater civic engagement. IAF affiliates state-wide emerged in Texas, partially turning around the once-grim history of restricting their rights and opportunities for women, economic have-nots, and Mexican and African Americans, as the body of this chapter details. Like other southern states, U.S. Congressional intervention in the

1940s and the 1965 Voting Rights Act reduced restrictions and the poll tax. Attempts at more voter suppression continue into 2019. Centuries of this less-than-democratic history shaped the state's ability to realize its claim to democracy.

Not surprisingly, people's current public participation in politics is low compared to other states, no matter the indicators used to measure participation. According to the Annette Strauss Institute for Civic Life at the University of Texas at Austin, the state ranks #47 in voter turnout, driven largely by socioeconomic factors,[2] though lower Hispanic voter turnout captures more media attention. In presidential elections, when turnout is highest compared to midterm, local, and primary elections, only 55 percent of registered Texans voted in 2016 (compared with 70 percent in Wisconsin, the state where I grew up), and mid-term elections generated about half that percentage except in 2018 with its confidence vote for or against the sitting U.S. president and a race for U.S. senator from Texas. Only a third of Texans join groups, according to the report, and churches are the most common group that people join, although a mere quarter of the population, 26 percent.

Unhealthily low participation rates result from centuries of history, which we cover in the first part of this chapter. Obstacles to participation began to drop after World War II, thanks partly to Congress, to Mexican American civil rights groups, and to growing civil-society pressure within the state. As Michael Lind sees it, both traditional southern elites and modernizing business elites eventually sought federal public investment to grow the economic infrastructure and host military bases, but adhered strongly to the concept of a low tax, limited government.[3]

In this historical chapter, I advance two arguments, organized into the two major sections of the chapter. First, the Texas IAF emerged amid the political flux of the immediate post-civil rights era in the 1970s with the confluence of growing Mexican American political muscle and the still-resistant local business-government alliances that left segregated neighborhoods festering with limited infrastructure and ensuring flood disasters in places lacking infrastructure like west San Antonio with its not-yet-tapped faith- and identity-based communities. Thanks to the moral and ethical rationales that come with faith and justice work (developed in Chapter 4), volunteer leaders roused and demanded responses from recalcitrant city bureaucrats and politicians. Civic entrepreneurs, like in the IAF, seized and expanded political spaces that began to open up in Texas cities. The half-century-old MALDEF, the Mexican American Legal Defense and Education Fund, challenged (and continues to challenge) structural obstacles that impede democracy, such as local at-large districts in favor of single-member districts in many cities and states,[4] thereby providing leverage and space for community organizations like IAF affiliates to gain a stronger voice in city councils, including San Antonio and other Texas cities. See Box 2.1 that summarizes success stories from Texas IAF founding lore along with their practical civic and strategic details. Recall the IAF rules from Chapter 1 to see the early "radical" language and tactics of the last quarter of the twentieth century.

My second argument focuses on the absence of civic education in Texas social studies curricula—a gap that IAF affiliates fill. The Texas Essential Knowledge and Skills (TEKS) state standards for public education emphasize facts and dates in history and government using a standardized testing system that prizes memorized responses to multiple-choice/multiple-guess questions, rather than the Civics Standards found in the National Assessment of Educational Standards (NAEP) voluntary test which contains four criteria, besides "content knowledge" to include "experience, skills, and motivation" (the latter of which could include relevant local-regional political institutions and processes).[5] According to the above-cited Texas Civic Health report, besides low voter registration and turnout, only 14 percent of Texans have ever contacted a public official. In IAF affiliates and among primary and secondary volunteer leaders (see lingo in Chapter 1) in their member institutions, many forms of participation have become normal and routine: voting, contacting officials, and meeting with them. Leaders know their representatives. This chapter incorporates some basic civics: changing political institutions. I also include an elaborate section of websites at the end of the chapter under the heading "For Further Reflection" listing the many statewide media outlets, think-tanks, and government websites, both in local IAF cities and the state. In a typical assignment in my former courses, students completed a form with names and other information about their city council representative, county commissioner, school board trustee(s), and state legislators. Alas, the majority of students were clueless before the assignment. Not so for EPISO and Border Interfaith leaders!

In this founding lore, we can appreciate the radical tactics, effectively deployed in a different era. At the UTSA archives, I read and took photos of the provocative language used in 1970s and 1980s COPS/Metro, such as a non-dated resolution criticizing a utility "monster [that] continues to inequitably suck the blood of the elderly" and a flyer for the 9th Annual

Box 2.1 IAF Founding Lore

San Antonio was a particularly fertile place in which Mexican American leaders emerged, including Ernesto Cortés, Jr. in the Mexican American Youth Organization (MAYO).[6] However, Cortés parted ways with identity politics and founded the first IAF affiliate in 1974, Communities Organized for Public Service (C.O.P.S., though I will use COPS from here on) in San Antonio with a large Mexican-heritage population that lived on the west side of the city, absent conventional city infrastructure such as sidewalks and drainage for flood control. COPS's early years are well documented, and its achievements have become stories told and retold in foundational IAF studies.

Ernesto Cortés, Jr., San Antonio C.O.P.S. early years. Staudt photograph, courtesy UTSA Archives.

Every year, floods caused deaths and housing destruction in San Antonio. In 1974, torrential rains caused particularly bad crises, even sweeping away a bridge. Crises often galvanize political action, and COPS provided constructive action and practical strategies for solutions. From the book by Mary Beth Rogers, Cold Anger, COPS leaders' dialogue with City Manager Sam Granata is worth quoting. After

> *"... five hundred angry COPS members" confronted him with facts and figures ..., "COPS leaders told the city manager they were not interested in any of his long-winded explanations. They wanted 'simple yes or no answers' to their questions. Why was the West Side so neglected? What had happened to the bond money? Would the city rectify its past mistakes?"... Granata "admitted to the shouting audience that the city had just flat 'dropped the ball'."[7]*

So much for fair and professional management, part of the myth and occasional reality in modern government. When COPS leaders went to City Council, their case was persuasive. COPS used confrontational tactics that Alinsky and Chambers would celebrate (recall Chapter 1). The mayor ordered staff to come up with a new budgetary plan to finance drainage. This achievement is what the IAF calls a "win," that is, a victorious achievement of goals which also strengthened the COPS's ability to demonstrate power for respect and recognition. COPS acquired power, such as multiple people, multiple member institutions, and research that it developed on its own, before pushing the program, or a strategy design to win, as per an IAF rule: "power before program." The win buoys hope and motivation for subsequent goals to be addressed.

To exercise leverage for influence, IAF affiliates once used strategies and tactics from the creative to the mundane. Among COPS tactics in San Antonio, leaders pushed for a counter budget to fund still-limited infrastructure projects on the west side which needed and deserved equitable funding compared to other parts

(Continued)

***Box 2.1** (Continued)*

of San Antonio. Among creative tactics, COPS focused on two big institutions, a bank and department store, and went to department stores, "trying on everything and buying nothing. Then, they lined up at the teller windows ... changing hundreds of dollars into pennies and then back again into dollars."[8] Here too, we see confrontation, creative, dramatic, and semi-humorous tactics reminiscent of Alinsky's discussion of the Tycoon Department Store and Mr. Snoot (again, Chapter 1). While Alinsky was still alive and organizing in Chicago, he even threatened to bring enough people to lock themselves in all the public restrooms at O'Hare Airport; the threat alone was enough to achieve victory (reminiscent of Chambers's rule about threats). Remember, readers, this was an earlier era when social movement activists and the IAF used drama and creativity in their public tactics.

In this and other IAF affiliates, equitable funding to address flooding became a potent call. The presence of ordinary people-leaders plus priests, nuns, and pastors pushed agendas toward victories in early years, though with less disruption and confrontation once the organization gained respect and its seat at the table in subsequent decades. IAF affiliates pursued, and continue to pursue, then and now, Get-Out-The-Vote (GOTV) efforts to educate voters about their positions and to increase turnout, particularly in districts where a new representative will engage with the whole community (i.e. become relational) rather than only with their donors.

Convention on November 7, 1982, in which "C.O.P.S. Demands a Future: 'No permanent Underclass in San Antonio'."[9] This was tough, effective language for a state that had long privileged the "haves" in the White population.

Historic supremacies: White, wealthy, male

Non-Texans (as I once was) may not appreciate the size, scope, and patriotism of the state in the larger U.S. context. Texas is huge, second largest in land size (after Alaska) and second largest in population.[10] For this section, I want to stress how Texas prides itself on being a former republic (1836–45); its Lone-Star flag flies very close to, but underneath the U.S. flag in many public places including schools at all levels. The biennial *Texas Almanac*, issued every other year, is probably the longest[11] of any state almanac.

Throughout their history, Texans have lived under "six flags" (U.S. since 1845; Confederate States of America 1861–65; Republic of Texas 1836–45; Mexico 1821–36; Spain 1519–1821; and France 1685–90;) which one sees on the floor of the State Capitol rotunda. When Texas flew the Mexican flag, once-original inhabitants welcomed "illegal immigrants" from Tennessee and other states who settled in the place, contrary to Mexican law from 1830.[12]

In Austin, the state capital, the Bullock Texas State History Museum devotes the second floor of three to the pre-republic and independence periods. When I visited, the thousand-miles of borderlands with Mexico hardly got attention. Mexico outlawed slavery in 1829, so when the opportunity to legalize slave labor arose in the Texas Republic, politicians seized the opportunity and once again, after US annexation and secession, in the Confederacy era.

Leaping forward from this historical section, readers should know that Texas history is continuously drilled into students' heads, no doubt more than state-history drilling in other states. Students are required to learn about Texas both in middle school and in one of two required American Government courses in public universities and community colleges. Readers should consult the scores of Grade 7 social studies "standards" focused on Texas history, heroes, and geography.[13] Besides pledging allegiance to their country, Texas law since 2001 requires that underage Texas students also pledge allegiance to their state: "Honor the Texas flag; I pledge allegiance to thee, Texas, one state under God, one and indivisible." When I see and hear this ritual, I get a queasy feeling, wondering if it detracts from the national U.S. loyalty pledge. My home state, Wisconsin, has no such state loyalty pledge, and I doubt that any other states do either.

Although its borders and boundaries changed throughout history, Texas has always been big enough to distinguish itself by regions, such as the Great Plains, the Gulf Coastal Plains, and the Tropics of the South Texas Rio Grande Valley among other more elaborate regional categories. Even though once-state Comptroller John Sharp defined a sizeable 43 of the 254 counties in the "border" region in his well-known book *Bordering the Future* in 1998, the borderlands region is rendered near invisible in contemporary Texas textbooks despite the uniqueness that has always come from the interdependence of Mexican and US cities and towns along the border.[14]

For some, Texas history and pride feel like a "state of mind" as the song "Lone Star" (aka) "Texas State of Mind" goes with revealing lyrics: "It doesn't matter how far I go; that lone-star is all I see; no matter how many miles I put between us." This historic mystique works its way into numerous symbols of pride and even campaign slogans. One 2018 U.S. Senate campaign slogan featured "Tough as Texas," emphasizing freedom and strength. While settlers of all backgrounds might have required toughness and strength to survive, those with African American and Mexican heritages experienced little freedom, but rather avid state-legitimized discrimination, segregation, and slavery.

The so-called Progressive Era of 1900–20 hardly exhibited progressiveness in its current meanings around social justice and democracy. Texas practiced racial and ethnic segregation, resistance to women's suffrage, poll taxes that disenfranchised poor voters, tenant farming, and alcohol prohibition. Historically, the poll tax of $1.50–$2.00 to exercise the equal right to vote could represent a whole day's wage.

Opening political opportunity in the mid-twentieth century and beyond

In one-party dominant systems, the plight of Texas for most of the late nineteenth through the mid-twentieth century, the spring primary elections to nominate the Democratic Party candidate become the major contest. So if the law could inhibit non-white candidates, incumbents could virtually guarantee white supremacy. The "White Primary" became law in the early 1920s, but Dr. Lawrence A. Nixon, El Paso dentist and member of the NAACP, filed lawsuits and finally prevailed when U.S. courts outlawed such policies in the 1940s and the 1965 Voting Rights Act prohibited poll taxes. The American G. I. forum, a Mexican American civil rights and veterans' organization founded in 1948, challenged poll taxes and the denial of burial spaces by white-only funeral homes.

The League of United Latin American Citizens (LULAC), founded in 1929 and faulted for its assimilation orientation, worked for civil rights and filed society-changing lawsuits on jury selection, equitable educational funding, and residents' access to public education regardless of citizenship status.[15] Multiple LULAC Councils exist in many communities around the U.S. (El Paso has ten), but its base does not operate like the IAF affiliates. Founded a half century ago in 1968, the Mexican

American Legal Defense and Education Fund, modeled on the NAACP, calls itself the "nation's leading Latino legal civil rights organization" on its website. MALDEF advances civil rights, policy reforms, and structural changes in many issue areas, but as a legal organization, it mobilizes no local base as does the IAF.[16]

A major political institutional reform opened the political opportunity structure. Beginning in the 1970s but adjudicated through the 1990s and even now, the at-large local election system changed to geographic district-based systems thanks to MALDEF lawsuits. Advantages in an at-large system accrue to wealthier sections where voter turnout has always been higher than elsewhere and campaign contributions therefrom, generous. Some cities feature a mix of at-large and district-based seats, with a majority to the latter. The number of city council seats varies in each city, so obviously also the number of votes necessary for a majority to pass ordinances. Cities also began to hire professional city managers to avoid the administrative challenges that politicians with limited experience governing big bureaucracies might produce.

Political parties: Fissures and shifting ideological agendas

Political parties, for all their flaws, have historically served as mediating institutions that incorporate newcomers into political life. Their major task is to recruit and promote candidates who offer a loosely coupled ideological, issue, and policy agenda to voters. Candidates for county and state offices, including the fifteen-member State Board of Education, run in partisan races. For better or worse, most city and all school board elections are nonpartisan, a so-called "progressive" reform earlier in the twentieth century. Without issue-oriented campaigns, nonpartisan elections permit personality-based campaigning with victory often going to the candidates who generate the largest campaign donations, reported and transparent but not capped in Texas, unless countered by organized voters who understand the issues behind billboards, Facebook "boosts," and thirty-second television ads.

Statewide in the twentieth century, Texas shifted from the one-party dominance of Democrats, to a brief era of competition and choice, and then one-party Republican dominance. If one imagines a continuum from left to right with a bell-shaped curve at the center, Democrats once leaned slightly left of center, emphasizing proactive government, greater inclusiveness, and participation (in the U.S., known as liberal), and Republicans once leaned right of center, emphasizing individual choice and limited government (called conservative).[17] Ironically, southern Democrats once tended to vote conservatively, more so than northern liberal Republicans. (Yes, the labels can be confusing!)

Women and people of color began to seize more political and economic opportunities, achieving victories in civil rights, including women's rights, the U.S. Equal Pay and Equal Employment Opportunity laws of the mid-1960s, and advances in women's ability to control their bodies and plan families. In party-factionalized Texas, some Democrats opened up to include and recruit more women, Mexican and African Americans, while other Democrats remained relatively conservative. The Democrats were not the only party with fissures, however.

In the 1960s and 1970s, state political culture opened to more than White people. As Benjamin Márquez's definitive study about Mexican Americans in Texas analyzes, political mobilization occurred via civil rights, aligned with Democratic Party and Anglo elites therein, ultimately gaining successful integration. However, he says, "The incorporation of Mexican American activists and politicians into public life proceeded steadily even as vast socioeconomic disparities between the races remained intact. Electoral and community organizing gradually came to occupy distinct spheres of activism. Civil rights organizations grew less influential in party affairs and were replaced by ethnic caucuses and party leaders."[18] As this book shows, without attention to the connections between class, ethnicity/race, and gender, an inequitable status quo prevails.

The short-lived Raza Unida party held its first national convention in El Paso, 1972, and nudged greater party responsiveness and more diverse elected officials in nonpartisan elections. In conservative Democratic Party Texas at the time, Raza Unida reminded politicians to stop taking Mexican Americans' votes for granted without offering policy concessions.

Beginning in the 1980s, in the US generally, moderate Republican conservatism began to shift toward embracing fundamentalist religious constituencies, along with people resentful or anxious about civil rights and women's equality. Scholars and pundits called this "the southern strategy" to turn conservative Democrats in the south away toward ultraconservative White Republicans. Younger readers may be surprised to know that Republicans once supported the Equal Rights Amendment and women's right to choose abortion in consultation with their doctors during their first trimester in accordance with the 1973 Supreme Court *Roe v. Wade* decision. Nationally, the traditional Republican focus on individualism changed drastically in the 1980s during the Reagan and especially the George H. W. Bush presidential years.

Texas opened up in the 1980s and early to mid-1990s with the election of statewide Treasurer and then-Governor Ann Richards, covered well in Mary Beth Rogers's 2016 book. Also, journalist and humorist Molly Ivins said that Ann Richards was a "great politician" who also happened "to be remarkably good at governing;" and an " 'OK, let's work this thing out' kind of governor rather than a 'Do it my way or I'll break your kind.' "[19]

Ann Richards, Bill Hobby (Lieutenant Governor),[20] former Governor Mark White, and U.S. Republican Senator Kay Bailey Hutchison worked well with Texas IAF affiliates, supporting proactive public investments in quality workforce training and water, sewers, and road infrastructure in borderland *colonias*. They visited people and places outside of the capital city, Austin. The IAF also developed working relationships with political appointees in important state agencies, like the Texas Education Agency (TEA) that understood the importance of raising learning expectations for all students, regardless of their ethnicity or household earnings, for a solid economic future in the state. That was a time of pragmatic bipartisan centrist relational action to respond to Texans and forge practical solutions, including the issues that emerged from broad-based community organizations like the IAF. In the twenty-first century, bipartisanship and party competition have been lost to one-party dominance.

Not unsurprisingly in a changing socio-economic structure, parties evolved and people disagreed on polarizing issues, producing factions and breakaway movements. Nowadays people notice polarization within the Republican Party, once filled with business-friendly moderates but who now contend with hardline Tea Party activists who together can paralyze the passage of bills in Congress, even with a Republican majority in the House and/or Senate. The Tea Party movement began in 2009 and surged during the Obama presidential administration around the curious combination of extremely limited government approaches to, for example, health care, and yet of the big-government imposition of traditional ideas about family and sexuality. One can peruse the state's major political party platforms over the years to see how the Republican (Grand Old Party/GOP) Party seemed to take cues from the HULU-adapted novel written by Margaret Atwood in 1985, *The Handmaid's Tale*. Witness the recent struggles within the Texas Legislature in 2017 over students' school bathrooms. Had the strict bathroom bill passed, heavy governmental intrusion would have been necessary to police children with their birth certificates, and the gender label thereon, when students passed through checkpoints at doors to school restrooms.

Lest people assume that only Republicans are divided between the Tea Party and the moderate Republicans, Mary Beth Rogers colorfully analyzes intra-party factions, with names attached, in both parties and shifting allegiances over decades of recent Texas history in her 2016 book. In interviews with lawyer and moderate Republican Tom Luce, she called our attention to how small numbers of Tea Party voters who turn out at high rates can influence the Republican nominees for office at the state and national levels. Let me quote a few sentences in full from her book: "When I looked at the primary turnout numbers, the winner got only 3.5 percent of the vote that Republicans usually pull in a general election," Luce recalled. "That means that some 3.5 percent of the voters, the hard right of the Republican Party who control the primaries, also now control the state of Texas."[21]

In a state with low turnout generally and one-party dominance, we might predict ominous trends unless countered with voters who understand the way primary elections can warp ideological camps and shift the center of political gravity in extremist directions. Aggravating these trends even further is the way district boundaries are drawn by partisans in the legislature (whether Republicans or Democrats) after each Census, often known as "gerrymandering" for the strange lizard-like boundaries that tend to favor the incumbent, strengthen the dominant party, and reduce electoral competitiveness. As Texas author Lawrence Wright analyzes after what he calls the "most fractious" legislative session in 2017, this was a plan developed in 2003; after previously helping to organize fellow candidates and party infrastructure, Speaker of the House and ultraconservative Tom Craddick was quoted from an interview saying, "It wasn't just about winning elections. We had a redistricting plan" that created a permanent Republican majority and created a model that was replicated in other states.[22] In one-party dominant systems, voters cannot rely on the textbook-stressed "checks and balances" among the branches of government that could foster more voices and policy choices in between elections.

The Texas legislature

The Texas Legislature meets every other (odd-numbered) year, for a restricted number of days January through May, unless a special session is called. The Texas House consists of 150 representatives and the Texas

Senate, 31 senators, who earn just $7,200 annually and thus require other salaries, mainly in business and the legal profession (the two largest occupational categories of Texas legislators). Texas permits two weeks of early voting, a generous amount of time, though it requires voters to register a month before elections. Until recently, my bellwether home state Wisconsin restricted voting to election day only, but now permits early votes with the municipal clerk. Wisconsin offers an open primary which allows greater fluidity than the Texas-style closed primary that forces voters to declare a party affiliation, thus affecting both primary and run-off elections. Wisconsinites turn out at far higher rates, as noted in the 70 percent cited earlier.

The state legislature also placed new, but surmountable identification obstacles to voting into place, criticized as voter suppression because virtually no evidence existed that non-eligible people had fraudulently voted. Critics appealed the move, but by 2018, courts clarified decisions to leave the government-issued picture ID system in place. Three decades ago, the Texas Legislature required that all high school principals host a deputized voter registrar on campuses, but the 2018 Texas Civil Rights Project report, complete with a map, noted only selective compliance, particularly the way the law is ignored in the lower Rio Grande Valley and its majority Mexican American population.[23]

To bring us up to contemporary times, as the *Texas Tribune* state-wide media source noted with graphs and charts, the legislature is largely "White, Male, Christian, and Middle-Aged."[24] Women, Mexican Americans, and African Americans are underrepresented in this majority-minority state. The Texas Legislature provides an excellent website to track bills, hearings, and details about legislators and their districts.[25] However, bill tracking is complicated to follow, and one must know the bill's number, title, and year to locate items in its search engine. Well-paid lobbyists, ex-legislators among them, draft some of the bills. Lobbyists are skilled masters of this process, watching for opportunities to influence bills in their various stages or at hearings. Thirty-one senators serve in the Texas Legislature with four-year terms, while 150 house members serve two-year terms and operate in continuous re-election mode unless their seats are safe for re-election, sometimes without opponents. Thanks to partisan and racial gerrymandering, many seats count as safe.

The enormity of money in Texas politics cannot be overstated. Drawing on the National Institute of State Money in Politics Industry Influence, political scientists categorized contributions to state legislature candidates in 2014. In Table 2.1, see a condensation of contributions

Table 2.1: Top five interest groups and party contributions*

Finance, Insurance, Real Estate	$68.4 million (65% to Republicans)
Labor	$59.7 million (82% to Democrats)
Health	$52.1 million (61% to Republicans)
General business	$54.5 million (68% to Republicans)
Lawyers and Lobbyists	$37.6 million (51% to Republicans)

*Source: Anthony Champagne, Edward Harpham, and Jason P. Casellas,
Governing Texas (New York: W. W. Norton, 3rd edition, 2017), 2014 data, p. 195.

from various sectors and the political parties and candidates to whom
sectors contributed.

From finance, insurance, and real estate, then health, then health business and general business, and lawyers and lobbyists (categories as listed
in source),[26] we see overwhelming amounts going to the dominant Republican Party. With numbers like these, it is no wonder that some people
believe their votes cannot counter the way money talks in politics.

Besides getting sympathetic politicians in office, wealthy donors
also pay to play in the gubernatorial political appointment process
of Texas. To be appointed, contributions during the 2014 and 2018
governor's race have reached as high as $700,000–$1 million with
data available on websites like OpenSecrets.org.[27] Republicans also
find the pay-to-play system burdensome, despite the empty talk of
ethics reform. In 2017, Representative Lyle Larson (R), from Bexar
County where San Antonio is located, introduced HB3305, a bill that
would have capped campaign donations to $2,500 or less for those
appointed to state boards and commissions.[28] While it passed the
House, it failed in the Senate. In 2018, Governor Abbott (R) supported
Larson's ultra-conservative opponent in the Republican primary election, who was also supported by Empower Texans, a conservative
group. Though Larson won re-election, he is unlikely to reintroduce
such a bill in future legislative sessions.[29]

The State Legislature exhibits flaws. The map link shows the House
district sizes and shapes (https://tlc.texas.gov/redist/pdf/house/map.pdf).
The Senate districts are supposed to represent approximately 800,000
people each. Beginning in 2019, the legislature will begin to propose
re-drawn boundaries to prepare for the 2020 Census results, and from
that, create new boundaries in 2021 unless an (unlikely) independent
redistricting commission is established such as exists in several states.

El Paso's District 78 is divided into two distant locations, on both sides of the Franklin mountain range, discussed in January 2020 testimony. In Texas, the dominant party leaders draw the boundaries, and only in the most gerrymandered lines would legal challenges be successful for possible lawsuits or federal intervention. Like money in politics, voters may wonder if the deck is stacked against the fair representation of people's voices. The Texas Legislative Council provides detailed demographic, income, and education data on each House and Senate district, with the ease of a click.[30]

In sum, the historical political institutions of Texas once restricted but eventually opened to a wider, more inclusive public. When the Texas IAF was founded a half century ago, Texas was a very different place, dominated by Democrats with nearly 10 million people, that is, less than half its current size of almost 28 million. After a brief competitive, two-party state system, Texas reverted to one-party dominance, this time under a factionalized GOP in which Tea Party zealots could swing primary nominations, and money seemed to be able to buy elections and appointments unless organized people changed the way the system inhibited their voices.

Meanwhile, the Texas economy, its opportunities, inequalities, and demographic diversity have shifted. Will the statewide network of Texas IAF affiliates be able to mount bipartisan support and moral narratives to build a more ethical Texas democracy? As we see in the section on Texans' well-being below, many inequalities continue or grow, aggravating the possibility of a fairer future for state residents. Besides, Texas participates in a global economy with the largest Mexico trade volume among states of over $90 billion with Mexico (2017 figures). This is a result of the 1994 North American Free Trade Agreement (NAFTA), now awaiting the uncertainty of a U.S.-Mexico-Canada Agreement (USMCA)[31] and the densely interdependent borderlands cities and towns for the over 1,000 miles that Texas shares with four states in Mexico. However, national security procedures stifle and delay the movement of goods and people in this economic interdependence due to controls established after the eastern coast tragedies of September 11, 2001. Additionally, since 2017 the state has contributed $800 million annually for the federal responsibility of "border security" using rhetoric that resonates well with the fears generated during campaign seasons and budget-making times. Can local IAF affiliate policy victories counter this system, with progressive ordinances that leaders push in supposed local democracies?

The Texas one-party system, under the label of pre-emption, interferes with and suppresses local ordinances deemed business-unfriendly.

In a recent lawsuit, the Texas Public Policy Foundation aimed to fight the paid sick leave ordinances passed in some Texas cities in 2018, as pushed by a collaboration of social justice organizations (not including the IAF).[32] The conservative, business-oriented American Legislative Exchange Council (ALEC) also wines and dines legislators in Texas and other states with cookie-cutter legislative models to inhibit progressive initiatives.[33] The state has denied the ability of local democracies to pass progressive ordinances on such matters as living-wage standards, health and environmentally-unfriendly fracking inside city limits, and even the reduction of plastic bags that, once discarded, sully the landscape.

Open pockets of democracy and policymaking still exist; it takes power—organized people or organized money—to locate such pockets and to fine tune their strategies into winnable goals, sometimes diminishing or diluting impacts. For example, while living wage ordinances cannot be passed for all residents, as happens outside Texas, Texas city and county governments can still act to increase their employees' average wages, as has happened due to IAF pressure in El Paso and other cities. That is all well and good, but wage theft continues to be a problem for approximately a tenth of Texas low-income workers, who are not paid the legal minimum wage or paid as promised for overtime, for which numerous bureaucratic and criminal solutions have been put into effect in 2011 statewide and locally thereafter in El Paso and Houston (see Chapter 7 on collaboration over a narrow ordinance).

The social and economic well-being of Texas residents

True to its "limited government" label, Texas invests little in people and ranks low in most measures of well-being in social, educational, opportunity, and health. Here I focus on state rankings, but in the section below focused on IAF affiliate locations, I provide a chart with county data. Using 85 metrics, *U.S. News & World Report* provides up-to-date state rankings; current 2018 figures rank Texas at #36.[34] When I first moved to Texas in the late 1970s when Texas was in the bottom five on many indicators, I heard the running joke, "Thank God for Mississippi" (or the state of Texas would at the bottom). Nowadays, states in the bottom quarter like Texas could substitute the Mississippi joke with Louisiana, at the very bottom of most lists of well-being.

As noted earlier, Texas regions are meaningful in a state this size. The borderlands (43 counties) are almost half the size of all the non-Texas borderlands put together (79,423 square miles compared to

187,854) in John Sharp's *Bordering the Future*, once updated (but hardly changing) on the Texas State Comptroller's website. Sharp's rankings contained the special index: "Where We Stand" (if the border region was the fifty-first state) with pages listing fifty-two numeric indicators, among the following.[35] (I have put the contrast with Texas non-border counties in parentheses when contrasts are striking.)

If the forty-three-county Texas Border region were the fifty-first U.S. state, it would rank:

1st in poverty
1st in schoolchildren in poverty
3rd in female-headed households as a % of all households
3rd in death rate from diabetes (compared with 25th in non-border counties)
46th average annual pay (compared with 11th in non-border counties)
50th in manufacturing (12th in non-border counties)
51st in personal income (21st in non-border counties)
51st in construction (23rd in non-border counties)

Especially startling figures emerge on education and economics. As is obvious, many workers earn depressed wages in the borderlands. Women fare even worse, especially Mexican American women who earned 37 percent of White men's earnings in El Paso.[36] Economic factors in the borderlands like these make fundraising for community organizing difficult.

Until 2005, the *Texas Monthly* magazine published "Where We Rank," and Texas metrics compare poorly with other states, a result of the limited-government philosophies: 50th in the percentage of population with health insurance; 50th in number of high school graduates age 25 and over; 3rd in percentage of population that is malnourished; 2nd in teenage birth rate; 2nd in the amount of toxic and cancerous manufacturing emissions. The list goes on and on should readers wish to consult more detail.[37] Ironically, given the high rate of teen birth rates, most funding for sex education in Texas focuses on "abstinence only." And when the opportunity arose to expand Medicaid coverage in Texas under the Affordable Care Act in 2010, Texas declined even as Republican governors in New Mexico and Arizona accepted the expansion and its federal subsidies. I recall the public story of Border Interfaith Leader Carliene Quist at an Accountability Session in El Paso. Once jobless, she needed health care and was told by officials that the only way to get help was to get pregnant. She did not.

To make Texas more competitive in ways that benefit the have-nots and protect people's health, how can Texans counter anti-democratic tendencies? Besides issue-based voting and increased voter turnout, the answer lies in community organizing and pressure from a broad group of civil society activists. Below I provide place-based coverage of IAF affiliate communities.

IAF affiliates in Texas

The history of the Industrial Areas Foundation helped shape its evolution in Texas, as others have analyzed[38] (also see Chapter 1). Nationally, IAF's size and scope led to remarkable achievements, such as the Nehemiah Housing Program, which facilitated affordable housing for thousands in a once-desolate part of New York City. Could the IAF achieve comparable victories in a conservative state like Texas, even in a one-party dominant system?

Besides the founding stories and achievements covered earlier in this chapter, IAF's early period in the mid-1970s–1990s seemed poised to change Texas with growth and expansion. By 1990, Texas IAF affiliates included eleven organizations:[39] Austin Interfaith, Allied Communities of Tarrant (ACT), Communities Organized for Public Service (COPS), The Metro Alliance, EPISO, Fort Bend County Interfaith Council, The Metropolitan Organization (TMO), Valley Interfaith, The Border Project, Gulf Coast Organizing Project, and the Dallas Commission on Justice and Peace. The IAF has shrunk to seven affiliates since then, even as its large metro regions have begun to expand outward to surrounding suburbs and counties, such as in Dallas, Houston, and Austin.

It is difficult to estimate the size of each IAF affiliate, for measurement criteria vary: By number of member institutions, current or lapsed in their dues? By the number of volunteers who participate as primary, secondary, and tertiary leaders (see lingo in Chapter 1)? By the number of people who belong to each congregation that represents the bulk of member institutions? By the number of residents in each Catholic territorial vicariate, even if residents have lapsed in their faith or do not affiliate with a parish?[40] In each IAF affiliate, the number of member organizations expands and contracts with changing clergy and up-to-date dues paid to the IAF; thus, the size of each affiliate can only be estimated. Let me give an example from EPISO, which called itself the largest community organization in El Paso by the year 2000, claiming

50,000 people. I have no doubt that it was the largest community organization, but the estimate was based on the size of congregational member institutions, not on turnouts and number of volunteer leaders.

At the time of this book's preparation, nearly thirty years after Rogers's *Cold Anger* in 1990, IAF affiliates' closures, building, and rebuilding processes have occurred: Four 1990s IAF affiliates consolidated into two affiliates, and three IAF affiliates closed. However, new organizations have emerged: Arlington Mansfield Organizing Strategy (AMOS) (but not yet on IAF's map), Border Interfaith, The Border Organization in Del Rio (its Webb County affiliate in Laredo no longer operates), and West Texas Organizing Strategy in Lubbock. As we can see, IAF presence has tilted toward the urban east, north, and central parts of the state with their larger populations.

Statewide, the Texas IAF network achieved major successes. At its Austin statewide convention in 1990, the Texas IAF drew 10,000 participants.[41] I saw a video cassette (remember those?) with powerful, three-station news coverage from Austin's major TV channels panning the crowd and recording the public promises that prominent politicians made. In subsequent trips with EPISO and Border Interfaith to Austin after 2000, I was part of meetings on the Capitol steps and lawn of over a thousand people, who subsequently met with members of their state legislative delegations. These large gatherings occur during every legislative session, after earlier but smaller statewide meetings of organizers and teams of leaders from each affiliate who develop policy priorities and strategies. As a reminder of the first part of this chapter, the 1990s were different political times in Texas.

Among historic policy successes, IAF contributed to funding for unplanned settlements called *colonias*; the Investment Capital Fund for Alliance Schools; quality work-force training centers (see Chapter 8) with state matching funds; and the expansion of the Children's Health Insurance Program (CHIP). Although some successes ended, other funding continued—notable during hard times when the legislature sought cuts wherever it could.

The initial success tends to get more attention than defense and budget protection in subsequent legislative sessions. For example, the EDAP (Economically Distressed Areas Program) was passed in 1989 for local governments to fund water and wastewater services in *colonias* which, according to the Texas Water Development Board in 1996, numbered 1,453 settlements totaling 343,321 people.[42] Statewide relationships made it possible to network relationships for funding water

Texas I.A.F. Network

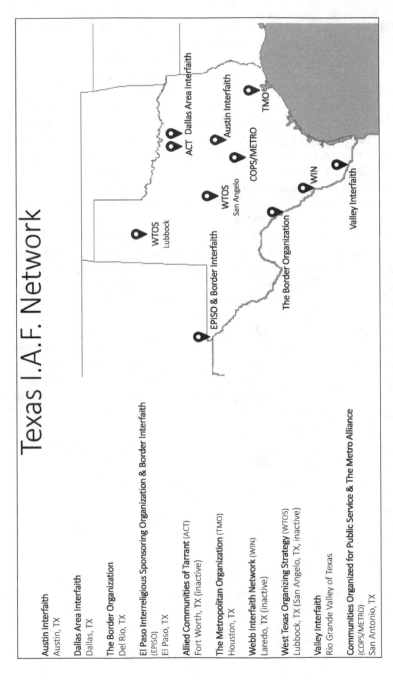

Austin Interfaith
Austin, TX

Dallas Area Interfaith
Dallas, TX

The Border Organization
Del Rio, TX

El Paso Interreligious Sponsoring Organization & Border Interfaith
(EPISO)
El Paso, TX

Allied Communities of Tarrant (ACT)
Fort Worth, TX (inactive)

The Metropolitan Organization (TMO)
Houston, TX

Webb Interfaith Network (WIN)
Laredo, TX (inactive)

West Texas Organizing Strategy (WTOS)
Lubbock, TX (San Angelo, TX, inactive)

Valley Interfaith
Rio Grande Valley of Texas

Communities Organized for Public Service & The Metro Alliance
(COPS/METRO)
San Antonio, TX

Texas IAF Affiliates Map. Staudt, with layout assistance from Stephanie Espinosa.

and sewer services in *colonias*, mainly affecting the 43-county border-lands (in this 254-county state), but augmented with relational power that IAF affiliates exercised with each of their own representatives and thus adding up to considerable bipartisan voices of support. In 1995, the state legislature passed the Colonias Fair Land Sales Act to "curb CFD's (Contracts for Deed) as a method of finance by requiring developers to record contracts in county registries ... and document services provided, such as sewage, water, and electricity."[43] And continuing on from their founding in the 1990s, six independent workforce training organizations emerged in partnership with community colleges and employers for high job placement rates especially in the growing health professional field (see Chapter 8). For the first of these, Project Quest, former Governor Ann Richards pledged a half-million-dollar start-up commitment.[44]

Moving up to the twenty-first century and one-party rule, one might question whether the Texas IAF had a seat at the state table as once existed earlier. When Governor Rick Perry refused to attend the dele-gates' assembly on September 8, 2002, at which 10,000 volunteer lead-ers would be present, local affiliate leaders pushed back at his excuse (a Cowboys football game) and local media around the state covered the outrage. In "VI [Valley Interfaith] Pans Perry," Lubbock WTOS Leader Rev. Davis Price was quoted: "Governor Perry, do not fumble our invi-tation. The real game on September 8 is here in Austin."[45] In one-party politics, however, progressive organizations began to play more defen-sive than offensive games. Texas government also fought the Obama administration over health and other measures, with scores of lawsuits by the Texas Attorney General.

The IAF, like other organizations, tackled legislative cuts in educa-tion budgets and various bills hostile to immigrants. Leaders and organizers worked behind the scenes with moderates in the business community to defend against the worst of proposed policy extremes. However, as Tea Party representatives and money shaped the legisla-tive agenda, it became difficult to grow relationships and to create wins. Despite the opportunity that the 2010 Affordable Health Care Act offered to states for the expansion of Medicaid, Texas declined, unlike the Republican women governors in New Mexico and Arizona at the time, as noted earlier. That left IAF affiliates to work locally to expand health care to avoid even greater burdens that increased emer-gency room visit costs would create for local taxpayers' support of their county public hospitals.

IAF operates in mainstream cities, some more accurately called metro-regions, including Houston, Dallas, Austin, and San Antonio, but also Lubbock, surrounded by suburbs (and ranchlands). The borderland cities include El Paso (some would also include San Antonio in Bexar County) and the smaller fragmented communities of south and southwest Texas such as Brownsville, Weslaco, and McAllen in the South Texas Valley, plus moving westward in Laredo and Del Rio. Those cities are surrounded by *colonias*, or unplanned settlements in which people organized over years to secure conventional public utilities like safe water and sewer services (that most everyone takes for granted in the rest of the U.S.) thanks in part to more effective IAF statewide coordination. Almost half of the IAF affiliates are located in the borderlands.

IAF cities, counties, and contexts

IAF-affiliated broad-based organizations, nestled in the landscape of major Texas cities, organize high-profile Accountability Sessions, meet continuously in ongoing relationships with officials, and achieve "wins" in local government. Recall that sociologist Norton Long's concept of the "local ecology of games" (Chapter 1) is useful here: he focuses on "major institutional sectors of the city—including labor unions, business, government, religious organizations, political parties," which occupy "a common territorial field and interact with one another."[46] In criteria outlined below, most IAF affiliates earned a "seat at the table" in local government decision-making, winning results that respond to broad-based interests about which I elaborate in Chapter 1.

I view an IAF seat at the table to include such observable indicators as "wins" (i.e. majority votes) for new city ordinances or county resolutions; at least three-fourths of candidates invited who appear at Accountability Sessions and the pre-forum briefing sessions; GOTV efforts in targeted precincts that produce victories for candidates who are responsive to community issues; coverage in the major print media outlets; official consultation for crisis responses such as hurricanes or for priority policy areas such as education; and community leaders' accessibility to periodic relational meetings with the IAF leaders. IAF victories do not occur in a vacuum, for other organized forces in an increasingly crowded field of issue-organizations in Texas, effective electoral campaigns, and exciting candidates such as in the 2018 race between the incumbent Senator Ted Cruz and challenger Beto O'Rourke all work to increase turnout as well. Additionally, strong IAF affiliates host websites and post on Facebook to develop strong and weak networking ties.

Comparative county data

Table 2.2 lists major socio-economic features of Texas counties with IAF affiliates. The table includes the two largest ethnic groups (unless one ethnicity surpasses 90 percent), the median county household incomes, and the density of civil society, as measured by nonprofits per 10,000 people in the population. The ethnic category names use the nomenclature of the *Texas Almanac* source, 2018, with "Anglos" referring to Whites or people of European heritage and "Hispanics" referring to people of mostly Mexican heritage. Only in a few big cities in Texas does the Black or African American population reach double-digit figures. Asian Americans represent 4 percent of the whole state population.

From the table, we glean basic insights. In big cities, Texans consist of people with multiple ethnic identities, from Hispanics (Mexican Americans primarily), Anglos (Whites), and Blacks (African Americans), except for the Texas-Mexico borderlands, primarily Hispanic with largely English-Spanish bilingual people. Both Lubbock and Austin contain mostly Anglo (White) populations. We can see a marked contrast in median household income ranging from the high of over $58,000 in Travis County (Austin) to a low of some $24,000 in Hidalgo County, the center point of the fragmented smaller cities where Valley Interfaith organizes. Indeed, the borderland county median household incomes are approximately half those of Austin and second-wealthiest Houston. A measure of central tendency, median household income disguises inequality; we have no GINI indexes of inequality such as what international institutions report for the nearly 200 countries in the world. However, we do know what figures the U.S. Census reports about the poverty rate, which ranges from the highs of nearly one third of the population in the south Texas borderlands to surprisingly high rates of nearly a quarter of the population in Dallas and El Paso. Dallas is equivalent to a borderlands community in regards to poverty.

Another relevant factor for analyzing the ecology in which cities operate (recall Norton Long) consists of the density of registered, tax-exempt nonprofit organizations, which include a whole slew of entities from foundations and hospitals to community organizations. The figure is a rough measure of civil society organizations and monetary resources to support them. From the chart, we see Austin, the Dallas-Fort Worth area, and Lubbock among the more densely packed nonprofit areas, but borderlands communities, less than half those rates. Not surprisingly, Austin, as the state capital city, shows the highest median income

Table 2.2: Texas cities and counties with current or recent IAF affiliates

City, County	2 Largest Ethnicities	Median County Income (% poverty)	Nonprofits/ 10,000
Austin, Travis	Anglos 50%, Hispanic 34%	$58,362 (12%)	55.9
Dallas, Dallas	Hispanic 39%, Anglo 32%	$53,186 (23%)	42.6
Del Rio, Val Verde	Hispanic 80%, Anglo 17%	$34,100 (21%)	23.1 (south)
El Paso, El Paso	Hispanic 81%, Anglo 13%	$32,614 (23%)	23.1 (south)
Fort Worth, Tarrant	Anglo 50%, Hispanic 38%	$48,727 (14%)	42.6
Houston, Harris	Hispanic 41%, Anglo, 32%	$55,088 (17%)	35.5
Laredo, Webb	Hispanic 95%	$29,778 (32%)	23.1 (south)
Lubbock, Lubbock	Anglo 56%, Hispanic 34%	$38,557 (19%)	45.1 (west)
San Antonio, Bexar	Hispanic 60%, Anglo 28%	$52,353 (16%)	35.0
Westlaco, Hidalgo	Hispanic 91%	$24,579 (31%)	23.1 (south)

Sources: US Census Bureau Quick Facts, 2017 figures; *Texas Almanac*, Texas State Historical Association, nomenclature for ethnicities, income, 2015 figures; Brown, Jo, and Andersson, *Texas Nonprofit Sector*, Texas A&M University (2013: 22). Besides the four major cities, I cite their divide for the rest of the state into 4 composite regions: west, east, south, and north (and classify El Paso in the south). Their data sets of 2010 come from the National Center for Charitable Statistics; its categories do not allow a targeted focus on social justice organizations (which would not fit in religion, in human services, or in public benefit, but cut across those and other categories). Black or African American populations in each city are highest in Dallas (25%), Harris (20%), Tarrant (17%), Travis (9%), Bexar (7%), and Lubbock (8%). All figures rounded off. For comparative purposes, US median income is $55,322, with 13% of persons living in poverty. Table construction based on early 2018 IAF affiliate lists from www.swiaf.org (some of which have now closed).

and nonprofit density because of its capital city location, with perhaps opportunities for collaboration in IAF terms. However, the density figures may also show the possible competing organizations that could drain away IAF membership institution potential unless IAF and others would find ways to collaborate more and share their victory (or loss) claims—a challenge, as we see in Chapter 7. IAF groups operate in a semi-vacuum of civil society terms in the borderlands for they are the primary social justice organizations in the region.

Let me briefly describe each place, for as any political ethnographer would emphasize, context matters. In power analysis terms, commonalities exist across cities. Most big cities' business communities work with and help fund the campaigns of their mayors and city council representatives to create business-friendly climates, historically and in the contemporary era. Harvey Molotch labels them "growth machines."[47] Most cities also host big nonprofit organizations; their tax-exempt status prohibits campaign endorsements and contributions. Nonprofit directors and staff sometimes become spokespersons (or "advocates" in IAF terms) for their clients, many of whom remain voiceless. Ethnic groups, such as Mexican American and African American civil rights and identity groups, also exercise political muscle in most cities, as do women's and feminist organizations. Little formal collaboration exists between these groups and IAF affiliates, though leaders overlap in multiple organizations.

Labor organizations represent just 5–10 percent of city labor forces. Statewide, the AFL-CIO counts a growing number of individual members reaching just under a fourth of a million in Texas. The National Nurses United and Service Employees International Union (SEIU) organize enthusiastic drives in cities with highly profitable hospitals like those in El Paso that, ironically, cater to a wealthy international patient clientele from Mexico, while (ironically) El Pasoans without insurance or money cross the border into Mexico to use its lower-cost hospital, dental, optical, pharmaceutical, and medical services. Teachers generally join associations like the Texas State Teachers Association, which is part of the National Education Association (NEA), and AFT (American Federation of Teachers) local affiliates, which interact with school board trustees. As an anti-union, right-to-work state, Texas-based teachers do not have the authority to engage in collective bargaining.[48] Big cities also became home to single-issue-based groups in health, education, the environment, and various multi-issue, multi-institutional broad-based member institutions besides those affiliated with the IAF.

Below I briefly describe each city in which IAF organizes. Readers should also consult the section at the end of this chapter, "For Further Reflection," for the websites of each of those cities. In those websites, one gets descriptions of the mayor and city council representatives, the size of the council and its geographic districts (mixed with at-large representatives in some cities), government departments, and more demographics on the cities. Local strategic action requires knowledge about these political institutions.

City by city

Houston is the huge, high-growth region in the bayou near the Gulf Coast and is subject to the periodic hurricanes that are hitting that region more and more due to climate change. From writer Lawrence Wright, we learn about Houston's size. It is not only the third largest metro region in the United States, but also its sprawl encompasses nine counties and 10,000 square miles (nearly the size of Massachusetts). The city itself is over 600 square miles.[49] The area is so large that the IAF affiliate TMO (The Metropolitan Organization) holds meetings in different regions therein.

Houston's city council contains a mix of at-large and geographic districts. While Houston is touted, for better or worse, as a city without planning and zoning, its government has a Planning & Development Department, Plan, and a large Planning Commission. After Hurricane Katrina survivors arrived in Houston, former Mayor Bill White called TMO Organizer Renee Wizig-Barrios to do what IAF does best: organize people, thus illustrating IAF's place at the table.[50] However, after another huge hurricane hit, Hurricane Harvey, major news outlets like *Texas Monthly* and *Texas Observer* warned of the city's inadequate follow-up at its one-year anniversary. [51] The entire *Texas Observer* issue contains full coverage of Hurricane Harvey's one-year anniversary, in "the impossible city."

Houston's economy is diverse: once oil and gas dominated, it is home to the Johnson Space Center and operates the world's largest medical complex and second-busiest port in the U.S.[52] Houston is a magnet for migrants from the mainstream US and elsewhere. The city offers a Welcoming Houston website from its Office of New Americans & Immigrant Communities, ten tips to make the city more welcoming, and an immigrant rights hotline.[53] Houston is the only place in Texas to which the late Anthony Bourdain traveled, as shown in the ten seasons on

Netflix of *Parts Unknown* totaling eighty episodes on Netflix (Season 8, Number 5) to show its diverse ethnic and immigrant heritages. Houston achieved the status as the most multi-cultural city in the state; I noticed on one of my trips there that their public buses displayed instructions in six languages, including Vietnamese and Urdu.

The larger **Dallas-Fort Worth-Arlington** metro region may be best known to Texans and non-Texans as the place of hub airplane connections in the DFW Airport, which began operating in 1974. Nowadays, the "Big D" may be famous for the name attached to its major football team, the Dallas Cowboys. In his chapter 7, Texan writer Lawrence Wright, author of *God Save Texas,* also analyzes Dallas, and its turning point after JFK's assassination in 1963 when it began to transform itself. Dallas, with its geographic district-based council, is a magnet for migrants from the mainstream US and elsewhere, just like Houston, with a combination of high-end professional jobs coupled with entry-level $10-an-hour jobs for many as well. Lawrence Wright calls the greater Dallas area "the most unequal big city in America" with pockets of poverty and racial segregation, a derogatory phrase backed up with methodical research from the Urban Institute.[54] A big banking center and headquarters home to large traded companies, Dallas shares the major airport hub with Fort Worth, supposedly where the West begins in popular parlance. In his definitive book about the city, historian Harvey Graff said Dallas is a place of extreme inequalities and multiple myths, lately the "Dallas Way," promulgated by its business boosters in conjunction with elected officials. But like other historians, Graff wrote nothing about Dallas-Area Interfaith, the IAF affiliate, with its thirty-some paid member institutions totaling a 90,000-person base that achieved major goals and is featured in Chapter 3.[55]

The high-growth magnet city of **Austin** is home to the state Capitol, a striking pink-granite building that resembles the U.S. Capitol. After all, Texas was once an independent republic (1836–45) and before that, part of northern Mexico (and still before that, home to indigenous peoples prior to colonial settlers from Europe, mainly Spain). The city is also home to the state's second-largest public university, the University of Texas at Austin, with current (2017) enrollment at over 50,000 students, just after the land-grant Texas A&M University in east Texas with almost 70,000 students. Austin holds a reputation of building, thinking, and being "green," with its beautiful Hill Country surroundings and building codes to protect the environment.[56] As T-shirts proclaim, "Keep Austin Weird," with its free, open atmosphere and the country's live music capital. In recent decades, that weirdness has become branding for a market niche of costly festivals like SxSW with educator badge prices beginning at $345 and platinum badges at $1,150. On his El Paso visit to push a statewide Hispanic Leadership Network, I heard current Governor Abbott publicly joke about living in the "People's Republic of Austin," as if it were China! In the more or less gerrymandered political system of U.S. and state legislative districts, Austin falls in the more gerrymandered category: so extreme that Jon Stewart's *Daily Show* featured a story about the way lines got drawn to turn the larger metro region into one with majority conservative representatives.[57]

Lubbock is a smaller conservative city of over 200,000 people in the ranching and oil country in northwestern Texas, the bottom of the country's central plains. As IAF leaders there emphasized in interviews, there's more land than people in southern plains. Once known as a "dry" city (i.e. prohibiting alcohol), people voted "wet" to allow alcohol sales in a 2009 referendum. Lubbock continues to be a conservative place of fissures within Protestant denominations over cultural-war wedge issues, such as same-sex marriage equality. Lubbock is home to Texas Tech University, with almost 40,000 students and a branch in El Paso for its medical school and health programs.

The Texas borderlands differ from the rest of the state: like occupied country. When I drove the near six hours from El Paso to Lubbock, I encountered a routine Border Patrol checkpoint on U.S. Highway 62 East, like those checkpoints that exist on all the major interstate highways (I-10, I-25, U.S. 70) going north, east, and west in what the Department of Homeland Security defines as the 100-mile border zone.[58] Three armed, burly guards, one holding the drug-sniffing dog, asked about my citizenship but not for my documents, probably after hearing my accent and seeing my complexion and license plate which evoked no red-flag crime "hits" among my family and friend networks in their sophisticated near-instantaneous technological surveillance databases. After that, I passed through the grim towns of Southeastern New Mexico, punctuated in between with pump jacks gouging the earth and emitting the taste and smell of sulfur. Once energy companies drained oil fields, fracking began with heavy water use and earthquake consequences. And then I passed out of the Mountain Time Zone into Central Time Zone. Imagine the width of Texas: west of Denver and east of St. Louis.

El Paso and **San Antonio** lay claim to a rich historical heritage tied to Mexico, with El Paso over 400 years old and San Antonio celebrating its 300th anniversary in 2018 with greater fanfare than usual in the annual spring Fiesta San Antonio. Their Mexican American populations are large, but only since the 1980s have diverse representatives of Mexican heritage been routinely elected to public office.[59] In *Bordering the Future*, 1998, an unsuccessful effort to target Texas investment in the borderlands after historic economic investments in cattle then oil and gas booms, former Comptroller John Sharp drew a line around forty-three so-called border counties to include San Antonio's Bexar County (probably to increase political clout from representatives there), though it is a four-hour drive from there to Brownsville and a 2.5-hour drive to Laredo.

El Paso has been my workplace and home for forty years, so while I have plenty to share later about the place, here I limit remarks to its special feature as THE largest metropolitan region in the world through which an international territorial line runs.[60] Among the safe big cities in the U.S., as measured by FBI crime statistics, El Paso ranked among the top ten safest cities depending on the year (despite the rhetoric that emanates from Washington, D.C.). The population is home to over 80 percent people of Mexican heritage, but several wealthy White men exercise extensive power and represent the region as gubernatorial political appointees on statewide boards. Just like the bicultural/binational marriages of the nineteenth century, one of them married into a wealthy Mexican border family. A businessman who co-chaired El Paso's Education Summit (see Chapter 7) bemoaned to students in one of my seminars that "there was once a time when a few businessmen could get things done" (motioning with a few fingers), but now, he said, "things are more complicated." A weak, but growing civil society (including the IAF) adds to complications.

Though big at nearly at 700,000 people, El Paso also interacts symbiotically with the 1.5-million population of Ciudad Juárez, Chihuahua, Mexico. Many relatives, friends, and working people cross the border both ways given the quarter-million worker maquiladora export-processing manufacturing enclaves in Ciudad Juárez. El Paso's interdependence with Mexico resembles that of the smaller border cities of Del Rio, Laredo, and the semi-urban string along the 1,000 miles of the South Texas border with their counterpart cities in the Mexican states of Tamaulipas, Nuevo León, and Coahuila. Each US city and town, like their cross-border counterparts, shares interdependent economies but extreme inequality gaps from one side of the international borderline to the other with the tenfold legal minimum wage differential through 2018.[61] Proximity to Mexico did not deter historic lynching, killings, and beatings of Mexican Americans such as in San Felipe del Rio (now **Del Rio**) as political scientist José Angel Gutiérrez pointed out in the previously cited, latest of his books about Chicano politics in Texas. The borderlands' political, cultural, and economic atmosphere is far different from mainstream Texas.

Concluding reflections

Texas is indeed a flawed democracy with its still lagging political participation compared to other states in the country. Considering the long haul of history, many groups had been disempowered, from Mexican and African Americans, to women and economic have-nots. When people from these groups rose to amass power, such as in EPISO during its origins in El Paso, the status quo was threatened with resistance, some of which came from conservatives in the Catholic Church.

Broad-based organizing, as in the IAF, has the potential to empower people and their voices and thus provide the kind of experiential civic education that does not happen in Texas public schools. We also saw how women's health issues, present in the IAF origins stories and later (covered in future chapters) have been muted in the state and in Catholic Church ideology as sources of IAF funding. Women, too, may be reluctant to raise body issues in the mixed-gender house meetings that sometimes occur in churches. To its credit, EPISO did not acquiesce to pressure from conservative Catholics who sought to capture its social justice agenda.

IAF arose in a competitive political opportunity structure that began to open in major Texas cities in the 1970s through the 1990s, not only to the IAF affiliates but also to Mexican American civil rights organizations, identity groups, and women's organizations. Thanks to MALDEF's legal work, groups pressed cities and large school boards and moved them toward geographic district-based local elections, which gave place-based organizations like the IAF the opportunity to develop relationships with a majority of representatives on city councils in some cities. City councils are officially "diverse" in their descriptive representation, but that does not necessarily mean that diverse people respond to constituents such as people of color, economic have-nots, and women with substantive representation. Texas still ranks near the bottom in indicators of well-being.

Statewide leaders, mostly Democrat but some Republican as well, demonstrated responsiveness to organized constituencies like the IAF during a relatively brief semi-competitive period of bipartisanship to address *colonias* infrastructure, educational reform, and workforce training. However, twenty-first-century Texas government became a non-competitive one-party system lacking checks and balances and marginalizing the voices of the minority party and many broad-based organizations including the IAF. The power of money is overwhelming for both elections and political appointments. In state interference over local control, called pre-emption, the legislature undermines some of the hard-fought local victories for social justice and environmental organizations. The statewide IAF has gradually sought to expand into counties surrounding the big cities, incurring success in 2018 as noted in Chapter 1 and elsewhere in this book. Local affiliates, besides providing genuine civic education, have earned places at the tables of their urban cities. But their leaders and organizers could benefit from a fairer, more competitive set of political institutions that passes ethics laws with teeth.

For further reflection

Cities with IAF affiliates: Websites for local government information, pictures, maps

Austin: http://www.austintexas.gov/
Dallas: https://dallascityhall.com/Pages/default.aspx
Del Rio: http://cityofdelrio.com/
El Paso: http://www.elpasotexas.gov/
Houston: http://www.houstontx.gov/
Lubbock: https://ci.lubbock.tx.us/
Rio Grande Valley cities of Westlaco, Brownsville, and McAllen: http://www.weslacotx.gov/; https://www.cob.us/; http://www.mcallen.net/
San Antonio: https://www.sanantonio.gov/

Public policy foundations

Center for Public Policy Priorities (CPPP), left of center: http://forabetter texas.org/
Texas Public Policy Foundation (TPPF), right of center: https://www.texaspolicy.com/

Statewide media and investigative city media

Austin Chronicle
Quorum Report ($)

Rio Grande Guardian
Rivard Report (San Antonio)
Texas Monthly
Texas Observer
Texas Standard (public radio)
Texas Tribune (daily)

Major state political parties

Democrats: www.txdemocrats.org
Republicans (GOP=Grand Old Party): https://www.texasgop.org/

Other

Texas Legislature https://house.texas.gov/; https://senate.texas.gov (see various citations)
Council of State Governments, for comparative perspectives in four-US regions https://www.csg.org/
Texas State Historical Association (searchable website) http://tshaonline.org
Texas Almanac, published by the TSHA
Bullock Museum https://www.thestoryoftexas.com
Texas Demographic Center, www.txsdc.utsa.edu
Texas Education Agency https://tea.texas.gov/
Texas Secretary of State https://www.sos.state.tx.us/
Texas State Library Archives Commission https://www.tsl.texas.gov/
Texan Bill Moyers on ALEC (http://billmoyers.com/episode/full-show-united-states-of-alec-a-follow-up/)

Notes

1. Clippings, carbon copies, and other documents: thanks to the EPISO office, El Paso, for access in June 2018.

2. Jay Jennings and Emily Einsohn Bhandari, *Texas Civic Health Index*, Annette Strauss Institute for Civic Life, Moody College of Communication (Austin: University of Texas, 2018).

3. Michael Lind, *Made in Texas: George W. Bush and the Southern Takeover of American Politics* (New York: New America, 2003).

4. See MALDEF President Thomas Saenz's testimony in 2017 outlining many accomplishments of this half-century old organization through

the current era. https://www.maldef.org/2017/09/testimony-of-thomas-a-saenz-president-and-general-counsel-maldef-before-the-democratic-policy-and-communications-committee/

5. The NAEP (National Assessment of Educational Progress), a federal voluntary effort to assess knowledge at Grades 4, 8, and 12 around the country in various content areas at basic, advanced, and proficient levels, defines civics to include knowledge, skills, experience, and motivation (the last, often related to local/regional topics) while Texas social studies standards includes knowledge alone (dates, names, places).

6. José Angel Gutiérrez, *Albert A. Peña Jr.: Dean of Chicano Politics* (East Lansing: Michigan State University Press, 2017).

7. Mary Beth Rogers, *Cold Anger: A Story of Faith and Power Politics* (Denton: University of North Texas Press, 1990), 110–112.

8. Section on Granata from Rogers, pp. 111–4. Quote, p. 114.

9. UTSA, Special Collections, John Peace Library, "A Guide to the C.O.P.S./Metro Alliance, 1954–2009," MS 346, Box 6.

10. *Texas Almanac 2018–9* (Austin: Texas State Historical Association, 2018), with 27.8 million people compared to California's 39.2 million, but double California's growth rate. 2016 figures, p. 19.

11. Totaled 752 pages, for 2018–19!

12. *Texas Almanac*, 35.

13. Texas Social Studies Content Standards by grade level can be found in the mammoth Texas Education Agency website: http://ritter.tea.state.tx.us/rules/tac/chapter113/ch113b.html Accessed July 1, 2018.

14. Oscar Martínez, *Border People* (Tucson: University of Arizona Press, 1996). In my *Border Politics in a Global Era*, I counted the rare number of times that TEA's curriculum "standards" mentioned the border, borderlands, and Mexico (Rowman & Littlefield, 2017), Ch 2. In a 2016 survey of over 1,400 borderlanders, similarity is found for a number of indicators with respondents on both sides of the border; see Alfredo Corchado, "Common Ground: Poll Finds US-Mexico Border Residents Overwhelmingly Value Mobility, Oppose Wall," *Dallas Morning News*, July 18, 2016. http://interactives.dallasnews.com/2016/border-poll/. Accessed July 19, 2016.

15. For the definitive scholarly study of LULAC's history, see Benjamin Márquez, *LULAC: The Evolution of a Mexican American Political Organization* (Austin: University of Texas Press, 1993).

16. Benjamin Márquez argues that MALDEF's early dependency on Ford Foundation funding shaped its strategies in "Trial by Fire: The Ford Foundation and MALDEF in the 1960s," *Politics, Groups, and Identities*, 2018 (on line).

17. As noted in the Acknowledgements, to most of the world, liberalism stands for classic liberalism from centuries past: limited government and maximum market/capitalist activity (not proactive government as in the US).

18. Benjamin Márquez, *Democratizing Texas Politics: Race, Identity, and Mexican American Politics, 1945–2002* (Austin: University of Texas Press, 2014), 172.

19. Molly Ivins calls Richards one of the few (her adjectives!) "efficient," "practical," and "hardworking" Texas leaders in her book, *Who Let the Dogs In? Incredible Political Animals I have Known* (New York: Random House, 2004), 172. According to Ivins, Richards lost her re-election bid in 1995 for several reasons: President Clinton's re-election coattails dragged her down, 120,000 more registered Republicans moved into the state, and George W. Bush "ran a helluva campaign," 174.

20. The Lieutenant Governor holds a strong, powerful authority, presiding over the Texas Senate.

21. Mary Beth Rogers, 2016, p. 127.

22. Lawrence Wright, "The Future is Texas," *The New Yorker*, July 10, 17, 2017, p. 43.

23. James Slattery, *High School Student Voter Registration: How Texas Still Fails to Engage the New Generation of Voters* (Austin: Texas Civil Rights Project, July 2018). https://texascivilrightsproject.org/wp-content/uploads/2018/07/2018-HSVR-Compliance-Report.pdf Accessed Aug. 1, 2018.

24. Alexa Ura and Jolie McCullough, "Meet your 84th Legislative Session: White. Male. Middle-Aged. Christian." *Texas Tribune*, January 14, 2015, Accessed July 1, 2018. https://www.texastribune.org/2015/01/14/demographics-2015-texas-legislature/

25. Texas Legislature: https://capitol.texas.gov/Home.aspx

26. Anthony Champagne, Edward Harpham, and Jason Casellas, *Governing Texas*, 3rd. ed. (New York: W. W. Norton 2017), 195.

27. Open Secrets (campaign contributions): www.opensecrets.org . One can check by state and year.

28. His bill passed the House but not the Senate. Ross Ramsey, "Texas House Approves Ban on 'Pay-to-Play' Appointments," *Texas Tribune*, May 6, 2017. https://www.texastribune.org/2017/05/06/texas-house-approves-ban-pay-play-appointments/ Accessed Sept. 15, 2018.

29. Josh Baugh, "Incumbent Larson Wins Despite Challenger Getting Governor's Backing," *San Antonio Express News*, March 7, 2018. https://www.expressnews.com/news/politics/texas_legislature/article/Incumbent-Larson-poised-to-overcome-12733646.php Accessed Feb. 1, 2019.

30. https://tlc.texas.gov/about. The late Daniel Elazar, an authority on federalism, categorized the fifty U.S. states by their political cultures in *American Federalism: A View from the States* (New York: Harper & Row, 1984): moralist with civic cultures, traditionalist with hierarchical roots in the deep south, or individualistic with a market-oriented approach. Texas has been called a combination of the latter two.

31. NAFTA, renegotiated in 2018 and renamed US-Mexico-Canada Agreement (USMCA), has yet to be considered in the US Congress.

32. Texas Tribune panel September 28, 2018: CPPP and Austin City Council Rep District #4 versus TPPF and champion of pre-emption, state House Representative Paul Workman (who was defeated in the 2018 mid-term elections).

33. For an excellent hour-long discussion of ALEC, see Texan Bill Moyers. http://billmoyers.com/episode/full-show-united-states-of-alec-a-follow-up/

34. "Best States," *U.S. News & World Report*, 2018, https://www.usnews.com/news/best-states/rankings. Accessed Oct. 15, 2018.

35. John Sharp, *Bordering the Future: Challenge and Opportunity in the Texas Border Region* (Austin: Texas State Comptroller, 1998), 197–200. For a 2006 update, see the UTEP Institute for Policy and Economic Research, https://digitalcommons.utep.edu/cgi/viewcontent.cgi?article=1027&context=iped_techrep

36. Manucla Romero and Tracy Yellen, *El Paso Portraits: Women's Lives, Potential and Opportunities: A Report on the State of Women in El Paso Texas* (El Paso: UTEP Center for Civic Engagement and YWCA Paso del Norte Region, 2004).

37. *Texas Monthly*, "Where we Rank," May 2005, pp. 171–2. https://www.texasmonthly.com/articles/where-we-rank/. Also see Cal Jillson, *Lone Star Tarnished: A Critical Look at Texas Politics and Public Policy* (New York: Routledge, 2014).

38. Edward Chambers, *Roots for Radicals: Organizing for Power, Action, and Justice* (New York: Continuum Press, 2003); Mark Warren, *Dry Bones Rattling: Community Building to Revitalize American Democracy* (Princeton: Princeton University Press, 2001), and a Texas overview in the Texas State Historical Association with its fine search engine https://tshaonline.org/handbook-search-results?arfarf=Industrial%20Areas%20Foundation .

39. Rogers, 1990, p. 209.

40. Once when I asked a priest from a large Catholic parish and EPISO member institution about how many people belonged to the

church, he asked if I meant those who joined the congregation or those living in the vicariate.

41. Warren, 2001: pp. 6–7.

42. Sharp, *Bordering the Future*, 1998, p. 127.

43. Sharp, p. 92.

44. Rogers; Warren, 2001, p. 5.

45. Steve Taylor, "VI Pans Perry," *Valley Morning Star*, August 28, 2002. Located, with other clippings, in the UTSA Archives, op cit.

46. Marion Orr, "The Changing Ecology of Civic Engagement," *Transforming the City: Community Organizing and the Challenge of Political Change*, edited by Marion Orr (Lawrence: University Press of Kansas, 2007), 3.

47. Harvey Molotch, "The City as a Growth Machine: Toward a Political Economy of Place," *American Journal of Sociology* 82, no. 4 (1976): 309–332.

48. Kavitha Mediratta, Seema Shah, and Sara McAlister, *Building Partnerships to Reinvent School Culture: Austin Interfaith* (Providence: Annenberg Institute for School Reform, Brown University, May 2009).

49. Lawrence Wright, *God Save Texas* (New York: Alfred A. Knopf, 2018), p. 82 and chapter 3.

50. Jeffrey Stout, *Blessed Are the Organized: Grassroots Democracy in* America (Princeton: Princeton University Press, 2010), 71. Organizer Renee Wizig-Barrios, no longer affiliated with the IAF, told Stout that in visits to the Astrodome, a television star and televangelist spoke in "surrealist, patronizing" tones to traumatized people.

51. Mimi Schwartz, "Troubled Waters: A Year after Harvey, has Houston Learned Anything?" *Texas Monthly*, August 22, 2018 https://www.texasmonthly.com/news/harvey-anniversary-houston-preparing-next-big-storm/ Accessed Nov. 7, 2018; "Hurricane Harvey, One Year Later," *Texas Observer*, special issue, August 27, 2018.

52. Wright, 62.

53. City of Houston Welcoming Immigrants: http://www.houstontx.gov/welcoming/?fbclid=IwAR2mvosZ-4AnpMb_e8CcE20n9ofLOpyTg_O5brnpoTvOam-_s0c7V7pwo34 Accessed March 1, 2019.

54. Wright, 176. Rolf Pendall with Carl Hedman, *World's Apart: Inequality between America's Most and Least Affluent Neighborhoods* (Washington, D.C.: Urban Institute, June 2015). https://www.urban.org/sites/default/files/publication/60956/2000288-Worlds-Apart-Inequality-between-Americas-Most-and-Least-Affluent-Neighborhoods.pdf Accessed July 1, 2018.

55. Harvey Graff, *The Dallas Myth: The Making and Unmaking of an American City* (Minneapolis: University of Minnesota Press, 2008); Michael Phillips, *White Metropolis, Race, Ethnicity, and Religion in Dallas, 1841–2001* (Austin: University of Texas Press, 2006); Jillson 2012.

56. William Scott Swearingem, Jr. does not mention Austin Interfaith in *Environmental City: People, Place, Politics, and the Meaning of Modern Austin* (Austin: University of Texas Press, 2010). Neither does Larry Cuban in his book *As Good as It Gets: What School Reform Brought to Austin* (Cambridge, MA: Harvard University Press, 2010) at a time that Alliance Schools were part of such reform.

57. Jon Stewart, *The Daily Show*. This segment is no longer on line, but I used to show it in my Teaching Democracy class, to great shock and laughs from students.

58. Melissa del Bosque, "Checkpoint Nation: Border Agents Are Expanding Their Reach into the Country's Interior," *Harper's Magazine*, October 28, 2018 https://harpers.org/archive/2018/10/checkpoint-nation-cbp-search-and-seizures-civil-rights-abuses/ Accessed Nov. 1, 2018; Kathleen Staudt and Irasema Coronado, *Fronteras no Más: Toward Social Justice at the U.S.-Mexico Border* (New York: Palgrave USA, 2002).

59. Rodolfo Rosales, *The Illusion of Inclusion: The Untold Political Story of San Antonio* (Austin: University of Texas Press, 2000). El Paso elected Mexican American Mayor Raymond Telles, Jr. in 1957; President Kennedy appointed him U.S. Ambassador to Costa Rica.

60. One might ask, what about San Diego? San Diego's core is about 17 miles north of the border; the urban sprawl spread southward toward the border and Tijuana.

61. Kathleen Staudt, *Border Politics in a Global Era: Comparative Perspectives* (Lanham, MD: Rowman & Littlefield, 2017), Chapters 3–4.

Chapter 3

"Dallas Area Interfaith: A Strong Multi-Ethnic Coalition"

Dallas as it is, Dallas as it should be....[1]

*L*et me begin with an inspiring story of the multiple achievements (called "wins" by many in the IAF) in which Dallas Area Interfaith (DAI) Leader Brenda Shell has participated. For over twenty years, she brought and continues to bring talents, skills, and networks to DAI's power in Dallas: "I knew everybody," she said.[2] IAF views networks and followings as important for its leaders. More recently, Shell and others dealt with feral dogs in neighborhoods. "People were afraid of getting out of their cars; an army veteran was mauled to death." After she and other leaders talked with a former DAI organizer, he said, "let's get together and do something about this." Together, she and other leaders worked to get the police department to appoint an assistant chief to coordinate efforts with animal control to reduce the number of wild dogs that roamed neighborhoods.

I share other DAI leaders' stories below, but Shell's story allows us to understand DAI's history and accomplishments in turning around schools, particularly at Franklin D. Roosevelt High School, with organized support from her church, impacting other schools and school board trustees who, pressed to support after-school programs, now institutionalized them in many schools in the district.

The Dallas Independent School District (ISD) labeled Roosevelt a "low-performing school." Crisis labels like low-performing can lead to school closure without some turnaround. Besides that, the neighborhood was changing. Shell described a mostly African American school in the South Oak Cliff neighborhood that her son attended in the mid-1990s. Growing numbers of Spanish-speaking students enrolled, learning English while learning other content. Shell said, "Some of the kids felt they were taking over our school. New teachers [perhaps some of them bilingual] spoke with accents that the kids couldn't understand well." At Roosevelt, she said, "the district had moved and shuffled principals and teachers around," so it was difficult to develop stable relationships. However, the parent liaison staff person had been there for three years, *so with DAI-acquired skills, Shell began to work with her and a principal who cared about the students and parents. Turmoil peaked at the school when a student was shot to death in the hallway. In this ongoing crisis context, Dallas Area Interfaith organizing was born at multiple levels: organizing parents, doing community walks, and connecting churches with the schools.*

Brenda Shell came from a small town in Texas where teachers were involved in kids' lives, unlike in Dallas ISD with its big central-office bureaucracy and high administrator and staff turnover. The size of the DFW region meant that with traffic, many working parents couldn't get home until 6 pm. "Kids had nowhere to go after school was out." Her church adopted a school; she and other parents talked to other ministers to get involved. Parents walked the neighborhoods and learned the issues. The principal called parents personally, unlike nowadays when automated phones "call" homes. Teachers took report cards to parents' homes, personally. Developing relational power and targeting school board trustees, teachers organized together with parents and DAI leaders from other areas to get a big "win, finally convincing them to create after-school programs."

Now Roosevelt is in far better shape, with a health science academy that integrally became preparation for both college and technical careers. From Roosevelt's website, we can also see various safety and identification measures in place.[3] Leader Brenda Shell says the school is now community centered. Alumni from the school are connected; they visit the school and line up to welcome new students.

Shell's church, Cedar Crest Church of Christ, stopped out of DAI for a while, then re-joined when she told the new minister, "have I got the thing for you!" As is evident from the church's website, the connection with DAI is celebrated as are interfaith relationships with other congregations. Cedar Crest offers a variety of programs, from Spirit Sundays twice annually with Roosevelt High School to urban farming and the Theater Ministry, as is obvious from the church's dynamic website.[4] Shell says that "churches have to change for people to come and to get younger people in, but the Bible doesn't change." DAI, she said, gave her the "skills to improve my community and to live out my faith tradition." DAI put Shell in relationship with people she "would have never known outside of DAI." She and other leaders put DAI's "vision for a divided society" into practice and in so doing, she says they are "reclaiming their faith."[5] We take up analysis of community organizing as faith-based or broad-based in the next chapter.

Framing the chapter

From a city with a southern political history, despite a location in the northern part of the state, a pair of dynamic and skilled women organizers, a wide variety of Black, Mexican American, and White leaders, and previous organizers have achieved many goals with relational meetings, community walks, and remarkably large action events numbering in the thousands at each sitting. Dallas Area Interfaith (DAI) is a relatively new Texas affiliate, born in the early-to-mid-1990s, a decade or two after the others. DAI was not part of historic IAF lore from the *Cold Anger* book of 1990, but this chapter seeks to make Dallas part of twenty-first century lore. Perhaps DAI's newness and strength in the IAF scheme contribute to its dynamism.

DAI is one of IAF's four strongest organizations in Texas with over thirty paid member institutions which, together, total approximately 90,000 people. DAI communicates widely: it is featured in the city's primary media outlet; its website is informative, and its Facebook posts, periodic. DAI's round logo frames the inner circle with the area cities that DAI represents: Dallas, De Soto, Garland, Richardson, Grand Prairie, Irving, and Plano. Southern Methodist University hosted DAI's founding event in 1994 with 3,000 attendees according to local media coverage. At the Dallas Area Interfaith (DAI) offices, with a sign outside that it is part of the Katrina Support Network (many New Orleans 2005 hurricane refugees moved to Texas), I paged through binders each containing three-inch-thick print media copy coverage year by year, mainly from the *Dallas Morning News.* DAI spawned the sixth IAF-affiliated comprehensive, but independent 501c3 nonprofit high-quality workforce training center, Skill Quest (covered in Chapter 8).

So how can DAI be absent from various Dallas history books and the curriculum of many universities in the larger metro region? In *The Dallas Myth,* a critical analysis of the elite and its rhetoric published in 2008, former University of Texas at Dallas historian Harvey Graff does not mention DAI.[6] Even the published IAF books contain little about Dallas.[7] DAI's inspiring work made me determined to feature their work in a whole chapter early in the book in order to reveal both IAF processes and the kinds of local, integral public policy issues that can strengthen democracy and accountability in a region: housing, health, public safety, education, and immigration.

This chapter highlights policy, policy implementation, and policy changes that have meaningful impacts on people's everyday lives.

Recall Chapter 2's characterization of Dallas, shaping past and present, yet also the changed political opportunity structure with reformed local city council institutions and a thriving economy (for some, not all) with likely resources available to invest in a constructive social justice organization. Box 3.1 contains a timeline of DAI's accomplishments over the decades—one that the body of this chapter narrates with interviewees' presentations of meaningful actions, focusing on process as well as outcome.

As in many big cities, Dallas residents have much about which to get angry, but DAI provides a way to channel anger "cold" (rather than "hot") for strategic change to achieve participants' interests, IAF style (as Chapter 1 discussed). North Dallas, a world apart from the city's south, includes a prosperous enclave-like city called Highland Park with its own independent school district. Like other Texas cities, the historic Citizens' Council nominated and funded hand-chosen candidates whose philosophy about government involved traditional notions like "the best government is that which governs least" i.e. limited taxing and spending, and especially miserly spending in communities of color.[8] Local citizens' councils operated in other Texas cities, but rarely did any of those councils feature broad-based representation.

Yes, in 1995 Dallas elected African American Mayor Ron Kirk, but as informed voters know, the election of one woman, one Mexican American, and/or one African American does not change the political culture. Rather, representative majorities change political cultures, along with critical masses of diverse people who use their organized, numeric, and relational power to press government for policy changes in between elections. Besides, those elected from underrepresented groups do not all think alike. Nor do politically underrepresented women. Ideologies vary among people in groups once marginalized in the US political process, as do ideologies among men and/or White people.

During the 1930s and thereafter, in the book *Blue Texas,* Texas Christian University historian Max Krochmal documented the outright violence against working women and men—White, Black, and Mexican heritage—and the decades-long struggle to build a civil rights coalition by the 1960s.[9] Of course, Dallas is not unique in this regard. Before U.S. policies incentivized export-processing manufacturing in countries like Mexico and the Global South, manufacturers in the U.S. north gravitated toward low-cost labor in the U.S. south to make businesses "competitive," including in Dallas. The 1940s anti-union "right-to-work laws," both the Taft-Hartley Act and its Texas versions, made it difficult for

Box 3.1 DAI Milestones

1990–1995	*Initial organization: DAI Sponsoring Committee*
1994	*Governor Ann Richards and state representatives at founding convention: committed $1 million for job training*
1994–96	*Community Policing Campaign: Dallas Police Chief Ben Click signed agreement to work with DAI*
1996–99	*Campaign for after-school programs: initial funding from Dallas Parks Department and subsequent funding for elementary schools from Dallas ISD*
1997	*Alliance Schools begin at Roosevelt HS, ultimately totaling ten Alliance Schools*
	Grawler Park Recreation Center funded
	Work Paths launched (first IAF-facilitated workforce training program)
1997–2002	*Citizenship classes in DAI member institutions*
	Local INS office established to speed processing
	Helped support funding for affordable homes in South Dallas from city and Nations Bank
2001	*Get-out-the-Vote (GOTV) drive to pass DISD bonds*
2005–2006	*Organized relocated Hurricane Katrina survivors in Dallas and Collin Counties, "winning $52 million in housing vouchers. Katrina Survivors Network focuses on employment, job training, access to health care."*
2005–2006	*"Campaign to increase funding for police officer recruitment and training"*
2006	*Funding for indigent health care in Collin County, with improved eligibility requirements.*
	Civic Academies on public school finance
2007	*Statewide IAF work to improve Children's Health Insurance Program (CHIP) standards and children's Medicaid.*

(Continued)

Box 3.1 *(Continued)*

	Worked with Dallas police and consulate on Mexico picture IDs (the Matrícula Consular)
	Civic Academies on financial markets; on taxation
2008	*Plano Forum on immigration reform*
	GOTV and walks to support Parkland Hospital bond vote
2009	*Local and statewide work with IAF on state matching funding ($15 million) for job-training programs*
2010–2011	*"Know your Rights" workshops in DAI congregations*
2011	*Head Start closure, then placement of stranded children in public schools*
2012–2013	*Durable Medical Equipment (DME) Exchange*
	Statewide work aimed at expanding Medicaid coverage
	Booklet and education workshops on eligibility and financial aid in insurance exchange
2012	*Skill QUEST, a stand-alone workforce training nonprofit with first graduates*
2014	*Rally for local action on immigration reform*
	Wage-theft and worker-rest-break campaigns begin
	Workshops with DACA candidates
2015	*Neighborhood organizing around DME, Skill QUEST.*
	Statewide work for matching funds ($5 million) for job training
2016	*Strengthen Rental Housing Codes*
	Renewed community-police relationships
2017	*Work with Dallas PD on training and reporting wage theft*
	Statewide work on matching funds ($4.3 million) for job-training

Source: Condensed and quoted from DAI Annual Reports, 2015, 2016, 2017 (Dallas, DAI).

working class people to organize and use the power of numbers in face of employers with their power of money. Dallas history books analyze the deep racism and deliberate efforts to divide and rule people based on ethnicity and race. Additionally, some of the most extreme of religious fundamentalist ideologies—dispensationalists—find resonance among the populations of north and east Texas.[10]

Until the early twenty-first century, some Dallas law enforcement officers acquired bad reputations: beating or killing persons of color, giving "Driving While Black" a frightening reputation. In 1973, a turning point that galvanized the Mexican American community, Dallas Police Officer Darrell Cain killed twelve-year-old Santos Rodríguez in the backseat of the squad car playing Russian roulette, yet served only two and a half years in prison after his conviction.[11] Law enforcement's reputation is still questionable, as we are reminded every time a police officer kills a person of color. No doubt rogue officers still exist. Yet everyone, whatever their ethnicity, race,[12] gender, or sexuality, has an interest in professional police officers who maintain public safety with fairness and justice.

Despite continuing power imbalance, business has begun to share some power with organized others, including broad-based community organizations like DAI's multi-ethnic, multi-racial institutional alliance, as evidenced by the recent and past achievements that leaders revealed to me, more fully narrated below. DAI can be called the first multi-racial issue coalition in modern Dallas history.

DAI leaders change policies

DAI takes a well-deserved place in community organizing in the state, offering a multi-issue array of public policy crises common to social justice work in its confrontation with a status quo resistant to change. Below I share volunteer leaders' and IAF organizers' stories, their pathways into action, their achievements, what they offer as key DAI policy achievements, and their descriptions of still-existent obstacles that millions of people face in one of the most inequitable cities in the country and state. In so doing, I provide background on policy issues and their relationship to people's everyday lives.

Keep in mind the segregation and inequality in Dallas, with poverty rates comparable to the borderlands as the table in Chapter 2 showed. The challenge to good governance is enormous. The DFW larger metro region is fragmented, complex, and one might imagine, nearly ungovernable: fourteen cities of over 100,000 persons, plus scores of towns under that number, thirteen counties, and fourteen school districts. Such fragmentation creates challenges not only in targeting goals, but also in DAI's strategizing for achieving wins in targeted locales. DAI sought and gained a place at the table in those locales where DAI power exists: power is located in the member institutions and their skilled leaders. They tend to be in Dallas and Collins County, as stories reveal below.

In the late twentieth and twenty-first centuries, Dallas politics opened up to competitive elections and some progressive initiatives, thanks to community organizing, civil rights struggles, MALDEF, and ethnic/racial and women's organizations that together pushed structural changes in local government such as geographic district-based elections. Ironically, then, neighborhoods in geographic districts provided leverage to people who live in neighborhoods segregated by ethnicity and wealth. The Urban Institute puts Dallas (and Houston) in the top five U.S. cities for neighborhood inequality.[13] In the interviews, DAI leaders called my attention to the Urban Institute study just cited, demonstrating their knowledge of the wider research that they can use for leverage in making their claims for local policy change.

DAI participants, like other IAF affiliates, listen to people's concerns in small-group sessions called house meetings, do practical research, and take action on the minutia of government about which the majority of city dwellers may be oblivious, such as annual budgets, policy implementation (or the lack thereof), and fixable flaws in political representation and government. These continuous and time-consuming processes get no special lines in timeline lists of accomplishments, such as Box 3.1. Leaders who use IAF organizing skills not only change public policies, but also improve people's confidence in themselves and their own public voices. In the U.S., the state of Texas falls near the bottom for voter-turnout figures (see Chapter 2). With IAF organizing, people learn and practice how voting matters for turning out unaccountable politicians who work primarily for their campaign donors.

My interviews with DAI people offered many insights. Participation in DAI, said Organizer Josephine López Paul, "teaches ordinary people how to have a say in their lives."[14] Leader Adriana Corral said she was once voiceless, too shy to speak. But now she's not afraid.[15] Through DAI, people see and experience the importance of voting: as Leader Brenda Shell said, people "stopped believing that their vote doesn't count." And Leader Deborah Smith talked about her church getting "souls to the polls," even watching election returns as votes are counted together with congregants at potluck suppers.[16]

Josephine López-Paul, Senior Organizer, Dallas Area Interfaith. Photograph courtesy Josephine López-Paul.

Deborah Smith, Dallas Area Interfaith Leader. Photograph Kathleen Staudt.

Some DAI leaders, like Barry Lachman, M.D., and retired environmental engineer Leader Myron Knudson, both engaged since DAI's inception, also bring expertise and skills to their community organizing work with others.[17] As someone who worked in government, Knudson knows the importance of getting bureaucrats out of their offices to observe what goes on. He even cited a passage in the Social Gospels to that effect during our interview. We saw in Chapter 2 the difference it made when politicians traveled from Austin to borderland *colonias* to witness the despicable governmental neglect of residents' road, water, and sewer problems. In Dallas, or anywhere actually, it made a difference to get politicians and administrators out of City Hall and into neighborhoods to see neighborhoods and talk to residents living there.

DAI recruits leaders, young and old, like the younger Samanda Gronstal who energizes her networks and gets them involved, bringing greater age diversity to the organization.[18] She and her DAI colleagues took some of the pictures used with permission for this book.

Samanda Gronstal, Dallas Area Interfaith Leader. Photograph courtesy Samanda Gronstal.

Interconnected policies and their everyday impacts

The sections below reveal the kinds of local policy wins that IAF affiliates like DAI can produce to make meaningful changes in people's lives, from housing and health to immigration and public safety. Leader Brenda Shell's story in the chapter's opening section offers insights on historical education policies with campuses in crisis: "the community saved the school," she said. Below I share other policy stories that emerged from my interviews in mid-2018.

Housing conditions, health, and developers

The organizing around Dallas housing issues epitomizes what organized people can do to expose the flaws of limited local government oversight along with the continuing power of business and real-estate developers with long-standing and overrepresented power and influence in Dallas. However, the IAF is not only about exposure and criticism, but also about crafting constructive solutions in strategies for change. As a reminder from earlier chapters, Harvey Molotch and others write about city politics and their "local growth machines" that have tended to dominate public decision-makers.[19] The crisis in the conditions in rental housing emerged as a major DAI focus in 2016–17, as we see below, but a focus that became surmountable with demonstrations of power, civil dialogue, and compromises that people agreed upon in negotiations over solutions.

As DAI leaders and organizers heard in small-group meetings (called "house meetings" that I share here in this chapter), some Dallas residents rented substandard older houses that had not been inspected for decades, despite obvious violations. Residents lived in shacks within the city where open sewage, rats, and inside mold made healthy life near impossible. Landlords, some of whom could more accurately be called slumlords, did not respond to residents' calls and complaints, despite collecting rents of $600–700 a month. Perhaps landlords were waiting for developers to buy up the land and properties to make way for gentrification in a part of Dallas with downtown skyscrapers in clear sight. Elsewhere, north of the Love Field airport, which sits smack in the center of the city, residents lived and continue to live in housing near the airport and experience high air pollution-related asthma rates. Neither the landlords nor the city exercised accountability to residents. Who benefitted

Dallas house in need of city inspection. Photograph Kathleen Staudt.

from the neglect of properties and of air quality? Certainly not the tenants. No penalties were in place to fine landlords who neglected tenants and housing repairs. The thirty-year-old City of Dallas Housing Code lacked anything of substance to enforce.

Organizer Josephine López-Paul gave me a practical, but moving, account of the process as did other DAI leaders who count this victory as one of their most important in recent years. It took a year of organizing, starting with a small group of DAI leaders and growing to large public actions. After doing the research on antiquated and unenforced inspection codes, along with assessing model codes used in other Texas cities, DAI leaders and organizers met with individual members of the city council, as did the landlords' association members. At a city council meeting, DAI brought two hundred leaders to the audience, while the landlords brought a hundred, to discuss a new, model inspection code. With obviously changed power dynamics, representatives of the Apartment Association of Greater Dallas decided it wanted to meet with DAI to negotiate a new code. They reached a compromise. Although the word "compromise" has negative connotations for some, "to the organizer, compromise is a key and beautiful word" for its pragmatics in a "free and open society."[20] Non-IAF protest groups might have picketed City Hall, spoken to the media to shame the landlords and city, and refused to enter the building where decisions get made. In contrast, IAF affiliates like DAI leaders and organizers, worked to construct solutions that produced a majority vote (a "win") and thereby achieved their goals.

Afterwards, the Association stood with DAI around a revised proposed code, and the city council passed the new code with a 12-1 vote (the one opponent wanting a stronger code). The code not only passed, but city representatives budgeted fifteen inspectors to do annual inspections. A 311 line was put into place to report problems. Most importantly, the new code contained "teeth." If landlords failed to comply with the required changes after inspection, they faced a $1,000-per-day fine. According to the former code enforcement prosecutor, then city council representative Adam McGough, the new rules included "the strongest AC regulation in the state."[21] DAI will continue to follow up to make sure the code is enforced. In this issue DAI pressed not only to change policy, but also to insure effective implementation. All too often, policy changes are announced with fanfare, but they result in what some have called symbolic politics, designed mainly to appease the public and produce quiescence.[22]

Because regional hospitals have an interest in healthy people, including the reduction of asthma, the area hospitals supported DAI on health-related issues. Leader Dr. Barry Lachman, a medical doctor and congregant in DAI member institution Temple Shalom, had long been concerned about people without suitable access to health care, even when he attended medical school in the northeastern U.S. before moving to Dallas. He cited the chronic asthma problems affecting 200,000 people in Dallas, 80 percent of them young, due in part to indoor mold. Dr. Lachman worked with the local Environmental Protection Agency (EPA) office to develop procedures for home visits to provide respiratory education; he says he "wants to take this show on this road" with community partners elsewhere as other Texas cities face similar problems. Lachman said he has been called a "distinguished troublemaker," a label with which he happily identifies. DAI has also participated in public education about and support for relevant hospital bonds that respond to people in their member institutions and the wider public.

Getting out the vote

IAF strategies also focus on nonpartisan election issues, such as bonds and "get-out-the-vote" (GOTV) efforts to educate voters on the issues and on representatives who do and do not respond to their constituents. Oftentimes, as I know from living in El Paso with its extremely low voter turnout, many residents are clueless about the opportunities and burdens of passing bonds, that is, targeted public loans with long-term lower-interest payments. Whether people vote or not, bond passage (or failure) means that all residents are affected through the gain or loss of improvement opportunities and the increase or decrease in property taxes, especially if the property tax base and its value do not grow.

In the Dallas area, DAI educated voters with civic academies and GOTV campaigns to include Dallas ISD bonds (2001), indigent health care in Collin County (2006), and Parkland Hospital modernization (2008). (See one of the front-cover pictures on a Get-Out-The-Vote group in DAI.) Leader Myron Knudson told me the story of a challenging bond election. He said the Parkland CEO at the time credited DAI for the win, with its large public actions about health and quality hospital care and its voter mobilization, helping to produce an overwhelming 85 percent vote in support of passage. (Note that usually bond elections produce low turnout and close margins of victory or failure.) Parkland Hospital, the county public hospital, needed new equipment that would fit in its fifty-year-old building, too old to accommodate that equipment. Leader Knudson explained more to me. Parkland's political-appointee board members saw their primary mission as keeping taxes low rather than to improve health care. Although public entities, their decision-making processes were not transparent, and contracts were sometimes let on a handshake. After the bond passed with its associated public education, board processes began to operate more professionally with contracts and metrics. Knudson, an engineer by training, uses evidence to buttress his points (as we see below in the section on the police department). In the past, he said, the hospital emergency room wait times averaged thirty hours, but after hospital modernization, staff reduced wait times to an average of three hours.

In the cases above, I've outlined how DAI leaders and organizers listened to crises that people expressed in member institutions, which then prompted action. DAI leaders and organizers researched, strategized, and organized action to produce concrete and constructive results. In another practical effort, IAF and DAI in particular organized Get-Out-The-Vote (GOTV) campaigns, especially when politicians behaved as if beholden mainly to those who made campaign contributions to their election and re-election campaigns or to developers' ambitions to gentrify neighborhoods with little regard for where displaced people could find affordable housing.

Myron Knudson, Dallas Area Interfaith Leader. Photograph by Kathleen Staudt.

In one of these practical examples, as Organizer Josephine López-Paul explained, the city zoning commission denied license renewal to a Montessori school that residents valued for their children. A city councilwoman and Mayor Pro Tem,[23] aligned with developers, opposed the license renewal and thus the expressed interests of constituents in her district. Elections are not only about choice and accountability, but they also offer opportunities for candidates and voters to send messages to one another. In her bid for re-election in a crowded field of candidates with no clear majority for each, the two front-runners went into the run-off elections a month later after the regular election, which typically draws lower turnout. Twenty DAI women leaders, committed to talking with twenty voters each, reaching potentially four hundred, walked neighborhoods to "get out the vote" in the regular and run-off elections, thereby increasing turnout by 150 percent. The Mayor Pro Tem lost the run-off by 379 votes. Council renewed the Montessori school license soon thereafter.[24]

Juxtaposing safety, immigration, and identification

Public safety and immigration rights have become huge issues for residents all over the state, including high-crime Dallas. In 2017, the Dallas murder rate was the highest in Texas and in the top twenty-five of U.S. cities. At the same time, police officers' shootings of suspects, particularly persons of color, cannot be tolerated as the Black Lives Matter movement reminds the public after each tragic killing. Some people need protection from the police, while others seek police protection: a tangled juxtaposition.[25]

DAI organizers and leaders heard about safety and crime issues from leaders in their member institutions. As examples below reveal, these issues included slow responses to 911 calls, traffic stops that could result in jail without a government-issued picture identification card, speeding traffic near schools, and robberies and domestic violence about which residents feared making reports, including fears of revenge from those who wronged them. Many people live in fear: afraid to take their children to school, afraid to drive their cars. I talked to DAI leaders and organizers about these matters, and their voices emerge below.

How DAI forged a consensus over better community-based policing

DAI leaders voiced a variety of examples for why stronger relationships with police departments became necessary (see Box 3.1 on the Timeline), from the mid-90s efforts, to the 2005-2006 efforts for more police recruitment and training, to the very recent current efforts in 2016 and beyond, after heightened immigration enforcement and fears in the community. These examples range from domestic violence to theft at check cashing sites, anti-LGBTQ violence, and traffic safety. Over a twenty-year period, from DAI's creation in the mid-90s through the writing of this book, we see the persistent efforts to build a mutually beneficial relationship emerging around community-based policing. This long-term relationship needed continuous renewal and rebuilding, as with any and all public officials where turnover is typically high.

Leader Adriana Corral started working with DAI when her child of seven years attended a primary school without readily visible traffic signals that warned speeding motorists to slow down. She said "Drivers did not pay attention, people were scared to walk with fast cars nearby, and someone was nearly run over." Drawing on learned skills from DAI, Corral talked with the principal, networked with other parents in the Parent Teacher Organization (PTO) she headed, and successfully got her city council representative to get road bumps and flashing lights by the school within a month (rather than the usual year-long delay). Often the first step of potential leadership development involves issues like these: traffic safety near schools—fixable, but complex and time-consuming to address. Once new leaders achieved their goals, the "wins" spurred them to deeper and wider involvement.

A decade before heightened immigrant enforcement, DAI pushed for more police officers and better pay, given the shortages of officers in Dallas compared to other cities. Safe communities are those where residents trust the police and the police are trustworthy. The police depend on residents' reports for accurate crime control, witnesses, and information. Because professional law enforcers have an interest in working with city residents, law enforcement agencies around the country have tried to practice "community-based policing" since the 1990s. Yet police departments are often hard pressed to recruit officers and fill vacancies, especially with low entry salaries and dangerous work. In city government, police and firefighter expenses typically represent the biggest-ticket items in the city budget, as much as a third to three-fifths of the expenses; their salaries and benefit packages become contentious during budget-making season. Turnover is high in cities with low officer salaries if and when trained officers move to other cities to earn higher wages. The City of Dallas had a reputation for high crime and insufficient numbers of police officers.

A decade before (2005–2007), DAI leaders engaged in practical IAF-style research with impacts on their meetings with the city manager and council representatives. As data-oriented Leader Myron Knudson said, "we learned that in Fort Worth, with its lower-crime rate, the city counted 5.1 officers per 100,000 in population, but in Dallas, the figure was 1.8 per 100,000." DAI leaders talked to the city manager[26] and worked to get 800 more officers hired, partly with a bonus for recruitment.[27] Having worked many years in bureaucracy, Leader Knudson knew the kinds of constructive arguments that could nudge change. "I'm a good bureaucrat," he laughed, revealing an important insight about evidence-based policy reform to tweak rationales and identify specific strategies for change, with attention to enforcement. Currently, Dallas police officers earn a starting salary of $60,000, plus the possibility of overtime.

To fast-forward a decade later under heavy immigration threats, Leader Adriana Corral and others subsequently felt dread and fear after Immigration and Customs Enforcement (ICE) hyper-enforcement in long-term cooperation with local law enforcement especially after 2016. She said that others shared these fears in her Catholic congregation, a DAI member institution. After her initial feelings of hopelessness and despondency, Corral told me that she asked herself: "What am I going to do? I cried; I couldn't sleep; I was feeling hopeless." Soon thereafter, when the Texas state legislature passed a bill, meant to prohibit so-called sanctuary cities, known as SB4 (Senate Bill 4), Corral called Organizer Josephine López-Paul who told her "we have to organize. Come to the Police Department Headquarters for a large meeting." Corral said she thought "Whaaaat? I'm scared, but I will go." In what might be the second-most important accomplishment (the most important in some DAI leaders' eyes), DAI built on its relationship with the Dallas Police Department from previous interactions, organized public actions with police leaders, and got public commitments from them to deepen what elsewhere is called "community-based policing."

A heavy presence of immigration agents made Dallas a frightening place to live. According to Pew Research Center data from 2017, the Dallas area had the highest deportation numbers in the country, due to the assignment of more agents and the removal of some previous restrictions on detainer orders. ICE agents deported more people (16,520) than in larger cities with likely more undocumented people such as the New York-New Jersey area (2,576 deportations).[28] Before outlining DAI's enormous achievement in public declarations from three police chiefs to accept the parish-issued picture ID for routine traffic stops and crime reports, though, let me weave together the complex background on immigration and law enforcement in the Texas state context just to show how courageous these efforts were against the intimidation posed by state law and federal enforcement.

Leader Adriana Corral's story about parish picture IDs is visualized and told in an HBO/Vice News six-minute newscast on August 9, 2018,

Box 3.2 Background on Immigration and Local Law Enforcement

When the Texas state legislature roused and polarized the public about undefined "sanctuary cities" and then passed bills into laws, such as it did with SB4 in 2017, it deepened a wedge between local law enforcement and residents. Harsh federal enforcement and SB4, called the "Show Me Your Papers" law, continue to be contested in courts. "Sanctuary" evokes the image of medieval churches which offer protective shelter from abusive monarchs— an image at far odds with the reality in Texas. SB4 was supposed to ensure that local law enforcement released those imprisoned with detainer orders to ICE.

In the contemporary period, the rhetoric of "sanctuary city" made it seem as through local law enforcement did not cooperate with the federal government officers but instead sheltered dangerous people that ICE agents sought for possible deportation. Perhaps few people would object to Detainer Order releases, though it is important to understand the nature of the crime for which someone is jailed: misdemeanors or traffic citations, such as changing lanes without a clicker or a broken headlight. These offenses differ from serious, violent felonies. The police and sheriff deputies sometimes stop a driver or car based on the person's looks or the type of car a person is driving, and then the driver is asked for a picture identification while the officer checks for outstanding warrants. In some states, the overrepresentation of persons of color in traffic stops has been so large that state monitoring agencies review citations to detect possible racism.

SB4 threatened to penalize officers who did not enforce federal immigration politics. If and when police officers interacted with people over a traffic infraction or crime report, officers could ask for identification and check databases for legal presence, subjecting people to possible incarceration and deportation.[29] This would likely increase the pool of people jailed for lack of picture ID, rather than focus on or round up dangerous people. To the extent that the federal government envelops local law enforcement into doing federal immigration government work on city streets, and given the

(Continued)

Box 3.1 (Continued)

tendency for some police officers to stop persons of color, SB4 at the state level could incentivize immigrant and racial profiling.

The legislation was supposed to address the relatively narrow issue of prisoner release if and when law enforcement was presented with ICE detainers rather than to induce more police surveillance and checking for identification and citizenship. With explosive and threatening language, the state would have trans-formed local law enforcers, who are paid by local taxpayers, into behaving like federal immigration authorities on the streets of Texas. For better or worse in readers' minds, local Texas law enforcement had regularly complied with federal detainer orders with one or two exceptions among the 254 counties in Texas.

And to back up on heavy-handedness in the background to SB4, hidden behind the closed doors of bureaucracy, one also finds opaque decisions that illustrate the hardening state policies to trap undocu-mented people. As DAI learned in its listening sessions, some parents feared traveling to church or taking their children to schools in case they were stopped without identification. Once a law enforcement officer, then an IAF leader and organizer, and now in DAI, Organizer Socorro Perales explained to me the long-term political strategies of ambitious politicians seeking national political office.[30] These elected leaders can nudge change made behind the closed doors of bureau-cracy in executive agencies,[31] such as the Department of Public Safety (DPS). By bureaucratic fiat in 2008, the DPS forbade the renewal or granting of driver's license holders to those without citizenship or on no pathway to citizenship.[32] The inability to get driver's license IDs aggravated non-citizens' risks, creating the sort of crises that bubbled up among DAI leaders in house meetings and led to the culminating public action of thousands with police chiefs when increased numbers of ICE agents deported residents at higher rates.

---

with over 70,000 views as of early 2019.[33] In the video, she responds to interview questions on the difference it makes to have an ID: "Oh my gosh, it's like day and night. To enroll your kids in school, to go to a doctor, open a bank account. If you don't have that, it's really hard." She and members of her parish did outreach on the procedures for getting

Socorro Perales, Dallas Area Interfaith Organizer. Photograph courtesy Socorro Perales.

a parish picture ID, which involves checks and months of membership. In a sacred space like San Juan Diego Catholic Church, in which people feel safe, it is also moving to see the priest announce the procedures. Corral said that 1,600 people signed up, and more people joined the church. Others interviewed in the video included Organizer Josephine López-Paul, the Dallas police chief, and other officers about the public pronouncement that people may use the parish picture ID at the officer's discretion. Besides this achievement, the video shows DAI's effective communication via video and news.

In addition to DAI leaders' fears about living in shadows, my interviews with other DAI leaders brought out other safety concerns. Among these issues, we learn about people's need to report domestic violence and theft in multiple languages, with the legitimate expectation of speedy responses. Leader Samanda Gronstal said both the police and phone number 211 needed more bilingual officers (Spanish, Vietnamese) who "understand multiple points of view." She told a horrific story of an abuser who set a truck on fire with his partner inside; it took forty-five minutes for the authorities to arrive; the woman burned to death in the meantime. In another story, Gronstal and her friend, a nun with a walker, stayed late at the Catholic school where they used to work. After leaving, they heard gunshots and called 911, but were told "the address doesn't exist." Imagine the fear (including the fear about incompetence regarding street addresses in the 911 system)!

Samanda Gronstal, Dallas Area Interfaith Leader "selfie" with other DAI leaders.
Photograph Samanda Gronstal.

In large cities like Dallas, residents seek safety, but fear calling the police to report crime or serve as witnesses in court cases. Yet people experience crime. Let me provide a few more examples that came from interviews with other DAI leaders. Many people, especially those living paycheck to paycheck, do not establish bank accounts to receive direct deposit of their paychecks. Why? Banks charge monthly fees if customers lack minimum account balances—hardly affordable to many working in low-wage jobs. Leader Fr. Mike Walsh described to me the fears people face when they use corner-store facilities to cash checks on their paydays. Carrying cash, he said, some face the risk of "robbery outside the store or of being followed by home-invaders who take their money and threaten physical harm if a report is made." Invaders warn, "We know where you and your family live."[34]

And a chronic issue all over the state involves delayed responses to reports of domestic violence that may result in tragedies like injury and murder; victim-survivors fear calling the police, or police arrive too late.

Rev. Michael Walsh, C.M., Dallas Area Interfaith Leader. Photograph Kathleen Staudt.

Leader Gronstal said, "This is part of system failure." In addition to women, the usual victim-survivors of domestic violence, LGBTQ people question whether they can assume equal justice and response if assaulted or a victim of theft; they want justice too. Just as residents have an interest in safety and professional policing, so also do police departments have an interest and stake in people's reports. Yet some residents hesitate to report crimes.

To respond to these fears and concerns, DAI engaged in long-term relational power with police chiefs to permit residents to use picture IDs from a credible source. After the long-term process of building a consensus around strategy, in 2017 DAI leaders held an "action" with three police chiefs in different cities and 1,500 people strong in the audience, displaying the power of numbers with people of faith. DAI's member institutions include many Catholic parishes, and the bishop—like other bishops elsewhere in the US—has long articulated the basic dignity of all people, regardless of their citizenship status.[35] Many DAI leaders express a public interest, not only self-interest, in immigrants' rights to live without fear.

DAI leaders know and repeat Biblical injunctions, Old and New Testament, about "welcoming the stranger." Leader Dr. Barry Lachman recalled his own family's immigration background, with grandparents from Romania who arrived under very different U,S. laws than the system now in place. He wondered "Why is it a crime to seek a better life?" People also shudder in remembrance of Nazi profiling and checkpoints during the 1930s and 40s, the Holocaust, and the challenges people faced gaining entry into the U.S. in exodus from Hitler's regime. Dr. Lachman made global reference to the apartheid-like segregation of north and south Dallas that evoked Cold War-era language: the "Berlin Wall of the Trinity River, the north-south divide."

True to form, IAF organizations developed consensus over issues and strategized for wins in multiple steps on the ID issue. One initial step, albeit incomplete for everyone living in fear, was to work with the Dallas Police Department to accept the Catholic-parish-issued picture identification card. Such ID cards, not issued lightly or to anyone who walks in the church doors, can serve to verify identity to police officers in traffic stops. DAI sought police chiefs' public affirmation that they would accept the parish ID card if drivers could not produce a government-issued ID card during a police stop. In past policy practices, people without a government-issued ID could be jailed, perhaps facing detainer orders by federal officials. If police officers accept a parish ID, then interaction could proceed and if warranted, a citation issued, rather than going to jail with its possible deportation consequences, leaving children to the vagaries of a problem-infested foster-care system in Texas.

As those who study policy know well, street-level bureaucrats, like police officers, welfare social workers, and teachers, can exercise discretion based on their judgment in particular cases.[36] According to DAI Organizer Josephine López-Paul, "we taught them their own policy." On traffic stops, the policy calls for officers to examine government-issued identification. However, the police department's own policy document also indicated that other forms of identification could be accepted at the officer's discretion. "There was the nuance," said López-Paul. In the large public meeting, police chiefs committed to policy, at the officer's discretion, to accept the church-issued picture ID. The clarified policy, accepted at the highest levels of police chiefs, gave once-fearful local residents more confidence about interacting with police officers and reporting crimes they experience or witness. However, fear has not ended in Dallas, for the parish ID was only a partial solution for Catholic congregants, not for the non-Catholic and secular populations. And one can only wonder if and when police chief pronouncements trickle down to supervisors and officer levels.[37]

The Catholic parish ID is only one small step toward community-based policing and reducing, not totally ending the dark days of people's fears about many things: long-overdue federal immigration reform; delays, foils, and heavy fees in the naturalization process; and what public administration scholars call the "devilish details" about policies made behind closed doors such as what occurred in the Texas Department of Public Safety about driver's license renewals, as discussed above. Under multiple U.S. presidents, but especially since 2017, the federal-level Department of Homeland Security has made it abundantly clear that family separation, putting children in detention, and confusing non-English-speaking parents into signing English-language documents about leaving their separated children comprise acceptable "practiced policy" unless judicial orders forbid such deception. While a Catholic parish ID is an incomplete solution for everyone, residents face somewhat less fear in their interaction with the Dallas-area police departments. We learn here about the enormous energy necessary for local solutions, however partial, for problems that the U.S. Congress has been unwilling to address. This enormous energy involves persisting, drawing on the leaders' multiple strengths, and weaving through the ways that the self-interest of fearful people can become the public interest of a large community organization like Dallas-Area Interfaith. However, the public achievements are always tentative, requiring follow up. And there is always more to do.

Visual images pack a punch. I was stunned to see pictures of the large DAI 1,500-person action of uniformed officers who respected the call to prayer that generally begins and ends IAF meetings and actions. The DAI website contains this striking picture (https://www.dai-iaf.org/) as does its most recent *DAI Annual Report.*

A change in self

We have covered a variety of policies above, from housing inspection and health to education and safety. Through DAI, leaders learned civic skills and details about the process of pushing constructive reforms: public speaking, moderating meetings, building turnout for actions, getting out the vote, following up in relational meetings with officials, and organizing events, among others. However, one of their most important skill acquisitions consisted of a changed sense of self and the place of self in society. Leaders learned courage, confidence, and self-respect. They discovered their strengths and talents. They developed new frameworks for understanding systemic issues and policy change. As Leader Adriana Corral said too, "I started seeing stuff differently."

Leaders have come to expect respect when meeting in small groups with their representatives, like any other constituents, professionals and business owners alike. In several interviews, leaders told me that occasionally, public officials showed up as much as thirty minutes late to a relational meeting or an official tried to control the meeting. Note that IAF affiliate organizers and leaders ALWAYS come to meetings on time with their agendas, which are distributed to all who attend and they introduce themselves and their member institution. Rather than stewing in silence at what can be deliberate humiliation in a hierarchical and unequal society, the organizer encourages leaders to call the representative to task at the meeting about the disrespect shown the attendees. IAF earned a "place at the table" and the place is an equal and respectful one for its leaders.

Faith connections

In the next chapter, we examine the faith-based connections to people's participation in IAF organizations. In Dallas, leaders brought up the faith theme over and over. Again, Leader Adriana Corral: "We're not alone; we are people of faith. I can stay home and cry, or do what I can do to help." As noted earlier, Leader Myron Knudson referred to the Social Gospel story, a metaphor for officials to get out of their comfort zones and go to the streets to learn, or in the Biblical story, to gather people for the feast. Father Walsh, who worked with the big IAF organization in Los Angeles and in Little Rock, a challenging place for grassroots organizing, said about Dallas, "God gets me to the right places." New Leader Jenny Zacarias told me that while she knows and understands poverty from her childhood, her situation is now far better.[38] Still, she re-committed her life. In confession, the priest encouraged her to be involved with DAI, so she agreed. "I always equated power with money, but learned the idea that power can be acquired with money AND organizing: I've seen it! So many systems are set up and designed to keep people poor." Samanda Gronstal, a young leader, initially wondered about getting involved after Sr. Consuelo and others announced the social justice call and a House Meeting at her church. "Once you start, you see the connectedness of issues." Gronstal, while acknowledging the difficulty of "keeping bridges strong between multi-racial leaders," is hopeful for the future and DAI's growth. She says that "Hispanics bring youth to DAI."

Whatever their background and faith, one senses an unmistakable solidarity and commitment among DAI leaders. One also senses that leaders believe that they have been "called" to do social justice work and that DAI is the right organization in which to do that work. We take up these issues in the next two chapters, one on faith and purpose, and the other on pathways into social justice organizing and leadership. Yet we see in this chapter how leaders' self-interest can turn into DAI's organizing agenda and thereby tap the power of the many toward achieving public interests in an improved Dallas.

Concluding reflections

In this chapter, we have seen DAI's achievement of multiple wins with a wide variety of leaders who brought skills to the process and/or who have been changed in the process of organizing for social justice. Crises often emerged in house meeting stories that instigated strategizing and organizing toward solutions. One might compartmentalize public policies as neat and separate categories, such as in textbooks or campaign policies, but this chapter shows their integral connectedness as policies affect residents in their everyday lives. For example, housing inspections and health are tied. DAI organizing created an inspection code with teeth and enforcement as did its support in a bond election for long-overdue public hospital modernization. Dallas developers, like those in most cities, exercise power with money, but their agendas can be surmounted with people's concerns. Such counter-balance requires constant vigilance.

DAI most certainly occupies a place at the table (recall Chapters 1 and 2), despite the size of the metro region and the existence of many other nonprofit organizations and groups. Its organizers, both women working on a base of past organizers, both men and women, bring skill, enthusiasm, and dynamism to their work to identify more and more leaders and achieve DAI goals. With leaders, organizers have found ways to integrate women's issues and family violence into DAI's public safety agenda. DAI achieved many goals over the years that made and continue to make life and democracy better in the city; however much more needs to be done in those regards. DAI regularly holds accountability sessions, pursues GOTV efforts, and enjoys relational power through its many meetings with officials. Its leaders are truly diverse, not only in their identities and religious affiliations, but also in their skill sets. Leaders and good organizers make DAI strong.

Professional police officers are fundamental for people's safety, yet they exercise discretion with both beneficial and tragic impacts. Police killings, without the obvious due process of law that all people deserve, bear heavily on the Black community. Hispanic people also worry about police profiling that can result in deportation. Police officers' traffic stops can break apart families if people are jailed for trivial offenses and then released to ICE on detainer orders that could result in deportation. Hopefully, the commitments DAI received resulted in thorough dissemination throughout the police force and in training. Getting out the vote always matters for securing representatives who listen and respond to their constituencies as well as providing a rightful voice to voters, most all of them informed voters with DAI affiliation.

Dallas remains a huge, fragmented, and divided city. DAI's victories always need follow up, even as new issues and crises emerge from small-group listening sessions. As elsewhere, prosperous people vote at high rates, so pushing for more equal voices and voting remains a constant struggle. Whether "distinguished troublemakers" or moms dedicated to make a better life for themselves, their kids, and their neighborhoods, DAI leaders have made a problematic city better, slightly less problematic in the gains made for hospital modernization, better schooling no matter their location, and the mechanisms to live in decent housing.

With its two dynamic women organizers, DAI offers perhaps the gold standard for what IAF organizing can be elsewhere in the state. To invoke the epigraph for this chapter, DAI works with the metro region as it is, moving it toward Dallas as it should be.

Notes

1. This phrase takes off from the combination of empirical and normative in Saul Alinsky's famous quote, "As an organizer I start from where the world is, as it is, not as I would like it to be." *Rules for Radicals: A Practical Primer for Realistic Radicals* (New York: Vintage), xix.

2. I interviewed DAI Leader Brenda Shell on June 17, 2018. Elsewhere in this chapter, I refer to this interview.

3. https://www.dallasisd.org/roosevelt

4. https://www.cedarcrestcoc.net/church-ministries.html

5. The vision is on p. 2 of DAI's 2016 *Annual Report.*

6. Harvey Graff, *The Dallas Myth: The Making and Unmaking of an American City* (Minneapolis: University of Minnesota Press, 2008). Graff subsequently moved to Ohio State University. Michael Phillips,

White Metropolis, Race, Ethnicity, and Religion in Dallas, 1841–2001 (Austin: University of Texas Press, 2006); Cal Jillson, *Lone Star Tarnished* (New York: Routledge). For an analysis of the special relationship African American religious leaders developed with political authorities, see *The Accommodation* by journalist Jim Schutze, originally published by Taylor in Dallas (which appeared to bow to pressure from the establishment that the book created a negative image) but later Citadel Press (https://www.dmagazine.com/publications/d-magazine/1987/march/the-accommodation/).

7. However, Mark Warren in *Dry Bones Rattling: Community Building to Revitalize American Democracy* (Princeton: Princeton University Press, 2001) contains an analysis of Dallas, especially its work on racial justice in the city and in organizing.

8. On the "limited government" phrase, see https://www.washingtonpost.com/news/volokh-conspiracy/wp/2017/09/06/who-first-said-the-best-government-is-that-which-governs-least-not-thoreau/?noredirect=on&utm_term=.e049b7dd236b).

9. Max Krochmal analyzes police brutality in support of Ford Motor Company and other manufacturers in *Blue Texas: The Making of a Multiracial Coalition in the Civil Rights Era* (Chapel Hill: University of North Carolina Press, 2016), Chapters 1–2.

10. Michael Philipps, *White Metropolis: Race, Ethnicity, and Religion in Dallas, 1841–2001* (Austin: University of Texas Press, 2006). An extreme form of evangelical fundamentalism, dispensationalists follow a nineteenth-century prophetic belief in seven stages of mankind toward a specific end, connected with the nation-state of Israel, of rapture, tribulation, and the second coming of Jesus: https://www.theopedia.com/dispensationalism; https://www.christianitytoday.com/history/issues/issue-61/dispensational-premillennialism-dispensationalist-era.html

11. Lauren Silverman, "How the Death of a 12-year Old Changed the City of Dallas," https://www.npr.org/sections/codeswitch/2013/07/24/205121429/How-The-Death-Of-A-12-Year-Old-Changed-The-City-Of-Dallas, July 24, 2013, Accessed 11/2/18.

12. I hesitate to use the social construct "race," as do many social scientists and anthropologists, but defer to common usage.

13. Rolf Pendall with Carl Hedman, *Worlds Apart: Inequality between America's Most and Least Affluent Neighborhoods* (Washington, D.C.: Urban Institute, June 2015). https://www.urban.org/sites/default/files/publication/60956/2000288-Worlds-Apart-Inequality-between-Americas-Most-and-Least-Affluent-Neighborhoods.pdf Accessed 7/1/18.

14. Interview with Lead Organizer Josephine López Paul, July 16–17, 2018. Elsewhere in this chapter, I refer to this interview.

15. Interview with Leader Adriana Corral (with a surname pseudonym I assigned), July 16, 2018. Elsewhere in this chapter, I refer to this interview.

16. Interview with Leader Deborah Smith, July 17, 2018. Elsewhere in this chapter, I refer to this interview.

17. Interviews with Leaders Dr. Barry Lachman and Myron Knudson, both on July 17, 2018. Elsewhere in this chapter, I refer to these interviews.

18. Interview with Leader Samanda Gronstal, July 18, 2018. Elsewhere in this chapter, I refer to this interview.

19. Harvey Molotch, "The City as a Growth Machine: Toward a Political Economy of Place," *American Journal of Sociology* 82, no. 2 (1976): 309–332.

20. Saul Alinsky, *Rules for Radicals* (New York: Vintage, Random House, 1971), 59.

21. DAI 2017 *Annual Report*, p. 3. Councilman McGough was the former code enforcement prosecutor.

22. Murray Edelman, *The Symbolic Uses of Politics* (Champaign-Urbana: University of Illinois Press, 1964).

23. A Mayor Pro Tem is like a vice-mayor who steps into leadership when the mayor is absent.

24. Interview with Organizer Josephine López-Paul.

25. On race and racism, IAF's relationship with police departments is a complex one to develop and strategize around. Residents obviously need protection against violent crime and theft, including domestic violence. Policy analysis is very much about defining problems and their scope, then developing solutions consistent with those problem definitions along with strategies to achieve those solutions. How IAF research defined the problem about the Dallas Police Department became part and parcel of the solutions posed. Was the problem over-policing or under-policing, a sub-question for which is: what is the appropriate level of policing in which communities? Too many Black men especially, also women, have been killed by police officers. An international media source, *The Guardian*, was the first in 2015 to gather data on police killings of suspects, perhaps innocents—a problem of which the FBI only gathers "voluntary" data from police departments around the U.S. And the FBI voluntary database, always reporting fewer than the more than 1,000 police homicides annually, titles their tables

"justifiable homicides"; they were recorded separately from murder rates because, by definition, killing of innocent victims or mistakes, or prior to a charge and due process of law, do not exist. https://ucr.fbi.gov/crime-in-the-u.s/2016/crime-in-the-u.s.-2016/topic-pages/expanded-homicide. There were 171 murders in 2016, Dallas, but police killings were recorded separately and not by the city https://ucr.fbi.gov/crime-in-the-u.s/2016/crime-in-the-u.s.-2016/tables/table-6/table-6-state-cuts/texas.xls https://www.theguardian.com/us-news/2015/dec/31/the-counted-police-killings-2015-young-black-men; https://www.theguardian.com/us-news/2016/dec/15/us-police-killings-department-of-justice-program; https://www.theguardian.com/us-news/2017/jan/08/the-counted-police-killings-2016-young-black-men. Some IAF affiliates have begun interacting with their county, city, and state representatives about restorative justice that would ease re-entry of those released into the workforce to gain living wage jobs. Now, in Texas, Austin is among the few cities to have passed an ordinance for "fair-chance hiring," which removes the box on application forms about past convictions until a later stage in the hiring process.

26. The city manager's position at the helm of governance in the weak-mayor cities of Texas can be crucial for good governance.

27. 600 in DAI's 2017 *Annual Report*.

28. Stephen Young, "Dallas Area Had Highest Number of ICE Arrests in the Country in 2017, New Study Says," *Dallas Observer*, February 14, 2018. https://www.dallasobserver.com/news/ice-arrested-more-people-in-dallas-than-anywhere-else-in-2017-10367404. Accessed February 5, 2019.

29. Even before the state Sanctuary Cities law and court attention, ambitious local law enforcement practices resulted in deportations until civil society pushed back. Former El Paso sheriff, the late Leo Samaniego, set up checkpoints outside the city limits targeting older vehicles and asking not only for a driver's license and proof of insurance, but also for Social Security cards and citizenship documents. Both the IAF organizations and the Border Network for Human Rights met with him, queried candidates running for sheriff about the policy, and met with newly elected former Police Chief Richard Wiles who ended the practice and penalized deputies who harassed people. Samaniego's practice resulted in approximately 800 deportations. According to the story one grandpa told at a Border Interfaith Accountability Session, while legally living in Westway *colonia* and taking his grandchildren back and forth to school, he was stopped seven times

in three months by the same deputies! See analysis in Kathleen Staudt and Josiah Heyman, "Immigrants Organize Against Everyday Life Victimization," in Rich Furman, Greg Lamphear, and Douglas Epps, eds., *The Immigrant Other: Lived Experiences in a Transnational World* (New York: Columbia University Press, 2016), 75–89.

30. Interview with Organizer Socorro Perales, July 17, 2018.

31. This is the so-called fourth branch of government at national and state levels.

32. https://www.dps.texas.gov/DriverLicense/LawfulStatusDLID.htm

33. See https://www.youtube.com/watch?v=M2TgqL0kkFU

34. Interview with Fr. Mike Walsh, July 17, 2018. Elsewhere in this chapter, I refer to this interview.

35. U.S. Conference of Catholic Bishops and Conferencia del Episcopado Mexicano, *Strangers no Longer: Together on the Journey of Hope* (Washington, D.C.: USCCB, 2003).

36. Michael Lipsky, *Street-Level Bureaucracy* (New York: Russell Sage Foundation, 1980).

37. *Inside Bureaucracy*, the classic book about public administration by Anthony Downs (1967), cautions against assumptions that policy pronouncements at the top reach the bottom of hierarchical institutions, such as government (or that reports at the bottom reach the top without serious editing and selective information loss). My work in higher education was a constant reminder of this as well. The challenge facing university presidents pushing policy change, many joke, is like "herding cats."

38. Interview with Jenny Zacarias, July 17, 2018.

Chapter 4

"Voluntary Organizations with a Purpose: Faith-based or Broad-based?"

A gain, let us start with a brief story, this time from a member of the clergy at an Austin Interfaith member institution. He speaks to key themes of this chapter.

When Rabbi Alan Freedman arrived in the city, an active member of the synagogue reached out about community-based social justice work. With the synagogue's eventual affiliation in Austin Interfaith, Rabbi Freedman said that congregants "can effectuate real changes in real people's lives on a local basis." He theorizes that "theologically liberal religion has a large issue: to define what the church means to people in their lives. The IAF focuses on community building; it is an institution that can also provide purpose and meaning in congregants' lives.... Reform Judaism shares cross-currents with IAF issues." Rabbi Freedman believes those issues provide a way to strengthen commitments both to people's faith and to their community.

Rabbi Freedman says that "IAF brings attention to issues they [congregants] didn't know were of meaning to them." Austin Interfaith supplies details about local policy issues. "There's no debate about the value of the issues, just how much money to throw at them." With Austin Interfaith, he said, we are "getting into the weeds" and learning about city budgets. After that learning, "people can make up their own minds."[1]

With these eloquent quotes from Rabbi Freedman, we can see the purposeful activities that clergy and lay leaders can open to their congregants through IAF affiliation: ways for individuals to learn and to have meaningful impacts on a wider world that needs repair, a world that requires in-depth, practical civic education in local democracy. As for why congregants participate, that is, their motivations and organizational incentives, we cover the purposeful incentives in this chapter that supplement IAF's focus on self-interest for its paid organizers and unpaid leaders (see the appendix to this chapter and Chapter 5). In a crowded field of media sources, on paper and online, whether well-educated or not, IAF participants learn details about local government agencies and change strategies when they belong to IAF member institutions. Temple Shalom offers gender-balanced clergy, with a woman Associate Rabbi and a woman Social Justice Fellow. However, we see in this chapter that far from everyone in IAF faith-based member institutions commits to active social justice work. Rather, congregations offer special niches—such as music, youth education, and/or social justice work—for members to practice their faith in action.

The City of Austin is a well-off, mostly highly educated community (albeit amid internal inequalities) compared to the rest of the state (see Chapter 2). The city is relatively progressive, with social justice policies in place thanks to a critical-mass majority of city council representatives. Austin is also a place of dense nonprofit options including Interfaith Texas,[2] perhaps confusingly similar in name to the IAF affiliate, but IAF's Austin Interfaith is the action-oriented community organization for justice work. One question this chapter asks is whether we should call IAF affiliates faith-based or broad-based organizing. Perhaps the word "purpose" responds best to IAF organizers' and leaders' motivations to participate in the IAF, thus the reason for the chapter title.

Framing the chapter

Faith-based narratives offer powerful language, stories, and metaphors that resonate with community organizing for social justice. The 1950s–1970s civil rights movement and its leadership, including clergy such as the Reverend Dr. Martin Luther King Jr., drew on Biblical stories like the Old Testament chapter of *Exodus* to move large numbers of people to think and act differently about racism and White supremacy. In the 1960s and 1970s many clergy—priests, rabbis, and pastors—took courageous risks, not only in civil rights struggles, but also in anti-war protests. Later, just before his assassination, King focused more on economic justice, a phrase used to address the rigid inequalities that intersect with race, gender, and ethnicity in U.S. society.

In that era, faith-based narratives resonated with the formative experiences of many Americans. Clergy carried moral authority beyond the ideologies, policy platforms, and opportunism of U.S. political parties. Does the faith-based narrative still move people to think and act in accordance with social justice? Many religious denominations in the U.S., with aging congregants, have lost members. Have congregations changed—or changed enough—alongside other changes in US society, presumably a society less prejudiced and more tolerant (though events after 2016 might call that into question)? Reform Judaism welcomed those changes, as have some but not all Christian denominations. This chapter grapples with these difficult issues: both the line between sacred and secular and the typical struggle that voluntary organizations face in recruiting members and maintaining their interests in single- or multiple-purpose organizations. Ultimately, I argue, IAF affiliates and faith-based congregations provide a sense of purpose to people living in the radically individualistic United States.[3]

In this chapter I address the strengths, weaknesses, and fissures of religious institutions in Texas and the US. I then move to the moral and ethical rationales for challenging public policies and policy change, for IAF social justice work uses such rationales, including moral narratives and language. I deepen the discussion from Chapter 1 contrasting charitable service and justice work, focusing especially on immigrants and refugees who enter Texas from Mexico and Central America. As an IAF unpaid leader for twenty years, my worry involves the decline of religious commitment in US society, especially among younger people, and what sort of purposeful associations might replace or augment spiritual institutions.

Faith denominations

The member institutions of Texas IAF affiliates reflect a great variety of religious denominations. However, they are not representative of Texans' religious affiliations, given the overrepresentation of Catholic churches and the underrepresentation of Baptists and its outlier numbers of twenty-six schisms.

In the first graphic, see the clarifying sizes and shapes for the contemporary IAF period, using one of my favorites—a Word Cloud—to show the predominant faith institutions in four of the large IAF affiliates that list paid members on their websites (other IAF affiliates do not list member institutions or post websites): Austin, Dallas, Houston, and San Antonio. All of them—except San Antonio—have approximately one-third non-faith institutions such as labor, neighborhood, health, and schools as member institutions. Two of them—Austin Interfaith and Dallas Area Interfaith—use the word faith in their name, but the other two do not: the oldest IAF affiliate in Texas, Communities Organized for Public Service (COPS) in San Antonio and The Metropolitan Organization (TMO) in Houston. As easily discerned, IAF member institutions are overwhelmingly Catholic, after which comes mainline Protestant denominations, themselves divided into many denominations.

Texas IAF religious denominational strength. Staudt formatting, courtesy Wordle.

Table 4.1: Texans' religious affiliations[4]

Baptist (26 associational types)	4,590,000	+
Catholic	4,673,000	+
Church of Christ (3 types)	394,065	−
Episcopal (3 types)	148,439	−
Lutheran (9 types)	272,066	−
Methodist (7 types)	1,314,445	+
Mormon (2 types)	300,591	+
Non-denominational (2 types)	1,546,542	no data
Pentecostal/Charismatic (17 types)	677,083	+
Presbyterian (13 types)	183,290	−

Source: 2010 figures, *Texas Almanac 2018–19*, Austin: Texas State Historical Association, 2018.

I condensed the voluminous data about Texans' large denominations to which over 100,000 people affiliate in Table 4.1 below in order to show the many, many faith denominations and the numbers of their parishioners in 2010. In comparison with IAF affiliations, we see some mismatch: an underrepresentation of Baptist and Pentecostal institutions in the IAF affiliates across the state, but an overrepresentation of Catholic churches, as noted above. One might wonder how those faith affiliations jibe with race and class. From my observations, Mexican Americans predominate in many of the Catholic congregations, and Whites in Texas-wide Baptist congregations. The source for this chart also shows extreme fissures in some denominations, such twenty-six types of Baptists and seventeen types of Pentecostals/Charismatics, also differentiated by racial/ethnic labels. The table's plus and minus signs on the right also show whether growth and decline has occurred in Texas since 2000.

Although religious ideologies often trace their founding to what anthropologists call an "origin story" or a person in a particular time and place, schisms have occurred over the centuries, and whole groups break away to form newly named groups based on what outsiders might view as minute differences or as twenty-first-century American political wedge issues. Depending on denomination, people celebrate founders such as John Wesley, Martin Luther, John Calvin, and others, but even after their once-unifying spiritual and storied force, divisions emerge within denominations. Perhaps one can infer an unmistaken resemblance—the internal conflict and exit—with political parties and factions therein over time. Surely, however, there is much common ground among faith traditions.

In Texas, Judaism is estimated at only 60,645 members, less than half of the 2000 figure, and most members are affiliated with the Reform tradition. I believe this is an undercount, based on synagogue membership counts from Jewish Federations in Texas cities.

Searching for purpose in the twenty-first century

Scholarly studies offer insights about why people join and associate in "voluntary organizations" (to use a perhaps antiquated term), which lack authority to compel affiliation: churches and community organizations.[5] Such studies provide insights to answer questions like: Why do people join and stay involved? How do organizations maintain people's interest? (The next chapter highlights IAF organizers' and leaders' stories answering some of these questions.) While the IAF stresses self-interest (what might be called economic or what scholars would call "material" interest), the category into which both churches and social justice organizing fits is "purposive": that is, organizations with a single purpose or multiple purposes, the latter subcategory of which has been called "ideological." Have some churches become a collection of "interest groups," wondered Reverend Kevin Young,[6] a reflective United Methodist Church pastor? (I appreciated his use of political science concepts, which he said came from his undergraduate major!)

Rev. Young's church in Lubbock affiliated with the West Texas Organizing Strategy (WTOS) when it first began two decades ago but underwent a lull for some time before Organizer Emilee Bounds (see her opening story in the next chapter) arrived to re-build and reorganize.

Rev. Kevin Young, Leader, West Texas Organizing Strategy. Photograph Kathleen Staudt.

She and WTOS leaders hope to connect the Lubbock east-west divide including celebrations on the east side like Juneteenth (June 19, 1865, when Texas finally ended slavery) and the Methodist congregations on both geographic sides of Lubbock. Most cities in Texas seem to have geographic divides based on ethnicity/race and economics.

Rev. Young's congregation is an aging one, though large numbers of Methodist youth were attending a summer conference in June during the days I visited Lubbock. A specific church staff member reaches out to university students at nearby Texas Tech University. Rev. Young, like Organizer Emilee Bounds, says churches need to change: "can we re-invent the whole? Move away from a more singular focus on the two Sunday morning services" (beyond their different liturgy and music)? "What are other organizations doing about things people care about? How can we be in ministry with them?" These are compelling questions that I hope many readers reflect on. Some religious institutions are adaptable and open to change, as we see here.

Rev. Young's church provides space and various services that fill needs in the surrounding area. He said, "This is homeless central; 70–100 families come here for food vouchers. We offer a Food Bank, space for Alcoholics Anonymous and PFLAG, a legal clinic, and connections with Texas Tech University" (which more recently reached out to broader communities with its LGBTQIA center).[7]

Rev. Young talked also about fissures in the Methodist church, especially around the 2016 election, and after that, consecration of Western

Region Bishop Karen Oliveto, who happens to be married in a same-sex relationship. A conservative think tank, the Institute for Religion and Democracy (IRD), highlights and disseminates information about fissures in various denominations. In IRD's blog, titled "juicy ecumenism," the IRD author connects the bishop's ordination to the consequent congregational loss of funding,[8] but perhaps this is more of a threat to smaller churches, unlike Rev. Young's larger church, which pays its membership fees to WTOS (typically 1–2 percent of net revenue). Despite the ways that distant forces deliberately foster divisions, Methodism emphasizes inclusiveness, love, and faith in action.[9]

Divisions like these, aggravated by conservative foundations, remind me of the ways that traditional Christianity long excluded women—and still excludes women in Catholic and other denominations—from serving as clergy. In my childhood, the conservative Wisconsin Lutheran Synod of my parents' church excluded women, not only from serving as clergy, but also from serving as ushers or even passing the collection plate. U.S. churches have come a long way toward greater inclusiveness, but still have a way to go.

Some churches change; others remain static. Yet common spiritual and moral grounds exist among them. Let us briefly look at the national scene on religious trends.

Consider these highlights from national studies dealing with religion and politics in the U.S., however rare those studies may be. Those studies that exist often focus on the rise of conservative Christian evangelical groups, some of which became active in the Tea Party movement that gained a foothold in the Republican Party as long as a decade ago.[10] In sociology scholar Arlie Hochschild's detailed interviews with people in southwestern Louisiana, where natural resources and people's health have been undermined by heavily polluting petroleum and gas industries, otherwise-kind people openly blame those "getting ahead of them in line for prosperity" for their ailments and static opportunities rather than dangerous industries and a state government that gives industry free reign to foul the environment. Business-friendly Texas policy closely resembles Louisiana's light regulation of pollution especially in east and coastal Texas. Beyond in-depth studies like Hochschild's, other survey research illuminates religious trends with large samples of trend data. The Pew Research Center, for instance, covers religious differences and trends in the US, including the decline in religious affiliation, as does *American Grace*, whose first co-author, Harvard political scientist Robert Putnam, is famous for his articles and book on democracy and social capital.

In *American Grace: How Religion Unites and Divides Us*, a 673-page tome, Putnam and David Campbell analyze quantitative national data and surveys on trends in religious affiliation[11] from the rising numbers of new Catholics (so-called "Latino Catholics" compared with "Anglo Catholics"), to the numerically declining mainstream Protestant faith traditions such as Episcopalians, Presbyterians, and multiple synods of Lutherans among others. However, Putnam and Campbell deserve some criticism: they do not unpack all of the traditions under the "evangelical" label, from fundamentalists to the Evangelical Lutheran Church in America (the latter, a progressive mainstream Protestant denomination). Moreover, Putnam and Campbell seem curiously unaware of the IAF and of faith-based social-justice organizing traditions since 1940 and thereafter, or of Judaism, neither addressed in their book.

In more recent large-scale surveys in the US with sample sizes above 35,000, the Pew Research Center reports two-thirds of respondents who loosely call themselves Christians and/or religious, though they do not attend or belong to a church. They also report on growing numbers of respondents who call themselves Agnostics and Atheists (under 10 percent) and "nones," meaning no religion, a growing identity among youth.[12] How do people identify with religion, if at all? If a faith is claimed, do they practice their faith in an institution, in solidarity with others, regularly, or only once or twice annually for holidays or milestone life experiences such as a wedding or funeral? Even the so-called "religious" commit themselves in highly variable ways.

The decline in religious affiliation occurs not only in some forms of Protestantism and perhaps Judaism, but also in Catholicism when considering youth. WTOS member institution Christ the Savior Cathedral in Lubbock sounds an alarm on its website, citing a survey showing that 80 percent of Catholics will stop practicing their faith by the age of twenty-three.[13] Many mainline Protestant churches have experienced a decline in members and a corresponding increase in the average age of members. With demographics like these, the future of those denominations predicts neither growth nor healthy maintenance. And if the IAF affiliates rely mainly on faith-based organizations, wherefore the IAF in future generations?

As noted above, in three of the strongest and most transparent IAF affiliates in Texas to list this information on their websites, about a third of the dues-paying members consist of non-religious organizations. However, many of the non-faith member institutions, such as health clinics or schools, do not have a similar stable base of participants as do faith-based congregations. Even in schools, once children graduate, parents also graduate from participation on those campuses. As noted in Chapter 1, to be addressed again in the concluding chapter, the IAF has spread to many other states in the US and several countries with similar declines in religious affiliation. Thus, the affiliation of nonprofits or schools may be a trend in the future.

It may be that US society is but a generation away from most respondents identifying themselves as "nones," that is persons with no religious affiliation. In Montreal, Quebec, Canada, where 95 percent of the population in the 1950s attended Mass, the figure has gone down to 5 percent, as church space is being "re-purposed" into "temples of cheese, fitness, and eroticism." Historian Gérard Bouchard "noted that playfully subverting the original function of churches was the result of a deep distrust of religious authority. Feminism is very strong here," he said, "and people remember what the church did to their mothers and grandmothers."[14]

The author of the article went on to interview new occupants of ex-church buildings about why people left: "The church opposed divorce, censored books and bullied women to reproduce, and in the 1960s, a generation rose in revolt, a period known as 'The Quiet Revolution.'" Mr. St-Georges, fifty-four, of the Théâtre Paradoxe, recalled being told that when his mother was ill and already had nine children, the local priest insisted that she have a tenth: him. She died shortly thereafter. "The clergy crossed the line into people's private lives, so people rebelled."[15]

In the US, the decline of religious adherents is not so marked (at least, not yet). From the Pew Research Center's large sample, again approximately 35,000 respondents, the figure averages 36 percent who attend weekly, down from 39 percent in 2007. However, once broken down into age, denominational, and other demographic groups, we see marked drops in youth participation and therefore, predictable future trends. Only 17 percent of the under-thirty crowd attend weekly. By denomination, Jehovah's Witnesses, Mormons, and Evangelical Protestants attend weekly at the highest percentages of 85 percent, 77 percent, and 58 percent respectively. (Pew bundles so-called "evangelicals" differently than other studies.) Those who earn $30,000 or less annually and those with a high school diploma or less education attend in the largest proportions.

In a long list of views about which the Pew Research Center asked questions, including those about same-sex marriage and scientific views about evolution ("God's design" was labeled the unscientific response), the weekly church-attending survey respondents showed less tolerant attitudes.[16] The national survey results offered a veritable goldmine of information, though not-Texas specific, including some predictable views: for example, that far more self-identified conservatives than self-identified liberals attend church weekly and that the majority of weekly attenders consider themselves anti-abortion. Other views were not so predictable: 40 percent of weekly attenders agree that "homosexuality should be tolerated". People's attitudes are changing; levels of education have gradually increased. U.S. Supreme Court decisions have legitimized long-sought human rights. Will more clergy and congregations match such changes?

Despite the stability of church institutions, albeit a declining stability, results like these do not bode well for future community organizing based on self-proclaimed faith member institutions unless church attenders trend more toward compatibility with civility, legal rights, and educational awareness that includes science. Yet every time people hear of scandals in the church hierarchy—bishops routinely transferring rather than removing child abusers, for example—people shake their heads in disgust. Their faith may be shaken, perhaps not so much as their distrust in the hierarchical institutions, which lack accountability for crimes. So, going back to the faith-based versus broad-based label for the IAF: Perhaps the label of purposeful, broad-based social justice organizations can accommodate those who desire impactful meaning in their lives through social justice work.

Whatever the label, faith- or broad-based organizing, people in the wider public respond to ethical and moral rationales for challenging public policies and proposing changes in those policies. To this topic we now turn.

Ethically driven policy debates

Social justice organizations like the IAF and enlightened churches offer space to frame reasoned arguments for policy reform in moral, philosophical, and ethical terms. "Moral" space holders, once conservative Catholics and fundamentalist Protestants, had in the past claimed themselves as the sole guardians of morality in U.S. politics and policy change. Some conservative Texan public officials have gone go so far as to say that "atheists" cannot and should not represent the wider public, criticizing local progressive officials, despite the non-establishment clause (of a religion) of the U.S. Constitution.[17] Do reasonable people with a moral core get caught between two extremes? As one commentator analyzed,

> For decades, the two wings of U.S. politics have dealt with spirituality in opposite ways. The God-wielding right proudly trots out organized religion to defend its views, and the secular, postmodern left keeps even non-religious spiritual experiences so quiet as to imply it's silly or shameful to have them. That dichotomy has resulted in rightwing dominance of the spiritual space in the U.S.

People who operate with a moral and ethical code should claim or re-claim that space, I believe. However, many of them mute those codes in public speech and spaces. Mary Beth Rogers, author of the earliest Texas IAF book, wrote in the Prologue about a conversation with a colleague on what drew her into politics. She said that she told this colleague, for her,

> "it was both the excitement of the game and the teachings of the Methodist church." Pause. Did I really say that? Should I continue? In my political circles, you always handled a discussion of religion and politics cautiously because in the Bible Belt, anyone who mixed religion and politics was either a scoundrel, a soft touch, or a fool.[18]

Perhaps people's search for democratic civic process and meaning could couple with a spiritual place, at least in moderate or progressive denominations rather than with right-wing evangelicals or conservatives. Postmodernist anxieties can be found mainly among the highly educated and/or occupants of higher education work, as Chapter 8 addresses, on one of many reasons why the IAF and higher education institutions do not mesh well.

In broad-based and nonprofit organizations that seek policy change, or in justice and advocacy organizations, leaders must carefully deliberate the rationales for why change is sought. Let us consider rationales driven by values or ethical claims.

Among many rationales used to critique or change policies, some resonate with faith-based narratives. Deborah Stone in *Policy Paradox: The Art of Political Decision-Making*[19] focuses on effectiveness, equity, freedom, and security, several of which constitute value-laden and complex philosophical principles. In her discussion, equity alone contains eight different practical applications, and security, four applications. To these we could add ethical, moral, and faith-based principles that emerge from new or renewed interpretations of social justice for people within and beyond national borders coupled with the imperatives to act in everyday life ("faith in action" as this is often called). Policy analysts often use the effectiveness criterion, coupled with cost/benefit calculations. Rationales need not be limited to one principle.

Moral narratives offer ways to cut across and through the extreme party polarization of contemporary U.S. and Texas politics. In mid-2018, many people reacted emotionally and intellectually to the separation and detention of children from their families seeking asylum from violent and impoverished countries. Who was not touched by the pictures? By the sounds of children crying for their parents? By a one-year old, bottle in hand, sitting before a judge in an immigration court? Surely a moral dimension should evoke some generalized response. For specific Biblical verses and stories, interpretations vary, depending on those who interpret with fundamental terms and those with a broader understanding that takes into account metaphor, science, historical memory, and Biblical pronouncements. We saw that play out in mid-2018 about this very issue of refugee children separated from parents in detention facilities.

Witness also the use of and reaction to former Attorney General Jeff Sessions's reference to Romans 13 in June 2018 on obedience to the law for order, a verse used in antebellum and Apartheid regimes of the past in the U.S., South Africa, and elsewhere. Yet just a few verses later in Romans 13, one reads, "whatever other commandment there may be, are summed up in this one command: Love your neighbor as yourself. Love does no harm to a neighbor. Therefore love is the fulfillment of the law." One part of Romans offers rhetorical leverage for a conservative racist agenda, while the other part offers a humanist and inclusive agenda, especially when preachers interpret "neighbor" to mean people from various ethnic groups, other sides of borders, and/or halfway around the world. Cynical critics might point to the ways proponents and opponents selectively cherry-pick varying passages to serve their agendas, including even the American Revolutionaries versus the British Loyalists at the birth of the nation.[20] Back then, Sessions might have been aligned with British loyalists! Given these seemingly sacred pronouncements, one can understand the discomfort that secular people experience when politicians link the sacred to public policy.

In public policy terms, the language of faith resonates with progressive social justice issues that focus on reducing inequalities and exploitation, welcoming strangers (immigrants), and compensating labor fairly. That faith-based language can move and inspire people, as it moves me in my own Presbyterian faith, albeit raised Lutheran. While this chapter does not seek to impose labels upon people with different perceptions of what is meaningful to them, the discussion, I hope, does provide an airing of over-lapping commitments and still-remaining secular-sacred tensions in this era of declining spiritual faith, but growing economic inequality in the U.S.

Consider a mainline Protestant Prayer of Confession, quoted below, with a strong emphasis on inequality and action rather than on compla-cency, from the biennial General Assembly of the Presbyterian Church of the USA in 2018 and spoken at the Sunday service of University Presby-terian Church in El Paso on June 24, 2018. This moving narrative struck me as a call to justice. It inspired me to know that this moral statement on inequity came from a large national assembly attended and supported by people of faith.

Box 4.1 Prayer of Confession, Presbyterian Church of the USA, 2018 General Assembly

"Leader: Children of God, shaped by both faith and history, let us confess our sin so that we stand ready to follow God's call.

People: God of promise, forgive your people when your dreams of shalom for all are co-opted by yearnings for earthly kingdoms.

Leader: When your call to be a blessing to all peoples is corrupted by grasping after wealth that privileges some and disadvantages others.

People: Give us the courage to name the sins which continue to distort our lives, the attitudes that some are better than others, the complicity in systems that are unjust and the complacency with institutions that diminish the common good.

Leader: As we cross into the future you set before us, re-form us.

People: Make us bold to live into your vision of a community that welcomes all as kin."

As far back as the 1970s, Texas IAF founder Ernesto Cortés, Jr. used Biblical figures and stories in heavily Catholic west San Antonio and in meetings with clergy in other cities as more Texas IAF affiliates formed. He called Moses and Jesus among the best "organizers." That label for a sacred-secular connection, which might seem almost sacrilegious to some, evokes metaphors applicable to everyday lives. In statewide IAF seminars, participant-leaders read and present readings in small groups from Greek myths, political-historical texts, Hannah Arendt, and Old and New Testament Biblical stories to pose questions, even performing role plays to foment wider discussions.

Consider the example from the Old Testament story of Jethro and the complaining Moses: from the story used at an IAF training session, participants acquire the obvious take-away that one individual cannot solve all the problems, cannot do it all. That is, IAF needs the power of multiple leaders and multiple institutions.

In another New Testament story used by Houston-based statewide senior organizer Elizabeth Valdez, participants prepare a letter like one of Paul's letters to the Corinthians: what and to whom would you write about your community? (I draw on her practice in the final appendix to this book: A Letter to Texans.) Note that all the chapters in First Corinthians offer comprehensive coverage of issues that we may or may not agree with, but stress using one's gifts for public service, far more than its Chapter 13 on "faith, hope, and love" (the last being most important), so beautifully read at weddings (for couples who might drop out of church soon after the ceremony and honeymoon).

IAF meetings generally start and end with an inclusive prayer for its secular, non-denominational public work for social justice. Chroniclers of early foundational IAF work, such as the earlier cited Mary Beth Rogers and Mark Warren, devote whole chapters to the theology of organizing. Yet the largest and strongest three of the four Texas IAF affiliates, as noted above, also draw on secular nonprofit organizations for approximately a third of paid member institutions which, like the Workers' Defense Project, offer a stronger base of people on wages and work issues. The significance of this trend is key: these clinics, schools, and other nonprofits broaden the base of IAF work, but typically do not offer a stable unpaid leadership pool, as do congregations. The development and sustenance of unpaid leaders may be more likely in congregations with long-term members. Yet outside of Texas, in states with growing IAF strength, secular-sacred issues emerged which are likely to be encountered elsewhere. In a new IAF affiliate located in a large swath of a mountain state, participants—half of whom came from faith-based institutions, and half from other institutions—debated whether to begin the meeting with a prayer in 2018.[21] Why or why not? A moment of prayer produces a quiet pause for reflection, maybe for inspiration. After discussion, participants agreed to open in prayer. So perhaps community organizing via the IAF can be called faith-based or broad-based, depending on those who participate and their openness to others. However, the Biblical references may evoke some pushback, particularly among younger people like the "nones," as I address later in this chapter.

For the spiritually inclined, that is for those who seek meaningful lives that touch beyond family and household, commitment to social justice offers a comprehensive ideology and set of interconnected goals that serve as motivations and incentives to join. Note that this is not an explicit self-interested, or material incentive, as emphasized in IAF practices. Clergy members committed to IAF affiliation offer a way to define larger life meanings through community building. Recall Rabbi Freedman's comments about congregational membership in Austin Interfaith giving congregants an opportunity for meaningful community involvement, for learning, and for relationships with those from other walks of life.

Importantly, social justice work might appeal to only a minority of members in a church. In my own Presbyterian church, an IAF member institution, only a half-dozen people can be called core or secondary leaders, but as many as twenty evince tertiary leadership by attending Accountability Sessions unless the session is held at the church, which could draw as many as a hundred, more than half the Sunday service attendance. In various congregations, some congregants resonate with the choir and music; others, with youth education; still others, weekly service only. While churches do not take particular stands on issues, their social justice ministries sometimes fall on deaf ears, the ears of a few, or face resistance in a congregation. In an Austin interview, I appreciated a Lutheran pastor's frank comments.

Austin Interfaith Leader Pastor Tim Anderson, once monolingual as he grew up in segregated Chicago, served in Peru and acquired an internationalist sense, becoming fluently bilingual. He hosts a Spanish-language service with his congregation, a member institution of Austin Interfaith, in which not all congregants participate in social justice work. What is the "rub" he faces, as he calls it? "Congregational participation. The ELCA (Evangelical Lutheran Church of America), 95 percent White, is culture-bound." Regarding the IAF, middle-class members ask him: "is this what church is about?"[22] Pastor Anderson categorized different types of congregants. Some are suspicious. Others, especially the Spanish-language congregants, "get it" or respond "I'm here; I'm ready," while still others "adopt the American individualist mindset." Yet others are busy, he said: IAF work is extensive and labor-intensive; it takes time and commitment that people do not always have. As for Pastor Anderson, "I remain involved. Austin Interfaith leaders provide 'ground truth.' You get the actual perspectives from people in different neighborhoods. The system hasn't worked well for everyone." Pastor Anderson, like many clergy, understands the largest systemic constraints that people face in the state and country. To his congregation, he offers the option to learn and work in solidarity with others around the purpose of social justice. But I sensed, as I do in my congregation, that he must respond to the diverse people in church. This may extend as far as avoiding a direct "ask" for people to participate in the IAF, as happens in some Catholic congregations where an invitation to participate in social justice organizing from the priest or a sister (nun) would be welcome. Recall references to this in Chapter 3 and in subsequent parts of this and other chapters.

Pastor Anderson's insights could probably apply to many Protestant denominational members affiliated with the IAF, as in my church. There, our outreach time, talent, and resources connect with over forty nonprofits, only one of which is Border Interfaith, on both sides of the border. Congregants serve as leaders, not IAF style, but on nonprofit boards of directors, among other tasks. The social justice work makes some people anxious, except for calls to engage in informed voting. Denomination and institutional processes matter, as I discuss in governance issues below.

Governance in churches

Church governance matters as much as IAF governance in community organizing efforts, alluded to in Chapters 1 and 5. I was struck when listening to interviews with IAF leaders and their responses to my question about "their story" including how they got involved in the IAF affiliate. Among Catholics, many made positive reference to an invitation: "Father asked me" or "he suggested I get involved." In many Protestant denominations, such conversation might be relatively rare. Indeed, in house meetings, congregants in my church hesitate to reveal private matters to others in small-group sessions. The sense of individualism is strong even as people identify with their faith community.

I sometimes find myself the lone Protestant, a Presbyterian, among all Catholics in EPISO planning meetings. The differences in church organizational culture amaze me. The Presbyterian Church of the USA practices internal democracy in a relatively non-hierarchical setting. At my church and other congregations in the regional, geographically based Synod of Tres Rios in southwest Texas, parishioners elect a twelve-member, three-year termed body of "Elders" (whatever their age, one from my church was seventeen), who serve on what is called the Session. The pastor reports to the Elders who represent the policy-making, deliberative body. In other words, the Session becomes like a Board of Directors in a nonprofit organization, but as people joke with Elders like myself, "once an Elder, always an Elder" for its lifelong commitment. The Session spawns numerous committees, co-chaired by Elders who meet monthly and recruit volunteers to assist with fellowship, liturgy, and other responsibilities. In good democratic practice, committee members discuss matters thoroughly, so thoroughly, that when a motion and second is made, it often passes by consensus or perhaps with one or two voting no or abstaining.

As is obvious, Presbyterian governance involves time-consuming, laborious commitments. The nomination process for identifying new Elders, then putting candidates up for election by the congregation, is also laborious but democratic. A discernment process also exists for hiring new pastors; call committee members interview the candidates and propose their choice to the congregation whose members then vote. This is very different from the Catholic Church or even the IAF: the Catholic Bishop—himself appointed in the hierarchy—appoints and rotates priests, with ratification from the Vatican, and in the IAF, the organizer is assigned from above (see the next chapter).

Though on-the-ground organizing has evolved from the late Saul Alinsky's principles, as noted in Chapter 1, he was a decided secularist with an instrumental vision about strategies to build large bases through institutional coalitions. Alinsky even supported individual rights to birth control and abortion, but rarely made that public in early days with the mostly Catholic Chicago Back of the Yards neighborhood where he said large families aggravated their economic plight: "that instant I would have been stamped as an enemy of the church and all communication would have ceased."[23] The Catholic hierarchy clings to principles that may not be believed or practiced. Kentucky Diocese-based Bishop John Stowe, once an EPISO leader, recently wrote a strongly worded Op Ed "questioning the logic of supporting a president who, while against abortion, clashes with church teaching on a number of other issues. We cannot uncritically ally ourselves with someone with whom we share the policy goal of ending abortion."[24] Stowe was and continues to be a courageous man who seeks social justice.

My knowledge of internal decision-making in a Catholic parish is one of an outsider who interacts with many priests, nuns, lay leaders, occasionally the bishop in the El Paso Diocese, and IAF leaders from Catholic institutions, including in the borderlands nonprofit world, a place where people take the Biblical calls to "welcome the stranger" seriously. I meet people who take a year, two years, even a lifetime to offer service to immigrants, such as what happens at El Paso's faith-based Annunciation House.

The Catholic Church consists of a hierarchy of men, centered on priests in parishes; they report to bishops, who report to archbishops, cardinals, and ultimately, the pope. The current Pope Francis, progressive and tolerant, is the first pope from the Global South (Argentina). The Vatican itself uses an opaque process to select the popes and their different ideological and religious leanings within the faith.

Typically, Catholic parishes have various "ministries" in which people are involved, ranging from social justice to "life," "peace," and a curious one I found in a South Texas IAF member institution, "courage" to abstain from attraction to the same sex. The current bishop in El Paso is committed to immigrants and humane immigration reform and enforcement. He also supports social justice work and communicates this support to the territorially organized vicariates in the region. At a parish, if the priest is committed to social justice and opens the door to IAF dialogue, then the IAF organizer can work with him to build a core team of leaders who act on their self-interests, IAF style, and put their faith in action. If the priest views social justice work as irrelevant, too complex or political (in its negative interpretation), then IAF affiliation is impossible. So we see diverse interpretations of doctrine.

Catholic dioceses promote voting with "faithful citizenship." Before the 2016 elections, Catholic media and bishops' quotations emphasized the priority of life—usually pre-birth life—in remarks about making choices about whom to vote for. Despite a probable consensus among bishops in the hierarchy, save Bishop Stowe and perhaps others, Catholics disagree among themselves and act similarly in their private lives about the 1973 *Roe v. Wade* decision from other religiously affiliated women, as studies show.[25] The church puts the brakes on feminist and/or reproductive justice work in IAF affiliates, as do the Catholic Campaign for

Human Development grant funds. In impoverished communities, the IAF affiliate may depend on this money for its budget and dues. However, some volunteer leaders from Catholic churches might also object to any focus on reproductive health, if they accept admonitions from the religious hierarchy.

As readers no doubt conclude about this disciplined community organization and its achievements in Texas, the IAF is not a transformative "radical" organization, in the sense of getting to the roots of problems. Even IAF's reformist efforts are not as comprehensive as progressive people might seek in women's and gender equality issues for example.

Radical to reformist

With policy change, the opportunity exists to address problems systematically to embrace large numbers of people. The word "radical" was once tinged with connotations of revolutionary upheaval that sought to transform society by getting to the roots of problems.

"Radical" can refer to both means, such as strategies and tactics, and/or ends, such as goals and achievements. IAF can hardly be called radical in its end goals, which could range from challenges to unregulated capitalism, the neoliberal global economy, pay-to-play politicians and appointees. The pay-to-play system was aggravated in the 2010 *Citizens United* Supreme Court decision and other seemingly unsurmountable systems that critics emphasize or for which many younger people long solutions. Yet radical IAF tactics from decades ago pushed IAF power against established power, such as those cited in Chapters 1 by Alinsky and in Chapter 2 by Cortés with his COPS sit-ins disrupting exploitative businesses in order to provoke negotiation and resolution toward people's self-interests.

Compared to those early tactics, the IAF has moved from a somewhat confrontational direction to relational work with officials, even avoiding confrontation with developers' agendas that promote public-risk, private-gain bond issues. Perhaps this signals a mature stage of IAF organizing and/or their "seat at the table" (see Chapter 2). The IAF still uses prominent tactics such as direct questions in Accountability Sessions with an expectation of direct responses, which some candidates try to avoid. Clergy and volunteer leaders may be uncomfortable with the perception of IAF's confrontational reputation, however reformist it may be in the twenty-first century, given the mix of congregants discussed earlier in this chapter. Growth in IAF affiliate member institutions seems to top off at forty, even in the strong IAF affiliates. Why? Wariness, time investments, and dues contribute to leveling off. Words like "radical" or even "power" from the titles of Alinsky's or Chambers's books may be off-putting to cautious people. Once involved in IAF processes, however, cautious clergy or volunteer leaders would realize that many IAF practices exude civility, centrism, and reformism. Indeed, once involved, they would realize that volunteer leaders have the primary voice in local affiliates' strategies and goals.

The radical search for causal roots consumes much time, talent, and paper. Many academics write reams about such topics. More and more young people view unregulated capitalism as the source of many problems, a more "radical" perspective and hardly amenable to pragmatic politics at the local and state levels. Instead, the IAF identifies causes and their solutions with doable strategies and goals that affect large numbers of people; it cannot solve all societal problems. Ironically, while Alinsky and Chambers use the word "radicals" in the titles of their books, radical-others may view community organizations as offering little more than practical band aids, albeit better than service, that perpetuate the larger roots behind contemporary capitalism or neoliberal global economies. Yet the counter to that critique is compelling.

Surely critics of unregulated capitalism would find some common ground with the IAF in empowering new and larger numbers of leaders who begin fixing serious policy-related problems in people's everyday lives, step by step, win after win. People's empowerment is the essence of IAF work with training new and diverse leaders—a long-term historical tradition in American politics ranging from suffrage movements to civil rights struggles and anti-war movements. Everyone, nevertheless, has limited time and priorities that fit with their worldviews. To identify common ground is not necessarily to commit to participation in the IAF.

As the IAF states for its organizational mission in the latest IRS 990 tax form, which all tax-exempt nonprofit organizations that generate $50,000 or more in revenue must complete, the IAF is committed to "identifying, recruiting, training, and developing leaders ... The IAF is indeed a radical organization in this specific issue. It has a radical belief in the potential of the vast majority of people to grow and develop as leaders, to be full members of the body politic, to speak and act with others in their own belief. And IAF does use radical tactics: one-on-one individual meetings whose purpose is to initiate a public relationship and to re-knot the frayed social fabric."[26]

This is a laudable, noble mission statement, but it is quite compatible with mainstream American-style democratic pluralist politics, an underlying theme of many government textbooks. Small-group and face-to-face meetings are used in a variety of leadership settings and trainings, not only in the IAF, but also in work, nonprofit boards, and educational settings. They ought to be used in lots more organizational settings for effective bonding and communication and in grassroots politics. In subsequent chapters, we see stories of how people trained in the IAF model apply those skills in other settings in collaborative and committee work to pursue pragmatic reforms.

Pragmatic reforms for Justice v. Service and Charity

The justice-service distinction sets the IAF emphasis on justice apart from nonprofit advocacy and service work. IAF aims at systemic change building on its power base of volunteer leaders and prospective leaders. That work may overlap with civic academies about political processes and doable reforms that inform people, called variously Public Academies, Civic Academies, or Parent Academies. In places with immigrant communities, such as in many Texas locations, as part of its empowerment work, IAF leaders offer "Know your Rights" presentations. Vulnerable people are often more willing to attend such events in the safe and sacred places of religious congregations. Affordable and accessible heath care has also been a priority.

El Paso's IAF affiliates worked with officials on expanding health care access. Given the large underinsured population and the state's refusal to expand Medicaid after the complicated 2010 Affordable Care Act (ACA), EPISO and Border Interfaith collaborated with the University Medical Center to offer workshops on ACA sign-up in both Spanish and English. At an El Paso County Commissioners' Court meeting, El Paso's IAF organizations worked all day to build a majority, needing one more vote, with stories and testimonies supporting the construction of health clinics in the underserved, outlying areas of the county. They only needed to move one commissioner to change his mind and he ultimately voted to support the clinics in a 3-2 vote. In partisan county elections, only one commissioner was a Republican, but Democrats disagreed on measures with fiscal consequences. Yes, Medicare for All might be optimal, but in IAF practice, one starts with what is and where people are, then pushes forward. Besides, universal Medicare cannot be achieved from local and state levels without massive constituency support from all over the country.

In policy outcomes, though, IAF affiliates always lean toward justice, like the above policy to expand health care with the voices of people who articulate their interests. In another example, Border Interfaith worked with the city manager to improve flood control with proper inspection systems, rather than merely city clean up thereafter, and to compensate residents fairly. After a major 2006 flood that destroyed fifty homes in a poorly regulated area, the city sought to compensate residents on their value of their homes after destruction—i.e., nearly value-less, except for the land—rather than on their appraised values before the flood, which residents would need to move into comparable housing. A Texas Rio Grande Legal Aid lawsuit upped the ante. Who could fault a community organization for this work? "The devil is in the details," as a public administration axiom goes. IAF's practical politics pay attention to these details as well. IAF is not about direct service or charity, even though many church-goers feel more comfortable performing such tasks.

IAF training offers workshops on the contrasts between "Service and Justice." I have attended various workshops over the years in which clergy present their different faith-based perspectives on service and justice. The Biblical Old Testament Book of Amos is famous for its reference to letting "justice flow down like water." Not coincidentally, the title of Mark Warren's definitive 2001 book about the Texas IAF is *Dry Bones Rattling: Community Building to Revitalize American Democracy*. This reference, too, comes from the Old Testament Book of Ezekiel on the awakening and activating of a people. In Hebrew, the translation of "rattling" can mean "spirit" or "wind."

Besides periodic Biblical references to justice, many Biblical and faith traditions also put value on service: feeding and clothing the poor. Both service and justice have value, but IAF affiliates lean toward justice-oriented systemic change so that people, for example with access to affordable health care who earn decent wages, do not need to depend on service and charity. The emphasis on justice work is another example of the multi-faceted IAF's Iron Rule of Self-Sufficiency which is taken up in various chapters herein.

With declining religious affiliation and hyper-individualism in states that practice limited government, one wonders where and in which mediating institutions people will be moved to do service OR social justice work. People's lives are no longer nested in mediating institutions that encourage face-to-face relationships of trust, what many sociologists and political scientists call "social capital," from civic organizations to sports clubs and the traditional parent-teacher associations/organizations in schools.[27] The previously cited Harvard political scientist Robert Putnam wrote extensively about the decline in relationships of trust and voluntary organizations which the IAF calls mediating institutions in its workshops on that topic, linked in part to the lack of time, including the rise of women's paid work outside the home. Instead of PTAs, bowling leagues, and sports clubs, we see people working and/or interacting with technology—phones and laptops, with buds in their ears—even in public places like coffee shops where they could talk face to face. While virtual communities exist on Facebook, Instagram, and Twitter, users offer support with a click and shed support or affiliation with a click, just as they affirm, affiliate, or criticize with an emoji. Relational power and trust rarely get built through superficial social media means.

Long-term social justice action and policy change require deeper connections, trust, responsibility, patience, time, and persistence—social capital—to get things done in the public sphere. Besides, multiple minds and eyes working together can produce a blossoming set of strategies, ideas, and reasonable rationales to frame social justice work. It takes time to build relationships to bring people to the table to forge workable solutions. Former organizer, now core EPISO leader, Alicia Franco frequently mentions in meetings the decade or more that it took to get multiple water authorities, the Texas Water Development Board, and both local city and county officials to work with leaders in *colonias* to craft cooperation and locate money for waste and wastewater treatment in our fragmented federal system of government. The imprimatur of clergy and of faith-based member institutions provides the credibility to draw people from different agencies and levels of government to a decision-making table. Yet faith-based connection may appeal more to the middle-aged and older communities.

What is it about religious affiliation that does not resonate with youth or prompt sustained commitment among adults? In an interview with political science professor Dr. Irasema Coronado, who calls herself a "cultural Catholic" and no longer attends church, her answers ranged from the exclusion of women in clerical leadership and the shocking abuse scandals to the continuous reiteration of "sin" for those who violated traditional precepts relating to sexuality, marriage and divorce, and remarriage.[28] Moreover, she said that when people seek to root milestone events like baptism, marriage, and funerals in the church, perhaps with a progressive priest whose church services they attend, they could run obstacles from the rigid vicariate geographic organization of the church.

Protestant churches do not organize on territorial bases, but experience fissures (schisms) in the decades-old cultural wars in U.S. politics. In this research, I learned about the all-too-many differences among Protestant faiths, even where the word "united" (or I supposed if absent, non-united?) is positioned in front of their denominational names. The only time the biennial General Assembly of the Presbyterian Church of the USA gets national press coverage is when it passes resolutions that welcome the ordination of LGBTQ pastors or church ceremonies of same-sex marriage partners. And a few people leave the church, unwilling to participate in inclusiveness, even though the U.S. Supreme Court legalized same-sex marriage in June 2015. In Lubbock I heard about Protestant church reactions in the same denomination after that court decision: one church mourned the decision and the other celebrated the decision. Young people exhibit more tolerance on civil and marriage rights, given the passage of laws and court decisions of recent years.

When youth—many of whom stop out, drop out, or never entered a church—consider leadership in an IAF organization, the process seems complicated. They feel they must join a church and then become part of its IAF core action team, unless they are part of a nonprofit organization or school that affiliates with the IAF. Some think all the discipline and rules emerge from another era: "antiquated" said a social justice activist unlikely to join an IAF affiliate.[29] And young parents with children may lack the time to participate in IAF affiliates and their many meetings.

Over the years in my upper-division political science classes, I have assigned books and readings from IAF writers and scholars such as Dennis Shirley and Mary Beth Rogers. Whether in small-group task forces or in larger class discussions, I remember students' decided discomfort around discussing political organizing strategies connected with faith institutions and Biblical stories, such as are covered in Rogers's *Cold Anger*. In graduate seminars, busy students—often both working and studying— rarely took the opportunity to attend big events like Accountability Sessions. In the doctoral seminars, educational administrator-students often expressed pre-conceived biases against organizations like EPISO, worried about interference with school management (see Chapters 6 and 7, including the content that people signed in the EPISO-led Alliance School Compact). Few professors even bring this sort of material into course design (see Chapter 8), but this section of my chapter points to the challenge of recruiting the next generation of IAF organizers and leaders, without motivations that might come with stipends or special youth-focused leadership academies and/or faith and affiliation. The Texas AFL-CIO organizes youth leadership activities, and statewide organizations like the Texas Freedom Network (TFN) try to build chapters on university campuses, with stipends to student facilitators and training for them. LULAC sponsors youth chapters on campuses; I shared the advising function as a faculty member with a community advisor for one year. However, leaders and organizational power bases in universities, like other nonprofits and public schools, can disappear after graduation unless full attention is devoted to leadership succession.

Despite my worries about the next generation of social justice leaders, IAF work to develop leaders is noble and central to its empowerment mission. Few advocacy-oriented nonprofits devote their mission to leadership development, that is, to identify and train people to acquire and use their own voices in public settings. Instead, professionals advocate on their clients' behalf, perhaps without real experience in the vulnerabilities people face. Here I recall the good work of battered women's shelter staff who eagerly welcome and celebrate volunteers for service work, with "clients" appreciating help, rather than justice work in policy reform amid the messy political process. In contrast, with the IAF, I have seen voices from the formerly voiceless become loud and clear in relational meetings with officials, in storytelling at Accountability Sessions, and in co-moderating big events, among other actions.

As noted several times in the chapter, faith-based institutions draw far more on aging congregants than on youth. Youth may be uncomfortable with IAF meetings starting and ending with ecumenical prayer. At a 2018 IAF Leadership Academy, with twelve under-thirty graduate students (of a total eighty-five participants), I facilitated a small group session at the end of Day 2, discussing how to build what the IAF calls a "core leader team." I know they acquired new skills and tools about community organizing from engaging sessions by senior organizer Sr. Maribeth Larkin on the "Cycle of Organizing" and "Power" and from Joe Rubio about "Pressures on our Families." The students came from multiple academic disciplines, soon to graduate and perhaps leave El Paso for upward mobility in places with better wages. Alas, movement toward the next step fell flat, as we see below.

Knowing the importance of "cold anger" (recall Chapter 1), all the students expressed passion and outrage about immigration injustices and Texas laws that increasingly constrict a woman's legal right to control her body. One student, active in the Democratic Socialist Alliance and

EPISO/Border Interfaith Leader Training Planning Team, 2018, with Adriana García, Organizer (front, second from left), Leader/Treasurer Eddie Chew, and Sr. Maribeth Larkin, Supervisor Senior Organizer (back, left). Photograph Kathleen Staudt.

Continuing the Revolution, worked to bring Democrats into the Bernie Sanders camp. Two participants worked on reproductive justice, with a young man saying, "I raise money for the West Fund." In the local IAF, always nonpartisan, reproductive matters have never emerged. Youth may not realize that denominations vary their teachings on the still-polarizing issue of legal abortion, with Catholics for Choice groups co-existing, ironically, with some—no doubt, only a few priests and none that I know—who think communion ought to be denied for these "sins." As for immigration, there are limitations to this work at the local level besides "Know Your Rights" presentations, although we saw in Chapter 3 what Dallas Area Interfaith did with picture IDs from Catholic parishes. When I met one of those "trained" students four months later, we discussed additional thoughts about the IAF Leadership Academy. He blurted out that most of the participants were "too old" and asked "why the IAF doesn't offer specific training for young people?" Perhaps his response was impulsive and immature, but it was also the kind of frank reaction that few people say aloud. I listen to varied reactions, not only because of my training as a researcher, but also as an IAF leader. This recent experience, plus the various class discussions about IAF readings over my teaching years, lead me to wonder from where the next generation of IAF organizers and leaders will come. At the same time, I recall from Chapter 3 the beauty of cross-age leadership and collaboration in Dallas Area Interfaith. While a comparative perspective is useful, context-specific aspects of each IAF city must be taken into account, such as the size of Dallas and the likelihood that young people will remain there for the more plentiful jobs than in El Paso.

Many younger people know little about religious denominations. The two issues around which most cohere is immigration (DACA youth, refugees) and women's bodily integrity, including freedom from violence. In El Paso, the Border Network for Human Rights, with its foundation funding, and the faith-based Hope Border Institute with its Catholic Campaign for Human Development funding, address immigration issues with speed, clarity, and protests.

Immigration reform and other borderland issues

The plight, insecurity, and vulnerability of immigrants escaping violence and poverty have galvanized many to "welcome the stranger," especially in the borderlands. Faith-based social justice leaders remind others about Biblical passages, referring to respecting and serving "the poor among us," offering "debt relief and forgiveness," plus fairness and other principled moral imperatives. Reinforcing this issue-based language and its rationales, the Catholic Church issued multiple bishops' statements on humane immigration policies, as have various mainstream Protestant denominations and Judaism[30]

IAF leaders do not shrink from using phrases with evocative adjectives that economists abhor, such as "decent" wages. Rather than avoiding the word "family," which in previous decades, conservatives and Tea Party advocates have claimed and sought to own, IAF leaders embrace the word and develop their "family agenda" and criticize "family-separating immigration policies." Youth may marry late, if at all. While the word "family" does not always resonate with younger people, I have met a few young leaders who are devoted to their parents and help translate or speak for parents at Border Interfaith and EPISO steering committee and Accountability Sessions. Strong motivations exist for residents in *colonias* without clean water or proper septic tanks to participate in member neighborhood organizations or congregations based on their family's self-interest. This chapter emphasizes purposeful, faith-based, and ideological incentives, but we see scattered examples of self-interest incentives throughout this book—the latter of which IAF principles stress.

Let us explore further the example of migrants crossing the border and the policy to separate parents from their children. Although the routine denial of asylum seekers was a crisis brewing over the years,[31] however less visible, photographs and tapes of crying children captured national attention, which crescendoed during summer, 2018. Thanks to faith-based institutions, but especially the Catholic Church with its many shelters (often with the name Casa del Migrante) along migration routes through Mexico, fewer people died on the journey than would have been likely without those shelters. Decades ago in El Paso, nonprofit organizations like Annunciation House, the Diocesan Migrant and Refugee Center, and Las Americas Immigrant Advocacy Center have provided legal assistance and shelter on their journeys. Bishops spoke with courage in their own locales and in Congress about the plight of migrants fleeing violence and poverty and decrying inhuman family-separation policies. However, in the 2016 presidential elections, bishops encouraged parishioners to vote for "faithful citizenship," which seemed to prioritize life before birth rather than whole lives after birth. Although dissent existed in Catholic media as noted earlier, the words of bishops carry weight with people pondering their decision to choose the candidate who promised to appoint judges against *Roe v Wade*.[32] By 2018, migrants' life issues came out loud and clear, as Bishop Stowe's earlier cited written remarks in early 2019 emphasized.

In a nondenominational church, Paseo, which hosted a bilingual service near downtown El Paso on June 24, 2018, titled "United in Lament and Prayer for our Migrant Neighbors," liturgists expressed sentiments against family separation, drawing on global perspectives about the root causes of migration. Let me quote some of the liturgy; the liturgist spoke and congregants recited bolded words in unison.

The message was strong; the focus was direct. Liturgy emphasized the radical roots of the global problem. But there was no organized call for action except flyers on where to bring food and clothing donations, a worthy service but not justice-oriented, as stressed in the IAF. Attendees sat next to their friends, without any structure for one-on-one meetings that might develop new relationships and subsequent house meetings. Only fifty people attended the church, which was not

---

Box 4.2 Liturgy on faith and migrant abuse

"Oh God, we lament the trauma that is happening to asylum seekers at the U.S. Border. **Lord have mercy.** *We pray for an end to separation of families, the desperation of parents and children, and the degradation of their dignity.* **Lord have mercy.** *We lament the violence and corruption that is forcing these immigrants to leave their home countries.* **Lord have mercy.** *We pray for an end to corrupt government, violent power structures, and poor living conditions in Central America.* **Lord have mercy.** *We lament the policy decisions enacted by our own US leadership that have led to the traumatizing of children and infants.* **Lord have mercy.** *We pray for humane and just legislation to be passed by congress immediately.* **Lord have mercy."**

---

affiliated with the IAF, but even if it were affiliated, the IAF does not address global neoliberal causes that push migrants to flee their countries, for the IAF does not organize around a national, much less global agenda. Non-Paseo congregants never met again, so the opportunities to develop relationships of trust disappeared into thin air. Perhaps the event soothed the pain of its participants more than afflicted or challenged those who perpetrate policies that foster violence and dangerous migration journeys. So here we see radical rhetoric, but no post-gathering goals and strategies.

Concluding reflections

In this chapter, we have examined the language of faith and spirituality in an extremely individualistic society where denominations divide over issues, from centuries-old to culture-war topics of today. The moral and ethical core of these religious voluntary associations evokes commonalities, especially associated with acquiring a sense of purpose and meaning to lives with faith and social justice affiliations. However, some denominations change little along with a changing society. As such, church buildings may shrink like what has happened in Montreal—re-purposed or empty spaces.

The challenges that faith-based organizations will face in the future involve declining religious affiliation, especially among youth. We see also that the resistance to acknowledging women and gender justice is a common thread tying together the discomfort young people share about churches, particularly hierarchical, male-dominated, and non-accountable denominations with histories of abuse. No doubt immigration issues evoke some discomfort in more conservative locales away from the border or where White people do not interact with people from the Global South or even people of color in the U.S.

In Texas and the borderlands, we saw in this chapter that people are motivated to participate via their membership in institutions affiliated with the IAF, around issues of both self-interest (such as *colonia* infrastructure) and purpose, ideology, and/or faith. These issues emerge in house meetings, then bubble up to IAF steering committees and create the bases around which to strategize and formulate goals that are achievable at the local and state levels.

Although some strong IAF affiliates contain the word "faith" in their names, others do not. And three strong IAF affiliates include nonprofit organizations in their coalitions, underlining a possible move toward broad-based organizing rather than faith-based organizing. The supposed radicalness of the IAF is its insistence on empowerment: that people find their public voice and work with others in relationships of trust to make change. IAF participants express an undying hope and faith in pluralist democracy. While this pluralist normative theme undergirds most political science textbooks, text authors often paint a cynicism-inducing picture of near-total elite control of the political process, thereby undermining hope.

In the next chapter, we hear the voices of IAF leaders and organizers, their motivations and their journeys into social justice organizing. The chapter resonates with issues raised herein. The appendix to this chapter draws on important analysis in political science about what motivates people to join organizations and what incentives exist to build and sustain those organizations.

Chapter 4 Appendix: A primer on self-interest and institutional incentives

Despite the purposive, faith, philosophical, and ethical rationales noted in this chapter, the IAF often stresses that organizers and leaders listen to and locate people's self-interests, whether from leaders and potential leaders or from institutions. In scholarly social sciences, the seemingly sound but slippery term "rationality" is evoked to understand attitudes and behavior. In a 1965 classic, *The Logic of Collective Action,* Mancur Olson, Jr. emphasized material rationality as the logic, though Olson also acknowledged that self-interested material and non-material factors also motivate joiners of organizations. Well, which is it—material or non-material? And to what extent—for which people who define rationality differently at various stages of their own development? Non-material incentives embrace a whole host of factors.

The previously cited policy analyst Deborah Stone criticized the rational model as typical of economists' individualist decision-making approaches that have overtaken the "polis" model to include self-interest along with rhetorical appeals, numeric metaphors, emotion, and those philosophical rationales analyzed earlier: freedom, security, equity, and effectiveness. She welcomed moral narratives as part of the polity. IAF uses moral narratives and stories, but clings to self-interest as a motivator. One could say that Olson's embrace of material and non-material rationality fits the IAF model. Almost anything fits! If I participate because I want to learn, interact with people across the usual class and ethnic borderlines in a community, and practice my faith, those could all be viewed as rational non-material incentives.

The IAF emphasizes self-interest to motivate and maintain participants and to solicit support or funding from investors, like banks and business people, for IAF affiliates. Besides volunteer leaders' self-interests, the IAF trains organizers and leaders to consider the self-interests of local businesses that may "invest" in IAF work. Recall the IAF iron rule of self-sufficiency. When local businesses and institutions invest, they attach no strings, unlike the many strings from government agencies. But does business investment in the IAF imply strings? One IAF rule I heard over and over, but did not see in Chambers's list (Chapter 1, Box 1.2) says: "no permanent friends, no permanent enemies." Such a rule may be hard to practice if organizations face difficult financial straits (taken up in the next chapter). Yet in my 2018 interviews with leaders, I listened to how they responded to a variety of motivations, from achieving self-interest to practicing faith in action and to learning or responding to loss. At some generic level, all of these could be viewed as rational, because individuals' perceptions of rationality differ. For reasons outlined above, I believe that better insights can be gained from a key source of political science scholarship, summarized below.

The best primer on motivation and incentives in creating and maintaining voluntary political organizations, including I would argue, congregations, comes from a classic book by James Q. Wilson, cited earlier. Voluntary organizations differ from government, which has the authority to compel people to comply with laws and taxes.

Wilson analyzed three types of incentives: material, "solidary," and purposive. Each incentive comes with consequences for commitment and long-term involvement, especially once individuals achieve their self-interested goals. Remembering that people participate voluntarily in their congregations and that congregations voluntarily decide to pay dues to IAF organizations, we must understand that these are voluntary organizations that lack authority over volunteer leaders and member institutions. It behooves us to understand what sorts of incentives will maintain, sustain, and even grow organizations.

Unions and professional associations, such as teacher groups, use material incentives. The phrase sounds like IAF-style self-interest. People join to obtain better pay, benefits, and legal protection. Union officers commit to the organizations, with full- or part-time pay or release from other duties, but the larger membership involvement is superficial, often limited to dues-paying, except in crises when they may be asked to join picket lines.

Texas is a "right-to work" state which prohibits collective bargaining and forbids unions from collecting dues from all employees although the so-called non-paying "free riders" benefit from gains that unions make. People who join organizations to achieve their goals may leave after they achieve individual success. I have observed collective self-interest with neighborhood groups, in *colonias* for example, that temporarily affiliate with an IAF affiliate but reduce or end their involvement once they achieve their goals. Those IAF leaders who live outside the *colonias* discuss *colonia* residents' self-interests and decide if the whole group will adopt them as an IAF goal. The same happens statewide with Texas IAF priorities: infrastructure problems in borderland *colonias* do not occur in Lubbock or Dallas or Austin, but with discussion and interaction among people who enjoy relationships of trust, the *colonias* issue became a statewide priority for over twenty years in efforts to fund the EDAP and assure that land-buyers building their homes had more secure title to their land than a sales deed. The transition from self-interest to public interest also occurs in other political NGOs, political parties, and in government itself. Similarly, health and education emerge as self-interest problems among particular groups (children, the aged before

Medicare kicks in), but informed leaders see the wisdom of support for public schools and wider health benefits, even if their children have grown or their Medicare safety net is in place.

James Q. Wilson uses the unusual word "solidary" (perhaps derived from social and solidarity), to describe incentives that attract potential members through the pleasure of associating with friends or trusted people, as well as through the status acquired from association. Joiners may make long-term commitments, but if friendship or trust breaks down, the relationship could be severed. The model of faith-based institutions is one of trust and fellowship in the church family and its clergy. People may drop out, stop out, or drop back in based on fatigue, health problems, and disagreement, whether in their congregation or the IAF. Yet congregations undergo change, clergy leave or are replaced, and people move, relevant especially in the territorially-based organization of the Catholic Church. The social aspect of solidary attractions limits a deeper commitment to issues, according to Wilson. With IAF's approach to leaders and the networks, the solidary incentive is relevant but superficial for long-term commitment.

Purposive incentives attract people interested in single or multiple issues and causes; Wilson categorized them into three subgroups. Purposive organizations, said Wilson, face the greatest difficulty in attracting joiners. However, once in, those joiners are likely to stay, especially if they achieve victories. In higher education over decades, I have long observed students and faculty motivated by a single-issue agenda, from civil rights, women, ethnic/racial, and LGBTQ empowerment to environmental stewardship. Wilson said that groups which attract and motivate people with comprehensive agendas should be called ideological; here was where he included religious congregations.

Based on interviews and experience, I believe that the incentives for long-term paid IAF organizers and seasoned core/primary volunteer leaders consist of ideological reasons, such as commitment to social justice issues, life-long learning, faith in action, or deepened democracy. The religious among them continue for faith-based reasons, especially the "faith-in-action" that clergy try to inspire among those who attend weekly services and more—every day, in-between services.

Beyond the single- and multi-purpose organizations, Wilson named a third subtype, redemptive groups, which organize not only around ideology but also around changing individual behavior to exemplify that ideology—so demanding that few join such groups and if or when they did, they might burn out and lose the work-life balance many aim to achieve in the advanced market-oriented economies like the U.S. Among some of the best organizers I have worked with (eight in all!), I worry that their 24/7 commitment to the work might be lived and understood as the third category and thereby induce burnout. Some leave for this and other reasons. Surprisingly, though, many continue for decades. We examine these journeys of paid organizers and volunteer leaders in the next chapter.

Notes

1. Interview with Rabbi Alan Freedman, July 25, 2018.

2. Interfaith Action of Central Texas, with its wonderful acronym iACT, is not affiliated with the Texas IAF or the IAF-affiliated Interfaith Education Fund. According to the website, "iACT cultivates peace and respect through interfaith dialogue, service and celebration" http://interfaithtexas.org/our-mission. In El Paso, the Dialogue Institute (www.thedialogueinstitute.org/elpaso, formerly the Institute of Interfaith Dialogue, and home of the Raindrop Turkish House) asks the question "How can citizens of the world live in peace and harmony?" They are inspired by Muslim scholar Fethullah Gülen, who is from Turkey but lives in the U.S. The Gülen movement established over thirty charter schools in Texas, including the Raindrop schools in El Paso. They participate in a new, or morphed, group called the Interfaith Alliance. These kinds of 501c3 nonprofit organizations do not focus on community organizing to build a base of volunteer leaders who work for social justice.

3. By the 1980s, Robert Bellah et al. joined social capital writers such as James Coleman and Robert Putnam, in harkening US roots to Alexis de Tocqueville's nineteenth-century book, *Democracy in America*, on the balance between community and individualism, in their book *Habits of the Heart: Individualism and Commitment in American Life* (Berkeley: University of California Press, 1985).

4. Texas State Historical Association, *Texas Almanac* 2018 (pp. 592–6; 2010 figures).

5. James Q. Wilson, *Political Organizations* (New York: Basic Books, 1973, 1995 second edition), Chapter 3.

6. Rev. Kevin Young, interview, June 2018.

7. On the many acronyms in this paragraph: PFLAG stands for Parents and Families of Lesbians and Gays. See the TTU website: http://www.depts.ttu.edu/centerforcampuslife/lgbtqia/index.php

8. https://www.umnews.org/en/news/married-lesbian-consecrated-united-methodist-bishop The Institute for Religion and Democracy, https://juicyecumenism.com/2017/02/03/lesbian-bishop/ Accessed July 15, 2018

9. United Methodist Church: http://www.umc.org/what-we-believe. In early 2019, another split occurred over LGBTQ issues.

10. Arlie Russell Hochschild, *Strangers in Their Own Land* (New York: The New Press, 2016). Also see Theda Skocpol and Vanessa Williamson, *The Tea Party and the Remaking of Republican Conservatism* (New York: Oxford University Press, 2012).

11. Robert Putnam and David Campbell, *American Grace: How Religion Unites and Divides Us* (New York: Simon & Schuster, 2010).

12. Pew Research Center 2015, 2016. http://www.pewforum.org/ (click on religion for multiple reports).

13. Christ the Savior Catholic Church, Lubbock: https://ctsep.org/

14. Dan Bilefsky, "Montreal Dispatch: Where Churches Have Become Temples of Cheese, Fitness, and Eroticism," July 30, 2018. https://www.nytimes.com/2018/07/30/world/canada/quebec-churches.html. Accessed July 30, 2018.

15. Ibid.

16. Attendance at Religious Services, Pew Research Center, Religion and Public Life. Accessed July 1, 2018. http://www.pewforum.org/religious-landscape-study/attendance-at-religious-services/

17. Sarah Smarsh, "How the American Left Is Rediscovering Morality," *The Guardian*, August 4, 2018. http://www.theguardian.com/us-news/2018/aug/04/american-left-morality-alexandria-ocasio-cortez-bernie-sanders Accessed Aug. 4, 2018. Saul Alinsky, founder of the IAF in 1940, had many labels, one of them "atheist." In *Rules for Radicals*, he said he supported birth control and abortion, but never would talk about "archaic" notions in early discussions with Catholics in Chicago (p. 94).

18. Mary Beth Rogers, *Cold Anger: A Story of Faith and Power Politics* (Denton: University of North Texas Press, 1990), 6.

19. Deborah Stone, *Policy Paradox: The Art of Political Decision-Making*, 3rd. ed. (New York: W. W. Norton) 3rd edition, 2012.

20. Lincoln Mullen, "The Fight to Define Romans 13," *The Atlantic*, June 15, 2018. https://www.theatlantic.com/politics/archive/2018/06/romans-13/562916/. Accessed July 1, 2018. UPC Rev. Tim Gray reminded me that Romans is a particularly complicated Biblical chapter to analyze because of its many probable authors.

21. Senior Supervisor/Organizer senior organizer Joe Rubio shared this at the EPISO/Border Interfaith Leadership Academy in June 2018.

22. Pastor Tim Carlos Anderson, Interview, July 25, 2018.

23. Saul Alinsky, *Rules for Radicals* (New York: Vintage, 1971), 143. Once in relationships of trust with priests and a Catholic Chancellor, he said he asked them, "How much longer do you think the Catholic Church can hang on to this archaic notion and still survive? Take a look out there. Can you look at them and tell me you oppose birth control?" The Chancellor "cracked up" and called it an unfair argument.

24. Cited in Michael J. O'Loughlin, "Bishop Stowe: Why the MAGA Hats at the March for Life?" *America: The Jesuit Review*, January 24, 2019, accessed Feb. 1, 2019, https://www.americamagazine.org/politics-society/2019/01/24/bishop-stowe-why-maga-hats-march-life Bishop Stowe also calls for LGBT inclusion in the church.

25. https://www.factcheck.org/2007/12/abortions-comparing-catholic-and-protestant-women/.

26. This comes from the latest IRS 990 on file with Guidestar.org, a website with searchable information on medium- and larger sized nonprofit organizations. Organizations that generate $50,000 annually must complete these forms. Once the minimum standard was $25,000 when earlier studies were done, discussed in the next chapter.

27. Robert Putnam is most famous for his book *Bowling Alone*, but for decades sociologists like Robert Bellah and James Coleman have also written about social capital.

28. Interviews with Dr. Irasema Coronado in summer 2018.

29. Interview with Asha Dane'el, September 1, 2018.

30. For selections, see Lois Ann Lorentzen, *Hidden Lives and Human Rights in the United States: Understanding the Controversies and Tragedies of Undocumented Immigration*, vol. 3 (Santa Barbara, CA: Praeger, 2014).

31. The Syracuse University Tracking System, TRAC, is located at http://trac.syr.edu/immigration/ . Accessed multiple times over the years, most recently Nov. 23, 2018.

32. See the National Catholic Register with various bishops' quotes. http://www.ncregister.com/daily-news/election-2016-u.s.-bishops-on-voting https://www.catholicnewsagency.com/news/can-a-catholic-in-good-conscience-vote-for-trump-76894

Chapter 5
"Organizers and Leaders:
Their Pathways In and Out of
Broad-based Community Work"

L et me start again with stories, this time two of them.

Claudia Santamaria is an educational leader whose life pathway allowed her to learn and apply skills acquired through an IAF affiliate and particularly in Zavala Elementary School, once deemed to be "failing" in official Texas parlance until it became an Alliance School affiliated with the IAF (see Chapter 6). Prepared to teach bilingual education, Santamaria accepted a position at a school in which few of her fellow graduates had interest—one with low standardized test scores, and high mobility (student transfer) and teacher turnover rates. During her second year, in a one-on-one relational meeting, IAF Austin Interfaith Organizer Kathleen Davis asked her about her "story" with the question "Why did you become a teacher?" Santamaria said, "It was the first time I had been ever asked!" She continued with nuance: she "evolved" her initial reason—initially, a shallow reason involving her position as eldest in the family--to the real reason. She came to the U.S. at age five and was thrown into English-only classes where she cried a lot and only learned to read finally in fourth grade. "I didn't want other kids to go through that pain."[1] Since Zavala Elementary School, Santamaria moved on to become an assistant principal, principal, and director of a big-district office that guided parent-engagement specialists on school campuses (see Chapter 6). She still sees herself as an IAF volunteer leader.

Doug Greco is a paid senior organizer in a large IAF affiliate, leading a team of new paid organizers who began relational work and action in surrounding counties.[2] When I asked for his story, he began with how his working-class background in northeast coal-mining country shaped his journey. He became a high school teacher at a "failing" high school in east Austin with high student absentee rates, low test scores, and constant principal turnover. In schools, he said, where social inequality can be marked, one sees through "a lens through which the world can be seen." After two years of leadership—building relationships and a core staff team at the school—teacher-leaders like Greco did

151

neighborhood walks and developed relational power with parent leaders. Together, after a staff vote to formalize the Alliance School relationship with the IAF affiliate Austin Interfaith, the teams built an alliance between teachers and parents around students' learning, an after-school program, and summer youth employment opportunities. The school left the failure warning list. Greco discovered that he liked working with adults, so he decided in 2002 to try out as an organizer (a formal stage in recruitment; see below) and then was hired. A few years later, he became a lead organizer for six years, took off time to earn two masters' degrees at distant distinguished universities, and eventually returned to organizing. He guides a new Central Texas Interfaith organizer team that is developing relationships with potential leaders outside the city in surrounding counties and achieving successes with Get-Out-the-Vote campaigns.

Building on the analysis from the last chapter, we see that experiences in their youth, both for Leader Santamaria and for Organizer Greco, made them receptive to social justice work in an established organizing model with track records of success. People like Greco and Santamaria (and no doubt many readers) understand the limits of reform led by traditional hierarchical and bureaucratic models without a civil society base and their voices, such as parent leaders. Drawing from the conceptual insights of the last chapter on motivations and incentives, it seems rather shallow to label these motivations material self-interest. Rather, deeper and longer-term interests have been at play in leaders' and organizers' self-selected recruitment and continuation with Austin Interfaith and other IAF affiliates.

Framing the chapter

Why do people join and remain in purposeful organizations like IAF affiliates? While some leave, many find the work fulfilling and use their skills in a variety of fields, including other organizations and workplaces. As senior organizer and supervisor, the late Sister Christine Stephens said publicly at a one-and-a-half-day IAF seminar of committed leaders that I attended in mid-2018, "one never gives up on the IAF." For some, like Greco, IAF organizing became a lifelong vocation that brought meaningful relationships, efficacy in large and effective local and statewide organizations, and social justice successes in their lives and the lives of others. Santamaria brought valuable relational skills into her work with parents and school staff. Many leaders stay involved over the long haul; witness the Dallas interviews from Chapter 3, with people who stayed on for twenty years and more. As we see in this chapter, some volunteer leaders decide to become paid organizers after a grueling training and probation period. Organizers constantly look for leaders who might want to become organizers as well, inviting them to distant trainings and state-wide sessions where participants often find it energizing to be in a room with 150–200 other people committed to social justice.

Besides those who stay involved, leaders move out of their IAF affili-ates, their cities, and/or even run for office. However, IAF principles require politicians to exit this non-government organization once in government elective office. Texas State Representative Gina Hinojosa, one of them, proclaims identity as a "mother, advocate, progressive" on her website who "volunteered with Austin Interfaith and was a key leader in the organization's successful efforts to require corporations that receive economic incentives from the City to pay their employees a living wage or higher."[3] Representative Hinojosa stopped out of Austin Interfaith, but if and when she leaves office, I would not be surprised if she once again participated in IAF, for the organizational power base resonates with her purposeful life-long commitments to justice, fairness, and equality. Working on their own, individuals can hardly make the sort of changes possible without the power of numbers and relationships. Those leaders and organizers who stop out or leave can apply the skills acquired in trainings and experiences to work for other organizations.[4]

Few community organizations besides the IAF exhibit the quality of relational power among volunteer leaders and between leaders and public officials. Leaders' learning surpasses what they might get in school, university courses, and most certainly, the TEKS/Texas Essential Knowledge and Skills state standards, where rote knowledge (like dates, names) is valued and tested but basic civics and experiential community learning are virtually ignored, as addressed in Chapter 2.[5]

This chapter analyzes the grassroots base of the paid organizers and the volunteer leaders who make IAF community organizing work effec-tive. After examining recruitment and pathways into very different lead-ership volunteerism and organizing careers, based mostly on interviews and on reflection about my own pathway, I deal with contradictions that can produce tension. The first exists between vertical forces: the opaque Texas IAF center and West-Southwest IAF—alternatively called the top or the institutional superstructure—and its grassroots IAF affiliate lead-ership base. One way the contradiction manifests itself is in the questions raised in local IAF affiliate leaders' minds about for whom the organizer works: local leaders or the IAF superstructure? The local pays their salaries, but the top requires regular reports and their presence at numerous distant trainings. This superstructure-base issue reinforces the struggles to generate revenue particularly in the weaker IAF affiliates located in lower per-capita income counties or those in the rebuilding process. Recall that the IAF Iron Rule of Self-Sufficiency states that no funds can be generated from government agencies with their "strings" attached, to assure autonomy and independence. Using IRS 990 tax forms, political science scholar Benjamin Márquez analyzed the monetary sources in Texas IAF affiliates from 1991 to 2000 and found contradictions with the Iron Rule: few member institutions paid their dues and the IAF depended heavily on particular foundations, such as the Catholic Campaign for Human Development (CCHD).[6] As noted in previous chapters, funding sources establish conditions for the use of grant funds, which potentially undermine self-sufficiency. In Border Interfaith, for which I view the treasurer's report on a monthly basis, CCHD funds currently in 2019 constitute a third of income—sizeable to be sure, but not dependency.

As a second contradiction, we look at the Iron Rule within the IAF hierarchy. IAF affiliates pay annual fees (sometimes called "technical assistance") to the IAF, IEF (Interfaith Education Fund) which reimburses local leaders' travel, and the Network of Texas Organizations (NTO). The criteria for these fees often lack transparency or accountability for decisions made by senior leaders at higher levels.[7] So one might ask whether the Iron Rule operates at the top level: the IAF superstructure depends on and burdens local affiliates in revenue generation to sustain itself. To be sure, those senior IAF officials also acquire external grants for the organizations beyond the CCHD.

A third interesting dynamic—a contradiction partially resolved— involves the ongoing shift from the senior men organizers of decades past at the national IAF level (Alinsky, Chambers, Cortés, Gecan) to a gender-balanced group of organizers in Texas. Archival documents at the University of Texas at San Antonio also show gender balance in the early San Antonio COPS volunteer leadership. Each IAF affiliate develops its own titles and decision-making structure, and from 1972–1982, women constituted four of the five COPS Presidents.[8]

Over twenty years of my unpaid leadership inside the IAF, I witnessed the move toward greater gender balance among IAF organizers in the mix of interviews for this book and in distant trainings and conferences. My use of the word "gender" emphasizes the

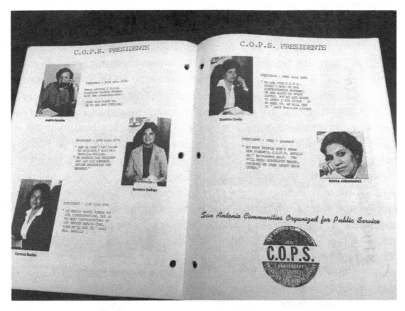

Early years C.O.P.S. presidents. Staudt photograph, courtesy UTSA Archives.

construction of behavior through social rather than biological sources, a socialization likely to affect organizing and leading styles.[9] Boys and girls, men and women undergo gender-specific socialization that intersects with age, ethnicity and race, class, and nationality. While the demographic shift toward gender balance has occurred, socially constructed training for organizers' style still emphasizes "toughness" in their presentation of self, public speaking, and interaction to underline their credibility and power. I witnessed this toughness at distant trainings. However, some of the IAF women organizers I have worked with and interviewed exude a genuinely friendly style, but still remain credible, powerful, and strong.

Relationality and context have been viewed as central to political women's way of interacting with others.[10] In a 2008 book about Latina "firsts" in Texas politics, a group of political science scholars emphasized Latina pioneers' different communication styles compared to men and to other ethnicities.[11] The first Latinas to be elected to various state and local offices tended to be embedded in dense social networks and brought complex community accountability relationships into their campaigns and decision-making processes. As a Los Angeles-focused analysis of Latino political agency remarks, "Latinas in leadership roles thus often (though not always) approach leadership in a gendered manner, using empathic sensibilities and other common female social skills to cultivate working relationships that can sustain collective mobilization."[12] Of course, one cannot generalize about large categories of people; exceptions to patterns can always be found. Moreover, the eras in which such studies are made must be understood. Back in the 1970s era with its overt discrimination against women in law and business—the typical occupations of state legislators—previous studies of the tiny percentages of women in U.S. politics found that women's pathways into office tended to come through voluntary associations. Two decades into the twenty-first century, we see younger and more diverse women elected to office. To the extent that women's different styles persist, the shift could be a godsend in the bully-intensive, harsh polarizing political world of the twenty-first century. In the IAF volunteer leader base, no shortage of women exists. Women have become the majority of congregants in many religious denominations; that is, women represent the larger pool from which recruitment occurs for IAF paid organizers and more volunteer leaders.

Although women are visible in IAF affiliates, policy issues that affect women—relating to domestic violence, sexual assault, and health—tend to be muted in IAF affiliates. However, these issues have emerged in Dallas Area Interfaith agendas, as Chapter 3 analyzed, framed via public safety. Two strong women organizers and many women leaders speak their minds in house meetings, interviews, and strategy sessions.

Whatever the contradictions and tensions therefrom, the stable and wide grassroots IAF base is what makes IAF special and effective compared with many other non-governmental organizations. A people-base requires committed work that other NGOs might not be willing to develop. In *Blessed Are the Organized*, Princeton theology professor Jeffrey Stout quotes Texas IAF founder Ernesto Cortés, Jr. stressing "the need for patient, indeed perpetual, micro-organizing as the basis required for genuinely democratic macro-organizing."[13]

The symbiosis between both top and bottom determines whose voices shape content heard in what kind of hierarchy—transparent or opaque—for IAF's effectiveness in achieving social justice agendas at the local and statewide levels. So from a perspective of institutional governance in this chapter, we examine the extent to which--even in a relatively flat hierarchy like the IAF—regional and statewide senior organizers and supervisors impose strategies and goals on those at the grassroots and if so, how, and how local organizers and leaders respond to the superstructure. These upward and downward processes are crucial to the achievement of effective statewide agendas and strategies.

In this chapter, I argue that recruitment, organizer training, rotation, and internal governance keep the IAF coherent on a superstructure state and regional level, but that IAF affiliates' unpaid local leadership base is as crucial to fulfilling the democratic accountability IAF claims for its institutional governance. Below we look at differences between organizers and leaders: who are they and what makes them tick?

Organizer and leader differences

As we learned from the stories of Claudia Santamaria and Doug Greco in the opening paragraphs of this chapter, some leaders become organizers like Greco while others continue to use skills in their own institutions and workplaces like Santamaria with her value-added IAF training and experience. Leaders and organizers undergo enough training to share the same IAF lingo and occasionally attend distant training workshops together, but the intensity of their commitments and obligations differs. Both titles—organizer and leader—involve different roles and tasks.

The recruitment and formation of organizers is one of IAF's most essential tasks, for it affects the IAF affiliates' strategic public work and organizers' subsequent ability to recruit new leaders who develop the ability and courage to speak with substantive content and moral authority in grassroots and relational work. The IAF places many demands on its organizers, but they are well compensated, earning more than a mid-level professor—if they and their leaders can raise enough money to support an organization to the tune of a $100,000–$300,000 or more annual budget on average (typical amounts in local nonprofit organizations with minimal staff). The institutional revenue-generating demands merit our consideration in this book: organizers "fire" themselves if they cannot work well enough with leaders to generate revenue for sustaining the affiliate, paying salaries, and submitting dues to the IAF, IEF, and TNO, as we cover below.

An organizer's work is fulltime and more. One-on-one relational meetings and planning meetings represent the core of organizers' work: connecting with people over the big "why" questions, learning their stories, like Santamaria discussed with then-Austin Interfaith Organizer Kathleen Davis. Organizers communicate extensively, usually face to

Emilee Bounds, West Texas Organizing Strategy Organizer. Photograph Kathleen Staudt.

face in the local setting. They also connect with fellow and sister organizers and with their supervisors on weekly bases through reports, emails, and phone conversations. Gradually over recent decades, most organizers moved from a face-to-face and phone-based communication culture to a partial email culture, with occasional Facebook posts and tweets in the bigger affiliates. In a typical day, organizers can have as many as three to six meetings: "as many as I can get," Lubbock-based Organizer Emilee Bounds said in an interview.[14]

Besides the horizontal communication in their locales, let us examine organizers' vertical communication with supervisors. Intensive vertical communication with supervisors keeps organizers focused on the statewide agenda and the commonalities across the state and region. Organizers also network with other organizers around the state, which provides them with ideas and strategies on which leaders might act in their local contexts.

Organizers' incentive structures differ from leaders, despite similar pathways into the IAF. The senior organizer is paid a good salary, equivalent to a high school principal's salary in the region, i.e. around six digits, while the leader is an unpaid volunteer with a network. The word "volunteer," however, does not adequately cover a leader's work in and with their network of people who trust them. Leadership is not based merely on individual dues as in other nonprofit organizations such as the former ACORN, the Texas Organizing Project, LULAC, or the League of Women Voters, but rather on leaders' experiences, networks, training, and public voice. The title "leader" merits special rank: special and deserved talent, reliability, and respect.

With nudging from organizers, leaders plan and implement IAF actions. In one of their most important tasks, leaders recruit, inspire, and remind their networks to attend the planned actions and follow-up. Member institution "turnout" is usually the number-one item on an agenda when planning actions; only through persistent sign-ups and reminders do IAF affiliates generate attendance that runs from the hundreds to thousands. I find it downright sad when other non-IAF civic organizations only draw five or ten to an audience for candidate forums— i.e. more candidates than audience members! Leaders also schedule relational meetings with public officials and attend in groups of three to five, usually with the organizer. The organizer does not speak for the organization to the media; rather, the leaders' voices reign supreme. After all, organizers come and go, usually rotated in five to seven-year terms, on their own volition or on re-assignment from above. Leaders live in their community; they and their base hold and own whatever power its IAF affiliate exercises. Yet without an organizer to nudge, give direction, and communicate, the entire local affiliate could fall apart.

Beyond that, an organizer's training is deep, and their mentoring from senior IAF supervisors, continuous (more on this later). Organizers are employees, perhaps better said 24/7 professionals, while unpaid volunteer leaders usually work in other jobs or in retirement, thus investing only partial or episodic labor and time to the IAF affiliate, stopping in and out depending on their other commitments. How are they chosen? Some self-selection is involved in showing interest and showing up to participate. However, organizers are constantly on the lookout for potential leaders: does she have a network? Is there anger about injustices? Is he willing to invest time and talent? To be a primary or core leader involves substantial time and labor commitments plus an understanding of the bigger IAF picture. New leaders display tentative commitment, as they undergo mentoring from the organizer, while seasoned primary and secondary leaders reflect confidence and maturity, perhaps mentoring new leaders about "how we do things" (*sine qua non* for socialization into organizational culture). Whatever the length of their involvement, leaders usually find the experiences to be "energizing"—a word I often hear and experience myself, although "exhausting," is also apt, whether

Alicia Franco, EPISO/Border Interfaith Leader. Photograph Kathleen Staudt.

one has been leading over twenty years or even over the forty years my colleague Alicia Franco has committed to the Texas IAF. She wore the organizer hat in multiple parts of Texas and continues to wear the leader hat in multiple member institutions in El Paso.[15]

The ideal and real organizers and leaders

Alinsky's *Rules for Radicals* in 1971 called for a miraculous set of ideal qualities in organizers (his words): curiosity, irreverence, a sense of humor and imagination, an organized personality, a well-integrated political schizoid (i.e. open to negotiation), ego, a free and open mind, and political relativity.[16] Look at any nonprofit management textbook or attend any leadership workshop, and one will find a very different set of desirable character traits, sometimes viewed as biologically born rather than made in their specialized, traditional roles like president, vice-president, secretary, and treasurer (more on this later) plus their individual members. Only a few decades ago, people assumed physical traits to be important: tall, lighter skin color, and male, for starters (one reason why the U.S. has lagged in electing women to office compared to European countries and those in the western hemisphere). As Chapter 2 discussed, Texas politics continues to over-represent White men in political office.

IAF organizers typically start as leaders, talented people who "want to make a difference." Existing organizers identify, approach, and call potential leaders to participate. Recall Doug Greco's story in the opening chapter. His leadership as a teacher no doubt called existing organizers' attention to his skills and networks. At large IAF affiliates, senior organizers work with and mentor new organizers. Consider the national IAF website and its detail about "Becoming an Organizer."[17] The site lists the "qualities of a successful organizer," different from Alinsky's list, but worth quoting fully:

> NATIVE INTELLIGENCE—not necessarily degrees, but the ability to think, reflect, communicate, challenge the conventional wisdom, make judgments in complicated situations, and show flexibility.

> ANGER AND EDGE—not temper, not ideological fervor, not an abstract commitment to "the people," but a clear sense of what's wrong, impatience in the face of that wrong, and a drive to address it.

> A WILLINGNESS TO CROSS RACE AND CULTURE—to be willing to work with people unlike oneself, people of other races, classes, orientations, faiths.

> A TRACK RECORD – some evidence, in high school, college, the local community, the workplace of attempting to relate to people and to respond to situations that seemed to demand responses; and some success in whatever field or career or endeavor has occupied the individual's time.

After a potential organizer submits an application and statement of interest, and undergoes individual meetings perhaps in a short distant training, they go through a paid "try-out" period of ninety days involving placement in an IAF organization. IAF is not only very selective but also demands much of its organizers. Institutional high expectations couple with careful guidance and mentoring from a senior organizer/supervisor in the try-out and, if accepted, continue in the actual place to which they are assigned. For the IAF applicant-trainee-try-out-intern turned organizer, the assignment reminds me a little of the old-style Peace Corps and the necessity for its volunteers to be flexible about place-based assignments. (I applied to go to South America, got an invitation letter for a probable African country, and landed in the Philippines.)

What interviewees' stories tell us

Let us consider the experience of a new, relatively young organizer in her early thirties, someone who already understood the demands of organizing from her previous work as an IAF leader. No doubt her parents' commitment to social justice also shaped her youth. Here we see the "call" to organize, one that involves an approach from key people like a pastor or organizer.

Emilee Bounds, whose parents were part of the founding convention of an IAF organization in Oklahoma, got involved in her parents' faith institution, the United Church of Christ. She spoke with her pastor about "making a difference," and the pastor responded to Emilee with an invitation: "come to a meeting." She told Bounds she wanted her "on my core team."

Initially, Bounds did not know what this all entailed. However, she learned how to do House Meetings through experience. She was moved while hearing the stories that people told about the pressures on their families. Once Bounds got to know the organizational model, she fell in love with the process of organizing. With about fifty others, she attended a grueling training in August, with interactions from 5 am until midnight, consisting of reading assigned material, discussions, one-on-one and relational meetings, and public speaking. One month later, she was among the select, invited to the labor-intensive try-out experience for three months where she acquired the habit of scheduling numerous one-on-one, house, and relational meetings.

As an organizer in Lubbock for six months when I interviewed her, Emilee Bounds had been meeting with the leaders and clergy, and developed deeper relationships with these people and other prospective leaders in efforts to rebuild the West Texas Organizing Strategy. She offered local training with an outside speaker known statewide, mainly to prepare, inform, and inspire potential new leaders. For Bounds, a typical day consists of three to six individual meetings.

Emilee also sets up meetings with leaders and potential leaders in nearby places, such as Midland, San Angelo, Amarillo, and other towns, but some of these trips involve hours of driving each way in the wide-open spaces of the west Texas plains. Lubbock leaders consider her "dynamic," a person always looking for and reading about new opportunities to re-build the organization. Bounds expects to hold more trainings for leaders and new leaders. Emilee and WTOS leaders exude hope about growth for various reasons, some of which involve a supportive Catholic bishop and a growing sense of efficacy—that is, the notion that one can make a difference—among an expanded group of leaders.

Rev. Price Davis and Janet Price, West Texas Organizing Strategy Leader. Photograph Kathleen Staudt.

As I learned WTOS history from seasoned leaders, I heard the initial Lubbock organizing convention drew over 1,500 people. Despite its location in a less populous, spread out, and conservative place ("more land than people," I kept hearing in interviews), several statewide elected officials came from the city and nearby places: among them long-serving Pete Laney and Tom Craddick in the Texas House, both also serving as Speakers of the House, each from one of the major political parties. IAF-style "relational power" with those officials had offered opportunities to achieve important goals in the state legislature, such as expanded eligibility and flexible registration procedures around the CHIP/Children's Health Insurance Program for low-income children, a focus in the early 2000s.[18] CHIP coverage and eligibility requirements continue to be an IAF focus, as state government tried to reduce the budget through opaque and complex procedures such as six-month re-enrollment requirements, thereby putting children at even greater risk. Places like Lubbock are ideal for IAF expansion, new leadership, and organized relational power.

Despite past glories, the number of paid member institutions in WTOS had shrunk over time. Through early summer, during Bounds' short tenure, the WTOS had no current win. But the relational process is as or more important than wins during the rebuilding stage. Leaders did IAF-style research to assess why the city council majority did not vote for an ordinance to regulate payday lenders, despite WTOS leaders having met with council representatives to get majority support and bringing a sizeable turnout on the day of the vote. The opponents to regulating predatory lending consisted not only of the payday lenders themselves, but also the banks that loan money to these third-party predatory lenders. The IAF "Power Analysis" tool allowed people to clarify and strategize for expected wins and occasional losses like this. The city council representatives who supported better regulation spoke for the semi-segregated economically distressed parts of the city, but the other representatives in west and south Lubbock ultimately decided it was not in their best interests to oppose the banks, potential campaign contributors, and re-election as incumbents. Perhaps their middle-class constituencies agreed; perhaps they did not, but need reminders in preparation for the next election.

As I know from leaders' stories in El Paso and from the statewide Texas Appleseed nonprofit organization in which volunteer lawyers use their skills for practical solutions, the multi-billion dollar predatory lender industry charges late-payers usurious rates, more than 500 percent in interest and fees, potentially resulting in car loss and the inability to earn a livelihood. I heard one El Paso leader speak publicly about his shame being scammed (one of the more than 150,000 Texans to lose a car from 2012–15 according to Texas Appleseed).[19] Nevertheless, when payday lenders operate under stronger regulations after city ordinances, they move to counties or to the Internet. In this current administration, the federal government moved to weaken regulations to protect consumers, among them military personnel, many young and away from home for the first time.

In another example and like others who made life-long commitments to social justice, Senior Organizer Sr. Maribeth Larkin joined and stayed with the IAF and its opportunity to learn "what it means to be responsible adults in a democratic society. IAF provides access to a diverse platform to organize broadly."[20] After forty years of organizing, now based in Los Angeles, she guides and mentors new organizers and travels to present at training workshops. She has returned to El Paso many times to assist at workshops.

Few organizers raise young children while organizing, though I know one such organizer in a strong Texas IAF affiliate. No doubt the usual strain of women's double jobs, including unpaid work in their homes, would bear heavily on the 24/7 demands of paid organizing jobs. Even in universities with their more flexible schedules, the primary child-care parent confronts challenges, so much so that relational support networks have been established like Mama PhD groups (after a book so named).

Without supportive partners who share child-rearing responsibilities, organizers' full 24/7 schedules would make for inevitable clashes.[21] Once children have grown, household workloads change. I asked a fellow leader and friend, the husband of a new organizer, about how his life has changed since she started organizing. He joked, responding with a smile, "she's on the phone all the time, emailing and talking."

Organizers communicate with one another via emails and phone calls, besides the relationships they develop at trainings away from their home bases. IAF is very much a talk culture due to relational trust building and re-building, on the phone or in personal meetings, but organizers to different degrees have slowly and selectively embraced the efficiencies of email communication as well, especially after trust relationships have been established. However, opportunities can go missed both within the IAF affiliate and with potential new leaders and partnerships when organizers ignore or respond late to emails.[22]

Organizers always push for events and leaders to gain validation and visibility in the primary newspaper source in their communities, but only the stronger IAF affiliates gain regular coverage in the main and alternative presses or use the freely available opportunity to post on Facebook to disseminate information. Elaborate websites exist in four IAF affiliates; even the West/Southwest IAF site does not always catch up with what affiliates accomplish or even whether some exist. When I first developed the Texas IAF map for Chapter 2 in spring 2018, it listed eleven affiliates, but as my research proceeded, I found that three no longer existed. Given the limited scholarly studies of the Texas IAF, newcomers and students may find it difficult to locate information, without websites and articles about the IAF affiliates, as I learned in some interviews when students sought sources to write research papers. IAF affiliates need wider exposure, especially for their public actions. Otherwise, they run the risk of looking weaker than other organizations like Texas Organizing Project or PICO National Network (now called Faith in Action, and in the state, Faith in Texas), that have an active electronic and social media presence,[23] although they may lack a firm leadership base equivalent to the IAF base.

Leaders, seasoned and new, come into IAF organizations through a variety of pathways. Some have been involved in charitable and service work in their churches, but long for ways to do justice work, that is, to foster policy and systematic changes for larger numbers of people than individual service and charity. An organizer may approach potential leaders because they have a network; people trust them. Clergy may suggest participation to them, asking: why not participate in the local

IAF affiliate? (A question like this more likely emerges in Catholic churches.)

In the past, some leaders had also been loosely involved in local political efforts, but became disappointed in weak, impotent political party machinery when it comes to issue-oriented work (despite the elaborate Texas Democratic and GOP platforms listed for further reflection in Chapter 2) as I learned in interviews. U.S. parties, after all, primarily work to elect candidates who hopefully articulate issue agendas, not to organize people in between elections as do some parties in other parts of the world. Political parties used to be important in neighborhoods, as mediating institutions with precinct captains who knew their neighbors and built relationships with them. In recent presidential elections, however, the two major parties seem to focus more on their national committees and fundraising apparatus.

Amazingly, in many interviews, leaders became involved after their positive response to an invitation: "I was asked." Teachers, clergy, colleagues, and others notice potential in people, especially those with networks and skills. Leaders also emerge from formative experiences in their families (like organizers Emilee Bounds and Josephine López-Paul, as we see below) or in their schooling, including theological seminaries such as long-time national head, the late Edward Chambers or Organizer Ramón Durán who has organized all around Texas.

Theological preparation may prepare people for skill sets similar to those of organizers. I am sometimes in awe of pastors who multi-task 24/7; their complex workload reminds me of IAF organizers, exuding flexible dynamism, generating enough revenue to keep the institution afloat, and inspiring people to enhance their learning curves. Several clergy in Border Interfaith became dynamic and eloquent co-chair leaders in the organization: Rabbi Larry Bach, Father Pablo Matta, and Lutheran Pastor Wayne Kendrick. Their faith leadership seemed as strong, creative, and eloquent as their IAF leadership.

The word "leader" sounds somewhat daunting. In traditional organizations, from PTAs to nonprofit boards, identity, and issue-oriented groups, members elect or select people to hold offices like president, vice-president, treasurer, and secretary for particular terms of office. This is an old, traditional model. Once those traditional leaders assume their offices, members tend to be treated like followers who participate sporadically unless appointed to committees.

In IAF affiliates, people become unpaid volunteer leaders when and after they get involved and trained through experiences and leadership academies. Some may have been voiceless in public before their involvement. IAF leaders grow in their confidence to exercise leadership with experience in pre-meetings, rehearsals, agendas, and script-writing for complicated public actions like Accountability Sessions. In this research, I also interviewed brand-new leaders, still quiet and nervous, requesting complete anonymity on my consent-to-be-interviewed forms (which I of course respected).

Leaders are not born; they mature with guidance, experience, and feedback from evaluation, which is part of every IAF meeting and action. How did the meeting go? Let's first respond with one-word reactions, the organizer says: "excited," "overwhelmed," "ready," etc. Then discussion ensues. IAF planning and steering meetings involve give and take, discussion over complex issues and strategies. I have always appreciated how, in El Paso's affiliates and their monthly steering committee meetings or in issue-focused committee meetings, leaders "agree to disagree" but then develop a consensus among people who share credibility and trust, then project a united front at public actions. At the local level, I have long seen evidence of the Learning Process approach, rather than the superstructure Blueprint approach, evoking concepts I introduced in Chapter 1. Inscribed in the book below, a long-time senior organizer describes the process further.

In *Blessed are the Organized*, senior organizer Elizabeth Valdez, based in Houston but working statewide in training and supervision, talks about leadership development. Leaders emerge from many walks of life, not formal professions, but from informal connectedness, such as rosary readers in parishes according to Valdez. To develop leaders, an organizer must

1. Identify those with earned entitlement.
2. Widen the range of topics on which these natural leaders can speak with authority.
3. Expand the scope of groups that recognize that authority.
4. Place leaders in situations "where what they say and do can be held accountable by other leaders and their own institution."

In this earned position, leaders speak with content and moral authority.[24]

Let us examine more stories of various leaders from my interviews and observations. A number of leaders, I found, brought a commitment to social justice far earlier than their IAF involvement, as is true when I reflect on unpaid Leader Kathy Staudt, i.e. my own case. Kathy is my community name; my academic and published first name is Kathleen, also my baptized name.

Staudt took faith messages from childhood church services and Lutheran parochial school seriously, noting contradictions in heavily segregated Milwaukee and household life. She was a daily witness to power dependencies in her parents' traditional marriage with her father-breadwinner and her mother, a homemaker. However, she stopped attending church at age fourteen in reaction to the rigidity of an extremely conservative Lutheran Synod and its failure to provide anything but a submissive place for women in the church. As a young teen, Staudt had no language for this obvious institutionalized injustice. During undergraduate days in the late 1960s and early 1970s, she was involved in extensive activism around the Vietnam War, civil rights, welfare rights, and women's "liberation" as it was called then (along with its relational Consciousness Raising small groups). After graduate school came academia and tenure, teaching courses, researching, and publishing. In her thirties, Staudt re-joined the (Presbyterian) church just before the birth of her first child, and the pastor baptized both her now-grown son and later, her daughter, neither of whom attend church as adults. She wanted to participate in and support the largest social justice organization in the El Paso region, a region with still-limited civic capacity. She also wanted to learn more about local politics, made possible with her church as a Border Interfaith member institution. She values her church, with its supportive community of people, which enriches and enhances spiritual sustenance to foster purpose and principles in life amid the complex, materialist/individualist society of the late twentieth and early twenty-first century U.S.

Dallas Leader Dr. Barry Lachman grew up in a conservative family in the northeast before he became a medical doctor. However, his father—who was against big government in principle—criticized the failure of local government in upstate New York to enforce inspection codes in old housing stock that was not maintained by landlords. "Nobody should have to live like that," his father told him.[25] Dr. Lachman, very involved in the development of a strong housing inspection code in Dallas (see Chapter 3), participated in social justice and the expansion of health care for his whole life, from medical school onward. His synagogue has long been a member institution of Dallas Area Interfaith.

Leader Leon Williams brought long-term commitment to human and civil rights before moving to west Texas.[26] A seasoned leader from Washington, D.C., Williams works in the Lubbock public school system.

Comfortable in the world of D.C. community politics, he was frustrated with organizations that lacked the relational power and power of numbers within IAF affiliates to achieve their agendas. After getting his master's degree from Texas Tech University, he became involved in Lubbock's WTOS through a nonprofit organization.

Several leaders, I learned, grew up in families where a parent ran for public office. Whether the parent won or lost the election, the political world came alive for them as children and young adults. Leader, then Organizer, then lead DAI Organizer Josephine López-Paul grew up in a New Mexico union family who participated in strong, conscious organized action to strengthen the rights of Mexican Americans. She worked as a teacher and became angry about struggles and losses in the teaching profession. Recall the "cold anger" from Chapter 1. López-Paul channeled her anger into constructive change strategies and wins in many locales where she organized. She was an organizer in El Paso in the early 2000s.

Other leaders underwent loss or anger about problems in their own lives and neighborhoods. In IAF terms, this is the self-interest that can begin to solve problems with both the power of numbers and relational power. As Chapter 3 highlighted with quotations from my interview with her, Leader Adriana Corral in Dallas worried about her children walking to school without traffic lights and speed bumps. With others, she organized to establish safer streets around the school. Her commitments grew to embrace a wide variety of issues, all connected to her faith and acknowledgement that people achieve more working collectively. Corral has recently been featured in a news story about the Dallas Police Department's acceptance of picture ID's issued by Catholic parishes.[27] Once Dallas Area Interfaith obtained public commitments from several police chiefs, leaders like Corral said, "I feel more confidence in case the police need a photo ID."

Another Adriana, with the surname García, first Leader and then home-grown Organizer in El Paso, sought something more than attending church and congregational ministries. "I wanted to put faith into action." Adriana García spoke with her priest, a former co-chair of Border Interfaith, and he suggested she participate. She now organizes for two IAF affiliates in El Paso, recently joined together in 2018.

In this section, with the voices of IAF organizers and leaders, we see various pathways into social justice work. It often takes an organizer who sees, then develops through one-on-one meetings, the leadership potential that may have lain dormant in leaders' lives.

While this chapter describes IAF organizational culture being built and re-built, the previous chapter alluded to changes in church organizational cultures. Recall from Chapter 4 that both types of formal institutions—congregations and IAF affiliates—are voluntary nonprofit organizations, lacking authority to compel membership such as what governments do with laws and penalties. Let us look deeper into non-IAF institutional cultures such as congregations and their changes. Such change may need to go hand in hand with changes in society and people's hunger for meaningful social justice work.

Organizational cultures: Amenable to IAF leader recruitment?

As mainline Protestant congregations undergo an aging church-going population, like my own Presbyterian Church, the reflective leaders among congregants consider ways to respond to a changing society to draw in people of all ages. Recall the phrase from both Organizer Emilee Bounds and Leader Rev. Kevin Young in the previous chapter to "make the church relevant again." Some former mediating institutions (like labor unions, drawing members from only a tenth of the labor force nationwide), are now less relevant to addressing people's concerns compared with earlier eras when families could rely on their neighbors, churches, unions, and even political parties, however imperfect such assistance once was, as IAF trainers note when they give workshops focused on "Pressures on Families."

No doubt clergy ponder the question about the right balance between continuity and change, inward congregational and external community action. My church offers two morning services, one with contemporary music and the other with traditional music. We are home to a Spanish-language service, but also incorporate Spanish into our liturgy for the mostly English-language congregants to learn. Our youth group is small, but celebrated and energized with interesting faith-based projects and summer camps. People exchange ideas and develop relationships in young adult and book groups. Like the Methodist church in downtown Lubbock, we too offer space to numerous community organizations like Alcoholics Anonymous and PFLAG that regularly use our rooms for meetings during the week. Like Methodist congregations in Lubbock, my church is an IAF-affiliated member institution, appealing to some but not all of the entire congregation (as Austin-based Lutheran Pastor Tim Anderson also analyzed in the previous chapter).

Graciela Quintero, West Texas Organizing Strategy Leader. Photograph Kathleen Staudt.

Another Presbyterian pastor-leader I interviewed had been involved in an IAF organization in the northeastern US, preceded by a neighborhood association which used the power of numbers to keep a money-laundering entertainment club out of their area. Once in west Texas, he hit the ground running as a seasoned IAF leader. He has long been a fine public speaker and exudes the confidence that comes from a lifetime of church and community leadership in a smaller city like Lubbock where people can more easily develop relationships with a variety of representatives.

Some academic fields and professions lend themselves to community organizing. Re-entry student Graciela Quinteros, a new leader, heard presentations from Organizer Emilee Bounds and another leader in her social work graduate seminar at Texas Tech University.[28] In most higher education institutions, social work has at least two tracks: clinical (individual) and community or policy, which fits into social justice organizing for systemic change (common in Mexico as well). Many "clients" who interact with social workers in nonprofit or government agencies could address some of their issues with policy change for greater economic security, such as living wages, and others, for a pathway to citizenship status. Even senior IAF Organizer Sr. Maribeth Larkin said about her past social work vocation, "I thought I wanted to do social work, but seven years of experience with providing crisis intervention and direct service for the poor was so frustrating that I nearly left my community." She asked herself: How could I "get the system to work for people?"[29] She became involved in the Los Angeles United Neighborhood Organization (UNO) (now called ONE LA) to work for wider systemic changes for people so that they would not need to go to social workers or government. Note that the emphasis on individual and family self-sufficiency also reflects the key IAF Iron Rule of Self-Sufficiency: never do for others what they can do for themselves. One should not have to depend on the vagaries of public policy and budgetary changes from election to election.

Before I knew the tasks of an IAF organizer, perhaps I could have called myself a university campus organizer, working with a faculty base to create two new programs and one center in addition to teaching, research, and writing. When my own children entered elementary school, I had a strong self-interest in quality education and caring teachers. Former Dean Arturo Pacheco introduced me to EPISO after including me in UTEP's participation with the late John Goodlad's National Network for Educational Renewal, pioneered in the 1980s, at the University of Washington. Goodlad's approach was a little like the IAF, but focused on educational leaders rather than a power base. It involved relational meetings and seminars to discuss readings (similar reading assignments to the IAF!) so important in crossing institutional and campus-community boundaries. Leaders from multiple educational institutions attended multi-day seminar retreats away from work to discuss timely books on educational renewal. The relationships from meetings led to fruitful partnerships, including one with the teaching-training magnet school at El Paso's Riverside High School. Before that, I knew little about EPISO, but with this network, I later visited Alliance Schools and Project Arriba, instigating my two-decade series of continuous community-based activities, from 1998 and ongoing even now.

In the late 1990s, I founded and directed the UTEP Center for Civic Engagement (CCE) and fostered a deep partnership with EPISO and Alliance Schools in a foundation grant[30] (see Chapter 8). Although the many lengthy meetings took time, along with travel time from campus and home to schools, the CCE legitimized my community-based work and efforts to identify and involve other professor-leaders and students. I sometimes found myself cross-pressured, though, working in a public institution yet also a leader in the largest community organization in the city, admired by some but threatening to others.

In this section, we have viewed overlaps between IAF leaders and organizers, but key differences exist between them, their roles, and institutional incentives and penalties. Unpaid volunteer leaders step in or step out of participation, unless their commitments are lifelong, but paid organizers are employees, responding to both their base and to their supervisors at the somewhat opaque state- and region-wide levels. As a political scientist, I believe the institutionalist perspective in this and the last chapter offers insights about the control, process, and discipline within a voluntary organization of a relatively few paid employees *vis a vis* the unpaid leaders that operate in fragmented multiple locales, such as what I cover in this chapter. How does the superstructure maintain coherence?

Institutional superstructure and grassroots affiliates

On first glance, the IAF seems to be a less hierarchical organization than most nonprofits with its thin national structure, divided into two geographic parts, Metro and West/Southwest, its regional and statewide senior organizer supervisors, and the Interfaith Education Fund (IEF) whose staff members raise money to organize large trainings and seminars and generate funds for these distant multi-day events. IAF affiliate fees to the IEF cover travel, food, and accommodations for these trainings.

To support this superstructure, the Texas IAF, the Interfaith Education Fund (IEF), and the Network of Texas Organizations (NTO) require annual dues, sometimes called "technical assistance" in budgets, the criteria for which are not clear. These mandatory fees, plus the expenses of running an office and meeting payroll, become potentially burdensome to the newer local IAF affiliates or those organizing in impoverished city locales in which IAF affiliates work (recall the table in Chapter 2 showing approximately half the average county incomes in borderland cities compared to mainstream counties). After twenty years of leadership, to me, the superstructure hierarchy seems opaque, without a clear board or decision-making structure. No board members' names can be found on the national IAF website either.[31]

Although relatively flat as an organizational hierarchy, compared to hierarchically steep organizations like the military or universities, the IAF exhibits some hierarchy like most formally organized NGOs but not informal social movements with their episodic marches and short lives. With an eye on this hardly visible hierarchy, along with the roles and responsibilities of people at its different levels, we can better understand the relationship between top and bottom, or cues from centrist directions and their symbiotic connections with and reactions from the grassroots.

Local IAF affiliates show an uncanny similarity in the issues and strategies they pursue across the state. How does that resemblance occur, despite the institutional concept of "House Meeting," the grassroots small-group bubble-up format of IAF process? Does this similarity imply that a superstructure of senior organizers, supervisors, and trainers imposes their views? If so, how, why and with what response? In local contexts, leaders and organizers might assess unique opportunities or challenges that move them to pass on the common IAF issues, strategies, and goals, such as proposed ordinances on payday lending, health care access, higher school expectations, infrastructure improvement, immigrants' rights, the ACA's Medicaid expansion opportunity, and campaigns to send thousands of postcards on DACA and immigration reform to congressional representatives.

While eerie commonalities exist, some IAF affiliates do not duplicate the common issues from "above" used elsewhere in the state. They tend to be the stronger organizations with an ability to exercise local strategic power *vis a vis* the state and IAF region. Recall from Chapter 3 the pioneering rather than replicative strategies in Dallas Area Interfaith (DAI) and its relational work with police departments and city staff on housing inspection codes. Another example comes from The Metropolitan Organization (TMO) in Houston with its ongoing continuous hurricane-cleanup cycles but path-breaking work to reform gun laws that people on both sides of a centrist safety perspective could live with. In the Box 5.1, I share a few words on Texas and guns.

Box 5.1 A Few Words on Texas and Guns

In recent years, the Texas Legislature approved gun laws that leaned away from centrist balance: open- and concealed-carry privileges to licensed owners in public settings, even on university campuses. Alas, the existence of too many guns and too much hot anger generates fatalities behind closed doors. In 2016, men killed 146 women intimate partners and 24 other family members and friends in those incidents, with 68 percent of perpetrators using a firearm.[32] Few IAF affiliates deal with family violence except as it interfaces with a public safety agenda: professional, speedy, and responsive police work, as Dallas Area Interfaith leaders voiced. Common-sense gun regulation requires challenging strategies in a state like Texas with its liberal gun laws, despite the mass shootings at Santa Fe High School (2018), at the Sutherland Springs Central Baptist Church massacre (2017), and the killing of five police offices in Dallas (2016). As I was finishing the manuscript, a shooter drove from Dallas to El Paso to murder 22 "Hispanics" on August 3, 2019, according to his manifesto on line. And three weeks later, a shooter in Odessa killed 7 people in the Midland-Odessa area. (See my Letter to Texans at the end of the book.) The Houston IAF affiliate, TMO, displayed public courage to put common-sense gun control on its agenda, with the consensus of its thirty-some member institutions and the scores of thousands therein. After the El Paso massacre, the Texas IAF network developed a strategy to take 100,000 signed postcards about reasonable gun reform bills from leaders in all the IAF Affiliates to Senator John Cornyn in his Washington, D.C. office because he did not respond to repeated requests for a meeting in Texas.

Despite the pioneering efforts in the strong IAF affiliates, we should ask whether the more common similarity suggests a kind of state centralism and if so, analyze the reasons behind it. Here an institutionalist perspective moves us to analyze the strategies through which the top affects grassroots processes that create similarity across affiliates.

One obvious reason for issue similarity across IAF affiliates is Texas political culture itself and its historical emphasis on limited government, the neglect of formerly politically marginalized communities (witness Chapter 2), and the inequalities thereby generated. Local IAF affiliates operate in a one-party state with a philosophy of limited government, which generates low-income people's common experiences: anti-union and business-friendly practices, complete with polluting industries no matter the health consequences. So perhaps the state itself encourages common reactions rather than IAF superstructure centralism.

A second explanation for similarity involves IAF institutional governance and specifically the careful selection, training, and rotation practices that reinforce discipline and control. Here I focus on several processes: extremely careful recruitment, probation, and initial training (as covered earlier in this chapter); ongoing socialization of organizers through mentoring, constant contact, and training; and the rotation of organizers.

At the superstructure levels, senior organizers keep statewide efforts coherent and allow statewide leverage to achieve statewide wins. This was especially effective for dramatic and pioneering gains during the 1980s and 1990s with a more competitive democratic era (see Chapter 2): financial support for infrastructure in *colonias* (water and sewer services), Alliance Schools, and high-quality workforce training centers. In the twenty-first century, IAF affiliate organizers and leaders continue to interact and meet over these continuing issues on their agenda to protect previous gains, though less IAF statewide attention is paid to some of the most dangerous threats to democracy, such as undermining "local control," in which the state undermines local ordinances through "pre-emption,"[33] and pay-to-play politics which aggravate the power of money far more than during IAF's younger stages. Is the centralism still effective? Does it address the twenty-first century's procedural threats to local control amid one-party domination? Let us look at the factors that keep paid organizers coherent and committed to the statewide agenda in long-practiced traditions of the near-half-century old IAF.

Organizer rotation

Earlier in the chapter, we discussed the highly selective recruitment process for organizers and their intensive training before assignment. Even volunteer leaders, mentored by organizers and periodically participating in statewide meetings and regional trainings, learn and adhere to IAF culture.

In yet another strategy to support centralism and consistency across the state, senior organizers rotate local organizers to different locales, either because the organizer sought a change of place (perhaps unable to raise enough money), or senior organizer-supervisors in the superstructure deemed a greater need elsewhere. Leaders, of course, remain grounded in their contexts and institutions. Like many arranged marriages, assignment from above can evolve into mutual respect (or not).

Leaders have little voice in choosing organizers before they arrive, unlike the more democratic process in some Protestant denominations and their "calls" to new pastors (see Chapter 4 on church governance contrasts). Rather, the state- and region-wide senior organizer-supervisors assign organizers based on a discerned match with the context. Once assigned, leaders can ratify choices at a subsequent local delegate assembly. Perhaps this is not unlike the Catholic Bishops who assign and rotate priests depending on discerned matches. The prevalence of Catholic theology students, sisters, and clergy organizers in the earlier Texas IAF perhaps established this organizational culture. In several IAF cities, leaders found out the organizer a few hours before arrival. With good will and respect for the IAF, local volunteer leaders give the superstructure the benefit of any doubt they might have. On relatively rare occasions, organizer-leader relations do not work out, but it could take some time before changes get made.

As several leaders said about organizers who ranged in effectiveness over the years, "Organizers make all the difference."[34] Some organizers bring greater expertise and experience than others in building the IAF affiliate with more member institutions and fundraising committees. Some exude relational personalities, others may be stiff or tough, even with the new volunteer leaders they identify, then mentor and/or meet with regularly. I have worked with eight organizers over twenty years. The rotation of organizers is similar to strategies used in some government agencies, like the State Department, which shifts Foreign Service Officers periodically to build loyalty to the organization rather than to the place and its people.

Distant seminars

Earlier in this chapter, we covered the careful organizer recruitment process, which supports centralism and consistency across affiliates. Some love the rigor and firm model, open to learning yet willing to subject themselves to a pre-existing paradigm. Some potential organizers sense the expectation of toughness and workaholic discipline in pre-official training and tryout experiences. One interviewee chose to exit before investing time and talent in what he called a "semi-hostile, cult-of-personality" setting. He believed the organizational training neither valued critical thinking about the IAF paradigm nor practiced the "relationality" that is preached in IAF lingo.[35] Others leave after a few years of organizing, but with their new skills, join other organizations which provide them with more autonomous leadership experiences. No data are available on the number of potential organizers lost in reaction to this atmosphere or on the turnover among organizers. I, for one, would never become an organizer. Despite the many rules in state higher education (see Chapter 8), the official tag "organizer" would likely curtail my freedom to join other organizations focused on issues the IAF does not address.

For those organizers who stay, there is continuous intensive socialization, constant training, and periodic seminars in which formal and informal cues signal preferred organizer behavior. However, once someone becomes a veteran organizer, they no doubt have attained the capacity to challenge and/or negotiate with the top or respond to local leaders. Let's look at some of the cues in a 2018 training found in Box 5.2 for the extent to which they reflect the Blueprint discipline or Learning Process approaches.

Box 5.2 Drama and Continuity in the IAF Training Format

Consider this seminar, resembling others I've observed over twenty years, from July 2018. Several times each year, the IAF offers multi-day learning opportunities to organizers and leaders consisting of organizing seminars on IAF strategies, insightful articles, or book lectures from their authors. Founder Ernesto Cortés Jr. is well read and acquainted with prominent writers. I have attended two trainings and four seminars over the twenty years with 60 to 200 in attendance and exciting cross-fertilization of ideas and exchanges over meals and discussion.

In a recent 2018 statewide seminar, author Michael Lind sat up front with Cortés, as is common in other seminars. Lind presented his[36] book with occasional questions and interruptions from the colleague alongside him. Cortés rarely started a comment or question with the microphone on, upon which audience members called out, "Ernie, the mic!" After the incisive question(s) and exchange, and Lind's conclusion, the floor then opened for discussion for a short time, always with the eyes and ears of the senior organizers. The next part of the training format consisted of small groups (mostly leaders, with an organizer-facilitator) who presented the chapter creatively (even in dramatic form) and raised questions for the author.

Occasionally, a leader or organizer presented in a less-than-confident voice and style, so Cortés engaged in Socratic Dialogue. On public display, participants watch and wonder: Can she respond with the assertive, confidence, and toughness necessary for IAF work? When this public drama involves a male-to-female confrontation, it creates a jarring reminder of long-time unequal gender dynamics.

The entire 2018 training process was enlightening, though my major take-away from the seminar was the similarity in format, separated over two decades. As a forty-year veteran of teaching, most of my colleagues changed their syllabi and pedagogy periodically, a Learning Process approach, moving away from near-total lecturing from the front of the room, as I once did as a rookie professor. The constancy in statewide IAF seminars has been surprising. Should the Blueprint approach continue or change? Perhaps on first exposure, the material is interesting and absorbed, but after repetitious experiences, some may find the approach pedantic.

In a 2019 statewide strategy meeting I attended, the atmosphere exhibited more exchange and collaboration. However, Cortés continued to be the center of a day-long training, giving an insightful keynote address on the economy and serving as the key respondent to education and health experts.

Organizers: Multi-tasking and high expectations

Successful organizers, having undergone rigorous training, have many responsibilities: the cultivation of new leaders, continuous coordination with them, fundraising, and the ongoing maintenance and growth of the IAF affiliation coalition, that is, of more member institutions that pay

Ernesto Cortés, Jr.: Keynote speaker at February 2019 statewide IAF strategy conference. Photograph Kathleen Staudt.

their dues. Without the paid organizer, an IAF affiliate would quickly dissipate, as volunteer leaders recognize in their willingness to work in a powerful organization with statewide reach, name recognition, and a track record of accomplishments. Nonprofit organizations need paid staff to pursue their missions—along with staff paid well enough to stay in an organization. However, some fundraising responsibilities fall on the local people—no problem in big cities with growing economies, but borderlands communities lack such growth or the corporate headquarters with their discretionary resources. In these sites of "global competitive-ness," as city and business boosters frequently characterize the places, corporate headquarters operate at a distance, with operations designed to extract low-cost assembly-line labor and cheap truck transportation from northern Mexico factories.

Indeed, those businesses that invest in IAF affiliates may be working at cross-purposes with social justice on some issues and in alignment on others. An IAF principle permits flexibility in these matters: "no permanent friends, no permanent enemies." Can weaker IAF affiliates take on the city's developers and growth machines? I sometimes wonder if they would, given the omnipresent need to generate revenue and maintain relationships.[37]

While the IAF organizer's challenge is tough, they are well paid, with salaries dependent on member institutions that pay their annual dues and on leaders who work in committees to raise funds from grants and local "investors," such as business leaders and bankers, in a deliberate use of market-based rather than "donor" charitable language. Organizers cannot do their work without these resources, a self-sufficiency rule to compel local accountability. Some IAF affiliates resort to Ad Books, which provide civic information coupled with full, half, and quarter-page ads that local businesses, hospitals, and clinics pay for.[38] In the weaker IAF affiliates, particularly in impoverished or new city sites, it can be a challenge to collect member institutions' dues, yet dues in the form of "technical assistance" to the superstructure must be paid, despite the vagaries of income by affiliate and in the county average income base. An affiliate would not survive long if the bulk of member institutions were in "arrears." The Iron Rule of Self-Sufficiency prevails in IAF affiliates' budgets, but we must ask: self-sufficiency for whom? Is the superstructure self-sufficient without local affiliate dues? While the Iron Rule principle is still evoked, it has taken multiple directions—some of them in contradictory ways.

IAF differs from other nonprofits, even social justice organizations, in the ways affiliates are supposed to own their organizations. Money raised for local affiliates tends to be local, not out of state, except for foundation funding and the Catholic Campaign for Human Development. With more diverse funding, found in the larger cities, IAF affiliates can guard against capture by the funder's agenda or what in nonprofit management is called "mission drift,"[39] yet every funder or foundation has its own principles such as the CCHD on matters of pre-natal life, discussed in Chapter 2. Local control remains the ideal. In the most recent 2019 Border Interfaith budgets to which steering committee members like myself have been privy, approximately a third of funds come from the CCHD, perhaps worrisome but not the sort of dependency noted in earlier studies.

IAF affiliates expect their member institutions to contribute 1–2 percent of net revenue as dues, but pass on at least ten times that percentage from the total budget to the superstructure. Recall that the IAF's "iron rule of self-sufficiency" means strict avoidance of dependency on government. Occasionally, individuals become "friends of" an IAF affiliate, but no individual membership dues exist. Yet some churches have difficulty meeting the annual IAF affiliate dues expectation, as do the secular member institutions such as school-based parent or neighborhood organizations.

As widely known in the nonprofit sector generally, nonprofit organizations face perennial revenue crises. And some legally registered "non-profits" dominate revenue streams. In the Texas A&M University-derived data from Chapter 2's Table 2.1 on nonprofit density in Texas and its cities, hospitals represent just 1 percent of all the 100,000-plus statewide nonprofits, but take in 42 percent of all nonprofit revenue. Figures like this give new meaning to cynics of the nonprofit sector and the labels that profitable hospitals claim.

A self-sustained IAF organization is as complex as any nonprofit organization, except that IAF accepts no money from government as noted above. If organizers cannot generate self-supporting revenue for the affiliate, the organization cannot survive. Remember the chilling, joke-like comment on firing noted earlier from an interview with a senior organizer: "organizers are not fired; they fire themselves if they can't raise enough money to sustain the organization."[40]

Grant funding comes from various sources, such as the Catholic Campaign for Human Development, foundations, Ad Books, and local businesses. Most foundation funding requires recipients to have the 501c3 tax-exempt designation that IAF affiliates secured and diligently follow rules for: nonpartisan with no political endorsements of candidates. IAF's own disciplined and trained leaders learn to follow 501c3 rules, but coalition partners, such as unions and professional teacher associations, might make public remarks that align themselves to candidates and parties, as I heard at a City Council meeting from a Lift-Up Alliance union partner. IAF affiliates fiercely avoid such alignments or entanglements, making collaborations difficult and occasionally problematic (see Chapter 7).

The IAF rule, "no permanent friends, no permanent enemies," reinforces the no-endorsement principle. As such, IAF affiliates avoid capture or co-optation by a party or representative. Besides, the IAF affiliates work to acquire "relational power" with whomever is elected to office in whichever political party. The beauty of the strong statewide power that existed in early years is IAF affiliates' ability to hold representatives of particular districts—whatever their party affiliation—accountable to the people who live within those districts. IAF leaders' relationships statewide have been crucial for forging bipartisan compromises statewide, including startling achievements in the 1980s and 1990s in a more politically competitive state regime. IAF's ability to continue those achievements under one-party governance depends on Texans' willingness to elect state representatives (150 in the House, 31 in Senate) who work relationally with all their constituents—not only those on the extremist fringe such as Tea Party activists who win primary elections and shift the party toward the right—and who work with colleagues in bipartisan ways in the legislature itself.

Organizers, alone, cannot do IAF work. They work to build a broad leader base in "power before program" principles. Readers who seek an outcome timeline might not understand the time it takes to build the power base of leaders and member institutions before even embarking on a policy agenda or re-building that base. Policy analysts and academics with local knowledge can list a host of evidence-based problems, based on previous, unacted-upon academic studies, census data, and so on. While a program could emerge from those studies, as happens in some think-tanks and nonprofits, reform usually requires the mobilization of constituency bases.

Organizers depend on volunteer leaders working in cross-member-institutional committees and on teams to strategize and act to win goals for their own agendas, which emerge in small-group "House Meetings" in member institutions and in civic academies. In order to formulate winnable goals, practical research may be necessary in what IAF senior organizers and trainers call the "cycle of organizing" in their workshops—research, action, and evaluation—but not the kind of research as traditionally defined in academia. Rather, organizers and leaders determine the scope of problems, the flaws in existing policies, what workable solutions could correct those flaws, and who makes decisions, how, and with what sorts of pressures that permit leverage.

Concluding reflections

As we see, the pathways into leading and organizing are diverse. A good organizer goes to the people where they are. She listens to them. She works with them to develop goals that are possible, not impossible.

He communicates; he meets constantly with people face to face, but he also answers emails and responds to phone calls. He constantly scans the environment, people, media, and readings for opportunities; in that way she is an organizational entrepreneur. However, the IAF's historical institutional culture has been based so much on oral and face-to-face work that opportunities may be missed without taking time for website, email, and social media development for better communication.

As we have seen in this chapter, the interaction between the top and grassroots, center and peripheries, and/or superstructure and base raises challenges in two-way democratic accountability. The opaque superstructure uses institutional tools and procedures to maintain coherence among employee-organizers' local work with volunteer leaders around similar strategies across the state. These tools consist of intensive recruitment, rotation, and extensive mentoring to include continuous training. Such coherence served the Texas IAF well during the heyday of 1980s and 1990s achievements statewide, as discussed in Chapters 1 and 2. However, the twenty-first century symbiosis does not guarantee effective use of time and talents over solutions in an organization that once counted many state policy achievements like Alliance Schools, *colonias* infrastructure, and workforce training before the turn of the century but work hard after the transition to one-party, extreme pay-to-play state government. However, IAF's local policy achievements, as Chapter 3 on Dallas analyzed, show remarkable regional power, given a more open and nonpartisan atmosphere, until such time as a more balanced group of representatives is elected at state levels.

The IAF manages to maintain a large group of highly talented organizers and leaders across the state. Nevertheless, local fundraising, a chronic problem in most nonprofit organizations, is aggravated in impoverished areas with the salaries paid to the organizer and the dues paid to the statewide structure with what may be perceived as an imposition of the IAF Blueprint format, guidance, and continuous training.

This chapter allowed us to differentiate between leaders and organizers in their reporting relationships. Volunteer leaders, identified and mentored by paid organizers, emerge from member institutions in the local base. Organizers work for both the leaders and the IAF superstructure, the center or top-level senior organizers who select, train, re-train, and assign organizers in rotation. We have seen occasional differences but many similarities in agendas—emergent from the grassroots base or from the superstructure—a superstructure that extracts value from the labors of those at the base in the form of technical assistance dues to the IAF, IEF, and NTO. A social justice organization dedicated to democracy and accountability ought to provide greater transparency within the hierarchy so that leaders know, understand, and exercise voice in decision-making and dues-assigning processes. Besides local-state transparency, the national IAF website contains no information on its Board of Directors, although the names can be found in Guidestar's IRS 990 forms. Good practice in nonprofit work requires open and transparent governance.

The IAF training model has been a type of Blueprint, changing ever so slowly, but its occupants have gradually begun to diversify with younger and more gender-balanced organizers. However, the grueling selection and training process may deter the energy, expertise, and diverse ways of networking that Alinsky once seemed to prize. Talent is lost when organizers and leaders leave. After departure, these skilled social justice leaders could migrate toward other NGOs that welcome diverse talents among younger people and address comprehensive concerns, including women and gender issues, such as CTWO (Center for Third World Organizing) in "communities of color," PICO National Network now named Faith in Action, and the Texas-based Deeds Not Words, with chapters in five Texas regions. Nevertheless, none has the long-term track record of the IAF with its strong disciplined model.

How will IAF's organizational culture adapt to the twenty-first century, alternative models, and partnerships? In Section III, the three next chapters explore IAF's connections with schools, higher education, and collaborations with other social justice organizations.

Notes

1. Interview with Claudia Santamaria, July 23, 2018, Austin. Kathleen Davis was an organizer in multiple Texas IAF locations and then went on to work in the affiliated Interfaith Education Fund, Austin.

2. Interview with Doug Greco, Central Texas/Austin Interfaith Senior Organizer, July 23 and 24, 2018, Austin.

3. Rep. Gina Hinojosa, http://www.ginaforaustin.com/about, Accessed September 17, 2018. I am not aware that any other current state representative or senator journeyed through IAF affiliates, but many have attended Accountability Sessions and met in follow-up meetings after they won office.

4. This study does not cover leaders who left IAF affiliates, no doubt a study that would be difficult to do. However, I have talked to leaders who left EPISO and Border Interfaith (who wish to remain anonymous), who departed for reasons relating to workload or concern with the organizer's sometimes-abrasive style with people. Obviously, all organizers have different personalities and orientations to their job. In the course of doing this study, I encountered some who were uncommunicative via email or untimely communicators (compared to academia, certainly). Over my twenty years of participation, I have interacted with many leaders who left, probably more than who came in (a net loss).

5. The National Assessment Educational Progress (NAEP) does voluntary testing nationwide and reports findings at the basic, advanced, and proficient levels, called the Civics Report Card. NAEP defines civics beyond knowledge alone to include experience, practical skills, and motivation to become involved in public affairs. See Chapters 2 and 6.

6. Benjamin Márquez, "Mexican-American Political Organizations and Philanthropy: Bankrolling a Social Movement," *Social Science Review* 77, no. 3 (September 2003): 329–46.

7. In the local monthly Border Interfaith Steering Committee meetings, the Treasurer duly distributes the budgets and reports on income and expenditures. Over multiple years in many meetings, I have raised questions about the fees structure for what continues to be a fledgling organization to which not all member institutions can afford their own dues. No responses came, but only in the last year, I learned that approximately 20 percent of gross income is assessed, so for example, $20,000 total would be paid IF the budget is $100,000. However, some years are lean years, with organizations dipping into reserves or loans, yet the $20,000 does not change, so the cut may become 30 percent or more of income. The criteria behind fees remind me of debates about tax policies: a flat tax (i.e. the same percentage for all) or a progressive tax in which those with greater resources pay a larger percent and those with less pay a smaller percent. Deborah Stone's *Policy Paradox* (see her work analyzed in the last chapter) contains a chapter on the multiple meanings of "equity." If the IAF superstructure sought to develop a more equitable dues-paying structure, her analysis could be useful. A redistributive approach is also possible. Witness the historic "Robin Hood" education funding that took from Texas property-rich districts and redistributed to property-poor districts, which evolved into the "recapture" system whereby property-rich districts pay into the Texas Education Agency for redistribution to property-poor districts amid the declining

proportional state contributions to local school districts. In the 2019 legislative session, which reflected more bipartisan cooperation than previous sessions given Democratic Party gains in the 2018 House elections and a new Speaker of the House, members achieved multi-billion-dollar gains for education thereby restoring some of the wrenching cuts in previous sessions (see Chapter 7).

8. UTSA Special Collections, John Peace Library, "A Guide to the C.O.P.S./Metro Alliance, 1954–2009," MS 346, pictures of the 10th Annual Convention, November 20, 1983, Box 6.

9. Note that this sociological definition is different from the Vatican's, Islamic, and Gulf States' objection to gender terms, as voiced in the U.N. conferences for women, especially in 1995 and thereafter. In *Forming Consciences for Faithful Citizenship*, the U.S. Conference of Catholic Bishops rejects the "ideology of 'gender' that dismisses sexual differences and the complementarity of the sexes" (USCCB, 2015: p. 30). I doubt that most Catholic reasoning would reject racial social constructions that reinforce difference among people based on shades and skin colors.

10. One of the first to call attention to these differences was Carol Gilligan, *In a Different Voice* (Cambridge: Harvard University Press, 1982) critiquing Lawrence Kohlberg's moral development scale based on samples of only boys and men.

11. Susan Stall and Randy Stoecker, "Community Organizing or Organizing Community? Gender and the Crafts of Empowerment," *Gender and Society* 12, no. 6 (1998):729–756; Terry Mizrahi and Jessica Greenwalt, "Gender Differences and Intersectionality in Community Organizing," *Journal of Community Practice* 25, no. 3–4, pp. 432–63. Also see Sonia García, Valerie Martínez, Irasema Coronado, Sharon Navarro, and Patricia Jamarillo, *Políticas: Latina Public Officials in Texas* (Austin: University of Texas Press, 2008). In one of the few books on Latino/a/x politics, Mary Pardo discusses the women's involvement in IAF affiliates in Los Angeles, pp. 26–31: See *Mexican American Women Activists: Identity and Resistance in two Los Angeles Communities* (Philadelphia: Temple University Press, 1998). Throughout the book, she richly describes women's effective and complex networking to achieve their goals.

12. Ralph Armbruster-Sandoval, "Latino Political Agency in Los Angeles Past and Present," in Sharon Navarro and Rodolfo Rosales, co-editors, *The Roots of Latino Urban Agency* (Denton: University of North Texas Press, 2013), 163. He draws also on Carol Hardy Fanta,

Latino Politics, Latina Politics (Philadelphia: Temple University Press, 1993).

13. Jeffrey Stout, *Blessed Are the Organized: Grassroots Democracy in America* (Princeton: Princeton University Press, 2010), 14.

14. Interview with Lubbock Organizer Emilee Bounds, June 2018, to whom I refer in other parts of the chapter.

15. I conducted a formal interview with Alicia Franco, but have talked and worked with her more times than I can count over the years.

16. Saul Alinsky, *Rules for Radicals: A Pragmatic Primer for Realistic Radicals* (New York: Vintage, 1971), 72–80.

17. See the IAF national website, accessed Aug. 1, 2018: http://industrialareasfoundation.org/content/become-organizer

18. Interview with Rev. Davis Price and Janet Price on WTOS's history, June 21, 2018.

19. Texas Appleseed, accessed July 1, 2018. https://www.texas appleseed.org/i-heart-justice-2017-fair-financial-services

20. In San Antonio, COPS paid member institutions include three orders of sisters in San Antonio. However, the average age of nuns in the US now is in the 70s, another example of declining religious trends.

21. The newer alternative social justice organization, PICO National Network (now Faith in Action), which adopted much of IAF's model, posted a two-part friendly video to recruit organizers on its website, with one woman featured holding a young child. See http://www.organizing careers.org/videos?id=0001 Accessed July 1, 2018.

22. This is based on my experience with different El Paso organizers and in this research.

23. I subscribe to various social justice organization listservs and pay minimal dues to several others in order to read their public communication.

24. Stout 2008, p. 101.

25. This is the same Dr. Barry Lachman from Chapter 3.

26. Interview with Leon Williams, June 21, 2018.

27. See this on You Tube: https://www.youtube.com/watch?v=M2 TgqL0kkFU&feature=youtu.be published August 9, 2018 and accessed September 17, 2018.

28. Interview with Graciela Quinteros, June 21, 2018.

29. Senior Organizer Sr. Maribeth Larkin is cited in Edward Chambers, *Roots for Radicals: Organizing for Power, Action, and Justice* (New York: Continuum Press, 2003), 26.

30. I led the Center for Civic Engagement from 1998-2008; Azuri González has ably directed the CCE since then. https://www.utep.edu/cce/ It was renamed the Center for Community Engagement in 2019.

31. I was able to find board names from the 2016 IRS 990 tax form on the Guidestar website which includes forms, budgets, and board members for all organizations that generate more than $50,000 in revenue.

32. Texas Council on Family Violence, www.tcfv.org. Accessed multiple times over a decade, but of late Sept. 1, 2018.

33. Daniel Vock, "The End of Local Laws? War on Cities Intensifies," *Governing*, April 5, 2017. http://www.governing.com/topics/politics/gov-texas-abbott-preemption.html accessed 11/14/18.

34. If an organizer does not work out well in the context, several leaders should direct questions to him perhaps in one-on-ones. I know of a case where this was tried thrice without response, but ultimately there is no procedure to contact the organizer's supervisor about the issue outside of evoking something equivalent to a "vote of no confidence" (a crisis procedure) in steering meetings. Instead, leaders may simply wait for the rotation.

35. Interview with Dr. Aaron Waggoner, ex-Border Interfaith leader, September 25, 2018.

36. Mark Warren's book *Dry Bones Rattling* names experts invited to speak, the overwhelming numbers of which are men. See Note 13, Chapter 8.

37. Benjamin Márquez, in "Mexican-American Political Organizations and Philanthropy: Bankrolling a Social Movement," *Social Service Review* 77, no. 3 (2003): 329–346, using IRS 990 forms, analyzes dependency on external support in the forms of gifts and grants during the 1990s, rather than from member institutions' dues, in several organizations including the Texas IAF grassroots organizations. He analyzes income streams rather than expenditures from the grassroots to superstructure, as I do here primarily.

38. UTSA's archives, op cit., provide copies of 8.5 × 5.5 COPS Ad Books from the 1977–79, and 1980–89, and 1990–98 in Box 2 of the 145-box collection. I recall EPISO's Ad Books of a similar size in the early twenty-first century. A former Valley Interfaith organizer showed me the multi-color 8.5 × 11 Ad Book which, I was told, generated $100,000. See the picture in Chapter 6.

39. Michael Worth, *Nonprofit Management: Principles and Practices*, 4th ed., Chapter 15 on grants and contracts (Thousand Oaks:

Sage Publications, 2017). I taught nonprofit management courses for many years.

40. Sister Maribeth Larkin, Interview June 15, 2018. This may sound harsh, but it frequently happens in nonprofit organizations and higher education programs: some staff must generate enough revenue to pay for their salaries and more.

Chapter 6
"Schools IN Communities:
Parents and Teachers"

Once again, let me share a story, this time from Montserrat Garibay, a former leader in Education Austin, a member institution of Austin Interfaith, and recently elected Vice President of the Texas AFL-CIO.

In my 2018 interview, Montserrat Garibay remembered her past public work in supporting early childhood education in testimony to the Austin ISD school board during tense 2009–10 budget-cutting times.[1] "The board wanted to cut the full-day program to a half-day. With both parents working full days, many would have had to pull their children from the program." She also acknowledged the importance of full-day programming for early-childhood teachers. Member institution Education Austin and the IAF affiliate Austin Interfaith packed the school board meeting with parents for a full audience of people with a stake in quality preparatory education for elementary school. "Moms found their voice!" Garibay said. A compromise was reached and full-day preschool continued. As always for any victory, this "win" has a back story.

Garibay credited the mentoring she received from Louis Malfaro, then head of Education Austin (1999–2010) and following that, President of the Texas American Federation of Teachers (AFT). As a teacher, Garibay had gone to him during one of the periodic immigration raids in Austin after she saw a frightened child hiding under a slide in the playground. "It broke my heart," she said. She told Malfaro that they need to provide information to the parents. He responded "YOU are Education Austin. Come and meet with an organizer." She started a pre-kindergarten task force; they recruited teachers, met with school board members, and began organizing with parents. Garibay understands relational power and the importance of one-on-one meetings to develop relationships of trust. Six or seven months later, she said, "parents spoke with one voice at the school board meeting. We stand with you." Garibay celebrated her own bilingual teacher during childhood: "she was our guardian angel." With a caring and skilled teacher, students were ready to learn in English-language classes the next year.

Montserrat Garibay acquired organizing skills in multiple community settings such as Education Austin in collaboration with Austin Interfaith.

Montserrat Garibay, Texas AFL-CIO Secretary-Treasurer, former Austin Interfaith Leader. Photograph Kathleen Staudt.

Her stories offered inspiring examples of parent-teacher alliances around students' quality education. Alas, in all too many schools, parents and teachers rarely interact except during report-card nights, around discipline problems, or in the preparation of snacks for birthday parties mostly in elementary schools.

The Education Austin merger of major teacher associations provides an unusual collaboration, the two biggest among them being affiliates of the AFT and of the National Education Association (NEA). In other cities, NEA and AFT sometimes compete with one another over recruiting members, especially when school boards seek to negotiate with one association. Moreover, local association presidents do not necessarily view their roles as empowering teachers as leaders, but rather as handling grievances and advocating for salary and benefit increases at school-board meetings or with superintendents and their cabinet officials.

Framing multiple layers of governance

I titled this chapter with the words Schools IN Communities based on a course I taught for several years and on the obvious point about schools as nestled in their neighborhoods, cities, and the state. Many public policies affect parents and students above and beyond educational policies. And no doubt many people find it confusing to understand the fragmented institutions that govern or influence educational policies, assessment, and pedagogy: teachers, parents, taxpayers, business, the statewide elected board, the legislature, and bureaucracy, and local districts with their locally elected school board trustees. Notice the potential but voiceless unorganized students on this list. Besides drawing from the University of Texas at San Antonio archives, secondary research books and reports, and both my interviews and observations, I offer case evidence from contemporary campus and district websites, along with field research on innovations in El Paso's large Ysleta School District, once home to the majority of thirteen Alliance Schools in El Paso at the elementary and middle school levels. I have shared countless conversations with EPISO primary leader, Dolores de Avila, once principal but now retired, of the model Alliance School, Ysleta Elementary School, featured in Dennis Shirley's volume of case studies.[2] Despite the innovative reforms I analyze in this chapter, much still remains to be accomplished if the talents of all students in the state are to be developed.

In this chapter, we cover topics related to the extraordinarily complex educational policy issue, the stakes in which so many people share for the Texas economy and democracy, and the twenty-first-century current state of former IAF-affiliated Alliance Schools model in three regions of the state: El Paso, the Rio Grande Valley (South Texas), and Austin. Recall that Chapter 3 touched on Roosevelt High School in Dallas via Brenda Stoll's interview. To better understand the massive historic shortcomings of Texas public education, see the appendix to this chapter where I summarize the pioneering results of the first federal effort to put Mexican American education on the national public agenda with its five-southwestern-state comparison, 1969–1974.

Teachers and parents have obvious stakes in educational policy and implementation, particularly the assessment of learning and performance. Members of teacher associations tend to be skeptical of standardized tests as the single way to measure performance, albeit a skepticism made difficult in a state that pioneered the so-called "Texas Miracle" in the 1990s and provided a model for the bipartisan Congressional passage of the No Child Left Behind Act. Teachers are skeptical of a "magic bullet" measure from a score calculated on one day from a test based mostly on multiple-choice/multiple-guess questions. Texan and national obsessions over testing peaked for about a decade until many Texas bipartisan non-government organizations (NGOs) pushed back, including against funding cuts. These NGOs included the Equity Center, representing half of Texas school districts, Texas Kids Can't Wait, listing almost forty Texas organizations on its website (none of them IAF affiliates or IEF), and Texans Advocating for Meaningful Student Assessment (TAMSA).[3]

Setting the stage for twenty-first century education amid fragmented governments

With constant reforms and new testing tweaks and standards, advocates and leaders in a wide variety of institutions—educational, political, and NGOs—tried and continue to try to change Texas educational policies. Some policies are hardly implemented with enough time to take hold before school district superintendents once again start searching for better jobs and pay.[4] Multiple governance institutions include the legislature and the partisan body of fifteen elected officials who meet quarterly in the State Board of Education (SBOE); policy implementation emanates from above, mainly by the Texas Education Agency (TEA, founded in 1949); and the local Independent School Districts (ISDs). Since 2007, the SBOE's Republican majority has implemented some controversial changes in curricular standards, some that became a laughingstock of the nation by comics like Jon Stewart and Steve Colbert, and more recently, the affirmation of Moses as an influence on the U.S. Founding Fathers.[5]

The locally elected school boards make key policy decisions about budgets and superintendents, with annual budgets amounting to a half-billion and more in the bigger districts. School budgets are the biggest-ticket items on residential property tax bills. When I attended school board meetings in El Paso, I always saw the two main teacher-association presidents who gave public testimonies. The presidents disseminate information to their members through Facebook, emails, and meetings in a discernable and readable form compared with the official minutes of the meeting which are posted on official ISD websites. I suspect that few people read the official minutes except for lawyers and business contractors.

When I taught upper-division political science classes on the students' menu for social studies certification, I required students to attend a school-board meeting and complete my three-page observation form. In class discussions thereafter, most students expressed surprise at the low public attendance that consisted of, besides themselves, the teacher association presidents, ISD administrators, and business contractors with financial stakes in the lucrative building and technology contracts. Students' bottom-line evaluations ranged from "boring" to "shocking" for the high-visibility incivility and factionalism that occasionally broke out.

For institutional facts and figures about educational policy and students in the state, in order to add civic education value to readers, see the Box 6.1 that follows.

Institutions and their accountability measures (or lack thereof in the past) affect the way school districts and campuses operate. In a book about Dallas in the 1970s, school officials had few institutional stakes in retaining and graduating students. Parents attended community meetings and at one of them, complained about the 300–500 students suspended because they did not pay a shop fee of $1.56. As one parent said at a public meeting: "Maybe $1.56 is just 'chicken feed' to you—but for some of us here, it's money to feed *children* not chickens."[12] No accountability measures existed back then for students' mastery of content or graduation. Rather, students were simply pushed out.

Elsewhere, as an Annenberg Foundation book and videos portray, past frustration and complaints—that is, hot anger in IAF terms—may lead nowhere. Long-term, persistent organizing and leadership development inculcate skill, relational and numeric power to provide follow-up.[13] The institutional incentive systems under which those Dallas principals worked in the past did not encourage high school completion; the prejudiced and vindictive among them expelled students for minor offenses.

Endless educational reforms

Texas public education underwent major overhauls in the 1980s, first motivated by the alarming reports from a commission headed by businessman Ross Perot who later ran as an Independent for U.S. president.

Box 6.1 Contemporary Public Education Statewide

In early 2019, Texas was home to 1,031 independent school districts (ISDs) with more than 5 million students enrolled, a majority of them Hispanic (state nomenclature). Most big cities enroll a majority Hispanic student body, or count Hispanics as the largest student group, such as Arlington, at 44 percent followed by 24 percent African American.[6] Districts have their own superintendents, who average three to five years on the job, and voters elect non-partisan school board trustees who make major policy and budgetary decisions. Big-city superintendents earn salaries equivalent to the U.S. president, around $400,000 annually plus benefits. School board trustees, unpaid despite the heavy workload in big districts, come from a variety of backgrounds. Some trustees attempt to use board experience as stepping stones to higher offices.

Over recent years, students of color[7] have become the majority of enrollees in public schools. Of the 5.4 million students in the Texas Education Agency (TEA) "Pocket Edition" for 2017–18, Hispanic students comprise 52 percent, African Americans, 13 percent, and economically disadvantaged, 59 percent of students, with an over-representation of the former groups in that latter category. The TEA classifies 19 percent of the students as English Language Learners, a rhetorical step up from the former deficit language, Limited English Proficient. The high school completion rate, recorded at nine of ten students finishing statewide, was once far lower. Total revenue for the schools amounted to $60.8 billion; half of it from local sources, 40 percent from the state, and 10 percent from the federal government. Total revenue per student was $11,392; most of it pays for staff salaries (typical in government), but the per-pupil figure offers a numeric benchmark against which to compare students in different districts and campuses. Although the rating systems and standards change every few years in decisions made behind closed bureaucratic doors, the TEA currently claims that 89 percent of campuses met standards with 4 percent "needing improvement" and the rest not reported. Each district and campus can be examined using this basic measure for comparisons.[8]

The TEA website is huge and difficult to navigate, but some district and campus websites include data on the content areas in which students met standards or not and the extent to which gaps closed between mostly ethnic/racial and income groups of students. For a peek at current school "report cards" and per-pupil spending, Texans who are curious can insert the school's name in a search link.[9]

School governance is managed partly through the State Board of Education, which meets quarterly with its fifteen unpaid representatives elected on partisan bases. On local school boards, unpaid trustees are elected on non-partisan bases. Many constituencies share stakes in quality public education that develops the talents of all students, not only wealthier students: from business to parents, labor, students, taxpayers, and educators. (In the next chapter, I cover a massive, multi-year effort to develop civic capacity for educators to collaborate with business over improved education in El Paso, including IAF leaders.) In various IAF affiliates around the state, parents, educators, and IAF organizers once worked to develop Alliance Schools, funded with annual multi-million-dollar investments that ended a decade ago, now replaced with incentives for a variety of public charter schools—some of them non-profit (in-district and out of district) and others generating profit and paying high superintendent salaries—with the rationale of choice, innovation, and competition.

In the twenty-first century, the Texas legislature shaped educational policy in various ways, from increasing content course requirements for high school, cutting state support for education in 2012 by over $5 billion, and raising the number of exams required for high school graduation to fifteen, later lowering this number. The Texas governor's office, in Republican hands since 2000, shares authority with both the state legislative House and Senate, with Republican majorities since 2002. The TEA is headed by a gubernatorial political appointee. In 2019, the state legislature finally increased state support for education with $6.5 billion of new funding.

With public pushback from teachers and parents, Republican and Democratic alike, legislators reduced the excessive number of tests students had to pass for high school graduation. In 2013, HB5 reduced the number of high school tests to graduate from fifteen to five in exchange for reducing what was called the 4 × 4 graduation

(Continued)

Box 6 .1 (Continued)

program that had required four years of English, math, science, and social studies, thus opening the door for more business, industry, and technical courses.[10] *Many Texans, still weary of school days devoted to test preparation and the tests themselves, seek to reduce the number of tests in middle and elementary schools, the level at which formally reported tests begin in Grade 3 and for which there is test prep in Grades 1 and 2.*

The business community remains wedded to standardized tests for accountability, despite parent and teacher concerns. In recent years, El Paso's IAF organizations pursued grassroots research listening sessions with hundreds of parents and teachers to discover that the number of testing days (pre-tests, diagnostics, mock tests, real tests, make-up tests, etc.) consumed 40–60 days of a 180-day school year, leading to widespread dissatisfaction among parents and teachers. They communicated findings to a governor-appointed commission on accountability in 2008 and to local school board candidates at accountability sessions.

The governor's statewide committee met in El Paso in their rotations around the state. When an IAF parent leader and teacher testified about her elementary school son, in special education and anxious about passing—being mistakenly given the regular test despite assurances that he would be given the special education test before testing day and thus failing—the state-appointee commissioners were chatting and laughing over their boxed lunches. To show the courage of the volunteer IAF leader, she stood up and loudly said to them in near tears "it may be funny to you, but it wasn't to us." The committee members quieted down, apologized, and started listening again.[11]

Dennis Shirley documented the ways that the statewide Texas IAF pushed for laws to improve the quality of education and teacher preparation.[14] Initially, this improvement relied on standardized tests, even for teachers. Now the IAF is but one of scores of effective statewide organizations and teachers' associations that seek better education and funding.

Lawsuits also provided grist and leverage for reform. In San Antonio's *Edgewood v. Kirby* lawsuit, which the Mexican American Legal Defense and Education Fund (MALDEF) filed in 1984, the ultimate judicial decision for the plaintiff incentivized legislators to tackle inequitable per-pupil funding based on sources largely from local property taxes. Residents in property-poor districts struggled to pay higher rates, but could not reach adequate per-pupil expenditures. Remember, Texas is one of seven states with no state income tax. Other states fund education through more progressive income taxes rather than regressive property and sales taxes. Obviously, property-poor districts could not fund education adequately without extremely high rates of collection per $100 valuation of property, the unit of measure in Texas. In a book about the *Edgewood v. Kirby* lawsuit, the narrative begins with the example of property-rich Richardson ISD, Texas, recruiting teachers with graduate degrees who filled libraries with the latest new books, while property-poor districts (like the semi-rural San Elizario ISD in El Paso County) attracted few teachers with graduate degrees; librarians combed garage sales on the weekend to stock campus libraries. Not surprisingly, most Richardson students went on to higher education, but only 15 percent of San Elizario students did at the time.[15]

After many lawsuits and a great deal of legislative tinkering, per-pupil spending became more equitable. However, in 2005, the legislature authorized local option to cap property tax rates unless local voters supported an increase via Tax Ratification Elections (TREs).

Besides funding problems, high-stakes standardized testing had taken a punitive approach to schools labeled failing based on students' test results. In 2002, with bipartisan support, The No Child Left Behind law reinforced high-stakes accountability systems that graded schools and students based on graduation rates and test scores of students categorized by ethnicity, language, and other factors. The gaps between groups should not exist if there is a focus on high expectations for all students. Hispanic students' scores differ from those of White/Anglo and other students of color except when controlled for household income levels. We in Texas and the U.S. frequently see standardized test-score gaps between ethnic/racial student groups, reinforcing public stereotypes, but gap analysis lacks the nuance of the often-muted household income sources for such gaps that regression analysis can provide, as Lizely Madrigal's dissertation revealed for Ysleta ISD in El Paso.[16] However, in the most recent iteration of educational reforms in Texas,[17] the numeric indicator for "closing the gaps" is computed into school ratings. Institutional indicators like these incentivize school administrators to address issues like these that affect their ratings.

Traditional school work with parents

Before I make a case for parent engagement beyond making cupcakes or volunteering to make photocopies to help teachers, I must describe the common and traditional practices whereby school staff interact with parents, tending toward top-down, individual, and peripheral ways. School campuses connect with parents at report-card events, grade and test results via the Internet, and individual meetings, more often than not, for disciplinary issues, evoking parental dread if they are called to the school. The Parent Teacher Association (PTA) campus and district organizations tend to be antiquated: dues, rules, lots of fundraising, and procedurally complex elections, although the Parent Teacher Organization (PTO) provides a more open structure, free of procedural complexities. See the testimony about PTAs in Box 6.2.

If districts pursue policies for parent involvement, they typically use a top-down model from the central district with federal pass-through funds, if available. In my graduate course on education leadership, I invited two ISD-office staff members to speak to my mostly school administrator students.

> **Box 6.2 Testimony from an Anonymous Affiliate Leader: Alliance Schools and Parent-Teacher Associations (PTAs), 2013–15**
>
> *"I worked with IAF Alliance Schools from 1999–2003 and observed how parent-teacher synergy empowered students' learning. None of those schools, most of them located in low-income neighborhoods, hosted PTA's. So I agreed to serve on the district-wide PTA board of directors in our largest school district in 2013. Board work required attendance at lengthy monthly board meetings and mass meetings of PTA officers and school principals. At times, it seemed like I was in a 1950s time warp, with priorities related to campus fundraising, complex campus PTA procedures, and attendance priorities, complete with annual awards for perfect attendance.*
>
> *I chaired the committee on Legislation, Safety, and Security—an unusual combination, to be sure, but one that could embrace important issues like civic engagement on state education reforms and district-wide policies to reduce bullying in schools. The district PTA president and her board allies seemed wary of actions deemed*

"political" rather than civic education, but our committee's state legislator panel was informative, even praised by the administration, as was a video and presentation from the district counseling supervisor on procedures to address bullying. As a PTA district board member, I was required to join a local PTA, which I did for a nearby campus in a lower middle-income neighborhood near my house.

One couldn't help but notice that campuses in higher-income areas have large and lively PTAs, with amazing fundraising capability to supplement teacher training, purchase playground equipment, and acquire extra computers in those chronic times of budget crises. Campuses with PTA presidents in higher-income areas benefitted from their seasoned parent leaders, confident in their ability to raise money and negotiate with campus administrators. Campuses in lower-income areas usually lacked PTAs for various reasons: not enough members who could pay dues and competition among leaders campaigning for campus PTA president. When the State of Texas issued new rules about when, which type, and where food could be sold after school—the major fundraising strategy in most schools—a crisis emerged.

I wondered if unique circumstances existed in our own city, or if such malaise and inequity existed elsewhere. So I attended the national PTA meetings held in Austin, Texas, that year, 2014, and was saddened with spotty substance in the program, usually focused on speeches from so-called expert consultants. Of course I had no deep immersion on PTA boards elsewhere, but the furious exchange of state PTA buttons in between sessions as the primary relational work was an indicator of the difference with the IAF model and Alliance Schools where parents' and teachers' own stories in house meetings fueled the campus-specific issues on which we worked.

Upon return, with a bunch of state PTA buttons, I still struggled to get the principal or PTA president from "my" PTA membership campus to respond even once to phone calls and personal visits with notes about my interest. My now-grown children learned on campuses with PTO's in which I was involved, the cheaper version of a PTA without the need to pay state and national dues. I longed for the kind of Alliance-School connectedness among parents, teachers, AND the principal for campus work that might inform and affect district policies."

The central office parental involvement staff demonstrated Spanish-speaking capability which is good, but switched verbal gears up an octave to talk (down) to us in patronizing joking mode. Let me paraphrase what they said: We offer workshops for parents, but our main goal is to get signatures as evidence of participation for federal grants. Although the parental specialists were open to ideas about workshop topics, they along with the US Department of Education owned the project, not the parents.

Of course, another opportunity for voice and accountability occurs in elections. Voters choose school-board trustees on either at-large bases in smaller districts or in geographic district-based elections, thanks again to MALDEF's litigation. Until spring local elections in Texas moved to November in 2018, voter turnout rates in some cities fell to single-digit percentages. Local media provide limited information about candidates before the election or school board decisions after the election, unless corruption scandals prevail in school administration (not unusual in Texas). At what point are electoral victories from minuscule turnouts even legitimate in an ethical sense? Should trustees wear a banner: elected with slightly more than half of single-digit voter turnout? Yet in the big districts, school board trustees help form and approve budgets of a half-billion dollars or more, and typically, the biggest line on local property tax statements goes to the school district, as noted earlier. Presumably, rational voters want accountability for effective schools and for their tax dollars.

Campus organization cultures matter in the overall climate about achievement expectations. In some neighborhoods with low-income and non-engaged parents, there is always a danger that second-rate education is provided. One used to hear comments from otherwise well-meaning teachers or administrators, to paraphrase: "after all look at this impoverished neighborhood. What can you expect from students raised here?" People who live in impoverished neighborhoods bear the burdens of policies that sustain low-wage jobs, inadequate health care, and infrastructure. Social justice organizations like the IAF may be able to address these more comprehensive issues.

IAF-affiliated alliance schools

Statewide, an IAF-initiated Alliance School network, formed in 1992 to change the campus cultures of so-called low-performing schools, secured resources from the Texas legislature for the Investment Capital Fund in 1995.[18] IAF organizers, according to then Southwest IAF regional director Ernesto Cortés Jr., "hold training sessions [known in El Paso as 'parent academies'] with parents and community leaders on everything from how to read a school budget and speak before the school board to how to negotiate with elected officials. They teach parents that accountability does not mean blaming educators and administrators, but taking responsibility for negotiating solutions in partnership with them."[19]

In Alliance Schools, over approximately fifteen years, parents and teachers worked together with principals in leadership teams to create broader accountability than standardized test scores, though tests remained the chief indicator of student and school performance. In Texas, once low-stakes accountability systems and tests with various acronyms (TABS, TAAS) transitioned into high-stakes accountability and new test acronyms (TAKS, now STAAR) when the Washington, D.C. decision-makers put No Child Left Behind into law.

Under conditions of both crisis and available additional resources, community organizations like IAF affiliates built alliances with schools over raising students' achievement levels and creating a college-going campus culture. The statewide Texas IAF worked to achieve financial support for Investment Capital Funds, which rose from initial funding of $2 million to $9 million to $14 million (in 1999) annually for competitive grants that averaged $40,000. Local grant-writing teams completed lengthy forms (twenty-one pages of instructions plus four appendices!) for TEA-awarded grants to districts, not to the IAF, which accepts no government money, for a total of 175 campuses. Like many government grants, evaluation evidence required numerical indicators of improvement, such as student test scores and increased parental participation compared to previous grant periods.[20] I had often wondered why the IAF and Alliance Schools wedded themselves to standardized tests to measure success, realizing finally in archival reading for this book that grant reports required such evidence, thus compromising IAF self-sufficiency rules but only indirectly. In archival reports I read from 1999–2001, large numbers of Alliance Schools could be found in several IAF territories: Valley Interfaith (sixteen, in four school districts), Austin (eighteen), and El Paso (thirteen in two school districts), the contemporary legacies about which can be found in the following section.

Borderlands alliance schools: El Paso and South Texas

While Alliance Schools could document improved test scores and increased parental engagement, ultimately their numbers diminished due to the growing state and district obsessions with standardized testing and periodic principal transfers to increase test scores. Consequently, teachers and principals had less time to work with parents, do community walks, and participate in other activities. During their heyday in El Paso, parent leaders pushed for new technology and innovative teaching and learning practices. School board trustees stepped up to remodel several old schools, supply students with computers, and support teachers' professional development. And unlike IAF faith-based member institutions with their stable numbers of congregants, when students graduated from schools, parent-leaders also "graduated," leaving no parent leadership. During the decade into the new millennium, after changes toward the one-party legislative process, funding finally evaporated.

How did Alliance Schools operate in different Texas contexts? What legacies did Alliance Schools leave? Dennis Shirley features successful case study models from Austin, Fort Worth, San Antonio, Houston, and El Paso's Ysleta Elementary School, with its principal, EPISO leader Dolores de Avila,[21] plus his in-depth analysis of three school cases in South Texas. Following case studies below, I highlight results from foundation-funded multi-year evaluations in Austin with quantitative data on students' test scores, but broader indicators showing mixed, though relatively successful results with systemic district-wide changes. Several schools and school districts institutionalized positive reforms, but none, I believe, with the elaborate parental engagement and thus source of new volunteer leaders from IAF Alliance Schools.

Like EPISO's birth in early 1980s El Paso, the IAF Affiliate called Valley Interfaith began in resistant and contentious times. Dennis Shirley analyzed three Alliance Schools in South Texas amid Valley Interfaith's comprehensive agenda for *colonias* infrastructure and a workforce training center.[23] Each school exhibited a unique model in the fragmented district turf: McAllen and the Pharr-San Juan-Alamo (PSJA) Independent School Districts, the latter's name making multi-town fragmentation evident. In the Alliance Schools that he studied in the late 1990s, the TEA classified more than 90 percent of students as "economically disadvantaged," eligible for subsidized school lunches, the state nomenclature for low income.

A new and better standardized testing system had been put in place in 1991 to replace previous iterations, called the TAAS, but all over the state, it took several years for teachers and students to prepare for and improve students' test-taking skills. No doubt English-Language Learners struggled more than others to pass these tests, but by 1997, Spanish-speaking

Box 6.3 Ysleta Middle School, an Alliance School

I had the opportunity to be a "mentor professor" at Ysleta Middle School, an Alliance School, for several years. It was an inspiring experience to work with friendly and caring teachers, the principal, students, and especially the parents. The middle school, located a few blocks from the border, enrolled approximately 450 students, almost all of them Mexican American and eligible for free school lunches, categorized by the Texas Education Agency as "Hispanic" and "economically disadvantaged."

*My first event at the school was the warmly welcoming nine-week report card assembly. Amazingly, the turnout was extremely large for a middle school: 150 mothers and fathers attended! I say amazing because my children attended middle and high school in other districts where parents lined up to collect the first report card, perhaps chatted a few minutes with a teacher seated behind a table, and then left. After Carla Cardoza, Assistant Director of UTEP's Center for Civic Engagement, and I said a few words about our own educational experiences, including as first in our families to go to college, small groups of teachers and parents met at round tables (like house meetings) in the cafeteria to discuss their hopes and dreams for their children. Parents, mostly with six to nine years of education (*primaria *and* secundaria *if they came from Mexico), had high hopes for their children. When teachers shared their educational backgrounds, many parents were surprised to learn that teachers often were first in the families to get a university degree. Common grounds existed for collaboration around student success.*

Many parents worried about whether their children would continue successful learning once entering the large Ysleta High School with its approximately 3,000 students. They discussed these worries in more house meetings at the school parent center and elsewhere. Parents, with the EPISO organizer, asked me to give a Parent Academy on what researchers discovered about success in high school through graduation and entry into college. I shared research findings about students who didn't pass courses and earn credits in ninth grade, sometimes making decisions to drop out of school as early as ninth or tenth grade. I emphasized the importance of students learning in

(Continued)

Box 6 .3 *(Continued)*

classes with high expectations: not just standardized test passage, but especially reading and writing for success in higher education.

Parents asked about practical suggestions I might have. Although I believe in high learning expectations for ALL students, rather than ability-tracked students, I know that the Advanced Placement (AP) courses prepare students for college, so I suggested that the middle school might offer more open-admission pre-AP classes. In the high school to which students would enroll (see next chapter), I had observed shocking differences between AP courses and regular courses: in relatively small AP courses, students read several books and did daily journal writing, while in much larger regular classes, in which the majority enrolls, students read a single book for the whole semester and watched an occasional film about a book.

Some time had passed before the EPISO Organizer asked me: Do you know what the parents did after the academies? I did not know. Parents went to the principal to ask for more pre-AP classes. She told them it would be hard to schedule more pre-AP classes, and besides, she did not have the budgetary resources. Well, organized parents, persistent and diplomatic in their relations with school officials, met several more times and eventually prevailed with more pre-AP classes as principals in the then-decentralized management model for the district had some room for budgetary maneuver. This may seem like a minor inexpensive gain, but the parental victory buoyed their sense of power, hope, and ability to increase success for students.

Fortunately, the entire district had been transforming itself toward preparing students for college, in part due to relationships among EPISO leaders, the superintendent, UTEP's El Paso Collaborative for Academic Excellence (see next chapter), and school board trustees. District programs supported students' pre-college preparation in many ways: the district subsidizes all high school students to take the SAT/ACT, required in most colleges for admission. The district also requires all graduates to apply to colleges and universities, write their three-page admission essays, and complete twenty hours of service-learning each year in high school. Every high school offers magnet schools within schools so that students focus in their coursework and preparation for higher education.[22] Programs like these help students make successful transitions to higher education.

Valley Interfaith Resource Guide. Staudt photograph, courtesy Dallas Area Interfaith archives.

elementary students could take the test in Spanish. The tests are largely multiple-choice/multiple-guess except for two grades that assess writing with five-paragraph essays. Readers should know that educators debate the effectiveness of high-stakes standardized testing, and Shirley himself noted ambivalence about that form of assessment over twelve pages of mixed results on the case-study schools from the mid-to-late 1990s test results appended to the book. In the twenty-first century of continuous reforms, evolving standards and new tests emerged known as the TAKS and the STAAR tests, derived from the TEKS.

School leaders faced daunting challenges regarding decisions about partnership with community organizations like Alliance Schools. Principals—gatekeepers who open or close doors for parental engagement with IAF affiliates—must get buy-in from teachers. Principals occupy the school's public face; they are subject to periodic reassignment and risk potential wrath from school superintendents and the unpaid elected school board trustees who make budgetary decisions. Student "mobility" rates, TEA nomenclature for transfer, as high as 25 percent, revealed significant turnover of students and parents who move in and out of particular schools. Despite these risks, the three schools described by Shirley opted for the Alliance model.[24]

The three school cases offer a study in contrasts, partly based on the grade levels. Elementary schools tended to offer a parent-friendly, single-classroom experience for students. At Palmer Elementary, staff and parent leaders created a two-way bilingual program, after-school programs, vigorous parental engagement to include teachers' home visits, and curriculum-based appreciation for home and cultural heritage. Middle schools represent challenging age- and grade-level issues as students and teachers transition to the secondary models of multiple classrooms and content-specialist teachers. At Alamo Middle, parents and teachers wanted to address different issues, including gangs and bullies through conflict mediation. At Alamo Middle, Shirley uncovered discord, including worries that voter registration opportunities made efforts too "political"—even though county voting officials use schools as voting precincts—or crossed the line separating church and state. In late 1999, teachers voted against renewing Alliance School funds, given their "additional workload, distraction from an academic focus, and uncertainty of results."[25] In both schools, test scores went up and down from year to year.

In the third school case, Sam Houston Elementary in semi-rural north McAllen, Shirley found the most comprehensive application of the Alliance School model, involving parents, teachers, and a community base of pre-existing House Meetings at St. Joseph the Worker Catholic Church. In this region, with many new immigrants, religion is of great significance for daily life as Shirley pointed out. Together, parents, teachers, and Valley Interfaith addressed pressing community issues that impinge on schools: an old building from 1920, then a move toward a new building with controversy about the merits and drawbacks of a more distant school; a workforce training program called VIDA (Valley Initiative for Development and Advancement, see Chapter 8) in partnership with a new community college in South Texas; better city garbage collection; and especially, a hands-on innovative curriculum that developed from students' interest in housing construction and from MicroSociety, a national model wherein children learn through experience: markets, currency, management, customer service, courts, and newspapers, among other tasks that deepened applied interdisciplinary learning. Although it adopted a risky strategy in hopes of improved test scores, based on active, innovative learning rather than teaching to the test, this school made steady improvements.

Let me fast forward to 2018: Sam Houston plus Carmen Anaya Elementary. I examined the current websites for the three schools, their districts, and charter school inroads into the Rio Grande Valley. Houston school continues a version of MicroSociety called Minitropolis and specifically named "Houstonville," as featured on the campus website. Houstonville "offers students a variety of real-world positions, from IBC Bank executives and tellers, city government, law enforcement, HEB, Walmart and Home Depot."[26] One might question whether such jobs promote college readiness. The parent "involvement" link goes to the McAllen ISD, which offers learning opportunities for parents from "trained professionals," evoking the traditional model discussed earlier. Each campus has its own Parent Training Specialist, suggesting the more typical top-down approach found in many parts of Texas. The McAllen ISD website contains no Spanish translation function, unlike the Pharr-San Juan-Alamo ISD, in a region where Spanish is the dominant language.

In contrast to the McAllen ISD site, I examined the PSJA ISD website and schools in 2018 on websites that contain a Spanish-language function.[27] The TEA Accountability System puts considerable amounts of data onto its websites and school websites, difficult to decipher for parents, teachers, taxpayers, and residents alike. However, in new formats each year with shorter "report-card-like" presentations, graphs show whether students have "met expectations" in pass rates for different content areas and in reduced gaps based on ethnicity. Some of the innovations promoted in Alliance Schools appear to have been internalized in school district policies, such as dual-language courses in which students learn content knowledge in both Spanish and English. We see the difficulty of sustaining reforms without the Alliance School imprimatur, funding, and parent engagement organizers.

Most startling on the PSJA ISD website, I found a school called Carmen Anaya Elementary. Anaya was a bold and dynamic IAF-affiliated Valley Interfaith leader during the time period of Shirley's research. You Tube links feature stories about her life, the school, and her granddaughter's pride in the family.[28] In no other district with Alliance Schools did I see a school named after an IAF-affiliate leader like this.

Despite the choices available among public schools in South Texas, charter school systems have made inroads into the area. Charter student enrollees generate formula funding from the state that could detract from public school budgets. The Texas Legislature and TEA also offer incentives for public schools to create in-district charters with greater freedom from regulation. IDEA, registered as a 501c3 nonprofit, is a charter school system whose enrollment has grown rapidly in South Texas. Since 2001, co-founder and CEO entrepreneur Tom Torkelson has grown the Rio Grande Valley charter schools from 150 students to 26,000 students at 39 schools. Torkelson's website claims to enroll 7,000–10,000 new students annually, from Pre-Kindergarten to Grade 12, though it does not offer mobility or drop-out rates. The IDEA website does not offer a Spanish translation link.[29]

This section on Alliance Schools in the borderlands shows some gains made at the individual campuses and in school district policies, not all of which could be attributed to the IAF model. However, the expansion of charter schools in the Rio Grande Valley necessarily draws students away from public schools and the formula-funding based on enrollment. The IDEA charter schools have begun to market themselves in El Paso, a large county that is home to nine school districts. Below we look at Austin, a wealthy mainstream school district.

Let us now turn to Austin's Alliance Schools. In 2009, the Annenberg Institute for School Reform at Brown University completed a six-year study titled *Organized Communities, Stronger Schools* focused on seven cases around the country, one of them in Austin, Texas. The report featured the IAF-facilitated Alliance Schools, comprising a quarter of the district's elementary schools and half of the district's high-poverty schools with up to 35 percent English Language Learner students.[30] The beauty of Annenberg's evidence-based evaluation is its comprehensive analysis of not only measureable gains, such as standardized test scores on campuses, in the schools' capacity to educate students, but also the Alliance School model's impacts on district policies, i.e. of systemic change with impacts beyond the Alliance School campuses themselves. Leaders, both staff and parent, along with Austin Interfaith organizers and a supportive superintendent, made these results possible. I summarize findings from the report below.

Austin is a bifurcated community, historically separated into the less-affluent east and more-affluent west by the Interstate-35, though more recent gentrification has begun to push eastside residents out of affordable housing in the city toward suburbs. The Annenberg researchers' map of elementary campuses amid this de facto economic segregation showed that the percentage of eastside students' scores meeting minimum expectations in the study's historic baseline data from 1995 TAAS tests (33 percent–38 percent) fell below half of scores from schools on the west side (72 percent–95 percent).[31] By the end of Annenberg's longitudinal evaluation in 2006, most high-intensity eastside Alliance Schools in Austin became comparable to westside schools.

After successes at Zavala Elementary School, where interviewee Leader Claudia Santamaria taught (see Chapter 5),[32] the network grew to almost twenty Alliance Schools. The Zavala origins story has been covered in great detail in Dennis Shirley's case study volume from 1997, but here it is worth noting that Zavala parents in East Austin organized within the Austin Interfaith umbrella to improve students' performance, get a public health clinic at the school after a nearby public clinic was slated to close, successfully obtained funds for the school to offer after-school programming, and sponsored community walks about reading. Teachers did home visits, as did the principal.

Austin Interfaith organizers and leaders pursued the typical IAF strategies to develop teams: house meetings, walks for success, and relationship building. Leaders learned about power and how it can be exercised for the public good. They attended Accountability Sessions with thousands of people in attendance over a decade, with some schools dropping in and out between 1996 and 2006. With the Investment Capital Fund, the TEA invested $1.9 million in competitive grants for after-school programs, teacher professional development, and leadership training, according to the 2009 Annenberg study.

As the state put more and more pressure on high-stakes standardized testing, the time available for teachers and students to work together diminished, leaving eight Alliance Schools in 2004. The Annenberg researchers developed elaborate and methodical research to evaluate the schools, using mostly quantitative data from test scores, hundreds of parent and staff surveys, and qualitative data from in-depth interviews. Annenberg researchers separated the Alliance Schools into high- and low-intensity involvement and documented gains from the experience.

District impacts also emerged, with Parent Support Specialists (some trained by IAF Leader Claudia Santamaria!). I examined the Austin ISD website in 2018 and found thorough school climate surveys available on line, complete with response rates.[33]

Recall Chapter 5's interview with Organizer Doug Greco and his entry to IAF as a teacher who subsequently trained to become an IAF organizer in an eastside high school, A. S. Johnston. This school was once deemed a failure by the district but is now an Early College high school, and was eventually renamed Eastside Memorial. The parent-teacher leader teams turned the school around after two years. Subsequently, the school's mission evolved into more college preparation. In partnership with community colleges, early-college schools allow students to earn both a high school diploma and an associate of arts (AA) degree by completing credits for the first two years of higher education with M.A.-level dual-credit teachers. Also in eastside Austin, the LBJ Early College High School's website features Parental Support that involves both leadership and service.[34]

Some Alliance Schools evolved into enhanced schools in which previous innovations have stuck and been institutionalized to improve students' learning and embrace parents in the process. Alliance Schools are not a magic bullet, but they pushed the TEA and legislators to step up to prepare more students for advanced degrees and certification programs. The Alliance School model added value and connectedness to neighborhoods. Alliance Schools operated out of a crisis standpoint that, with statewide IAF organizational support and leverage, gave legislators the ammunition to push for funding. And funding, perhaps, made the difference for campus and district buy in. When that funding evaporated, so also did Alliance Schools. But progressive reforms stuck in some places.

Concluding reflections

This chapter has covered a tremendous amount of material about the many constituencies and governance institutions in Texas education over the last decades, when the federal government finally discovered Mexican American students and their unequal educational opportunity from the 1960s onward. See the Appendix to this chapter on the *Mexican American Education Study* which documented the inequitable delivery of quality schools to students in Texas. Now Mexican Americans— "Hispanics" in official parlance—have become the majority of students enrolled in public schools amidst an incredibly fragmented and often partisan decision-making process about course content, assessment, and teachers' interests.

I analyzed the legacies of Alliance Schools ending a decade into the twenty-first century both in the borderlands—the Rio Grande Valley and El Paso—and in Austin. The results are mixed, but some innovations from teacher-parent alliances and relationships with local school boards have stuck and been institutionalized in schools and districts that aim to serve all the students with institutional incentives for accountability metrics. We see the importance of leadership within school bureaucracies with strategically placed professionals who understand the importance of parent-teacher relational work. However, schools continue to rely extensively on problematic standardized testing as the signature measure for performance. Central district staff vary in their desire to engage with the public, even in their websites as we saw with the South Texas ISDs. Much depends on leadership in the school districts, among the 1,031 districts in the state, each with its own organizational culture and rotating superintendents and principals. Few people, including the IAF, address the pipeline preparation of these educational leaders in higher education. Once a leader in education reform, the Texas IAF now shares support with other powerful organizations in Texas.

After decades of crisis-driven language and practices involving public schools, both political entrepreneurs and the wider public created a demand for alternative choices in the form of charter schools funded by taxpayers. But in the interim vacuum, community leaders attempted to build civic capacity connecting business and educators. To this topic we now turn in the next chapter, examining collaborations that involved IAF affiliates.

Appendix: The backstory, MAES, 1969–74

The historic 1960s baseline of poor-quality education for students in the state of Texas, as documented in the comprehensive U.S. Commission on Civil Rights *Mexican American Education Study* (MAES), printed in six volumes, 1969–1974, offers a comparison with four other southwestern states. One of its co-authors, El Pasoan Dr. Susana Navarro (see Chapter 7), armed with her first degree in political science, traveled with a team to gather evidence in the still-overtly discriminatory state; she was once even denied a room in a Corpus Christi hotel in the early 1970s. She later earned her PhD from Stanford University, headed the Achievement Council in California, and then returned to her home in the borderlands to found the El Paso Collaborative for Academic Excellence with its systemic urban reform initiatives to strengthen content standards, as analyzed in the next chapter.[35]

During the 1960s, before there were computers to reduce laborious work analyzing data on ethnicity and race, the U.S. Commission on Civil Rights (USCCR), conducted research in five southwestern states, including Texas. The USCCR published six extraordinarily readable volumes titled the *Mexican American Education Study* (MAES) (1969–1974). The volumes can be found in some reference sections of university libraries and law school websites.[36] I believe it should be required reading as a baseline to understand education for teachers, students, and the public in the southwest from Texas to California. Short of that, I will summarize some important findings related to students' different experiences with public schools, based on their color and ethnicity.

Various scholars, including Dennis Shirley and Larry Cuban, have called the US school system, with its racial/ethnic and income segregation, a "caste" system.[37] Segregation, also based on class and housing, was reinforced with man-made boundaries around "school feeder patterns" from elementary to middle to high schools. While some courts ordered busing to de-segregate schools, as did the 1954 Supreme Court's decision to desegregate "with all deliberate speed" over a ten-year period, this court-ordered strategy did not exist for income segregation. A 1974 US Supreme Court decision, *Milliken v. Bradley*, outlawed a lower-court decision to bus Detroit students, mainly African American school children, to its mostly White suburban school districts.

Prior to the MAES, most studies of equity in schooling focused on de jure and de facto discrimination against African Americans in racially segregated schools—separate and unequal funding. One can hardly get a high school diploma in recent decades without some knowledge of *Brown v. Board of Education*, settled in the U.S. Supreme Court in 1954, ordering school desegregation based on the case of Linda Brown, who lived closer to a "White" school in Topeka Kansas, but had to walk further to a "Black" school in the segregated city. Desegregation took many years to achieve. Little Rock's Central High School acquired national infamy when President Eisenhower called in the National Guard to protect nine enrolled African American students in 1957 as they integrated the school. And higher education institutions had their share of conflicts and lawsuits associated with integration, given the traditionally segregated Historically Black Colleges and Universities (HBCUs).

Despite attention to racial segregation, little awareness existed about ethnic and linguistic discrimination until the MAES's massive, readable study came out. Let me try to summarize its momentous findings.

The MAES researchers generated original material from questionnaires in 3,000 school districts in five southwestern states and their evidence demonstrated a grim numeric base. The official imprimatur of a U.S. government agency provided some leverage for survey response rates. Nowadays, one can open the Texas Education Agency (TEA) and campus websites and click on links for near-instantaneous uploads of standardized test-score results by grade and content levels, broken down by ethnicity and other factors for campuses, districts, and the state; per-pupil spending, high-school graduation rates, and comparative achievement standards among other factors. In the 1960s, with neither standardized tests nor content standards, such analysis was done by hand, making evidence-based claims of discrimination laborious, but ultimately necessary for policy change.

The six-volume MAES produced voluminous results, some of which stand out. First, in measuring high school graduation rates in Texas—named "school holding power" back then—holding was highest among Whites, next African American, and finally Mexican American students who averaged eight years before departure. Second, reading levels for Mexican American students averaged one-to-two grades lower than their actual grade levels, the lowest of all the ethnic groups. Bilingual education was undeveloped at the time. Third, grade retention was highest among Mexican American students who, by the time they reached middle school—sometimes called junior high school back then—made decisions to drop out when their classmates moved ahead.

Perhaps these findings come with no surprise, given parental poverty, low educational achievement, and job discrimination during that era, but one factor is especially important. As one full volume points out, Volume 4 of MAES, little to no bilingual education existed in that era, so many children struggled to understand course content in English. In fact, teachers punished students for speaking in Spanish not only in the classroom but also on the playground. Only with a limited federal funding impetus did school districts begin to experiment with the still-untried and untested bilingual education strategies. Nowadays, many schools and districts excel in offering not only bilingual education, but also standardized tests in Spanish for English-Language Learners at elementary levels and two-way dual-language classes so that all children learn content in two languages.

Probably the most troubling finding of the MAES came in Volume 5, focused on classroom observation and data-driven teacher-student attention patterns, positive to negative. One might have hypothesized that male students of color faced negative attention as is commonly documented in current studies, but back then, Mexican American children were simply ignored, whether naughty or nice. MAES attributed this neglect to the lack of teacher preparedness and Mexican American teachers. Few Mexican American teachers, principals, school-board trustees, and superintendents could be found in the data, though New Mexico was far ahead of the other four southwestern states.

Notes

1. Interview with Montserrat Garibay, Austin, July 24, 2018.

2. Dennis Shirley, *Community Organizing and Urban School Reform* (Austin: University of Texas Press, 1997).

3. Texans Advocating for Meaningful School Assessment, http://tamsatx.org, accessed Aug. 1, 2018, pushed back successfully against the Texas legislature to reduce the number of tests in high school, passing HB5 (House Bill 5) in the 83rd legislative session. See also https://www.equitycenter.org/and http://www.texaskidscantwait.org/. The 2019, 86th Texas Legislative Session, added $6.5 billion to education, restoring some of the cuts described later in this chapter.

4. David Tyack and Larry Cuban, *Tinkering toward Utopia: A Century of Public School Change* (Cambridge: Harvard University Press, 1995).

5. Links from the Jon Stewart era of *The Daily Show* are no longer searchable on its site, but the SBOE was taken to task in 2010 for challenging content on, for example, Thomas Jefferson for remarks about the separation of church and state and Dolores Huerta, of the United Farm Workers, for supposedly being a socialist. https://www.nytimes.com/2010/03/13/education/13texas.html

More recently, board members have become less partisan and more focused on real education content. In 2018, the board approved an elective Ethnic Studies course in high school which would allow teachers to focus on the heritages, leaders, and places of the majority of students in the region (Hispanic, African and Asian Americans, indigenous peoples). In recent years, a school district in Arizona underwent great controversy and legal challenges when it forbade ethnic studies courses.

6. Richard Gonzales, *Raza Rising: Chicanos in North Texas* (Denton: University of North Texas Press, 2016), 38–39.

7. This may be an odd phrase to some readers, but it is frequently used nationally and refers mainly to African American, Hispanic, and Asian American students.

8. Texas Education Agency, https://tea.texas.gov/communications/pocket-edition/. I have long been skeptical of the ways that the TEA reports drop-out and school completion, given more-than-a-dozen ways to classify a student's departure, which could be a transfer or some unknown other cause given lack of follow up. When the Education Summit was being planned in the late 1990s (see next chapter), schools regularly reported ludicrously low figures like 1 or 2 percent drop-out even though they lost as many as a third of 8th or 9th graders, depending on the cohort examined as research graphs in the Education Summit binder made clear (my files).

9. Campus searches can be done in the following: https://rptsvr1.tea.texas.gov/perfreport/src/2017/campus.srch.html

10. Morgan Smith, "A Possible Deal on Testing, Charter School Bills," *Texas Tribune*, May 23, 2013. https://www.texastribune.org/2013/05/23/governor-playing-role-in-testing-bill-talks/ Accessed Aug. 1, 2018.

11. Written and oral testimony provided for this meeting at UTEP, August 4, 2008. I was present and submitted three pages of written testimony, "Listening Sessions: TAKS and the Accountability System," buried somewhere in the bureaucracy (copy in my files).

12. Shirley Achor, *Mexican Americans in a Dallas Barrio* (Tucson: University of Arizona Press, 1978), 99.

13. See the Annenberg Foundation documentary video and book, directed by Susan Zeig, *A Community Concern*, 2009. The Oakland case in the video shows angry parents badgering a central-office bureaucrat about spoiled milk in lunchrooms and no toilet paper in bathrooms—the essence of hot anger that goes nowhere except for venting and defensiveness. Eventually the parents and teachers adopted a reformist relational model like the IAF, but in a PICO National Network organization. The PICO and IAF-style "cold anger" channels energy into leader teams, research, and winnable goals.

14. Shirley, 1997, chapter 2.

15. Gregory Rocha and Robert Webking, *Politics and Public Education: Edgewood v Kirby and the Reform of Public School Financing in Texas* (Minneapolis, MN: West Publishing, 1993).

16. Lizely Madrigal-González, who worked inside Ysleta ISD central office, was able to tap data not posted publicly on line, to separate

the effects of economic disadvantage, language, and ethnicity on test scores in her dissertation, "The Mexican American Education Study: Civil Rights, Opportunities, and Achievements after Forty Years in Ysleta Independent School District," University of Texas at El Paso EdD, 2011. The regression analysis showed that income surpassed ethnicity to explain the outcomes of standardized tests, information that was concealed in the public presentation of test outcomes.

17. Tyack and Cuban, 1995, on continuous reforms.

18. Geoff Ripps, "Alliances in Public Schools," *Texas Observer*, October 11, 1996, p. 13.

19. Ernesto Cortés Jr., "Making the Public the Leaders in Education Reform," *Education Week* 15, no. 12 (November 22, 1995): 1.

20. IAF, Network of Texas Organizations, http://www.ntotx.org/victories. Accessed Aug. 1, 2018. For the most comprehensive collection on the statewide Alliance School network, I read in the University of Texas at San Antonio (UTSA) archives, Library Special Collections, John Peace Library, "A Guide to C.O.P.S./Metro Alliance 1954–2009," MS 346, Box 106, Investment Capital Fund, September 1999; Request for Applications, Investment Capital Fund, 1999–2001; and (a no-surnames) Memo to Ernie, Christine, and Alliance School Organizers from Yvonne, Subject, Alliance School Updates, September 3, 1998. In Elaine Simon, Eva Brown, and Chris Brown, Strong Neighborhoods Strong Schools – Case Study: Austin Interfaith, prepared by Research for Action for Cross City Campaign for Urban School Reform, March 2002, authors cite 18 Alliance Schools in Austin, compared with 15 in the archival material. Schools opted in and out, accounting for the difference.

21. Shirley 1997.

22. See Pauline Dow and Kathleen Staudt, "Education Policies: Standardized Testing, English-Language Learners, and Border Futures," in *Social Justice in the U.S.-Mexico Border* Region, co-edited by Mark Lusk, Kathleen Staudt, and Eva Moya (Netherlands and New York: Springer, 2012).

23. Dennis Shirley, *Valley Interfaith and School Reform: Organizing for Power in South Texas* (Austin: University of Texas Press, 2002).

24. Mark Warren wrote about principals' reluctance to engage with community organizations in "Communities and Schools: A New View of Urban Education Reform," *Harvard Educational Review* 75, no. 2 (Summer): 166, saying that many educators are "suspicious about community engagement. They may fear having community activists interfere in 'their' domain

because they see them as uninformed or, worse yet, as potential disruptors pursuing a wrong-headed agenda."

25. Dennis Shirley, 2002, p. 62.

26. McAllen Independent School District: https://houston.mcallenisd. org/ Accessed 8/1/18.

27. https://www.psjaisd.us/

28. https://www.youtube.com/watch?v=BFVKmDYuVsQ; https://www.youtube.com/watch?v=jHaoJ3Au-e8 . See these videos about Carmen Anaya Elementary School.

29. http://ideapublicschools.org/. The Rio Grande Guardian features Superintendent Torkelson's Op Eds and ads. For a sample, see https://riograndeguardian.com/author/tom-torkelson/ . IDEA claims 61 schools in the Rio Grande Valley, San Antonio, and Austin, with 36,000 students, with plans to grow larger enrollment.

30. The nomenclature for English-Language Learners used to be labeled with deficit language: Limited English Proficient (LEP), and some teachers once called (patronizingly) young students *mis lepitos*. On the Annenberg study, see Kavitha Mediratta, Seema Shah, and Sara McAlister, *Building Partnerships to Reinvent School Culture* (with multiple cases, including Austin Interfaith, http://www.annenberginstitute.org/publications/organized-communities-stronger-schools. Accessed May 15, 2018. I thank the COPS/Metro Alliance Senior Organizer Walker Moore for calling this study to my attention at the beginning stages of research for this book, during an April 2018 meeting. Surprisingly, Larry Cuban's book on Austin reforms under the same superintendent makes no mention of Alliance Schools; *As Good as It Gets: What School Reform Brought to Austin* (Cambridge, MA: Harvard University Press, 2010).

31. Mediratta, p. 9.

32. Also featured as a case in Shirley 1997.

33. Austin ISD (plus see individual campuses): https://www.austinisd. org/announcements/2017-18-parent-family-survey-now-available

34. El Paso has six early-college high schools. In Austin ISD, see http://www.lbjearlycollegehighschool.com/?PageName=bc&n=232815.

35. See her brief biography for a UTEP award: https://www. utep.edu/liberalarts/people/gold-nuggets/2013-gold-nugget-susananavarro.html

36. See the University of Maryland Law School Library for pdf's: http://www.law.umaryland.edu/marshall/usccr/subjlist.html?subjectid=27

37. Dennis Shirley, 1997.

Chapter 7
"The IAF in Collaborations: El Paso's Education Summit and the Anti-wage Theft Lift Up Alliance"

"We're looking for the magic bullet."
Danny Vickers, business co-chair, Education Summit

"There is no magic bullet."
Various educators

This chapter tells the stories of two class-connected collaborations, the first focused on educational quality for all children, across classes, and the second on omnipresent wage theft within the working class. The lengthy collaboration on education involved a mostly middle-class professional set of community leaders, including EPISO, with the participation of business and education most prominent. The Lift Up Alliance involved unions, an employment lawyer, and a fledgling NGO, Justicia Laboral, once connected to the now defunct Paso del Norte Civil Rights Project, which was appended to the still-strong Texas Civil Rights Project. El Paso's IAF affiliates participated in both collaborations, even though both were fraught with time-consuming work and accountability complexity.

I could start this chapter with stories, like the beginnings of other chapters, and share so many intriguing quotes from the cutting-edge Education Summit in 2000, but the two quotes in the epigraph boil down their essence from both major forces—educators and businesspersons—who pursued civic collaboration around the complex project to improve schools for all children. Was civic capacity built? Twenty years after the Summit, business and education leaders still do not see eye to eye, but the dialogue continues with new language about charter school choices.

Framing the chapter: collaborative challenges

IAF affiliates, coalitions themselves of broad-base member institutions, occasionally join wider coalitions, a challenge to be sure. In any collaboration with good outcomes, one question always pops up: who can claim credit? In truly complex events, the credit is collectively shared. Yet other complications emerge in collaboration, as analyzed in this chapter.

EPISO participated in the ambitious, first-ever El Paso Education Summit in 2000, co-chaired by educator and CEO of the El Paso Collaborative for Academic Excellence (EPCAE) Dr. Susana Navarro (introduced in the last chapter) and binational border businessman Danny Vickers, president of the technology firm EDM International with 2,700 employees in Ciudad Juárez. Conference facilitator Christopher Cross, president of the Washington, DC-based Council for Basic Education and participant at other state and national summits said, "I'm not aware of any other community that has done anything as elaborate and as thorough and as comprehensive as this."[1]EPISO's then-Lead Organizer Joe Rubio had a place at the table, planning and participating in competing discourses about improving education for all children in the region and seeking to interject grassroots parental engagement as a crucial factor.

This chapter examines whether EPISO's participation was worth the labor-intensive eighteen-month planning time, two-day conference with over 300 influentials doing strategic planning for specific outcomes. I argue that EPISO's participation was worth the time and energy, albeit with its relatively marginal role within the planning and conference itself, but strategic role in follow-up. For the Summit itself, educators could take the lead in claiming credit for outcomes, though all the planners and participants shared collective responsibility. On the question of joint business-educator civic capacity,[2] the jury is still out in 2019 as I analyze toward the end of this chapter with the emergence of a relatively new business organization known as CREEED (Council on Regional Economic Expansion and Economic Development) devoted to education-economic links in local development and supportive of charter schools.

The other collaboration described in this chapter, the Lift Up Alliance, involved a dozen organizations working to reduce wage theft so commonly experienced by vulnerable workers who fear reporting the crime. While a bureaucratic solution (an ordinance, enforced in the city's purchasing department) passed, the victory was largely symbolic and the collaboration went unacknowledged in subsequent years of progressive media follow-up. Following internal rules of accountability, the IAF affiliates could not revive work on wage theft without damaging the time and labor commitments to other issues and strategies on its agenda. Most of this chapter focuses on the Education Summit, and that is where we begin.

Validating EPISO's seat at the table

The El Paso Collaborative for Academic Excellence (EPCAE), herein-
after called the Collaborative, launched in 1992 by Dr. Navarro and
housed at the University of Texas at El Paso (UTEP), engaged in systemic
education reform, with support from the National Science Foundation
and other funding agencies. The Collaborative's mission focused on
increasing educational expectations and achievement for *all students*
(i.e. not only the so-called Gifted and Talented, Advanced Placement,
or International Baccalaureate students in the ability-based top 10–20
percent of campus student bodies).[3] The Collaborative raised scores of
millions of dollars, mostly from federal government agencies, to provide
professional training for the region's teachers and administrators.

By the late 1990s, well after initial resistance to EPISO's founding (covered in Chapter 2), this IAF affiliate had a place at the public
table for its many achievements and respect in El Paso. It had worked
with statewide IAF leaders and state officials to bring water and sewer
public services to *colonias* in outlying areas, as noted in earlier chapters.[4]
EPISO generated state funds for Alliance Schools, particularly in Ysleta
Independent School District (ISD), where campus cultures changed
to focus on higher achievement with strong parental engagement (see
previous chapter). The quality workforce training center, Project Arriba,
had begun in the 1990s in collaboration with the El Paso Community College, UTEP, and the business community; a third of the board
consisted of local IAF leaders (see next chapter). Project Arriba moved
participants from poverty into middle-class salaried jobs, with certifica-
tions and degrees, especially in the health-care sector.

In 1992, EPISO Lead Organizer Sr. Maribeth Larkin had been
invited to join the Collaborative board, chaired by Navarro. The board
included the mayor, county judge (the equivalent of the CEO for the
county), Hispanic and Greater Chamber CEOs, presidents of both UTEP
and El Paso Community College, and TEA Education Service Center
#19 Director James Vásquez, who as a past San Antonio superinten-
dent famously led the 1980s struggle for equitable school funding in the
Edgewood v. Kirby case filed in 1984.

Side by side, in the mid-1990s, UTEP's Dean of Education Arturo
Pacheco joined UTEP to the National Network for Educational Renewal
(NNER), a relational model that the late University of Washington
professor John Goodlad and colleagues developed in the mid-1980s.[5]
At retreats, strategically placed professionals in the school districts and

university read and discussed definitive books in educational reform. I happily participated in these retreats and twice joined NNER activities in Seattle, particularly around the topic of my course, Teaching Democracy.[6]

Collaborations are fraught with risks and opportunities, as any institutional leader knows whether she or he works in government or nongovernmental organizations (NGOs). IAF affiliates face additional challenges. As coalitions of member institutions (ten to forty of them typically), IAF collaboration makes many demands on labor, time, and accountable decisions to their own members. Of course, IAF affiliates also stand to achieve gains through collaboration: visibility, prospecting for more leaders, and relational power with which to achieve further goals. But in any collaboration with other organizations that have their own boards, constituencies, and agendas, it is difficult for all partners to speak with a coherent, single voice while simultaneously responding to internal democratic principles without compromise.

Multiple community leaders took their places at the planning and implementation table to begin a laborious but fruitful process of ongoing civic-capacity building across broad sectors. Although this chapter focuses on an early twenty-first-century process, educators, business people, and IAF leaders still engage in discussions that have more recently morphed into choices between public and charter schools, discussed near the chapter's closing.

Education Summit planning

Summit co-chairs recruited high-profile people to serve on the planning committee, eighteen months in process, and to speak at the two-day conference in mid-February 2000. Speakers consisted of well-known business and academic leaders plus major public officials, from local to state and national levels. With professional planning staff based at the Collaborative, namely Joanne Bogart, staff paid meticulous attention to maintaining a balance of educators and businesspeople in both planning and invitation lists for the conference, attended by at least 300 mostly decision-maker leaders from the private and public sectors (with some media estimates at 350). People lauded both Summit planning and performance. Texas Education Agency Commissioner Jim Nelson—also a speaker—called El Paso's Summit a model for the rest of Texas. He said that throughout the state, people "cannot believe some of the things that are going on in El Paso."[7]

With *El Paso Times* publisher Mack Quintana on the Executive Planning Committee, Summit preparations and events received wide, continuous media visibility in front-page coverage and Opinion Editorials, in both the build-up and follow-up to the Summit. The Summit even had its own logo in this, the city's major newspaper, of a book embracing the word "Education" and symbols of El Paso's mountains substituting for M's in the word Summit. El Paso sits between the Franklin and Juárez mountains at the end of the Rocky Mountain range and start of Mexico's Sierra Madre range.

In the planning process, committee members voiced commitments to change, but with competing discourses about the strategies and rationales to achieve better education. The public media discourse differed from the sometimes tense confrontation in private planning subcommittee meetings, which I attended, and at which I took notes; the hat I wore was that of political science professor who taught a seminar on Border Politics for the educational doctoral (EdD) program, thus interacting with many educational leaders in the region.

The previous chapter of this book revealed the complexities of educational policy reforms and public school performance with its multiple policymakers and constituencies. Similar complexity emerged in preparations for the Education Summit. In summit conference planning, both fruitful exchange and ugly tension emerged. Of course, to have such diverse people sitting at the same tables together was an achievement in and of itself.

Consider these different perspectives and disagreements, though. One disagreement involved workforce versus college-ready education. Disagreement also emerged over the speed of "fixing" the schools, the efficiency of school management, and the material interests underneath articulated positions.

The chief division, in my eyes, involved disagreement over depressed wages in the binational borderlands versus employers' desire for a highly skilled, work-ready labor force. Recall from Chapter 2 that in El Paso's next-door neighbor city in Mexico, Ciudad Juárez, global corporations paid wages that ranged from a fifth to a tenth of US wages. This structural cloud overlays all borderlands communities in Texas. Historically, borderland business leaders had grown comfortable with low-cost plentiful labor in the region. The Education Summit planners and participants confined analysis and action to the U.S. side of the border. This is not surprising, given the two entirely different educational systems in Mexico and the United States. However, business leaders, including co-chair Vickers himself with his factory in Mexico, certainly understood these structural dynamics.

Let me illustrate these disagreements with what I heard in committees and read in the media. For some businesspeople, vocational education had been lacking, producing students not yet ready for the workforce. Said Randy Kuykendall, owner of the private, job-training Western Technical Institute, "many of the courses taught in the education system aren't relevant or are perceived as not relevant by the kids," so students become bored and fail to master language and algebra, whether to become "mechanics, welders, plumbers and technicians or go on to a four-year college."[8] Will Wautlet, car dealer, echoed some of these remarks to explain why his children attended private schools. "I think our public schools are inadequate. I don't think they're educating the children enough. I think their hands are tied because of all the laws and lawsuits. There's no discipline."[9] He, like conference co-chair Vickers, wanted to see more vocational courses for all students. "Business people think educators are out of touch and are too academic, even in high school."[10] According to CEO Wes Jury, El Paso Greater Chamber of Commerce, when he tries to attract new business to El Paso, "The Number 1 question they all ask is: Can you produce the young men and women in your community who will comprise our work force?"[11]

Lawyer Ray Caballero, who later ran successfully for a one-term two-year stint as mayor in 2001, focused on larger structural obstacles and used discourse from supply-demand economics. Caballero said that business people looked at the supply side, complaining about the few adults with high school, community college certificates, or college degrees. He said, "we're beating up on ourselves…. What about the demand side of incomes and job prospects in this region?" He also stated that we are "blind to Juárez" referring to the inequalities within and across borders and business stakes in perpetuating such labor conditions. Even TEA Region XIX director CEO, Jimmy Vásquez, hero of Texas educational equity-funding fame during the 1980s and 1990s, joined in: he quipped about "fudge factors" in discussions about cheap labor. "You reap what you sow."[12] Why would well-educated graduates stay in El Paso with depressed wages unless they worked in the public sector, Vásquez implied when challenging the business community about how the low wages they sowed reaped the departure of many educated El Pasoans from the region.

As I listened and obsessively took notes about these divisions with my ethnographic hat on, I also wondered if "translation" was sometimes necessary to understand jargon emanating from both business and educator sectors. Businesspeople interpreted words like "retention" positively, such as low employee turnover, while educators viewed retention negatively, as holding students back to repeat a grade. Phrases like "vertical articulation" seemed incomprehensible to all but educators. Businesspeople framed problems and solutions in "economic efficiency" terms: one businessman viewed the nine school boards and districts in El Paso County as ludicrous and expensive, calling repeatedly for district consolidation. However, this was a horrifying idea to most educational administrators and elected school board trustees and even to some parents living in school districts with the very organizational cultures they admired compared to the other eight ISDs in the county.

The Education Summit

At the conference itself, every participant received a binder with charts about students' achievement, data-driven evidence consisting largely of standardized results from the Texas Education Agency, broken down by ethnicity, race, economic disadvantage, and language (then framed in deficit language, LEP for Limited English Proficient[13]). All data consisted of numeric achievement indicators, such as standardized test pass rates, by year, high school completion, and comparative figures from other major urban areas in Texas. The data showed El Paso, with its largely Hispanic student population, ahead of big cities like Dallas, San Antonio, Houston, and Austin in test pass rates, lower gaps between ethnic/racial student categories, and higher graduation rates.

El Paso shined in test results, despite the fact that other Texas cities had long been home to more dynamic economies, higher wages, and lower unemployment rates at the time. The Collaborative emphasized content standards and professional teacher development; it had distributed catchy posters (in both English and Spanish) all over the schools and in classrooms reminding students, parents, and teachers of learning content standards by different grade levels. No doubt, the EPCAE's focus on content standards and professional training for teachers had partly paid off with outcomes like this, as did the Alliance Schools and their strong parental engagement programs. Of course some might question the connection between multiple-choice standardized test scores and the deeper learning (such as writing, researching, and reading) that prepares students for higher education.

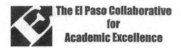
The El Paso Collaborative
for
Academic Excellence

TAAS: Passing Reading

	Academic Year				
	1993-1994	1994-1995	1995-1996	1996-1997	1997-1998
El Paso	70.9%	73.1%	76.9%	79.9%	83.2%
Ysleta	72.1%	54.5%	65.4%	85.2%	88.8%
Socorro	68.9%	73.1%	78.4%	81.2%	85.5%
Austin	70.7%	73.4%	74.5%	78.7%	82.2%
Corpus Christi	75.4%	75.9%	79.1%	82.9%	87.0%
Dallas	59.3%	62.8%	66.7%	69.1%	73.4%
Fort Worth	68.6%	68.2%	68.2%	72.0%	76.4%
Houston	65.7%	69.4%	73.1%	78.3%	81.4%
San Antonio	56.2%	56.9%	59.4%	65.9%	71.7%

Source: Texas Education Agency - Academic Excellence Indicator System Report 1994 through 1998

El Paso Collaborative for Academic Excellence comparative charts of standardized test scores in major Texas cities, in Education Summit binder, February, 2000.

At the Summit, distinguished and diverse speakers gave presentations. While Mexican Americans predominate as El Paso educator leaders, the powerful state-level policy elite is predominantly Anglo, even those appointed from El Paso. Businessman Woody Hunt, CEO of Hunt Companies and unfailingly an evidence-based decision-maker, made a keynote presentation at the Education Summit full of data about statewide performance gaps between groups based on ethnicity and other factors. Then and now, he consistently emphasizes the changing demographics in the state and the need for more college degrees among Hispanics. A *Texas Monthly* list of the twenty-five most powerful people in Texas recognized twenty-one White men (and two White women); of the twenty-five, only one of them from El Paso: Woody Hunt.[14] Hunt understood the shifting demographics in the State of Texas toward a Hispanic majority and its negative implications for economic growth if Hispanics did not graduate with quality education. National educator Katie Haycock focused on evidence-based identification of problems (such as unqualified teachers over-staffing low-income schools) and of solutions, such as putting teachers with proper content certification classrooms in all schools. In the large binder that all participants received, the Greater Chamber of

Commerce's mere two-page summary was underwhelming. "What is the Role of Business in Education and Workforce Development?" contained five key "facts," including the following: "El Paso's largest impediment to recruiting high wage jobs is the lack of a high skilled workforce."[15]

The Summit's three primary goals

At the event itself, three major goals emerged, succinctly condensed from 150 recommendations of the many subcommittee members. The approximately 300 participants on Day 2 used sticky notes, moving around to different parts of the conference room, to "vote" for their priorities on the walls. EPISO, assigned only thirty invitation spots, brought articulate parent leaders to participate at both days in various workshops where they emphasized the crucial roles of parental engagement with teachers and schools. In the highest-priority goal about a rigorous curriculum, conference attendees enriched that first goal to include "fluency in two or more languages." The phrase reinforced what many bilingual and dual-language teachers and researchers had long been pushing: students and community residents should recognize the assets of a bilingual and multi-lingual population. Below I quote the final three goals in full.

1. All students in El Paso should be required to complete a rigorous, college preparatory academic core curriculum, which includes fluency in two or more languages.
2. Ensure a sufficient and high quality teacher workforce, preK-12, in El Paso by preparing all teachers to teach rigorous, standards-meeting courses and by requiring all teachers to be certified in the subject areas which they are teaching.
3. Establish a regional campaign, led by elected officials, business leaders, parents and community members, which identifies education as among the community's highest priorities, that focuses attention on all students succeeding, and that encourages high levels of participation in school board elections and in educational decision-making forums.

Intended to provide credibility and leverage to various constituencies responsible for funding or pressuring to fund these goals, the Summit itself did not make funding demands. Of the three major goals, educators had already been acting on the first two, and at the Summit, participants reinforced their commitment, such as in UTEP's teacher preparation programs. However, the third goal dissipated, except for a chamber-designed survey for candidates to complete when running for school board and EPISO follow up, as analyzed below. Let me elaborate on each goal.

On the first goal, the Collaborative worked and continued working together with area school districts to promote professional development for teachers to focus on a standards-based curriculum. One could hardly find a school in the region without large, colorful posters of content standards displayed in prominent places, as previously mentioned. The Texas Education Agency, State Board of Education, and Legislature continuously addressed funding and revised content standards (the TEKS) and expectations for high school graduation, as covered in the last chapter.

On the second goal, reinforcing 1980s statewide reforms and state-mandated teacher- certification testing, UTEP's College of Education had been improving teacher preparation programs during the 1990s. The state had already required future secondary teachers to major in a content field and minor in education. UTEP also put student teachers in public school classrooms from their junior year onward with increasingly more hours, unlike other universities which required as little as two weeks in the schools prior to graduation. Dean Pacheco, part of the national Goodlad-led Educational Renewal movement, generated external resources to enable faculty and K-12 educational leaders to partner and coalesce around better collaboration for K-16 alignment and for cross-disciplinary alignment around teacher preparation among faculty in science, math, and social science.[16] Pacheco extended unpaid internship-like experiences and practice IN schools for three semesters before graduation; the requirements roughly modeled medical school training which puts future M.D.s inside hospitals before they acquire their final degrees. State government monitored teacher preparation programming with its certification examinations (albeit in standardized testing mode), with passing expectation rates at 70 percent and above for all ethnic and racial student categories.

At the time, regarding the third goal, EPISO facilitated the largest community-based model to encourage parental leadership and engagement in schools and in local elections. EPCAE staff also did parental engagement, namely by Pilar Herrera, with a more traditional model. Yes, some schools had their minimum-wage central-office-assigned parent specialists, but the more elaborate Alliance School model covered less than a tenth of schools in two of the three large districts. To expand the model, EPISO would need greater investments of time and monetary resources for parent engagement coordinators to grow more Alliance Schools or train the school districts' parent specialists who sponsored workshops and provided services. State funding still existed for the Alliance model, but the improvement of standardized test performance consumed more and more energy on campuses, squeezing out the labor-intensive relational work necessary to maintain or grow Alliance Schools.

Ad Hoc pilot-testing

No doubt scores of people, maybe more, acquired great ideas from the networking, relational work, summit committees, and the conference itself. Perhaps some pilot-tested those ideas and put them into practice. However, ad hoc efforts offer no substitute for institutionalizing full-fledged systemic change in how teachers worked with schools and parents, such as a district-led model like Alliance Schools, which Leader Claudia Santamaria (see her opening story in Chapter 5) helped support in Austin.

In one example, I taught Schools in Communities for UTEP's Teacher Education Department in three semesters of the early 2000s. The course included home-visit training, conducted by IAF organizer specialist Myrna Castrejón, and required three visits from each of the thirty-some students in each class. Despite my students' worries, none had problems in their home visits even though some of their mentor teachers in the public schools warned, or even scared, them about dangers. (A total of ninety students, with three visits each, equaled approximately 270 visits). In fact, most verbal reports and written papers revealed students' pleasant surprise with parents' hopes for their children and the ways they valued schools and reading.

Alas, UTEP faced constant limitations on hiring new faculty, so part-time instructors taught most of those Schools in Community sections and shared some of the same ambivalence about parents as mentor teachers in the schools, as I learned in occasional team meetings with them. It should be noted that part-time instructors may be among the most underpaid in higher education, busy putting together an over-full schedule of six or seven classes to include teaching at community colleges and chasing from one part of the city to another to create a low full-time wage, probably without health insurance. On funding constraints, over decades, the Texas Legislature has gradually reduced state subsidies to public higher education institutions. The next chapter addresses the many challenges met when attempting to connect higher education with community organizations. Innovative work in higher education usually involves faculty members' successes in obtaining external grants, though faculty incentives to write grant proposals tend toward research rather than community partnerships.

Among leaders in the business community, perhaps fatigue set in when they hadn't located their "silver bullet." However, the Greater Chamber of Commerce developed a survey, interview, and endorsement process for the motley group of candidates who run for the unpaid position of school board trustee. With low turnout in spring elections and limited campaign donations, few people knew or know much about the candidates or winners of these elections, at least in El Paso. However, EPISO followed up on the pursuit of Goal 3, as addressed below.

EPISO's follow-up, Goal 3: compacts/ *convenios* with parents

In the early 2000s, EPISO mobilized rallies and actions with hundreds of parents and grandparents to emphasize raising expectations and changing campuses to prepare students for a college-going culture. At these events, after hearing the major local speakers, such as Woody Hunt, UTEP President Natalicio, Danny Vickers, and El Paso Electric Company CEO Gary Hendricks, parents and grandparents signed "compacts," or *convenios*, in Spanish or English, (see graphic), in which they committed to support their children and grandchildren on pathways to higher education. I attended these dramatic events, buoyed with enthusiasm from the crowds. (Summit co-chair Vickers said they were like "revival meetings.") A cynic might wonder what difference it would make to sign such a document, but for me and no doubt for many parents and teachers, the signed agreement codified family support for a move toward higher expectations for all students in their journeys into higher education. Prior to Alliance Schools, few schools used such approaches, and whatever mentoring existed was individualistic, between counselor/ teacher and promising students.

A year after the Summit, in January 2001, EPISO organized an all-day Alliance Schools meeting "Creating a Pathway to College" with local leaders (again, the UTEP president, businessman Hunt and others) and external speakers (academic Seymour Sarason and IAF state leader Ernesto Cortés, Jr). Hundreds of parent and teacher leaders attended, but the number of Alliance Schools in the region had peaked and

Alliance Scholars Compact

The Alliance Scholars Initiative is a partnership between the Alliance Schools, the El Paso Interreligious Sponsoring Organization (EPISO), and the University of Texas at El Paso committed to developing a pathway to college for all students. As a team, we will create high expectations for all students and ensure that our students and those in our feeder system are engaged in a rigorous college preparatory curriculum. This pledge is a reminder to all of us engaged in this initiative that we have important roles and responsibilities to carry out. EPISO will continue to work with the Alliance Schools to provide leadership training and to organize a constituency of parents and community leaders who will hold the schools and school districts accountable to achieve high academic standards. The University of Texas at El Paso (UTEP) agrees to work with the Alliance Schools to make the university accessible to the community through the work of the mentor professors. UTEP also will work to ensure that every graduate of Alliance Schools who honors this Compact will be provided access to the financial and academic support needed to enter and succeed in college.

Principal's Pledge	Teacher's Pledge	Parent's Pledge	Student's Pledge
As a principal I pledge to	As a teacher I pledge to	As a parent I pledge to	As a student I pledge to
Meaningfully involve parents and members of the community	Prepare and deliver instruction which consistently challenges student learning beyond the grade level	Set high academic expectations for my child and expect that he/she will be engaged in rigorous college preparation	Pursue higher education. Apply for financial aid and scholarships
Develop and mentor leaders by providing training opportunities for faculty and parents	Development relationships with parents as partners and engage in conversation about their child's academic progress	Become actively involved in the school and work with my child's teacher in order to ensure academic success for my child	Accept the challenge to work at high levels of proficiency in all core areas.
Set high academic expectations for all students which will engage them in rigorous college preparation	Set high academic expectations for all students to be engaged in rigorous college preparation	Learn to advocate for my child and all children in the community by participating in leadership training with EPISO, school, and school district	Talk to teachers/parents about concerns/problems that I have and about my future plans
Organize a non-partisan constituency to hold the school district accountable for those expectations	Keep abreast of new knowledge in my field which I will share with students and parents	Hold the school and school district accountable to high academic achievement	Read continuously
Provide effective instructional leadership that will enhance achievement	Commit to continue my own learning and leadership development	Reinforce learning at home by encouraging good study skills and talking with my child about his/her academic future	Practice good citizenship
Commit to continue my own Learning and leadership Development		Support continuous reading at home and serve as a role model by reading myself	Take responsibility for my own learning
		Attend financial aid workshops held at my child's school	Engage in extra and co-curricular activities which will strengthen my social and academic development

WE PLEDGE TO WORK TOGETHER AS A TEAM TO ENHANCE _____'S ACHIEVEMENT AT _____ SCHOOL.

Dr. Diana Natalicio, President of UTEP   _EPISO Co-Chair_

Principal's signature   _Teacher's signature_   _Parent's signature_   _Student's signature_

_Date_____

Alliance Schools Compact form (English version), signed by hundreds of parents, principals, teachers, and students at EPISO meetings, 2001.

leveled off. They would soon evaporate due to the constant rotations of principals and superintendents,[17] the heavy time demands created by the federal law known as No Child Left Behind (NCLB), and the new, more complex standardized test, known as the TAKS. Test drilling and tutoring consumed enormous amounts of time and labor that could have been shared in parent-teacher activities.

Thus, the main follow-up to the Education Summit's Goal 3 rested with EPISO. After a few years, Vickers moved to California to start up another firm. Community-based leaders retreated to their own strengths and skill sets. However, more than a decade later, the business community re-grouped to form an organization, the Council on Regional Economic Expansion and Educational Development, CREEED (www. creeed.org), addressed later in this chapter. Similar debates exist now, nearly twenty years later, as then, between businessmen and educators about El Paso's supply of educated graduates and demand, with good local salaries.[18]

On Goal 1, besides the EPCAE's work, state laws also strengthened core-course credit requirements for high school graduation in basic subjects like math, science, English, and social studies. Yet tracking systems, deeply institutionalized in many schools throughout the United States with high expectations set for the students in "Gifted and Talented" and "Advanced Placement" courses, remained with some important exceptions where superintendents and district central office staff took heed of multiple progressive steps to strengthen students' education. Ysleta ISD was one of those districts. Local school board trustees can make a big difference.

Innovative districts, like Ysleta ISD with approximately 43,000 students at the time, offered options to students and parents among public schools, open enrollment, and open-access magnet programs in multiple career fields that required post-secondary education.[19] Teachers prepared students for college in these professional career-oriented programs. Additionally, Ysleta ISD subsidized SAT/ACT exams for all students. The district also required all students to apply to post-secondary institutions and write their personal essay for admission. The district developed and implemented policies for post-secondary preparation. Clearly, school board trustees and progressive leaders in district cultures can contribute to institutionalizing change to support quality education for all students; no doubt some of the progressive policies were threaded into Ysleta ISD culture as the district with the most Alliance Schools.

Readers may wonder what evidence supports initiatives like those covered here. In the early 2000s, the primary indicator of student success involved standardized test scores, questionable at best. Districts do not track students after high school graduation and their successes in higher education. Below, however, I offer several case studies. Many studies exist on students' persistence in higher education, but they are outside the scope of this book.

Additionally, federally funded programs like "Gear Up" opened opportunities for higher-expectation learning, using three models in El Paso. The UTEP and El Paso Community College models worked in more traditional top-down ways, out of higher education units, while EPISO in partnership with Ysleta ISD helped facilitate a community-based model with an Alliance School, Ysleta Middle School—the crucial period before high school, just before the riskiest year for students considering dropping out before high school graduation: 9th grade.

Alliance school success: Evidence from case studies

In the previous chapter, I shared quantitative measures of Alliance Schools' mixed, though mostly positive successes from Austin and South Texas case studies. Below I offer other case evidence of success from El Paso, limited to be sure and not as comprehensive as some readers might seek.

Case #1: In 2003, I had the opportunity to conduct part of the evaluation for Ysleta's community-based Gear Up model, using both quantitative and qualitative data. While the quantitative data showed only slight added value to students' performance from the Ysleta Middle School feeder pattern, compared to other middle school feeder patterns, the qualitative observations in classes helped me understand and interpret why. The internal tracking systems in high schools, elsewhere called "two schools within a school,"[20] continued to offer low- and high-expectation courses to students, depending on whether the courses consisted of Advanced Placement models. Higher standards for all students had yet to take hold in the early 2000s.

In a 9th grade English AP class, I observed a small group of a dozen students reading multiple books and doing daily journal entries to practice and improve their writing skills. All the students participated in energized class discussion. The comparison with a non-AP 11th grade English class could only be described as sad. An overly full class of forty students read one book over the semester. Rather than read the old classic, Nathaniel Hawthorne's *The Scarlet Letter*—admittedly, I despised the book, a required read in my high school—students viewed the 1995 Hollywood film *The Scarlet Letter* with Demi Moore. One student dared raise his hand to make an informative comment; I admired his courage but wondered and worried whether he would go on to higher education with this lackluster educational experience in an overly large class. Many factors intervene in students' journeys toward higher education or not, even the availability of money and wherewithal for university tuition payments to which this whole book and this chapter's stress on wages repeatedly refers. Despite the continuous, two-decade stress on high expectations for all students, emphasized by the Collaborative, central district office policy, and EPISO, the high school experience was mixed for the majority of students. However, below this section, I summarize yet more reforms that will likely make some difference over the next decade.

Case #2: Applied learning, like in the hands-on national model called MicroSociety, may have greater value-added staying power compared to the Gear Up experiences discussed above. Recall that Dennis Shirley's book emphasized applied learning in the Rio Grande Valley's Houston Elementary School, a school that also benefitted from multiple connections with church and the IAF-affiliate Valley Interfaith. In El Paso, former Alliance School Sageland Elementary School's MicroSociety also had staying power. In a fine master's thesis, Leticia Ibarra traced Sageland graduates through Bel Air High School and compared data on the senior students coming from each of three middle-school feeder patterns on several criteria: Grade Point Average (GPA), applications for higher education, and civic education, including high school student activities. The Sageland students outperformed the other students from different elementary schools.[21] At the time MicroSociety began in the early 1990s, a big investment of just under $200,000 was made to initiate the project, but the payoff in terms of student performance over six years was startling, maybe lifelong.

Some superintendent-induced setbacks

As much as people partially mobilized broad interest in schools in the post-Summit period, administrative greed set back the reputation of public school educators. Thanks to former state Senator Eliot Shapleigh's multi-year crusade about the scores of Bowie High School students transferred or suspended, beginning in 2007, public light finally shone on El Paso's biggest district's periodic crises, reducing public trust with the incessant media attention. The most devastating corruption case occurred with the former highly paid, EPISD Superintendent Lorenzo García, who directed his cabinet and some principals to "game" the system. He was ultimately convicted in 2012. Given the increasingly and extremely high-stakes standardized test system, the so-called low-performing schools could be closed and staff there, fired. At such a school, administrative directives led to the drastic reduction of the pool of student test-takers, transferring or ousting some poor test-takers, leaving the pool with those more likely to pass tests. Although anger was directed at García and the elected school board members who failed in their oversight function, the manipulation was an inevitable product of institutional incentives and penalties: high-stakes testing and high-end administrative contracts attached to bonuses for administrators who raised pass rates and penalties such as closing schools or restructuring them. The *El Paso Times* and local TV stations contained continuous and constant coverage of the scandal. The *Times* even won awards for their coverage. The TEA removed EPISD school board trustees and replaced them with a board of political appointees, one of them current mayor Dee Margo who used business principles to cleanse parts of the system. The board's selection of Superintendent Juan Cabrera generated some positive reforms—including open enrollment, more dual-language programming, and project-based learning—but also renewed public concern about flirtation with charter school partnerships and school closures.

It should be noted that charter schools offer mixed options. Some are innovative and engage parents, such as La Fe Preparatory in South El Paso. Others focus heavily on test-preparation and test-taking, pushing out low-performing test-takers or transferring them back into public schools. As such, these charter schools also game the system, but do so legally and are able to report high pass and graduation rates. The reality of both public and charter school outcomes is complex, generating many scholarly studies beyond the scope of this book.

Schools, whether public, charter, or private, require oversight. Community organizations and parents share the oversight function. It behooves all parents to understand the data that schools report about student performance, although it is often hard to fathom and opaque in decisions behind what is tested.

More and more educational reforms

Anyone involved in education knows that policy reforms are constant—so much so that by the time policy is implemented, or a new super-intendent takes charge, even more reforms are put into place before previous reforms have taken hold.[22] For IAF affiliates, the continuous turnover requires constant attention to relational work, building new or rebuilding old relationships. Testing companies constantly revise the instruments, and behind closed bureaucratic doors, the passing standards shift—50 percent correct to pass one year, 70 percent the next, and so on. Such decisions lack rationales and transparency.

Under conditions like these, it may be more useful to examine students' post-secondary outcomes in higher education: entry, persistence, grades, certificates, and graduation, certainly more valid measures than multiple-choice standardized test scores. The Texas Higher Education Coordinating Board (THECB) has developed databases and goals to track such outcomes in Texas universities and colleges. One of its latest goals is called 60 × 30TX, which stands for increasing the post-secondary certificate/graduation rates among the population aged between twenty-five and thirty-four years to 60 percent by 2030. El Paso's rate falls well below, at 29 percent.[23] To achieve these goals, schools must change campus cultures to foster the kind of achievement for all the students which would lead to post-secondary success outcomes: beyond the AP/IB group and beyond the high school standardized test pass rates. The IAF-facilitated but stand-alone workforce training center Project Arriba (see next chapter), with students' high graduation rates, strengthens El Paso's pathway toward THECB's goals.

Promising new initiatives have been put into place, such as Early Colleges, whereby 9th grade students enroll for four years and acquire both their high school diploma and a community college associate of arts (A.A.) degree. These initiatives put students on a college-preparatory track and cover two years of higher education tuition should students seek an associates or bachelor's degree and beyond. In regular high schools, teachers with eighteen content hours or masters' degrees in specialized areas teach "dual-credit" courses which earn higher education course credit for students and thus launch them into a semester or more of college without tuition expense. Such initiatives address part of students' economic struggles to fund their higher education and deal with some, though not all, of the obstacles they face acquiring credentials and degrees.

Philanthropic community foundations, especially those with plentiful resources in the four big cities of Texas, formed Educate Texas.[24] The expansion of school choice is part of their agenda, available for both public (including charter) and private schools. As discussed above, some public school districts also provide such choices with magnet programs and open enrollment. However, while charter schools—both profit and nonprofit—expand choices, they use public tax resources through per-pupil enrollment subsidies. Again, public oversight is necessary.

Revisiting business-educator-community civic capacity

Educational quality is tied to economic growth, and in the Texas future, more than half of new jobs will be tied to degree holders. In El Paso, CREEED was formed in 2013 by members of the business community, unwilling to cede the education narrative and strategy to educators alone. Perhaps this is a sign of growing civic capacity. Perhaps it is stubbornness, given the continuing disagreements about the supply of an educated workforce versus the demand to retain educated graduates with good salaries and benefits. Like Educate Texas, and in the interests of better outcomes than what public schools provide, CREEED seeks to expand school choices with charter schools. IDEA charter schools, operating in large numbers in South Texas, have been expanding their market niche in El Paso. The Rio Grande Valley already has thirty-six IDEA schools, but only a few exist in El Paso.[25]

CREEED connects education to El Paso's future economic growth, so it seeks a more highly educated population. However, El Paso's highly educated youth leave for the far higher salaries they can achieve elsewhere. UTEP graduates about 5,000 students annually; many teachers and health-care professionals remain, but more than half of computer science and other STEM (Science, Technology, Engineering, Math) graduates leave for better salaries and opportunities outside the region. Ultimately, then, a continuing disconnect exists in the yet-to-solidify civic capacity between educators and business people around producing better education outcomes, yet retaining graduates in a region with depressed wages. Unlike high-growth regions such as Dallas and Houston, El Paso has not yet become a magnet for professional migrants from other parts of the U.S.

I sometimes wonder how the Education Summit would have worked if EPISO had been leading the coalition of collaborative organizations, including higher education and business. No doubt EPISO's leaders would have carved out more relational meetings and long-term follow-up, but perhaps fewer people would have participated without the imprimatur of the university, business sector, and leading figures from local, state, and national NGOs and government agencies, such as what the Collaborative had the capacity to arrange. Even with the IAF at the lead, the larger state system's relentless emphasis on standardized testing would have undermined goals, space, and time for relational work and core teams on campuses and in districts. Such is the drawback of local social justice work in education without corresponding policy change at the state and national levels to reinforce or at least not contradict gains. Multiple placeholders at the table, including educators and business people, will still be required to supply highly educated workers who decide to stay in El Paso, especially at businesses that are willing to step up with higher salaries to retain skilled workers and graduates. The long-term project to educate all El Paso's children with high expectations sits amid an economy with long-standing low wages and wage theft, the topic to which we now turn.

Collaboration in the lift up alliance

Wage theft is a common problem throughout the state. Unscrupulous employers offer desperate-for-work people twenty or forty dollars cash for a full day's work. A legal minimum wage would have been $7.25 per hour times eight hours, or approximately sixty dollars per day. Or building contractors might promise overtime pay, but then refuse to pay for overtime hours or days. Even private employers engage in theft. Consider a recent case reported to me: An in-home health-care worker cared for a recovering patient, all day and night, seven days a week, even spending some of her own money for groceries. Is $200 a reasonable pay for seven days round the clock? No. Abuses like these are an unreported but commonplace crime, especially in the borderlands. Victims do not report because they are afraid to lose their jobs, which is forbidden under law. Moreover, how long and at what cost would it take to file for claims as well? The wheels of justice move slowly, if at all.

Thanks to El Paso State Senator José Rodríguez, the Texas legislature introduced and passed a law in 2011 that criminalizes wage theft. However, Wage and Hour laws, at both the national and state levels, have not deterred unscrupulous employers. Organized business tends to support laws like this because legitimate firms cannot fairly compete against employer-wage-thieves. Yet only one small business in the entire state, a roofing firm in El Paso, was charged and convicted of wage theft under that law for paying a roofing employee half of the approximate $2,700 he was promised. On appeal, the business won on a technicality, and the former employee was never paid.[26] A criminal remedy is time-consuming and costly to pursue, unless the victim gets pro bono legal assistance. (Recall from Chapter 3 that Dallas Areas Interfaith works with the Dallas Police Department to enforce the wage-theft law.)

Only two cities in Texas have passed ordinances to deter wage theft with civil remedies: Houston and El Paso. A city ordinance could deter wage theft, by preventing employer-wage thieves from contracting with the city and also removing their licenses to practice business. A city ordinance could also educate potential contractors about wage theft and its associated penalties.

A victim of wage theft must pursue complex, multiple steps to document and report their grievance to a small-claims court or the Texas Workforce Commission (TWC), which then determines whether theft has occurred, in order to provide due process of law to the parties concerned. If the theft has been confirmed, the victim is supposed to be able to collect past wages with the Justice of the Peace. However, without a city ordinance, the employer who refuses to pay faces no penalties; that is, it is a process without "teeth."

Over a two- to three-year period, EPISO and Border Interfaith participated in El Paso's Lift Up Alliance, a collaboration of approximately a dozen organizations and networks. Then-El Paso Organizer Arturo Aguila and EPISO Leader Eloiso de Avila steadily worked with the alliance and its participants, some of whom dropped in and out over the years of developing an ordinance.[27] Some participants in the network sought to march and carry signs in front of City Hall. Like other social movements, episodic action like this rarely generates action inside the building or relationships with a majority of city representatives prepared to support such a measure, for only a majority can pass an ordinance. Ultimately, Lift Up participants sought teeth in a local ordinance that would remove the wage thief's license to do business in the city, with expert advice from lawyer Chris Benoit. An ordinance passed in 2015 with a majority of representatives' votes.[28]

Nevertheless, in 2011, as noted above, with sponsorship from State Senator José Rodríguez, the Texas Legislature had already passed a law to criminalize wage theft.[29] Is criminalization the answer, given the years of delay, possible low priority in police departments, underreporting given employees' fears of retribution, and the costs and times of lawyers and courts? In a lone El Paso case, the employer was convicted and fined, but on appeal, the victim lost and four years later, still did not receive the money he was owed.

In a contrast to criminalization solutions, EPISO, Border Interfaith, and their many Lift Up El Paso partners' protracted collaborations sought to prevent wage theft and to recover wages for workforce-commission adjudicated victims by penalizing such employers and removing their licenses to practice business, plus any "offending company." Despite support from former Mayor Oscar Leeser, himself a businessman, the former city attorney and city manager cast an extremely risk-avoidant approach over the effort, with surveys and focus groups to solicit business and chamber leaders' viewpoints. Perhaps ironically, the El Paso Greater Chamber of Commerce publicly supported an ordinance with teeth, while the Hispanic Chamber did not, for the Greater Chamber, too, wanted to represent legal and ethical business practices and move away from the "cheap-labor city" designation chamber leaders in the last quarter of the twentieth century had promoted.

What did the multi-year efforts accomplish? I tried to find out who in the city was the duly-appointed "Wage Theft Coordinator" as the ordinance required. It took several phone calls, only to discover it was the Purchasing Department Director. He met with EPISO leader Eloiso de Avila and me in mid-2018 to discuss his careful compliance with the ordinance. On the positive side, every solicitation for a bid and contract between business and the city contains the six-page ordinance, so a preventive measure is in place. And a victim can come to the wage theft coordinator with evidence and documentation about a theft, for which an inquiry is made. No lists are kept of attempts and resolutions of these claims. On the negative side, "no city contracts have been cancelled or denied due to wage theft since the ordinance's passage in 2015, and no permits or licenses have been revoked, either."[30]

As we can see, there are many problems in deterring wage theft. The "win" for the collaboration was a bureaucratic solution without outreach to or coordination with the Texas Workforce Commission, itself lacking an adequate budget for enforcement. The IAF-Lift Up collaboration did not continue, and the investigative journalist interview with Justicia Laboral contained no acknowledgement about the time and labor that the IAF affiliates invested into coalition building toward a solution that involved more than episodic protests on the street. To re-start the Lift Up Alliance would involve time and talent from the unpaid IAF leaders, busy with their current agenda.

At its Steering Committee meeting, EPISO-Border Interfaith leaders discussed the de Avila-Staudt meeting with the purchasing director and possible follow up about this dilemma in 2018. The previous 2015 win achieved only "baby teeth" for enforcement, after all.[31] Leaders discussed the considerable investment in new relationships to develop an ordinance with stronger teeth, a TWC with funded proactive outreach, and relational work with the remaining Lift Up network to which victims could report claims to make sure all the evidence-based steps would be followed. Meanwhile, Border Interfaith and EPISO had other pressing action items on their agenda, an impending and always laborious Accountability Session—the second Accountability Session in 2018!—immigration work, Get-Out-The-Vote campaigns, follow-up schedules with officials once sworn into office in early January and relational, revenue-generating work for a possible twenty-first-century school built on the Alliance School model. It could not afford for its leaders to be spread thinner yet. So leaders reached the consensus to receive the report, but not engage in immediate action. After all, IAF affiliates cannot do all the social justice work in a big city.

IAF affiliates depend on other social justice organizations working alone or in alliance to develop a better strategy for what seems like a never-ending reality of reducing wage theft in a business-friendly state that worships limited government. Other big cities in Texas, home to more nongovernmental organizations and better fundraising opportunities, have the civic capacity to act on wage theft and other issues. One such stand-alone organization would be the Workers' Defense Project, which organizes and acts in Austin, Houston, and Dallas and participates as a member institution with IAF's Austin Interfaith and Dallas Area Interfaith.[32] Workers' Defense operates with staff and a worker base that have the wherewithal to prioritize issues like wage theft, workforce injuries, and paid sick leave with vulnerable low-income workers. If and when El Paso moves out of its economic doldrums—questionable given its unequal binational borderlands locale—EPISO/Border Interfaith will be able to work with other social justice organizations and/or recruit them formally as member institutions and thereby broaden its base beyond faith-based institutions.

Without outreach and practical research, IAF's seeming solutions—whether bureaucratic or criminal—resulted in what might be criticized a "symbolic politics," that is, the appearance of a solution but no real change in solving the problem.[33] Let me share yet another "meanwhile" about the El Paso roofing company whose owner was convicted, but who won on appeal, based on a technicality, and who is therefore "innocent" in the eyes of the law. Once I saw his signs in my neighborhood for his roofing work on two houses in September 2018, I checked his Better Business Bureau rating: Accredited business with an A+ rating.

Concluding reflections

Let me sum up major findings in this chapter on collaboration. El Paso's Education Summit was truly a remarkable achievement in 2000. It drew together high-level leaders from the educator and business communities and deepened the relationships between them. Civic capacity was thereby built, but rather than mobilizing community support (the lone participant of which was EPISO), a temporary consensus was upended with obsessive state and federally imposed standardized testing, both to measure performance but also seemingly designed to make public schools look bad. As time passed over a decade, fissures widened between educators and businesspersons with corruption in El Paso's biggest district where administrators gamed the system to generate more bonuses and to avoid school closures based on the high-stakes accountability system. By the time of Superintendent García's indictment and conviction in 2012, public school reputations produced a perfect storm, a perfect vacuum in which market-oriented claims could be made for charter schools inroads. It has long been debated whether charter schools can serve all students well.

In the Education Summit of 2000, the IAF Affiliate EPISO participated as a major player in planning and especially its follow up, thereby increasing its visibility and relational work with others to extend civic capacity even more. However, EPISO played a more minor role in the two days of the Summit, given the relatively small number of seats which it was allocated. Yet EPISO became the primary effective civic player to follow up on Goal 3 of the summit: to mobilize community interest in and participation in school improvements, with engaged parent leaders. Despite the time and energy expended, I believe that EPISO ultimately gained from its collaboration with the Education Summit. EPISO was accountable to its collaborative partners and to its own leaders and member institutions; its commitment to parental engagement was a longstanding effort, given EPISO's work with Alliance Schools and its place on the El Paso Collaborative for Academic Excellence board.

The Lift Up El Paso Alliance participants worked years to gain a concrete goal, a city ordinance to prevent wage theft with some enforcement teeth that can only be called baby teeth. The ordinance exemplifies symbolic politics that appear to address or solve problems but remain a mirage. Border Interfaith and EPISO pursued the collaborative alliance with accountability to its leaders and member institutions. However, if the IAF affiliates were to renew involvement, the time and effort could detract from its ongoing goals and strategies and thereby diminish accountability in its collaboration to leaders in IAF-affiliate member institutions. The IAF affiliates evinced commitment to social justice in its collaboration, despite no acknowledgement from former partners. To its credit, the El Paso-based Lift Up Alliance—including EPISO/Border Interfaith—obtained one of only two such ordinances in Texas—El Paso and Houston—that seem to have been blissfully ignored, especially by small-business employers who cut their costs through wage theft and do no contractual work with city government. One can only hope that the city's purchasing department has deterred some offenders through including the ordinance in its solicitations for preventive education. The experience with wage theft shows the long-term persistence and relational work necessary for social change to occur, even small steps of change, to address the unequal educational and wage structures in a community. A solid education for ALL students requires years of work to change district and campus cultures.

Educational policy and implementation are extraordinarily complex, as we covered in this and the last chapter. While civic capacity strengthened somewhat, supported with some innovative pilot programs, there is no substitute for systemic reforms that involve community voices, including parents. Systematic change requires an effective statewide strategy and responsive representatives, the latter of whom alas subscribe to the ideology of limited government, including limited support for public education. Can higher education institutions help fill part of the gap? To that topic we turn in the next chapter.

Notes

1. Quoted in David Crowder, "Summit to Tackle Education," *El Paso Times*, January 20, 2000, 1A–2A.

2. Clarence Stone is the political scientist known for *Building Civic Capacity in Educational Reform* and an NSF-sponsored ten-city study on educational reform, generating several books and edited volumes. See his edited volume, *Changing Urban Education* (Lawrence: University Press of Kansas, 1998) and his co-authored book with Jeffrey Henig, Bryan Jones, and Carol Pierannunzi, *Building Civic Capacity: The Politics of Reforming Urban Schools* (Lawrence: University Press of Kansas, 2001).

3. Mary Alicia Parra wrote a fine dissertation on EPCAE, "A Case Study of Education Leadership in Systemic Reform," (Dissertation, EdD, University of Texas at El Paso, 2002). Tracking systems have long been criticized in schools. See Jeannie Oakes and John Rogers, *Learning Power: Organizing for Education and Justice* (New York: Teachers College Press, 2006).

4. For the complete complex story, see Robert Wilson and Peter Menzies, "The Colonias Water Bill," in *Public Policy and Community: Activism and Governance in Texas*, edited by Robert Wilson (Austin: University of Texas Press, 1997), 229–274.

5. John Goodlad, *A Place Called School* (New York: McGraw Hill, 1984, 2004, 20-year anniversary edition).

6. Kathleen Staudt, "Democracy Education for More than the Few," in a book that emerged from the seminars, *Developing Democratic Character in the Young*, edited by Roger Soder (San Francisco: Jossey Bass, 2001), 45–68.

7. David Crowder, "Summit to Examine Skills Taught in Schools," *El Paso Times*, February 13, 2000, p. 1A–2A.

8. Crowder, Ibid.

9. Ibid.

10. Vickers quoted in Crowder, 2A.

11. David Crowder, "Summit Sets Top Priorities," *El Paso Times*, February 20, 2000, p. 2A.

12. From my voluminous notes taken at meetings.

13. I would cringe in graduate seminars when administrators discussed the patronizing discourse they heard in schools: *mis lepitos*.

14. Nate Blakeslee, Paul Burka, and Patricia Kilday Hart, "Power Company: Who Are the Most Influential People Determining the Fate of Texas—and What Do They Want?" *Texas Monthly*, February, 2011, p. 162–3.

15. All these documents and the binder are in my office.

16. Kathleen Staudt and Jack Bristol, "Educational Renewal Across College Borders: El Paso Strategies toward Change," *Making a Place for Change in Higher Education* (Washington, D.C.: American Association for Higher Education, 1999).

17. See Frederick Hess, *Spinning Wheels: The Politics of Urban School Reform* (Washington, D.C.: Brookings Institution, 1999), on revolving superintendents' agendas.

18. Lengthy committee meeting with CREEED CEO Eddie Rodríguez, August 23, 2018. CREEED leaders also write Op Eds on charters for the *El Paso Times*.

19. Pauline Dow and Kathleen Staudt "Education Policies: Standardized Testing, English-Language Learners, and Border Futures," in *Social Justice in the U.S.-Mexico Border Region*, co-edited by Mark Lusk, Kathleen Staudt, and Eva Moya (Netherlands and New York: Springer, 2012), 217–229.

20. Oakes and Rogers, 2006.

21. Leticia Ibarra, "Microsociety: Civic Education, Academic Achievement, and Higher Education Aspirations through Experiential Learning," M.A. Thesis, University of Texas at El Paso, 2001. I proudly chaired this thesis committee!

22. David Tyack and Larry Cuban, *Tinkering toward Utopia: A Century of Public School Change* (Cambridge: Harvard University Press, 1995).

23. http://www.thecb.state.tx.us/. The state does not do too much better in the likelihood of meeting the 2030 goal.

24. This effort was founded a decade ago to push student achievement toward post-secondary education certification and graduation https://www.edtx.org/.

25. http://www.ideapublicschools.org/. IDEA's charter school website does not have a Spanish-translation link, despite making inroads into the borderlands. Accessed Aug. 1, 2018.

26. Gus Bova, "'Landmark' Wage Theft Conviction Overturned by Texas Appeals Court," *Texas Observer*, September 6, 2018. https://www.texasobserver.org/landmark-wage-theft-conviction-overturned-by-texas-appeals-court Accessed 9/10/18.

27. As a Border Interfaith leader who attends monthly steering committees, I heard updates on the evolving strategy and I attended City Council meetings, testifying at one of them along with many others who voiced their self-interest, stories, and frustration at getting the money they were owed. On October 3, 2018, I talked at length with Eloiso de Avila before we met with the city purchasing director Michael Collins who is also the wage-theft coordinator.

28. Ordinance #018370 in 2015.

29. In the first case, the victim lost on appeal in 2018 (a technicality paperwork issue): https://www.texasobserver.org/landmark-wage-theft-conviction-overturned-by-texas-appeals-court/?utm_source=Texas+Observer&utm_campaign=2beddafdb2-EMAIL_CAMPAIGN_2018_09_07_02_35&utm_medium=email&utm_term=0_975e2d1fa1-2beddafdb2-34570011&goal=0_975e2d1fa1-2beddafdb2-34570011&mc_cid=2beddafdb2&mc_eid=e721e7d5a8.

30. Gus Bova, "Wage Wars," *Texas Observer*, June 13, 2018, https://www.texasobserver.org/wage-wars Lidia Cruz of the Justicia Laboral network (once affiliated with the now defunct Paso del Norte Civil Rights Project) says she gets thirty complaints weekly, but without documentation and due process, the process ends there. Bova's investigative report

also covers Houston, the only other city with an ordinance on wage theft, where unethical employers looking to cut corners subcontract with smaller employers who quickly disappear or go out of business when legal claims have been pressed. Houston's database of offending businesses had only thirteen employers (compared to El Paso's nine who received "final orders" to pay, but they are removed after five years), despite being a larger city.

31. EPISO Leader Dolores de Avila made this accurate characterization of a weakly enforced narrow ordinance in which government coordination falls through the cracks, without any proactive enforcement campaign.

32. http://www.workersdefense.org/industry-research/. I also interviewed a community activist/official in Austin about this who prefers to remain anonymous. Note that the Workers Defense Project is not a member institution of IAF affiliate, The Metropolitan Organization (TMO). Wage theft has a long history in the El Paso borderlands, especially Juarenses who crossed to work both in the formal and informal economies, but also El Paso-based workers: See Benjamin Márquez, "Organizing Mexican-American Women in the Garment Industry: La Mujer Obrera," *Women & Politics* 15, no. 1 (1995): 65–87.

33. Murray Edelman, *The Symbolic Uses of Politics* (Champaign-Urbana: University of Illinois Press, 1964).

Chapter 8
"IAF Affiliates and Higher Education"

O nce again, I begin with a story.

Dr. Mark Lusk, a bilingual social work professor who has served in administrative capacities at several universities around the country, decided to become involved in Border Interfaith after being approached by IAF co-chair Pastor Wayne Kendrick from Peace Lutheran Church. Dr. Lusk attended long-term trainings in San Francisco and Chicago and found them illuminating. "I saw the intellectual roots of the organization and its ties to faith." At the Chicago training, participants attended an Accountability Session action at a synagogue where he saw the "power of organized people."[1]

Although a core leader at his church, Dr. Mark Lusk decided not to continue active involvement in Border Interfaith for a variety of reasons. While he was surprised by some anti-scientific comments about evolution from the IAF organizer, with whom he met one to two times monthly, the main reason he did not continue had to do with over-work at the university, teaching, writing grants, researching, serving on committees, and monitoring new programs. "I stopped all peripheral activities to take control of my life." Besides, his main research involved interviews with refugees, not on Border Interfaith's agenda at that time. "With only so many hours in a day," he realized that "the organization was sucking up a lot of time without giving back.... My main point would be the opportunity costs of social activism: Uncompensated time with low returns on investment." Dr. Lusk said that activism lends itself to retirees, young wealthy college students, true believers, and not too many working-class individuals or active professionals. "There's also burnout, which I experienced and led me to narrow my work range to fewer mission-oriented activities."

Dr. Lusk believes "the IAF served me well," for students in his courses had always learned about social justice, but now learn even more, including about the IAF. However, he said most of his graduate students are atheists and feminists, rarely interested in the institutional church. [I might also note that UTEP, nationally recognized for "social mobility," serves a largely working class student population; a full 40 percent of students live in households with earnings under $20,000 annually.] Nowadays, Dr. Lusk continues to serve on various community boards; he responds to invitations to speak about his field research and expertise, "my greatest impact," he said.

With his extensive administrative expertise, and his work as a provost-appointed Faculty Fellow at UTEP's Center for Civic Engagement, he has designed and promoted faculty evaluation, tenure, and promotion guidelines to incentivize and reward faculty engagement for work with community organizations. As a mentor to junior faculty, Dr. Lusk encourages them not only to work with the community, but also to analyze, write, and publish articles about their work to build a credible record for their institutional evaluations and tenure and promotions.

Framing the chapter

In Texas cities with IAF affiliates, I have long pondered the loose or nonexistent ties between IAF and university faculty members and students. Perhaps in El Paso, EPISO and UTEP have been an exception, partly because the past UTEP-housed El Paso Collaborative for Academic Excellence invited EPISO to a seat at its table for the high-profile advisory committee and the Education Summit planning preparations (see Chapter 7). Since then, the EPISO/Border Interfaith-UTEP relationship has been sporadic, threaded with only a handful of professors, some who identify as an IAF leader and a few others who introduce the IAF as a community organizing model in their course curricula.

Why are so few professors and students connected to local IAF affiliates? I believe the answer has much to do with clashing "organizational cultures," a concept that refers to the values, ways of being, and incentives for task completion in institutional settings. In earlier chapters, we questioned the prominence of material self-interest as the key motivator, given the equally articulated emphasis on purpose, faith, and ideology found in some interviews. IAF culture is unique, even compared to other community organizations, with its disciplined model and carefully trained paid organizers and many more unpaid leaders. In public bureaucracies, most certainly state universities, we must understand the following two questions, broken down by three types of paid employees—what James Q. Wilson calls operators, managers, and executives[2] in his next significant book for this analysis, *Bureaucracy*—in the institution's political contexts: What are they expected to do? Why do they do that? Here I draw once again on scholarly studies of institutions, as in Chapter 5.

In the one main exception to the minimal relations between the IAF affiliates and higher education, we find community colleges. The IAF spawned, but never controlled or managed, high-quality workforce training centers like Project Arriba and Austin-based Capital Idea that place graduates in more-than living wage jobs. They do so in partnership with community colleges in San Antonio, El Paso, Austin, Houston, Dallas, and the Rio Grande Valley. These community-college cases illustrate the importance of identifying institutional interests in making partnerships successful. In workforce center partnerships with community colleges, the colleges generate enrollment and tuition, businesses especially in the health care sector obtain qualified/certified employees, local governments invest in economic development programs that generate long-term property and sales tax from employees earning middle-class salaries, and IAF affiliates sustain their continuing strategy to support people moving out of poverty into meaningful, living-wage jobs. We take up this issue toward the end of the chapter.

Universities and the IAF: Clashing organizational cultures

Sporadic relationships exist between universities and IAF affiliates, but they are uneasy and hardly cultivated. Ad hoc synergy also occurs. Students may learn or be inspired from a class presentation and seek experience in community organizations. University presidents usually claim that they seek to create campus cultures of inclusion that support student leadership development, both in classes and in student organizations. Yet we must ask what kind of leaders do universities cultivate? Student programming tends to focus on generic qualities: responsibility, communication, and instrumental activities that build individual career mobility. Nothing is wrong with that except that the scope of leadership training rarely includes broad-based social justice organizing. Perhaps this is understandable. After all, IAF uses more sacred than secular symbolism (recall Chapter 4), so public universities might steer clear of anything that smacks of religion even though the IAF promotes no religious agenda. Catholic colleges and universities, however, often require service and/or one or two theology courses.

University-based specialization and fragmentation

Higher education institutions offer a wide array of courses in the humanities, arts, and sciences, mostly within disciplinary boundaries. At the upper-division and graduate course levels, universities also offer inter-disciplinary Chicano, ethnic, African American and women/gender stud-ies that foster identity-based perspectives. Universities train journalists in a rapidly changing media arena. They facilitate other career-oriented expertise in teaching, health/nursing, business, and STEM (science, technology, engineering, and math) fields. The broad-based liberal arts umbrella potentially covers relevant material in history, public affairs, philosophy, and popular art.

In my Austin trip for this research, I interviewed one of the relatively few "public intellectual" professors at the University of Texas who has worked with community organizations and testified at the State Capitol about education bills for which she has expertise. I asked Dr. Angela Valenzuela about colleagues who might be involved in community orga-nizing, and she responded immediately about the "stunning absence" of such professors.[3]

She mourned how, prior to earning their PhDs, some graduate students seemed eager to make a difference, but once they obtained their highly competitive tenure-track faculty positions as assistant professors, they realized that teaching, steady publishing, and the quality of and respect for their research publications among colleagues and other academic reference groups would be what mattered for tenure and promotion to associate professor and ultimately full professor. Compared with other professionals, like lawyers and teachers, tenured faculty members may have more job stability because of the academic freedom principle (for their speech, discussed later) and their lesser likelihood to be required to meet "billable hours" standards in law firms. However, it should be noted that faculty members in some fields such as health must generate enough grant funding to pay part of their salaries.

At UT's LBJ School of Public Affairs, a graduate program with student research teams that write Policy Research Papers with research professors and professors of practice, I sought to interview professor Robert Wilson. With Ford Foundation support, he compiled an edited volume *Public Policy and Community: Activism and Governance in Texas* with IAF cases of what he called decentralized policy reforms of the 1980s–90s. However, he recently retired and moved away. The edited volume was externally funded research—highly valued in academia. Does collaboration depend on generating external resources? Only a handful of scholars have written about the IAF, often in peer-reviewed academic publications and thus not for the wider public; and main-stream studies rarely include the IAF (as has been noted in historical and education studies in previous chapter endnotes). Senior people inside the IAF or on an IAF board have written the major IAF books for a wider audience than academia.

Usually, academics research, write, and publish for other academics, thus limiting the impact of their ideas on the wider world. Only a small minority of faculty members do research on their own locale;[4] those of us in the borderlands have been fortunate to focus on this international place where globalization meets the local and matters greatly for people's quality of life in the comparative laboratory of two different political economies. Occasionally professors do something different or in addition to publishing in academic journals and books. Also at UT's LBJ School of Public Affairs, Dr. Victoria Rodríguez organized a conference in the mid-1990s that was meaningful but unusual for the way it relationally brought together scholars and practitioners about the topic of women in Latin American politics. Dr. Rodríguez featured not only scholars on the topic, but also *políticas* from Latin America.[5] Former Governor Ann Richards gave the keynote presentation. Now that is real accountability in research! The conference allowed researchers to share findings with subjects and people about whom they research for interchange and feedback on both sides.

In the social and health sciences, the approach that deliberately connects campus and community is labeled "community-based research (CBR)." Requests for Proposals (RFPs) from federal government agencies increasingly promote CBR as a way to share findings beyond academia, in partnership with non-government organizations and health agencies that might be able to use, apply, or advocate about findings to the wider public. Once again, let me say that externally funded research is highly valued in public universities, given the shrinking subsidies from state legislatures and the consequent rise in student tuition or what might be called "user fees" in public administration.

For my Dallas trip, I sought out professor-experts in regional history and/or in religion, given the dense concentration of private and public colleges and universities in the DFW region. But I found none who knew about, much less participated in, Dallas Area Interfaith until I told them. And recall from Chapter 6 that the whole book about educational reform in Austin during the time period of Alliance Schools made no mention of such schools or Austin Interfaith. Something is wrong with this picture, for it excludes readers and students from the comprehensive picture about history, schools, Texas politics, and non-governmental organizations in a region. It may reflect the research silos in academia: disciplines and interdisciplinary fields, even in Latinx Studies, as noted in earlier chapters.

Lest readers think professors are totally uninvolved with community, I must remind them that many professors do connect with organizations in applied teaching fields such as health, education, and business through internships and service-learning experiences. Dr. Angela Valenzuela talked about her involvement in teacher preparation programs with local schools. She and her husband, also a professor, work with a Saturday morning bilingual class of elementary-aged children using a culturally rich curriculum. She has had major successes in generating external grant funding for systemic change efforts in a cross-section of Texas cities to "grow their own teachers" who deeply understand the educational, cultural, and linguistic contexts. These externally funded efforts could have involved IAF affiliates if organizers and leaders networked with university people. I know many professors associated with centers, programs, and departments of women/gender, border/immigration, and ethnic/racial studies who maintain connections and relationships to community organizations that focus on mutual interests. Some of them write about the collaboration challenges but also learning gained in work with community-based organizations.

Professors behave like organizers when building research teams or critical masses of support for new programs across the internal institutional lines and hierarchies within universities. Higher education is like a miniature political system about which an IAF power analysis might be done. Who has power, why, how did they get it, from where, and with what resources? Despite the proliferation of ethnic/racial and women/gender/feminist interdisciplinary programs, few universities host centers focused on labor, class, inequalities, and/or poverty—the IAF's primary agendas. For a wide variety of reasons, universities in the UK, Europe, and Latin America focus far more on class than do universities in the U.S. Perhaps the disconnect between the IAF and higher education can be found in that absence.

IAF's narrow networks

For any engagement shortcomings in higher education, we must also ask if the IAF-higher education disconnect comes from the organizational culture of the IAF itself. Does the IAF welcome participation from those in higher education? Let us explore IAF's major books and my observations from seminars. I thread gender issues in this perspective.

The late Edward Chambers, a Catholic ex-seminarian with roots in working-class Iowa and longtime Executive Director of the national Industrial Areas Foundation who succeeded Saul Alinsky, wrote a "how-to" manual with assistance from Michael Cowen published in 2003 about the organizing process. He listed rules: a didactic set of guidelines called the "Universal Principles of Organizing" (see Chapter 1). Studs Terkel wrote about "Big Ed," as he called Chambers, in the Preface of that book.

In Chapter 6, Chambers reflected on his own experiences as an organizer, providing a moving account that could supplement Chapter 5 in this book for the early days of organizing. Chambers acknowledged male culture of his early days in 1950s and 1960s: "a machismo style with attendant bad habits.... with no place for women in our organizing." But "when we started the first IAF Training Institute, we cut women in on the same grounds and standards as we had for men."[6] He celebrated the many women leaders in IAF affiliates, though he quoted a peculiar case that came from a phone call to him from San Antonio.[7]

> [A]n angry voice said, "What are you teaching my wife in that training of yours? I didn't want her to go in the first place, and now she says she's not cooking every night unless some things change around here. What in the hell are you guys up to, anyway?" I asked to speak with his wife. She said, "I'm doing an action on him, just like you taught us." I explained to her that the actions were for the opposition, not your husband. "Oh," she said, "I'm very sorry. I'll only use what you taught me in public."

While Chambers seemed to recognize how economic dependency creates power inequality, he asked her to acquiesce to her husband and did not apply power-dependency concepts to everyday life, thus reinforcing the power hierarchy in marriage. The separation of the private and public was once a core theme in the IAF. However, in feminist activism, the personal and political are considered to be intimately tied and connected at their core.

Chambers wrote the book over fifteen years ago. We have seen in this book how the IAF affiliates in Texas have become more gender balanced, though an emphasis on "toughness" still prevails, especially in public performances. While toughness tends to be perceived as "masculine," the "relationality" so important in community organizing tends to be more

developed among women and requires an emphasis on mutually respectful conversation and empathy.[8]

In the twenty-first century, the IAF model embraces women organizers, though organizers' grueling training (see Chapter 5) may lean toward
the Alinsky and Chambers style. However, the strongest among women
may sooner or later draw on their own organizing style. Of course, the
male standard exists in many institutions, including higher education.
We can ask a rhetorical question to observe in many workplaces: Do
women adapt to the old models or broaden the models, especially after
they become skilled, experienced organizers? Do women professors?

As important as are the jarring gender dynamics in the San Antonio
call, Chambers's remarks in the book seemed wary of academics or even
anti-academic, perhaps part of IAF's organizational culture and training.
He said, "Academics and pundits love to throw around the term 'social
capital' and debate its nuances, but most of them couldn't organize a
block party. IAF's broad-based organizations are powerful social-capital
generators," acknowledging a concept in use by academics in their book-
length praise of the IAF.[9]

In a section entitled "What to look for in an Organizer," Chambers says

> Avoid Ph.D.s. They can't act. They get lost in writing books for
> one another. They are good at a certain kind of analysis, but
> never have a workable solution until the last chapter. For better
> or worse, at least a medical doctor gives you a prescription.
> Academic types are abstractionists. Does this make me an anti-
> intellectual? No, I'm just warning you about theoreticians and
> overrated so-called experts.[10]

While I agree with Chambers on some critiques, namely overly abstract
academic writing—and I could add more criticism—these comments
and others in Chapter 1's section on IAF rules simplify complexity and
rule out people and process with an extremely broad brush, including
some potential allies who teach the next generation of potential leaders.
Perhaps Chambers needed some education on how-to processes in higher
education, with which he had limited experience. If he were still alive
today, he could have read this chapter.

IAF spokesperson Michael Gecan wrote several books about his story
and organizing experiences, particularly the highly successful partnerships that the power of East Brooklyn Congregations created: affordable
housing. Gecan grew up in working, White ethnic immigrant Chicago

burdened with both mob power and the corrupt power of Mayor Daley's political machine, though also with one of the few remaining mediating institutions, the Catholic Church. Yet the church failed the neighborhood when its unmaintained firetrap parochial school burned and ninety-five children and nuns died.[11]

In his latest book published in 2018, *People's Institutions in Decline*, Gecan reiterates skepticism about academic obfuscation similar to Chambers: rarely visiting universities, with a one-day exception, and warning readers about "thinking critically from lofty academic or ideological distance."[12] I realize that academia has become the whipping boy from right, left, and center; I participate in some of that criticism myself, but with knowledge and experience that comes from working on the inside and with an organizer orientation from training in politics and public administration that began well before I even heard of the IAF.

Tension exists around the perhaps undeserved power of experts and "expertise." Having come of age politically in the social movements of the late 1960s and early 1970s, I understand the sometimes undue, unearned respect of those with authority. Besides that, graduate training teaches us to be critical, to challenge assertions, to ask for and validate with evidence, to clarify research methods, and to listen or read for logical flaws. In the IAF, relational power and the power of numbers are accorded more value than individual expert power. However, occasionally, in relational meetings, IAF leaders find it useful to refer to people by their formal titles for the moral or expert legitimacy they may provide: Rabbi x, Rev. y, Fr. or Sr. z, and Dr. Staudt.

The value of relational partnering

Let us unpack over-generalized and anti-intellectual remarks like those above. Of course, academia has been a male bastion for most of its history, but since the 1960s Equal Employment Opportunity laws, women have gradually entered the professoriate in greater proportions, even as full-time university positions have been shrinking for the rationale of cost-effectiveness. In universities that did engage with IAF, UTEP being the noteworthy example, it was primarily women who met with and partnered with EPISO organizers, from the El Paso Collaborative for Academic Excellence to the Center for Civic Engagement. President Diana Natalicio met with organizers upon request and regularly appeared in the community to give presentations when invited.

To community organizing, academics could bring something of value to education beyond the IAF-style short-term practical research related to action. In our interview, Dr. Angela Valenzuela noticed an IAF reluctance to draw on research to inform strategic thinking. At the same time, considering those IAF trainings and seminars with well-read and well-connected Ernesto Cortés Jr., organizers assigned intriguing academic books with authors from a variety of backgrounds: historians to theologians and news pundits, mostly men.[13] The quality workforce training centers like Project Arriba, Project Quest, and Capital Idea rely on scholarly and scientific cost-benefit analyses to demonstrate the rate of return on investment along with graduates' completion and placement rates. Great potential exists in better relations between the IAF and higher education institutions, perhaps fueled and expanded in ways that practice relational organizing and partnering.

Institutional expectations

In Chapter 5, we examined the institutional work structure of IAF organizers: their training, their placement and rotation, their reporting relationships, and the continuous socialization from all those factors to shape work behavior. We need to examine similar factors for professors, who undergo advanced study for at least four, up to ten additional years beyond the bachelor's degree primarily in research methods and some teaching experience before defending a dissertation for the terminal degree (for instance the PhD or EdD).

The search for academic tenure-track jobs is lengthy and potentially traumatic, with many judgmental eyes and ears in two-day interviews. Academic jobs have been shrinking all over the U.S., with underpaid part-time instructors filling in to teach. Assistant Professors are on probation for five years, also somewhat traumatic, during which time they are supposed to accumulate continuous research and publications, a good teaching record, external grants especially in science fields, and the least-important in assessment terms, service at both campus and community levels. At all levels, but especially at the tenured Associate Professor and (full) Professor levels, they are expected to participate in many committee assignments.

To determine if an assistant professor merits promotion to associate professor and the gold standard security of tenure after the probation period, many people judge candidates' work over several years both horizontally and vertically following the hierarchy of higher education:

external peer reviewers who assess candidates' research in their field of specialization, departmental colleagues, college and provost committees, the president, and Board of Regents. If granted tenure and promotion, academics generally become stable employees because other places to which one might apply rarely grant tenure unless the lateral move is to an administrative position. Unlike IAF organizers, who must work with leaders to generate revenue for their salaries, the academic is not required to raise their whole salary. An exception includes some health and medical fields where they may be required to raise a portion of that salary through external grants. With a "power analysis" cap on, one can see how politically charged the process can be unless decision makers adhere strictly to rules and professionalism. Still, one must always ask: who made those rules, for whose benefits and burdens, and with what standards? Even though academics acquire some autonomy, they undergo constant formal evaluation, each and every year before and after tenure. The wise academic learns the institutional incentives and penalties that shape their behavior and evaluation. The organizational cultures of academia tend to promote risk avoidance. There is risk in political activity, even as academics share constitutional rights to speech, association, and religion.

The principle known as "academic freedom" gives professors the right to speak and associate, including over unpopular topics. During 1950s anti-communist hysteria, Senator Joe McCarthy's hearings bullied international experts and filmmakers who lost jobs and got blacklisted from employment. Academics can lose tenure for cause, but are supposed to enjoy academic freedom about their areas of expertise.

Nevertheless, in academia, institutional rules and compliance trainings might send a chill on free speech to professors in their annual evaluations and the all-too-intimidating decisions about tenure after probation. Dr. Valenzuela reminded me to read the University of Texas Regents' Rules. Academic freedom is supposed to be well established to include an obligation to share expertise, yet the UT system sent "mixed messages" on the case that three women faculty members brought about the Texas law allowing concealed-carry guns on campus and inside classrooms.[14]

A considerable part of faculty evaluation consists of research and publication productivity in respected peer- or blind-reviewed well-ranked journals with high "impact factors" along with books published by prestigious presses, especially those publishers affiliated with universities. The quality of teaching is also evaluated, but the numeric criteria for evaluation are not as easily counted as are publications. Service, whether inside or outside the university, counts for little.

The busiest teachers are found in two-year community colleges, but they face little to no expectation about research productivity, even as their teaching loads are full, as many as four-to-five courses during a long semester, up to ten courses a year. In public research universities, professors teach two-to-three courses a semester. University institutions generally expect and reward a full research and publication agenda, optimally external-grant funded, making up almost half of their time. The "reward" may be a "meritorious" rating of 1–2 percent salary increases or a "course release" from external grant funding in which they "buy themselves out." Market language has infused academia along with other spheres of life.

As we can see, professors face competing demands on their time, and the pressure to raise funds can be as stiff as an IAF's organizer's pressure to fund the affiliate's budget to include their salary and benefits. Like the IAF, questions in academia must be raised about money: Who owns you and your research agenda? While lots of external funding of late comes from the U.S. Departments of Defense or Homeland Security, with particular military or border security agendas, little is available for community-based research except in the health sciences. Foundation funding is very competitive.

At many Texas universities, one is hard pressed to find any professor involved in the IAF. At UTEP, besides myself or Dr. Mark Lusk who stopped out of the IAF, one finds an occasional researcher like Dr. William Hargrove, community-based researcher in environmental health and director of a research institute. He interacts with community organizations and shares his research findings with people in the community once the articles are published. Affiliated with an Episcopal Church, a member institution, Dr. Hargrove underwent two-day IAF training. Bill counts himself as still involved, but does not attend the many labor-intensive steering and planning committees that make IAF actions possible. Besides, his church only periodically paid dues as a member institution. For Dr. Hargrove, the IAF public style, complete with scripted public meetings and borderline confrontation, may account for its limited appeal among the professoriate. He vividly remembers how a male organizer/trainer publicly "took on" a leader about her story. In academia, Bill says, professors lean toward civil discourse.[15] Given the issues raised in this chapter, I would add that bullying in academia has diminished but not disappeared.

Higher education programs encourage, even offer incentives for teaching faculty members to enrich their pedagogy. Many professors constantly fine-tune and tweak their course syllabi. One such example consists of academic service-learning and civic engagement programs. Such programs exist in over a thousand universities and offer opportunities for students and faculty members to connect with community organizations.[16] Professors can build a twenty- to thirty-hour community experience into their courses (i.e. about two hours weekly) as an alternative for a research paper, for partial course grades, or for extra credit. Besides the labor-light, but real-world-learning-heavy academic service learning, some fields offer supervised internships that range from twelve to twenty hours weekly for course credit in health, education, business, government, and the social sciences, or full-time at the graduate level. My Non-Profit Management course required mini-internships. To be sure, collaboration is a labor-intensive experience to assure co-ownership and voice (as previous chapters alluded to for IAF affiliates). Other scholars of community-based teaching have pointed out that unprepared students can be burdensome for those non-government organizations already stretched to capacity for staff supervision, space, and resources.[17]

As founder and director of UTEP's Center for Civic Engagement, and with support from the Deans' Council, as far back as in 2000, I proposed a new faculty evaluation policy with new criteria under the UT system's traditional criteria of research, teaching, and service. That is, under research, rules included evidence of "community-based research" and under teaching, evidence of "community-based teaching" to accord recognition and value to this labor-intensive work. I deliberated avoided additional language in the undervalued service section. However, in any hierarchical institution, a "leakage of authority" occurs, with diminishing compliance.[18] No doubt, busy deans selectively communicated such principles to department chairpersons and their tenured faculty who make initial promotion and tenure recommendations, depending on the discipline. In engineering, for example, the accrediting body values community-based work, so dean-level support would be stronger. And in "arts and science" colleges, English departments would find community-based work less appealing than sociology departments.

Policy compliance also depends on acceptance and co-ownership from other line administrators, such as departmental chairs and/or tenured faculty who evaluate their colleagues. On evaluation criteria, as organizers know, whether in the IAF or in higher education, persistence is necessary to achieve goals. More than a decade after my initial efforts, Dr. Mark Lusk, as provost-appointed Faculty Fellow, took up the task of getting more detailed rules in place, and successfully took his proposal to the Faculty Senate, which approved the policy, as did the provost and president. Under the able leadership of the Center for Civic

Engagement (CCE) Director Azuri González, field trips are arranged for faculty members to visit nonprofit organizations; tenure-track faculty also attend community-based research seminars with participation from mentor professors. Full response took a decade or more, but a word to the wary: changes in high-level university leadership can undo or undermine the acceptance of policies under their predecessors.

Let me deepen discussion of the organizational cultures that lead to "risk avoidance." In public universities—where many staff and faculty search for grants and gifts along with administrators who search for resources and support from the legislature—there are risks with offending donors or legislators, overbearing line administrators, and others. Such universities and colleges may regulate behavior via intimidating cues that discourage off-campus activities, especially if such activities are perceived as "political," a word that evokes negative connotations unless one understands its positive connotations (see Chapter 1) in small-d democracy.

Consider these examples of rules and procedures that may intimidate anxious professors. For one, faculty members may be required to seek line administrators' permissions to serve unpaid on nonprofit boards of directors or to do consulting work. The rule is understandable and reasonable, for it warns faculty about potential conflicts of interest, work burdens for unpaid board work and for paid work, of time limitations and the forbidden use of university equipment for non-university activity.

In another example, faculty and staff undergo annual compliance-with-rules training with its mixed semi-intimidating cues. Community engagement involves inevitable complexities which may be deemed "political" in the negative sense of the word. At some Texas public universities, compliance training consists of multiple-choice and true-false tests about content in on-line compliance modules. The training provides common-sense education about important legal and reasonable principles: the avoidance of conflicts of interest, the reminder of one's full-time job requirements, and the prohibited use of state equipment for private matters. Upon retirement after forty years, I began to happily ignore the emails which invite, with submission deadlines: "Renew your commitment to compliance."

Consider also the cues in the Political Activities Module that many faculty and staff must complete, derived from elaborate rules issued by the Texas Board of Regents who are gubernatorial political appointees.[19]

Test Question: "The term 'political activities' includes supporting or opposing legislation only." (Answer: false, because lobbying can go beyond specific bills.) However, the module makes it clear that education expertise can be shared. (Remember Dr. Valenzuela's citation of Regents' Rules!)

Test Question: "You should contact the Office of the President when providing information to elected officials." (Answer: True, perhaps to assure that the president is in the loop when institutional stakes are involved.)

At some point, these rules seem to cross the line of free speech and expression, even freedom of religion in the private lives of people affiliated with faith-based member institutions of community organizations.

Besides compliance modules, state law requires faculty members to complete quarterly reports for contacts with members of Congress, their staff, and/or federal officials. So when Congressional Representative Beto O'Rourke's chief of staff asked me (along with an orthodox economist) to present in 2016 at Congressman Beto O'Rourke's large Town Hall meeting about the controversial Trans-Pacific Partnership in 2016, we duly reported this contact in the online form, for the invitation to speak at the event was based on our research expertise. In another example, as a Border Interfaith leader, I periodically met with elected officials as a member of a church affiliated with the IAF organization. The first time I dutifully completed the form, I responded with the question of whether Texas still permits freedom of religion. Subsequent forms indicated that we need not report church-affiliated activity.

Despite my rather cautious analysis about the reluctance of busy professors to work in and with the community, training for new generations of faculty members may create a pool of people ready to do community-based teaching and research. Recent graduates have been not only socialized into community-based research but also recruited for their community-based interests. As noted above, institutional incentives have been put into place to reward or honor such expertise, including at annual celebratory events about community engagement. At least one-fourth of universities in the country operate service-learning, civic-engagement, and/or social-justice centers to facilitate students' experiential learning opportunities.[20] The most successful of those centers reform their institutional rules and procedures to acknowledge and value public work.

All this said, it is disappointing that academics do not seize the real opportunities they have to connect with communities to practice, apply, listen, and learn from others in their local community. Of course, few academics specialize in local research. Still, academics enjoy the good fortune of relatively autonomous jobs; attentiveness to institutions and rules provide space for public work that they can shrink or expand. Too many academics, I worry, spend too much time interacting with other academics about highly specialized research rarely read in the larger public. With more academic public-mindedness, perhaps our society could better address festering inequality, injustice, and growing authoritarianism.

The other side of the IAF-higher education equation is a seeming reluctance in the IAF itself for all the reasons analyzed in this section. If little value is accorded to expertise, partnership with higher education leaders may be challenging. Of courses, external resources can always facilitate partnership. An exception to these preliminary conclusions involves IAF partnership with community colleges. To this collaboration we now turn.

Collaboration between community colleges and IAF around workforce training

Contrary to the limitations of IAF-university collaboration, community colleges offer greater prospects for such partnership. They offer career-oriented programs in a variety of fields, especially health care, and students can acquire two-year Associate of Arts degrees that can be transferred to universities for careers that require a bachelor's degree in Texas, such as teaching.

In six cities, IAF affiliates facilitated the creation of high-quality, independent nonprofit workforce training centers with case managers to work with successful applicants and provide them with wrap-around services. The female participants who head households with children, in particular, need services while they attend classes. Together with business leaders in the cities, the workforce training centers place graduates in actual jobs. The professionals who manage the centers track participants' earnings before and after training in those positions and carefully document moves from impoverishment to living-wage jobs and more, from $10,000 annually to over $40,000 in typical scenarios. Over the years, these centers have produced thousands of graduates.

A fund is available in state government to match monies up to $5 million raised locally from city, county, and other sources. In every Texas legislative session, IAF organizers and volunteer leaders converge on the State Capitol to defend this fund and push for other issues on the

IAF agenda. With professional evaluators, the workforce training center directors report cost/benefit calculations that show how, for each public dollar invested, the Return on Investment (ROI) to the city and county over the long term is enormous in property and sales taxes, generally hovering around 1:20-plus based on my review of their annual reports. Consult the websites for annual reports on numbers, persistence, and graduation rates, before-and-after earnings, placement rates, and cost-benefit returns.[21] IAF affiliates organize people; they do not manage partially government-funded centers like these.

The centers, all of them 501c3 nonprofit organizations, list their boards of directors on websites. Some even post their IRS 990 forms that show nonprofit income and expenditures; as such, they are models of transparency. One can see who sits on those boards and their organizational affiliations. The boards draw heavily from the business community with whom IAF affiliates have built relationships, but leaders from IAF member institutions also serve, including rabbis, pastors, priests, and other community leaders. Board members assist the centers in seeking matching funds from city and county governments for economic and labor-force development. In my review of workforce training websites, I found a third or more of directors on boards, including the Vice-Chair, to be IAF-affiliated.

The cities and the centers operate in six places: Austin, Dallas, Houston, El Paso, the Rio Grande Valley, and San Antonio. Each has a unique name, mission, and history. The workforce centers offer evidence of the lasting, institutionalized accomplishments of IAF affiliates around the state, together producing thousands of graduates with certificates and degrees and earning middle-class salaries in stable professions. Their mostly 1990s founding stories are outside the parameters of this book.[22]

In a report for the Bill and Melinda Gates Foundation, El Paso's Project Arriba is featured as a strong example of a "community-based" post-secondary model, with mentoring, varied funding streams, support services, relationships with employers, evidence-based tracking of success, and more.[23] Why does this collaboration work relatively smoothly? Each institution in the partnership has an interest in maintaining and growing the partnership (an example of the IAF "self-interest" principle). The centers enroll students and provide wraparound services. Such close casework motivates students to complete the program in ways far deeper than the loose collection of counselors in higher education who each serve hundreds of students, if and when students are proactive about seeking assistance. The business community, as we know from the previous chapters, wants workforce-ready graduates. The colleges and universities, for enrollees seeking four-year degrees, have an interest in tuition and completion rates. The IAF affiliates continue their commitment to spread prosperity and living-wage jobs to a larger number of people in their communities.

The IAF affiliates also help to recruit students for the programs. The students and graduates often volunteer to "tell their story" at Accountability Sessions when candidates are asked if they will support these workforce centers at particular levels of funding support. Only a minute or two in length, the stories movingly illustrate the life-changing experiences of parents and the children who work in jobs that pay decent wages. Without middle-class salaries, these participants would be stuck in poverty along with their children, with only the rare among those children likely able to develop talents fully in the school system. With more matching funds, the centers could double and triple the thousands who graduate and contribute to economic development in their communities.

Concluding reflections

IAF affiliates and higher education institutions have only uneasy, distant, or absent relationships with one another. Their organizational cultures clash, or at least are hardly understood by those within each distinctive institution. As such, books about the IAF are rare in academic literature, including IAF's important contributions to reducing inequalities and working on class issues that generate living-wage or middle-class jobs. As or more importantly, the IAF is disconnected from a potential pipeline of young social justice leaders and organizer recruits. However, El Paso's IAF organizations developed stronger relationships with the University of Texas at El Paso over thirty years, primarily with several women academic leaders in the institution.

Part of the clash between the IAF and higher education institutions may be its avowed anti-intellectualism. However, IAF's anti-intellectualism at the national level, in its own self-described literature, has been tempered with the many male intellectuals invited to present their books in the West/ Southwest IAF region, which includes Texas.

The exception to this rule of the common IAF-higher education disconnect involves the community-college partnerships in post-secondary training with the six IAF-facilitated, but independent high-quality workforce training centers that have become institutionalized in the state. The participation of the business community on boards of directors exemplifies the relational work that produces positive outcomes of this training, such as high persistence, graduation, and job placement rates.

In other chapters, I have raised questions about the close relationships that sometimes exist between social justice organizations and the business community, relationships that might compromise the autonomy of IAF affiliates despite their principled rule I often heard articulated: "no permanent friends, no permanent enemies." If the philanthropic businesses are the same as the developers, will social justice organizers challenge developers when business advocates for bond issues that allow for "public investments and private gains" (the inversion of the "private investments, public gains" ideal) and contribute mounds of money to the campaigns of city council representatives that do their bidding? This is an open question. However, in the case of workforce training, we see how multiple self-interests—business, community colleges, and low-income residents—are served with these IAF-instigated and lasting signature projects to move impoverished people into middle-class professional salaried work.

Notes

1. Interviews with Dr. Mark Lusk, May and August, 2018.

2. James Q. Wilson, *Bureaucracy: What Government Agencies Do and Why They Do It* (New York: Basic Books, 1989). Besides his 1973 book cited earlier, I believe this one to be the next most relevant to this analysis. Alas, few scholars of public higher education draw parallels with U.S. government administration.

3. Interview with Dr. Angela Valenzuela, July 26, 2018.

4. Those of us who live, teach, and research in the US-Mexico borderlands have been able to connect the global with the local or to do comparative research. See my previously cited research on education (2003, 2012, 2010), political economy (1998), and NGOs (2002), but also books and edited volumes on violence against women and drug policy (2008, 2009, 2013). More recently, I have conducted modestly funded National Institutes of Health (NIH) community-based research with graduate students on environmental health, published in peer-reviewed journals tending to be more valued in academia (2012, 2015, 2016) and in a chapter (2017) where I analyzed the uncertain outcomes of community-based research (see reference list at the end of this book).

5. Dr. Victoria Rodríguez also published two books on the topic.

6. Robert Chambers, *Roots for Radicals: Organizing for Power, Action, and Justice* (New York: Continuum, 2003), 100–101; Michael Gecan, *Going Public: An Organizer's Guide to Citizen Action* (New York: Anchor Books, 2002) also narrates his own organizing experience. This integration of women based on existing standards reminds me of political scientist Judith Stiehm's path-breaking book *Bring Me Men and Women: Mandated Change at the U.S. Air Force Academy* (Berkeley: University of California Press, 1981). Questions constantly emerge therein: Whose standards? Why those standards?

7. Chambers, pp. 78–9.

8. Susan Stall and Randy Stoecker, "Community Organizing or Organizing Community? Gender and the Crafts of Empowerment," *Gender and Society* 12, no. 6, pp. 729–756; also see Chapters 5 and 2.

9. Chambers, p 68. Two leading book-length analyses of the IAF used the social capital concept: Dennis Shirley, *Valley Interfaith and School Reform: Organizing for Power in South Texas* (Austin: University of Texas Press, 2002) and Mark Warren, *Dry Bones Rattling: Community Building to Revitalize American Democracy* (Princeton: Princeton University Press, 2001).

10. Chambers, p. 110.

11. Gecan 2002. His background is similar to my own, but I was raised in Milwaukee, ninety miles to the north.

12. Gecan 2018, pp. 41–3; quote on p. 43.

13. Mark Warren names the distinguished authors in *Dry Bones Rattling*, p. 88: "On economic issues, guests included Barry Bluestone, James Tobin, Ray Marshall, Vernon Briggs, William Greider, Paul Osterman, Richard Freeman, Frank Levy, and many others. On education, seminars featured Terry Moe, Chester Finn, Howard Gardner, James Comer, Robert Moses, Richard Murnane, Henry Levin, and Deborah Meier, among others." On democratic politics, "Michael Walzer, Benjamin Barber, Jean Bethke Elshtain, Theda Skocpol, Robert Putnam, Richard Bernstein, and William Sullivan." On theology and religion, "Charles Curran, James Cone, Cornel West, Bryan Hehir, and Delores William." On race, "William Julius Wilson, Michael Dawson, Glenn Loury, and Thomas Edsall." I know academia is male dominated, but this list exaggerates such hegemony with twenty-eight men and four women. And little IAF interest seems to exist in women and gender topics.

14. See the *Austin American Statesman*, among lots of coverage: https://www.mystatesman.com/news/local/professors-have-academic-freedom-despite-whatsaycourt/1/. On appeal, UT lawyers argued that academic freedom lies in the institution not the person, yet outside the courtroom, reaffirmed the faculty members' academic freedom.

15. Interview with Dr. William (Bill) Hargrove, May 2018.

16. Campus Compact, https://compact.org/who-we-are/our-coalition/members/.

17. Randy Stoecker and Elizabeth Tryon, *The Unheard Voices: Community Organizations and Service Learning* (Philadelphia: Temple University Press, 2009). During UTEP's Center for Civic Engagement's early years, we brought Stoecker, a sociologist now at the University of Wisconsin, to meet with our faculty, community partners, and students. Stoecker founded and moderated the "comm-org" (community organizing) listserv and website, including its many scholarly papers. See, for example, my co-authored piece: http://comm-org.wisc.edu/papers2002/staudt.htm.

18. One of my favorite classics by Anthony Downs, *Inside Bureaucracy* (Boston: Little Brown, 1967), offered scores of laws and propositions to test in large-scale bureaucracies (like public universities, part of governments).

19. I printed copies, available in my office files.

20. Campus Compact (which also spawned state compacts such as the now-defunct Texas Campus Compact at which UTEP was a founding member for the founding event in University of Texas at Austin). https://compact.org/.

21. The websites for this organizations follow: Capital Idea (Austin): http://www.capitalidea.org/; Capital Idea Houston http://www.capitalideahouston.org/; Valley Initiative for Development and Advancement (VIDA), Rio Grande Valley http://www.vidacareers.org/; Skill Quest (Dallas) http://www.skillquestcareers.org/; Project Arriba (El Paso) https://projectarriba.org/; Project Quest (San Antonio) http://questsa.org/

22. See Warren, 2001, Chapter 6.

23. Maureen Bozell and Melissa Goldberg, *Employers, Low-Income Young Adults, and Postsecondary Credentials: A Practical Typology for Business, Education, and Community Leaders* (Workforce Strategy Center, October, 2009). I have a hard copy of the assessment, but it is available online: http://collegeforamerica.org/employers-low-income-young-adults-and-postsecondary-credentials/ Accessed Oct. 16, 2018.

Chapter 9
Concluding Reflections:
Wherefore IAF affiliates in Texas, the US, and the World?

"The world as it is…. the world as it should be."

In this book, I wove together the voices, stories, and experiences of Texas IAF leaders and organizers with scholarly studies, archival documents, and civic education about institutions, both government and nongovernment organizations (NGOs). Among NGOs, I included voluntary organizations with a purpose, such as faith-based congregations and social justice community organizations. This chapter's epigraph phrases, used in IAF trainings, have been adapted from Industrial Areas Foundations (IAF) founder Saul Alinsky, a proponent of organizing that starts with people in their places who work with hope to build a more just society. This book starts at the grassroots, using grassroots perspectives and a variety of research methods that complement and update books about the IAF written by its senior people, to show how local IAF affiliates operate and relate to their state organizations.

Toward hope, some justice and power

Together, scores of thousands of people in Texas work for social justice reforms in a disciplined manner via the Texas IAF affiliates. In so doing, they are working in the world as it is and win victories that build toward the world as it should be. For these mostly working- and middle-class people, each of those victories spurs them on to take on new goals—goals which bubble up from house meetings or down from state and regional IAF senior leaders. Hope moves grassroots participants, a sentiment that—coupled with skills, relationships, and the power of large numbers of people—can make a real difference for the public in this dark and polarizing era. It is nothing short of remarkable for people to join, then remain in those organizations amid the opportunity costs associated with work and households, given the sheer incentives toward individualism in US social life.

271

Thanks to the founders of the Texas IAF—among them Ernesto Cortés, Jr. and women like Elizabeth Valdez and Sisters Maribeth Larkin, Pearl Ceasar, and the late Christine Stephens—Texas is home to the oldest and strongest model of community organizing, a model that empowered many leaders and achieved social justice goals.

The IAF model works in twenty-four US states, sixty-five cities, and several other countries around the world. In this conclusion, I revisit the six questions from Chapter 1 and discuss continuing challenges in Texas, but also look beyond Texas, home to a powerful political-economic elite, for prospects to deepen democracy and reduce inequalities. I highlight an important recent precedent set in neighboring state Louisiana, where IAF state and local affiliates took on powerful business interests which had operated in collusion with past state government for billions of tax abatements. In so doing, Alinsky's use of the word "radical" has been restored for the win, but in a mature process that can appeal to broad-based people, even those Arlie Hochschild interviewed (recall Chapter 4) who racialized responsibility for problems actually produced by state industrial policies which trickled few benefits to working people, whatever their race or ethnicity.

In Texas cities, IAF affiliates have earned a "place at the table" of many local governments at the city, county, and school-board levels. Most local candidates and office-holders, perhaps once with initial trepidation, eagerly meet with the large cross-section of disciplined, well-organized people who seek constructive strategies for change. While the change does not always get to the roots of problems in highly inequitable societies like the U.S. and Texas, the process empowers people with civic education, voice, and the civility so desperately needed in today's polarized U.S. Moreover, many IAF-instigated public policy reforms produced meaningful changes that improve people's lives. At the state level, without a broad base of reasonable representatives who work on a bipartisan basis, meaningful change has been more difficult. Texas is dominated by one party, gerrymandering, and a primary election system that made harsh, extremist ideologues into party nominees and victors in this low-voter turnout state, near the bottom of all U.S. states.

Besides acknowledging the top tier of state and regional IAF leadership, we must appreciate those on whom I focus in this book: the long-term volunteer leaders and paid organizers at the grassroots level who work for not only their own interests but also the public interest in making society more equitable and just. A balanced proportion of leaders and organizers are women; and given the diverse urban and borderlands

locations of IAF affiliates, they also represent the state as it will be in
the next decade or two: a mix of primarily Mexican American, White,
and African American people. Those people are putting their ideas, principles, interests, and faith into action. In a twenty-first-century world
of social media congestion, people's relationships and commitments
in IAF affiliates involve so much more than a Facebook group, likes,
and comments among "friends" who are easily "added" and "deleted,
blocked, or removed" at a second's notice. Within IAF affiliates, people
build personal relationships of trust, responsibility, and commitment
to get things done together. Such interaction cannot be taken lightly.
The skills and sentiments learned have lifetime consequences for political efficacy and effectiveness even for those who stop out or drop out of
their local IAF affiliates. The use and expansion of relationships to build
trust and social capital to accomplish tasks together (see Chapter 1) and
expand the IAF have resulted in copy-cat practices in other community
organizations.

The national IAF's *2017 Impact Report* calls attention to the thousands of civil society institutions with which it works in those sixty-five
US cities and four other countries. The report highlights key victories
in Texas:

> Secured $27 million in food aid for Houston Hurricane Harvey
> survivors, through D-SNAP programs and protected thousands
> of renters from eviction. Passed a $5 million ACE grant through
> Texas legislature, funding high-wage, long-term job training.
> Revised Chap 27 of the City of Dallas Housing code, strongest
> tenant protections in Texas. Increased Bexar County and City
> of San Antonio entry wages to $14.25 per hour. North Texas
> negotiated the acceptance of parish ID's by three metro-area
> police departments. Leveraged $2 million in USDA funding for
> colonia water infrastructure in El Paso area.

These few lines of policy and budgetary achievements hardly do justice
to the difference made by empowered volunteer leaders and with people
in substandard housing and fear who live without adequate food, water,
and living wages: disaster-related food assistance (D-SNAP) in Houston,
tenant housing codes (Dallas), living wages (San Antonio), parish ID's
(Dallas), and water (El Paso). We covered these and many other issues in
the previous chapters, at far greater length, focusing on both process
and outcome. The analysis of process—like leadership identification

and development—is just as important as timelines and outcomes that required massive amounts of organizing work at mostly local levels.

The achievements affirm the importance of analyzing the IAF from grassroots on up, for it is local paid organizers and volunteer leaders who achieved these goals at local levels including tapping federal sources for local use. As for state-level achievements, the ACE grant that matches funds for quality workforce training centers continues from previous legislative sessions, when social justice people operated in the more-open space of a competitive political party system. Texas IAF ranks with California and New York among the most spectacular achievements, though Louisiana surely ranks with its cutting-edge challenge to petro-oil subsidies—a challenge that, won, will no doubt spread to other locales (as discussed below). Some states offer far more receptive spaces at the state level than Texas. Still, the Texas IAF continues and achieves, albeit with more obstacles than elsewhere, yet a strong people base.

Texas: Limited government, limited democracy

The political economy of Texas reveals a huge disconnect between those who hold power—who "pay to play" at the highest levels of power with campaign donations for their politicians—and the majority of people. Recall Chapter 2's chart on the biggest funder sectors in multi-million-dollar politics in the state. Moneyed power keeps its grip in what has become a one-party dominant regime that undermines reasonable, centrist-oriented civic dialogue, especially at the state level. In a state like Texas, social justice organizations try to counterbalance the paralysis at the top with active civil society at the grassroots and relationships with representatives from both parties who are willing to dialogue. IAF affiliates press local officials for policy changes that actualize the promise of democracy. However, all too often, IAF and local representatives are upended with state pre-emption laws that reduce local control in favor of the business-friendly status-quo that would allow injustices like miserable pay without benefits or fracking inside city limits, even when local representatives pass ordinances against such practices.

The Dallas Area Interfaith (DAI) case from Chapter 3 shows that it is possible to begin shifting from a city "that is" to a city "that should be" despite the challenges of its history, racial/ethnic divisions, and the steep road ahead in mending that division and inequality. While much remains to be done, DAI pursues a people-friendly organizer model. DAI's spectacular actions in the fall 2018 electoral season demonstrate what armies of empowered people can do in a huge Accountability Session, calling and walking to get out the vote (see Chapters 1 and 3). And similar actions in Austin Interfaith helped to increase voter turnout and flip a house district to turn out the champion of pre-emption laws in the state legislature (though ex-Representative Workman had many allies).

Many twentieth-century books on the Texas IAF focused on its admirable founders who built a strong, disciplined organization that has stood the test of almost a half century's time. Some IAF "rules" (see Chapter 1's list, which I re-visit later in this chapter) and institutional characteristics remain the same, from recruitment and training to the language used in IAF action, thanks to national guidebooks from the men who founded and led IAF nationally, from Saul Alinsky to Edward Chambers and Michael Gecan. However, the disciplined grid within which IAF works generates contradictions that produce tensions—tensions which may or may not be resolved in the continuous process of rebuilding and maintaining any NGO, including the IAF. As an organization, the IAF is dedicated to evaluating its actions, from meetings to Accountability Sessions and trainings. As a rule, the IAF also relishes tension at its actions, so as to avoid the boring groupthink that characterizes so much in hierarchical U.S. life. However, the juxtaposition of an imposed Blueprint-like grid creates contradictions that result in tension. As for whether IAF operations in Texas operate with a Blueprint or Learning Process model, I see tendencies in both directions; strong organizers and leaders at local levels lean actions toward a Learning Process model.

Contradictions, tensions, resolutions

In this book, I identified six potential contradictions in the form of questions based on the IAF organizing model and its collaboration with other organizations and public institutions, including higher education. My analysis was driven by concepts and theories from organizational studies that examine relationships within and between formal institutions. Let us consider them, one by one.

1. IAF Affiliates: faith-based or broad-based organizations?
   IAF senior leaders call the IAF broad-based organizing, though they use faith-based Biblical stories in some of the trainings. At local levels, IAF affiliates vary: the largest and strongest among them contain a mix of faith-based and broad-based organizations.

The smaller IAF affiliates, as in El Paso, draw entirely faith-based member institutions into their fold except for a short period when the American Federation of Teachers became a member institution. None of the IAF organizations pushes a religious agenda; however, their critique of problematic policies often taps both reasoned and moral arguments, based on stories that volunteer leaders discuss in house meetings. Words like ethical, fair, and decent wages should not be confined only to the religious in U.S. society. Ethical language need not be stripped from public policy analyses and rationales that all too often become confined to terms like "efficiency."

Religious commitment has been on the decline in U.S. society, as earlier chapters analyzed. For those IAF affiliates with religious-only member institutions, the pathway into volunteer leadership and perhaps even organizing comes through faith affiliation. If religious commitment declines even more in future decades, this pathway into organizing bodes ill for the strength of and growth in IAF affiliates. Moreover, discussions about revenue in previous chapters merit attention for the possible dependence of some IAF affiliates on Catholic Campaign for Human Development funding and the way that could shape the IAF issue agenda. The source, religious and denominational, prohibits organizing around specific issues related to "life," especially fetal life, and thereby inhibits attention to women's reproductive health (covered below in contradiction #4).

Chapter 1 discussed IAF's expansion, clearly well beyond Texas, the focus on this book, to half of U.S. states, but also IAF's expansion into other western countries such as Canada, the UK, Germany, New Zealand, and Australia. Those countries no doubt have been undergoing the same decline in religious commitment. The separation of church and state is a key principle in many western countries like these. Even though the IAF does not push a religious agenda, the IAF affiliates with the word "faith" in their names create that perception.

Given these considerations, I use the term "broad-based organizing" in the subtitle of this book. However, I appreciate the flexibility that local IAF affiliates' options provide in the names and recruitment strategies for member institutions.

2. IAF Collaboration in formal and informal coalitions
Collaboration is a tough challenge for any non-government or government organization. What seems simple can become extraordinarily complex with more steps, leaders, and participants. A classic book by

political scientists, *Implementation*, contains reprints of Rube Goldberg's cartoons to illustrate with comic relief the complexity of coordination across government agencies and community partnerships.[1]

Readers may need reminding that IAF affiliates themselves contain a collaborative coalition of diverse member institutions: synagogues, Catholic parishes, diverse Protestant churches, and for some, public schools and non-profit organizations like health clinics. At the state level, local IAF affiliates come together collaboratively and periodically for trainings and broader strategy meetings, adding to the complexity. Therefore, it should not be surprising that IAF affiliates take on collaborations with some deliberation.

In various chapters, we saw how IAF affiliates comprise diverse member institutions, even nonprofit organizations. Austin Interfaith's dues-paying member institutions, such as Education Austin or the Workers Defense Project, exercise independence, power, and visibility in their own right. Leaders in collaborations must tread lightly on practices given their nonprofit tax-exempt status. For example, labor/professional organizations like teacher associations can endorse candidates, but IAF affiliates cannot. In Chapter 7, we saw the collaborative strains in EPISO and Border Interfaith's participation in the Lift Up Alliance to prevent wage theft—an alliance that all but disappeared once an ordinance was achieved. However, collaboration can be in an IAF affiliate's self-interest. For example, the working-class base of unions and workers' defense projects help to broaden and thereby legitimize the IAF agenda for local ordinances on living wages and paid leave. EPISO devoted years to the Education Summit, a good match with its Alliance Schools and an opportunity to widen the base of parental engagement, even as the state's high-stakes testing system made it more and more difficult to build teacher-parent leadership teams in schools. In any and all of these cases from previous chapters, organizers and leaders must calculate their organizational interest in participation along with the costs and benefits therefrom.

IAF collaboration with higher education institutions has been limited, to the detriment of both sides of this equation. IAF could provide more community-based experiences to students and faculty. Higher education could provide background research, on which IAF-style research could build rather than re-invent, along with a potential pipeline of future organizers and student leaders, younger than the mostly middle- and older-aged congregants in IAF member institutions. Moreover, professors' research and teaching could make IAF work more visible in mainstream writing and publications about history, politics, and communities. Some IAF affiliates achieve external grants, but to broaden the funding base beyond the Catholic Campaign for Human Development, they could join with the considerable grant-getting capabilities in higher education which, for better or worse, incentivize external funding among faculty. Although the past anti-intellectual content of national IAF senior organizers is understandable, to deter people from reliance on experts and authority, the professoriate offers a wide cast of characters with whom mutually respectful collaboration could be possible.

Thus, I view collaboration as potentially useful, but complex for time and accountability reasons. External collaboration should not occur at the expense of local affiliates' accountability to member institutions. Local affiliates should be allowed to make decisions about collaboration.

3. Mix of top-down and bottom-up decision making

This third contradiction may be the most difficult tension to resolve. Statewide IAF senior organizers seek consistency and a unified force in legislative interaction, yet the organization is based on the principle that its issues bubble up from house meetings, not down from senior organizers and supervisors.

The superstructure of Texas IAF affiliates, part of the West/ Southwest IAF in a bifurcated national Industrial Areas Foundation, guides organizers and leaders with tried and tested processes used over the years and in other organizations, government and NGO alike: careful recruitment and selection, intensive training that continues during employment, and employee/organizer rotation. Trainee and organizer fatigue no doubt exists; an unknown number leave over the high expectations and rigid operating model. IAF leaders are essentially volunteers, motivated by self-interest and by purpose, not wages or monetary rewards, working in a hardly visible hierarchy with organizers. Organizers are not only accountable to the local leaders, but also to their senior organizer-supervisors and to what might be alternatively called the top, center, or superstructure that governs their work, reporting relationships, and continuous training. Local leaders neither select their organizers nor have a voice in planning distant training content, schedules, and pedagogy or how those distant trainings change over time.

IAF state and regional senior organizers pursue a disciplined formula for maintaining consistency and unity. The IAF selectively recruits, trains, and socializes paid organizers and volunteers to its language and rules that are reflected in its disciplined organizational culture—its way of doing and communicating "how we operate." That organizational culture may clash with contemporary realities and with other organizations, including local affiliates and the issues that bubble up from volunteer leaders in their member institutions. Local organizers interact regularly with their senior organizer-supervisors who relay and remind them about the IAF model and statewide agenda. The organizer could get caught between discordance from above and below, yet it is the volunteer leaders and member institutions below who raise money for local organizers' salaries.

IAF culture generates sizeable costs in the form of dues to the superstructure for training, technical assistance, and supervision. Fixed dues can be burdensome, especially to IAF affiliates in low-income communities like the borderlands or to those affiliates rebuilding former shells. This monetary contradiction creates a tension that pervades other contradictions; grassroots leaders have limited voice for redress about senior organizers' expenditures, dues, and training schedules. Organizers believe in and practice the IAF mission and work hard to facilitate fundraising to support their affiliate and assure that affiliate dues are paid to the IAF, the Interfaith Education Fund (IEF) (which reimburses some travel expenses for training), and the Network of Texas Organizations. The criteria on which these dues are based lack transparency. There is little voice for local leaders in such decisions.

One spillover contradictory effect in this informal, yet hierarchical superstructure shapes how and where organizers work in local IAF affiliates. Decisions about organizers' rotation ought to provide voice to local volunteer leaders and member institutions. The "who decides" questions are among the most fundamental in any organization, governmental or non-governmental.

Volunteer leaders can develop relationships with the statewide senior organizer-supervisors, but the superstructure is not immediately transparent. Even at the national level, the IAF website does not contain the names of its Board of Directors, but rather seven testimonials from mostly clergy. Of course, dedicated individuals can search, as I did, for board members' names and directors' salaries on Guidestar, the website containing nonprofit IRS 990 forms, but board directors' names should be easily available, certainly more than opaque, as they are on most non-profit organization websites.

4. Gender-balance and/or responsiveness to women's and gender-based issues

In yet another IAF potential contradiction, the founding fathers of the national IAF sought, trained, and used an assertive, even tough organizer style, discussed in earlier chapters: aggressive, driving, and ready to take on or call out people publicly and in training seminars. A style like this is not unique in the IAF; it is also found in other formerly male-dominated occupations. To succeed with this model, twentieth-century women often adopted similar styles, whether in government and politics, in higher education, or in community organizing. Yet in a model and with rules that stress relationship building, the old style may not work as effectively as in the early stages of organizational life.

To build social capital—i.e., relationships of trust to accomplish goals together—a conversational, listening, and mutually supportive interactive style may be better. Successful twenty-first-century IAF work depends, I believe, on a more gender-balanced group of organizers and perhaps the sort of relationality that often characterizes women's interactive styles. While caution is necessary in generalizing to large demographic groups like men and women, girls and boys still undergo socialization that prizes different gender-based styles. I have interviewed and worked with IAF organizers who exhibit gender-distinctive interactive styles. Women organizers in the twentieth century IAF no doubt adapted to the older, prized model of assertiveness and toughness, but the newer twenty-first-century women organizers perhaps epitomize the listening, socialized, and learned skills that produce success in relationship building yet assertiveness when confronting power and authority.

Besides gender-based interactive styles, the IAF works in highly different cultural settings in the diverse regions of Texas. Spanish-language capability is obviously a required skill for many organizers in the new twenty-first-century Texas. Relational work may require dense and personal communication styles and networks of both strong and weak ties, as discussed in previous chapters, adapted to context. Multiple models of leadership and organizing, beyond a paradigmatic Blueprint approach, resonate with varying cultural contexts and women's ways of interacting. In the twenty-first-century, IAF trends toward more women organizers and leaders, and toward demographic gender balance, thus resolving this contradiction and its tension.

Besides the issue of who organizes, female or male, issue agendas can or should cover gendered wage inequalities, reproductive health, and domestic violence. Perhaps such issues rarely bubble up in small-group house meetings because they may seem private, even shameful to those who have survived rape and domestic violence or legally terminated a pregnancy. Some current work is done with these issues, but in such a nuanced way as to be nearly invisible except to feminist eyes like my own and others. Yet these stories remain absent in IAF affiliates' work for various reasons. One is the heavy presence of the Catholic clergy and dependence on faith-affiliation money which may mute the open articulation of what generically might be called "women's issues."

At the same time as I analyze IAF on the silences around women's issues, we must acknowledge how the six Texas high-quality, IAF-spawned workforce training centers recruit women, often heads of household, who are well served with wrap-around counseling and services as they complete their degrees and certification programs while raising children on their own. The attentiveness to low-income women's interests is worthy, but muted rather than celebrated in IAF language and discourse. These graduates could become a future pool from which to strengthen commitment from younger people. Among potential young leaders and organizers, IAF could highlight this work or risk losing time and talent to other NGOs that openly support better women's wages, gender-equitable wages, and women's health.

Race and racism might also be viewed as potentially polarizing issues inside the organization, evident in how IAF affiliates operate in relation with police departments (recall Chapter 3). Earlier IAF books hinted that the IAF seemed slow to recruit more organizers and leaders from the African American community. This is not the case in the DAI's diverse leadership, nor in other twenty-first-century affiliates. And the representation of organizers and leaders with Mexican heritage is strong, as is the bilingual Spanish and English capability of many affiliated with the IAF. Texas has become a "majority-minority" state, that is, people of color

outnumber White/Anglo people. IAF's success in bridging boundaries across race, ethnicity, and language ought to bode just as well
for gender.

While the IAF recruits gender-balanced organizers, I am not
hopeful that it can deal with women's issues such as reproductive
health and violence. Leaders who identify as feminists invest their
energy into other organizations, in compartmentalized social justice
work. However, in our busy workaholic society, making time for
multiple organizations is a challenging feat at best. So either the IAF
or women's organizations will suffer the loss of committed participants without overlap in their agendas.

5. Generating revenue for local and distant operations
   In the IAF, like most nonprofit organizations, generating enough
   revenue to cover expenses while maintaining a safety reserve fund
   net is a chronic problem. Local IAF affiliates must not only cover
   their own expenses but also pay statewide dues. We have seen,
   especially in #3 above, the contradictions of an organization that
   celebrates self-sufficiency in its policy agenda and local affiliates,
   but not the self-sufficiency of its superstructure. Local IAF affiliates must raise revenue to pay their organizers, even though the
   organizers work as much for the statewide operation as they do for
   their local leaders. This contradiction produces tension, particularly in low-income counties. Statewide IAF dues collectors write
   grants and share some of the bounty in the form of covering travel
   for local leaders' training. However, they are dependent upon, not
   self-sufficient in, their relationship to local affiliates.

   Local affiliates use a variety of tactics to raise funds. They
   collect dues from their member institutions. Strong IAF affiliates
   can remove members in arrears and then reinstate them when dues
   are paid. This is not always the case for weaker affiliates who interact with member institutional core leaders to obtain partial pay or
   to wait for catch up on dues in arrears. Local affiliate committees
   visit with businesses and bankers for investments in their work.
   Affiliates sometimes produce Ad Books with civic information
   and ads for which businesses, hospitals, schools, or individuals pay
   a fee. As noted in an earlier chapter, I saw decades' worth of Ad
   Books in the UTSA archives for San Antonio's COPS in its early
   decades as well as a more recent elaborate multi-color version for
   Valley Interfaith. IAF also features "donate" buttons on its websites.
   And finally, organizers and leaders propose grants, some of which

become funded. The Catholic Campaign for Human Development has been relied upon as a primary funder in the weaker affiliates. All these tactics make for challenges to meet everyday financial responsibilities.

If local affiliates are to continue to pay dues using non-transparent criteria to the semi-dependent superstructure, their local leaders ought to have a voice in the actions, agendas, and budgets of the top-level operations. Internal accountability works in both directions.

6. Self-proclaimed and perceived IAF radicalism
   What does it mean to embrace the word "radical?" The word is both an adjective—as in "radical agenda"—and a noun—like an outlier who stands apart from the mainstream. The word, frequently heard in earlier contexts of the late 1960s and 1970s, evokes both positive and negative public reactions. Saul Alinsky used the word in 1946 and 1971 book titles; Edward Chambers used the word in his 2003 book title.

   For many, "radical" refers to reaching or digging to the roots-like origins of social problems. Radical goals—comprehensive, quick, and deep—are consistent with the effort to address the root causes of problems. Among root causes of massive problems we could include "globally competitive capitalism," which exploits the many to profit the few, or pay-to-play political rules and practices which privilege wealthy campaign donors and give them special access to politicians and appointee positions. The people called radicals pursue means to achieve those ends or that tend to stand apart from the mainstream processes of gradual reforms. The IAF pursues reforms in mainstream local and state politics.

   The language of radicalism—edgy as it is—seems less relevant in the twenty-first-century context, yet the wider public may assume that the old Alinsky and Chambers lore shapes today's IAF and its current practice in most Texas places with IAF affiliates. However, this *nom de guerre* does not characterize IAF's modes of operation in the twenty-first century.

   As a political scientist by training, to me the contemporary IAF approach evokes the pluralist ideal underlying many analyses of American politics. A pluralist political system is one wherein groups compete with one another for the policies they support; the greater their skills and voices, the more likely they win. Critics of the pluralist ideal warn about the way the political system is stacked against groups lacking elite support and money. The IAF has a stronger base than most groups in U.S. politics, so there is potential for, but no guarantee for altering power relations in a pluralism paradigm.

However one views the American pluralist politics paradigm, leaders in the IAF and its member institutions, largely religious institutions, persistently pursue long-term change. Admirably, local IAF leaders and organizers move with consensus, in a more or less democratically accountable framework which tends to avoid polarizing, provocative issues. The provocative issues could include wealthy business developers' use of public money for their private profit-making projects, women's issues, and the like. An avoidant agenda like this is safely reformist. The unwritten rule, "no permanent friends, no permanent enemies," frequently drilled in local leaders as a rule, may have turned such developers into permanent friends in some communities.

A truism in politics says: pick your battles carefully. Perhaps big industries and developers remain impossible to take on; unwinnable goals would be a waste of time in IAF thought and action. Moreover, those prominent business people may sit on workforce training boards and make annual contributions to IAF affiliates. Unwinnable goals—absent for understandable reasons, including the despair that could set in with failure—may perpetuate the long-term inequalities that fester in local communities.

In at least one locale, perhaps the IAF is becoming more radical, with pragmatic reforms now deemed "radical" as the center of gravity has moved right. Consider a neighboring state. In a potentially precedent-setting effort, Together Baton Rouge, part of Together Louisiana, worked with the East Baton Rouge Parish School Board to deny a $2.9 million tax break to Exxon Mobile. To some readers, this might seem like a drop in the budgetary bucket, but the "local chamber of commerce took out a full-page newspaper ad, warning of a rise of 'radicalism.'"[2] Here is what really seems radically undemocratic to me: Louisiana's politically appointed Industrial Tax Exemption Program board giveaway from 2008-2016—at a 99% approval rate, with no cost/benefit analysis—that totaled $10 billion in local tax exemptions, unbeknownst to most ordinary citizens. In 2016, newly elected Governor John Edwards—who succeeded Bobby Jindal—issued an Executive Order to allow local authorities to make their own decisions about tax abatements; IAF volunteer leaders used the opportunity, as did the local school board, to decide how to use their scarce resources. The IAF affiliate did research over several years, producing a fifteen-minute video (now viewed by 675,000 viewers) called "Why Louisiana Stays Poor."[3] The diversity optics included moderation by a man and woman, with a heavy emphasis on numbers and the state's comparative ranking on indicators of well-being. Recall Chapter 2 on Texans' sad joke, "Thank God for Mississippi," which has most recently turned into "Thank God for Louisiana," given its bottom-level ranking on well-being, despite the richness of its natural resources.

Hardly radical yet fundamental to democracy, IAF pursues not only policy reforms, but also restores a moral narrative to public discourse and ameliorates the worst excesses of unregulated capitalism. What may be unusual and special about IAF is how it puts people together from different ethnicities, income groups, and religious affiliations in relationships of trust around issues of class-based inequality, despite the social and economic segregation of U.S. society. Readers might wonder about high-attendance events that occasionally make candidates uncomfortable, but the response I offer is this: what is radical about direct action and insistence on public accountability? It is the essence of democracy. As important, IAF provides civic education in a state and country with little more than voting, monetized campaigns, and multiple-choice tests to students who study history and government in high schools. For the IAF, radical means people's empowerment (see Chapter 4).

Inequalities and class-based organizing in North America

Earlier chapters noted the inequalities that pervade life in the U.S. and Texas. Such inequalities are especially marked in cities and towns along the U.S.-Mexico border where three Texas IAF affiliates are located. Alas, despite the presence of borderlands IAF affiliates, the local and regional IAF operations pay no attention to trade and inequalities from one to the other side of the US-Mexico border. Many US-based border residents connect deeply and personally with friends and relatives on the Mexico side of the border. Article 33 of Mexico's Constitution forbids "foreign" involvement in its own affairs. However, the IAF has worked with nationals in other countries—Canada, the UK, Germany, Australia—to grow their own IAF affiliates. Can it do the same in Mexico?

The response is maybe, maybe not. Mexico's commitment to the rule of law is weak and its record with public safety, compromised. Despite cultural resonance, Mexico's relationship with organized religion is strained, both before and after Mexico's 1910 revolution against a thirty-year dictator, given pre-revolutionary, nineteenth-century collusion with capital and the post-revolutionary 1920s Cristero Rebellion against secularism in the emerging government. Perhaps the opportunity structure for the IAF model does not yet exist in Mexico, but the 2018 election of Andrés Manuel López Obrador and his new party, the National Regeneration Movement (MORENA) which has the majority in Congress, have committed to reduce inequalities, given that half of Mexico's population falls under the Mexican poverty line. He immediately doubled the legal minimum wage at Mexico's northern border to US$9 per day, which increased up to a million maquiladora workers' earnings in foreign-owned, mainly U.S. factories.

Inequality is an issue that resonates with progressive U.S. religious affiliations that take Biblical injunctions seriously. Yet churches and synagogues remain far from a united front. They, along with politicians, pluck verses from the Bible from different chapters in ways that justify their perspectives. With the IAF, perhaps more unity is possible around reducing inequality. IAF is first and foremost an organization about what I generically call "class issues" relating to wage fairness and inequality. The IAF is among the few organizations that identifies and recruits leaders from the working class—those earning a lower middle-income, working in blue-collar occupations.

Amazingly, the working-class description is hardly used in twenty-first-century America despite the very real group of people who have been marginalized in both major political parties and by the global economy itself. Despite the shrinking "middle class," the boundaries of which have always been illusory, and the trends away from upward mobility, the US hardly grapples with the word "class," although many obsess over race and ethnicity, which intersect with class inequalities. Class deserves a place in the public narrative. With constituencies that support identity politics and policy reforms, along with the decline of trade unions, it is surprising that more universities do not support centers for the study of class inequalities and poverty. Plenty of universities feature centers for business, entrepreneurship, and global competitiveness.

IAF makes laudatory contributions to US public life and democracy. Like any organization, it exhibits contradictions that produce tension. But most of these contradictions and tensions are soluble. Perhaps the contradictions could begin to be addressed by re-visiting Chambers's rules of organizing.

Re-visiting the 2003 IAF rules

In Chapter 1, Box 1.2, I listed IAF rules from former IAF national director, the late Edward Chambers. As I reflect on twenty years in my IAF experience with eight organizers, many hours annually in the locale affiliate, and both distant and local training experiences, I will re-categorize the rules on the following basis: (A) still operational, (B) complex rules that need greater clarity, given contradictions like those analyzed above, (C) good, sound common advice, and (D) rhetorical (non-operational) rules. Two rules seem more like homilies, found in category E. And I added a common, useful rule (F) which could be placed in category A or B.

A. Still operational

All action is in the inevitable reaction.
Action is to organization as oxygen is to the body.
Power precedes program.
Peace and justice are rarely realized in the world as it is; the pursuit, not possession, of happiness takes place amid struggle, conflict, and tension.

B. Operational rules that need greater clarity

The iron rule: Never, never do for others what they can do for themselves.
Your own dues money is almost sacred; other people's money starts controlling you.
The haves will never give you anything of value.
The law of change: Change means movement; movement means friction; friction means heat; heat means controversy, conflict.

C. Good, sound common advice

Every positive has a negative, and every negative a positive.
Anything that drags along for too long becomes a drag.

Have-nots should not be romanticized; they cheat, lie, steal, double cross and play victim just like the haves do.

Right things are done for wrong reasons, and bad things are often done for right reasons.

Given the opportunity, people tend to do the right thing.

D. Rhetorical rules

All changes come about as a result of threat or pressure.

Never go to power for a decision, but only with a decision.

The opposition is your best ally in radicalizing your people.

Power can never be conferred; it must be taken.

Avoid cynics and ideologues; they have nothing to offer.

E. Semi-theological homilies

Power without love is tyranny; love without power is sentimental mush.

Life force is about natality, plurality, and mortality.

F. Unstated, but useful rule

No permanent friends, no permanent enemies.

Let me elaborate more about these new categories—categories based on the analysis in my experience and this book. Readers may remember an affirmation of still-operational rules throughout book chapters. On category A, action-reaction-action constitute the dynamics of political life, neither fixed nor unchanging. A power base is essential before articulating goals and strategy. Alas, many budding policy analysts anticipate that a report will magically make change rather than be stored on a shelf or hard drive, eventually forgotten and/or discarded. Struggle, conflict, and tension, too: change is neither easy nor smooth. And that oxygen: to sustain themselves, organizations must be energizing, not boring.

As for category B, here we see rules about self-sufficiency and dependency that are fundamental to the IAF, practiced in some situations, yet not always practiced in its funding and dues-paying operations. Perhaps a clarification of these fine rules—still keeping them simple and memorable, or changes in dues funding, bottom to top, horizontally with member institutions, and diversification of grant funders—can move these useful points to category A. Additionally, the chapters on education show that Alliance School funding, which went to school districts and campuses, imposed evaluation requirements that tied IAF praise for its parent-teacher collaboration to improvements in standard-ized testing results in official evaluations to the Texas Education Agency, criticized both then and now as inadequate, non-comprehensive indi-cators of learning. Finally, from the "haves," IAF leaders seek "invest-ments" for local budgets and support on workforce training center boards of directors. The "haves" provide value therefrom. And while change is constant and often controversial, conflict is not absolute.

Moving to category C, I call these good pieces of advice, useful reminders to people. Perhaps it is my working class background, but these rules seem like common-sense tips my mother passed on about optimism, balanced considerations, faulty generalizations about catego-ries of people, and so on.

In category D, we see rhetorical rules that sound edgy and radical, like what Saul Alinsky wrote about. Perhaps these rules evoked the twentieth century IAF more than the twenty-first century. As analyzed throughout this book, I do not remember leaders threatening officials with anything stronger than encouraging strong voter turnout—pressure yes, but hardly a threat. On "taking power," what strikes me more about the twenty-first century is its negotiating ability, after having taken what I have called a seat at the table—a mature phase of an effective orga-nization, recognized for its power. Similarly, the good "research" done in IAF affiliates involves not only analyzing evidence independently of official interpretation, but also sitting with people in powerful institu-tions to acquire insights that can later be useful in formulating strategies and goals. Opposition, alas, may not be as clear-cut in the twenty-first century as the earlier crises over explicit racism, sexism, and classism and downright neglect of large, segregated parts of cities in the early days of the IAF. After 2016, of course, we did see a resurgence of overt racism, sexism, and classism. Common now, though, we often see leth-argy and apathy about institutionalized discrimination—a reason why stories from house meetings are so important to the IAF model. Finally, from Chapter 8, my dismay at the disconnect between higher education and the IAF should be clear. Yes, many academics are cynical—and yes, cynics breed apathy and a "why bother?" attitude—but not all academ-ics can be cast in that mold. And in my mind, denominations offer belief systems that could be characterized as ideologies. The organizational theorists on which I drew in Chapter 4 would agree.

In category E, we see odd statements about love. I call them homilies, but social scientists might simply put them in a catch-all residual cat-egory with items that do not fit elsewhere.

I added a category F for the rule that Chambers left unsaid: No permanent friends, no permanent enemies. I heard this many times from organizers and came to understand its usefulness in issue-oriented organizing that parts ways with the personalistic, patron-client loyalty politics in parts of Texas.[4] If it were on the official list, though, perhaps the rule would fit in category B. Why? The rule might conflict with the relationships built around the seat at the table of city politics.

It is now time to think ahead, not only with the IAF but also with a state that is undergoing demographic and likely voting shifts. Hopefully, the state of Texas will once again become a competitive, two-party system.

Toward a Bipartisan state future

The statewide IAF network's twentieth-century pioneering gains surpassed those of the twenty-first century so far: Alliance School funding, workforce training funding, and *colonia* infrastructure in the form of Economically Distressed Areas Program (EDAP) funding. Yet the IAF maintains or protects some past efforts, for example: matching funds for workforce training funds raised at city and county levels; EDAP's legislative advocates persist to renew and extend funding for *colonias*. The defense of hard-fought gains, even with less funding, can be as important under one-party rule as their initial achievement. Moreover, IAF's less-visible alliances with others in the background—even business— to prevent the most extreme, hateful legislation from passing is an achievement in and of itself. With ongoing relationships, statewide IAF efforts act regularly to prevent further reductions in health/CHIP funding that conservative leaders sought. In so doing, IAF joined a variety of other civil society organizations, making it difficult to ascertain which organization did what in how much numerical proportion. Like moderate business constituencies within the one-party system, the centrist IAF pushed back against extremism and incivility. Defensive work rarely generates the kind of visibility that IAF's offensive, proactive policy changes generated in the 1980s and 1990s.

The Tea Party faction in Texas may have peaked, given losses by incumbents and opponents' victories in the November 2018 election and thus opening opportunities for centrist dialogues to occur in civil, bipartisan ways. The statewide 2016 IAF strategy to expand its relational work outside the big cities into outlying counties and the rest of Texas achieved successes in 2018 and will become even more crucial in the future (more on this in the section below). Besides Dallas achievements, explained in earlier chapters, Austin Interfaith works in surrounding counties, like Bastrop, where the sheriff targeted Latino neighborhoods with checkpoints.[5] Their work to stop checkpoints gives people hope, skills, and wins.

An increasingly crowded field of community organizing exists around the state and nation. Organizing and its language can now be found in nonprofit organizations and party and candidates' campaign strategies. Many of my publicly minded students, inspired by candidates or simply looking for paid work with an upwardly mobile career path, have worked on campaigns and joined staffs of those candidates elected to office. This is worthy activity, of course, but it drains talent away from community organizing in NGOs like the IAF.

The November 2018 elections bore fruit from IAF's strategy to target suburban districts and surrounding counties to its four strong affiliates located in Dallas, San Antonio, Austin, and Houston. IAF affiliates hosted large Accountability Sessions, then large numbers of leaders pursued their traditional calls and walks to Get-Out-The-Vote in GOTV strategies. There is no substitute for voluntary organization leaders speaking face to face, as in the IAF affiliates, to encourage neighbors and community members to engage in informed voting compared to paid partisan canvassers. In the suburban districts surrounding all four cities, voters elected candidates who will likely be accountable to constituencies. In Dallas, five state legislative incumbents lost, partly because they refused to appear at the 2,000-person strong DAI Accountability Session. In Austin's gerrymandered districts, a major fan of pre-emption (as discussed earlier in other chapters) lost his seat. Accountability also won in Houston and San Antonio.

Of course, the November 2018 off-year elections became a watershed year for the doubling of voter turnout in many parts of Texas. Great enthusiasm emerged around El Paso Congressman Beto O'Rourke who traveled to all 254 counties in Texas, some counties many times, in his run for U.S. Senate against incumbent Ted Cruz. The enthusiasm drew lots more younger people to participate and vote than in previous elections. Moreover, unease with White House decisions in domestic, trade, and foreign policy matters also affected voters. Houston turned around not only state legislative seats, but also Congressional seats and judgeships. The latter can and should be a focus for overtly partisan judges.[6] Other organizations also rose to the challenge of the mid-term elections and will no doubt continue for the 2020 and 2022 elections. The state may once again have a competitive, two-party system that works in bi-partisan ways to achieve constructive policy changes.

The bigger picture: Social justice organizing in a crowding field

Although IAF is unique for its lengthy track record and solid leadership base, other organizations have emerged with equally important bases, such as the Workers' Defense Project (a member institute in both Dallas and Austin IAF affiliates), PICO National Network/Faith in Action, and the Texas Organizing Project, which endorses candidates and raises money to pay canvassers, unlike the reliance on voluntary leaders in IAF's Get Out the Vote activity. The League of Women Voters, with many chapters around the state, has begun to call itself bigger and bolder. Like other civic organizations, LULAC and the Southwest Voter Education Project encourage registration and voter turnout. Yet no other organizations run Accountability Sessions like IAF affiliates.

The unions, themselves collaborative coalitions like the AFL-CIO, nationally with over 13 million members, and the more recent Change to Win Federation, nationally with 3 million members, could offer collaborative opportunity prospects. Although unions use some of the same language and lingo as the IAF, unions target and recruit youth in summer Leadership Academies, something IAF could do.[7] However, unions also endorse candidates, thereby losing the opportunity to develop relationships with whichever candidate wins, like the IAF. Union membership may have reached an all-time low in the U.S. and Texas, drawing members from only 10 percent of the workforce, but it pursues youth development and uses techniques that many community organizations share in their training: civic academies, one-on-one relational work, and collaboration with other organizations that have overlapping interests. Alas, many union techniques used at the state level do not appear to trickle down to local teacher associations outside of the biggest cities in Texas, whose members are perhaps too busy teaching too many overly large classes per day. Some of the best organizers I have met in the southwest Texas borderlands affiliate with National Nurses United. A partisan organization, however, they endorse candidates and offered leadership for the statewide organization called Our Revolution, locally called Continuing the Revolution ("Bernie-crats").

IAF cannot do it all, obviously. And the IAF must choose rather than fight all battles, like any organization with mature common sense. Nevertheless, some analysts have criticized social justice organizing for its territoriality and lack of collaboration, even in the same terrain and issue areas.[8] On the national level, PICO once focused on the Pacific states and in California hosted federation affiliates in half the state assembly districts, but Faith in Action (PICO's subsequent name) has spread into half of the states and operates a national agenda and strategy that IAF lacks.[9] However, state achievements in Louisiana and the other near-half of U.S. states have made major wins, as the national Industrial Areas Foundation website proclaims. The faith-based Gamaliel Network and DART (Direct Action and Research Training) organize territorially in other parts of the country and so far have not moved into Texas. The tough challenge remains: how to negotiate collaborations with shared accountability and visibility? Drawing on Freud's notion, the "narcissism of small differences," long-time analyst of community organizing Peter Dreier faulted community organizations for their "exaggeration" of distinctions among models.[10] Does Dreier recognize the challenge of collaboration among coalitions like the IAF? I think not. On-the-ground experience makes those challenges ever-so clear.

IAF affiliates are not the only large NGO in the state. Besides countervailing tendencies like Tea Party chapters, growth occurs in potentially complementary NGOs with a justice agenda. Some nonprofit organizations promote secularism like El Paso's Join Us for Justice, affiliated with Americans United for Separation of Church and State, founded by two former Border Interfaith leaders. Other social justice organizations focus on immigration, like El Paso/southern New Mexico's Border Network for Human Rights and Austin's Tan Cerca de la Frontera. Young women and progressive men have affiliated with West Fund or Lilith Fund to support women's health and reproductive justice. Deeds not Words, an organization to which once-state senator and gubernatorial candidate Wendy Davis lent her name, draws on some of the same energy from youth. Besides traditional organizations like the League of Women Voters, one still finds chapters of the National Organization for Women or the Women's Political Caucus along with fundraising arms that drain revenue away from social justice into candidates who, if they win, might bring a social justice agenda to their work. The age fifty-plus crowd, affiliated with the American Association of Retired Persons (AARP), with its 38 million members, operates local community committees but without an organizing base like IAF affiliates and their regular actions. ACLU claims to be developing a community-based operation. However useful their rights-oriented tabling, investigations, awareness-raising, and monitoring protection at marches, they have yet to develop a local base of leaders like the IAF affiliates. I could go on; the list is long, especially adding in single-issue groups focused, for example, on the environment. As stressed through this book, episodic social movements quickly come and go, but a few develop into formal organizations like the IAF and offer long-term collaborative or membership-institution opportunities.

The field is already somewhat crowded for time, talent, and money. In the book, *A Shared Future*, we find an incredible array of data on the size and scope of community organizing: 189 local community organizing coalitions of 4,500 institutions, 3,500 of them religious, and 545 organizing staff, with 55 percent of them women.[11] People have a wide menu from which to choose, once territoriality is bridged or people turn to organizations that resonate with their priority issues.

Meanwhile, Texans' demographics continue to morph, with its two-in-five Hispanic population numbers soon to surpass the White/Anglo population. While poverty is dropping somewhat statewide, the South Texas borderlands poverty rate is double the state rate, given state and even IAF blindness to Mexico and the "globally competitive" labor that business touts from the Global South including Mexico.[12] Texas "as it is" could be a Texas that "it could or should be" once the state reduces the influence of money in political influence, voter suppression, and gerry-mandered districts. All Texans should act on these issues if the state's future is to be a prosperous one, with a small-d democracy wherein people work with civility, with others, and with their accountable representatives toward constructive solutions.

Notes

1. Jeffrey Pressman and Aaron Wildavsky, *Implementation*, 3rd ed. (Berkeley: University of California Press). Among many of Rube Goldberg's cartoon websites see: http://mentalfloss.com/article/54007/8-excellent rube-goldberg-cartoons.

2. Richard Faussett, "Daring to Say No to Big Oil," *New York Times*, February 5, 2019, B1. https://www.nytimes.com/2019/02/05/us/louisiana-itep-exxon-mobil.html . accessed March 1, 2019

3. "Why Louisiana Stays Poor," https://www.youtube.com/watch?v=RWTic9btP38; accessed March 1, 2019.

4. Kathleen Staudt and Irasema Coronado, *Fronteras no Más: Toward Social Justice at the U.S.-Mexico Border* (New York: Palgrave USA, 2002).

5. See Sean Collins Walsh, "Faith Group: Bastrop Sheriff Maurice Cook Targeted Latino Neighborhood," *Austin American Statesman* https://www.statesman.com/news/20180703/faith-group-bastrop-sheriff-maurice-cook-targeted-latino-neighborhood, Accessed August 1, 2018.

6. Matt Zdun, "State Appeals Court Says Austin's Paid Sick Leave Ordinance Is Unconstitutional," *Texas Tribune* https://www.texastribune.org/2018/11/16/appeals-court-blocks-austins-paid-sick-leave-ordinance/?utm_source=Texas+Tribune+Master&utm_campaign=db341b85cd-trib-newsletters-the-brief&utm_medium=email&utm_term=0_d9a68d8efc-db341b85cd-101202457&mc_cid=db341b85cd&mc_eid=3b3e7d7416 Accessed Nov. 19, 2018.

7. See Chapter 5 on my lengthy interview with Montserrat Garibay, which transitioned into conversation about the AFL-CIO.

8. Robert Fisher and Eric Shragge, "Contextualizing Community Organizing: Lessons from the Past, Tensions in the Present, Opportunities for the Future," in *Transforming the City: Community Organizing and the Challenge of Political Change*, edited by Marion Orr (Lawrence: University Press of Kansas, 2007), 193–217.

9. See Richard Wood's chapter "Higher Power: Strategic Capacity for State and National Organizing," in Orr, 2007, pp. 162–192. Alas, my major take-away from the chapter was that a tremendous amount of money was required for a multi-day experience in Washington, D.C., with meager results except for the empowering awareness that leaders acquired.

10. Peter Dreier, "Community Organizing for What? Progressive Politics and Movement Building in America," in Orr, pp. 218–251 (quote on page 222). I heard an IAF senior supervisor call PICO a "kinder, gentler" model that evolved after IAF's disciplined model.

11. Richard Wood and Brad Fulton, *A Shared Future: Faith-based Organizing for Racial Equity and Ethical Democracy* (Chicago: University of Chicago Press, 2015), 11. They say that a fifth of Americans are religious "nones," with no affiliation to a faith, and a third of youth under thirty claim "none." See their p. 12 (slightly different from previous chapters, due to different years and sources).

12. Alex Ura and Elbert Wang, "Poverty in Texas Drops to Lowest Levels in More than a Decade," *Texas Tribune*, September 13, 2018, https://www.texastribune.org/2018/09/13/texas-poverty-census-2017-lowest-levels-decade/?utm_source=Texas+Tribune+Master&utm_campaign=08cf60527c-trib-newsletters-the-brief&utm_medium=email&utm_term=0_d9a68d8efc-08cf60527c-101202457&mc_cid=08cf60527c&mc_eid=3b3e7d7416 Accessed Oct. 1, 2018.

Letter to Texans

Dear Texans,

Permit my audacity in writing a letter to you all like Paul wrote to the Corinthians. I know Corinth's location, on an isthmus, a place considered to be an internationalist global manufacturing site if one can call it that in the first century (twenty centuries ago!). Corinthians practiced many religions; some practiced none. And I know also that Paul wrote multiple letters to the Corinthians about different topics. I can't deal with all of them, and some topics are quite weird with historical hindsight. My letter to Texans focuses on the political economy of a huge globalized state with a political-economic elite that spends lots of public money to keep out the "others" yet maintain a business-friendly low-cost labor force.

Who are those others? Well, many come from the Global South, particularly Mexico, the Central American "violent triangle" of countries, and even as far south as Brazil or places in Africa and Asia. They are fleeing violence, guns—many, no doubt from the U.S.—and poverty. In this letter, I won't get into the historic colonial and post-colonial conditions that enriched some countries and impoverished others.

Texans, wake up! Soon our state will need people, especially young people, to grow our economy and develop greater prosperity for many. Let's think ahead. In 2030, will politicians develop incentives to attract migrants from the south? Those migrants will pay FICA tax, besides other taxes, and thereby help strengthen the U.S. Social Security system upon which many Texans will depend. By 2024, President Andrés Manuel López Obrador's (AMLO's) policies might have reduced inequalities, corruption, and poverty in Mexico, so perhaps those incentives Texas offers will necessarily be quite generous given the poor reputation the state has acquired for not welcoming the stranger. Notice that I used "might" instead of "will." AMLO has surrounded himself with former colleagues in the PRI after all. And who knows how two nationalists will clash from 2019–2021 and perhaps beyond?

To stay in Texas and its borderlands, people need good wages. Without living wages and professional salaries comparable to other parts of the country and North America, young people will leave. To induce women, Mexican Americans, and African Americans to remain in the state, prove to them that policies are responsive to them and their individual health needs, with the ugliness of still-close-to-the-surface racism, misogyny, and classism. Then the taxpayers who support schools—where in the future learning more authentically focuses on thinking, reading, and writing—will see other states reap the benefits of their school investments. And if wages paid by the mostly U.S.-owned foreign factories in Mexico continue to be low—low enough for *The Economist* to call Mexico's government to task for wage stagnation compared to other countries in the Global South—business will continue to have strong incentives to invest south of the border and pitch interdependent borderlands sites as places of global competitiveness with corresponding low wages on the US side of the borderlands.

Another wake-up call! The vast majority of Texans are tired of the "pay-to-play" system in politics. Far too much money is wasted on political campaigns with no monetary limits attached. Most of us would rather that money be invested in health care, such as Medicare. Speaking of health, Texas industrial polluters have a virtual free reign to destroy the environment and suck water from the earth for production with negative consequences for people's health. Who will pay for the costs of recovery and/or early death? Probably state government will absolve itself from the responsibility if the current system stays as is.

It is galling to think people can buy political appointments from the political party in power. Yes, we can identify the amounts they donate, a million dollars and more, for the top ten donors on sites like OpenSecrets.org, but who has time to look? Most families work two jobs and have to find safe day-care facilities for the children. Yes, I know that's a market niche for entrepreneurs, just like those charter schools who hire CEO-superintendents that paint public schools with the dirtiest brushes ever in order to increase their market share. Of course, some public schools deserve that negative attention. However, many schools and teachers do the best jobs they can with the limited resources available, despite being hamstrung by the testing and accountability system.

I had thought it was high time to expand Medicaid and get the 9:1 federal match dollars for that purpose, as conservative governors did after 2010 in New Mexico and Arizona, but in 2019 and beyond that option might be eliminated depending on court decisions in the wider U.S. Too many Texans are dying or suffering because they cannot afford health care. Because Medicaid expansion covers mental health issues, we could avoid the dangerous self-medication Texans pursue with alcohol and drugs, often violently endangering their family members in the process.

Raise and teach your children well, Texans! Encourage reasoning, civil discourse, and civic education inside your homes and the larger public community. Read and read more. Parents can model civic engagement during and in-between elections with leadership and participation in broad-based organizations with people from other walks of life, as in IAF organizations. Work for genuine choice in a two-party or multi-party competitive electoral system, without rigging the outcome through extreme gerrymandering. Yes, keep perfect ideal goals in mind, but work for what is possible and carry on.

Hope for the best and push until the better and best can be achieved. Consider Margaret Atwood's *The Handmaid's Tale*, one of America's top one hundred books, featured in the PBS Series *The Great American Read* in 2018 and even serialized on Hulu. As the central protagonist found etched in a closet by her predecessor in the cage-like room, *"nolite te bastardes carborundorum."* Pardon me for any offense, readers, but persistence and hope coupled with constructive cold anger and edginess will craft the socially just future we all deserve.

Kathy

P.S. One of 2019's massacres in Texas occurred in my home of El Paso, with twenty-two killed by a semi-automatic assault weapon that was easily obtained. More people were murdered in one day than the average number of murders annually in this, one of the safest big cities of the U.S. A young man drove all the way from a Dallas suburb to El Paso to act against the so-called "Hispanic invasion," to "send them back" as he wrote in his manifesto, using the demagogic language straight from the presidential campaign strategies of 2016 and 2019 (hopefully not extended into 2020). First responders did their courageous work, and hospital staff worked some miracles. By August 8, EPISO/Border Interfaith organized a respectful, solemn event, with small-group conversation healing strategies, an action agenda, and responses from many public officials, from Congresswoman Verónica Escobar and county commissioners Stout and Pérez plus county judge Ricardo Samaniego, to city council representatives Claudia Ordaz and Cassandra Hernández. Episcopal Bishop Dunn (NM, West TX) and Catholic Bishop Seitz (El Paso) prayed us in and out of the gathering. IAF West-Southwest supervisor/organizer Joe Rubio and Arturo Aguila came immediately to assist our leaders and organizer Adriana García, as did senior organizer Josephine López-Paul from the Network of Texas Organizations. We all need to move beyond sadness and grief to actions that will prevent massacres from happening in the first place. @ElPasoStrong

Reference List

Achor, Shirley. *Mexican Americans in a Dallas Barrio*. Tucson: University of Arizona Press, 1978.

Alinsky, Saul D. *Reveille for Radicals*. Chicago: University of Chicago Press, 1946.

————. *Rules for Radicals: A Pragmatic Primer for Realistic Radicals*. New York: Vintage, 1971.

Ambrecht, Biliana C. S. *Politicizing the Poor: The Legacy of the War on Poverty in a Mexican-American Community*. New York: Praeger, 1976.

Armbruster-Sandoval, Ralph. "Latino Political Agency in Los Angeles Past and Present." In *The Roots of Latino Urban Agency*, edited by Sharon Navarro and Rodolfo Rosales, 13–42. Denton: University of North Texas Press, 2013.

Bachrach, Peter, and Morton Baratz. "Two Faces of Power." *American Political Science Review* 56, no. 4 (1962): 947–52. http://www.columbia.edu/itc/sipa/U6800/readings-sm/bachrach.pdf Accessed June 19, 2019.

Baugh, Josh. "Incumbent Larson Wins Despite Challenger Getting Governor's Backing," *San Antonio Express News*, March 7, 2018. https://www.expressnews.com/news/politics/texas_legislature/article/Incumbent-Larson-poised-to-overcome-12733646.php. Accessed Feb. 1, 2019.

Bellah, Robert, et al. *Habits of the Heart: Individual and Community in American Life*. Berkeley: University of California Press, 1985.

Bilefsky, Dan. "Montreal Dispatch: Where Churches Have Become Temples of Cheese, Fitness and Eroticism," July 30, 2018. https://www.nytimes.com/2018/07/30/world/canada/quebec-churches.html. Accessed July 30, 2018.

Blakeslee, Nate, Paul Burka, and Patricia Kilday Hart. "Power Company: Who Are the Most Influential People Determining the Fate of Texas—and What Do They Want?" *Texas Monthly*, February 2011, pp. 86–95, 162–3.

Bova, Gus. " 'Landmark' Wage Theft Conviction Overturned by Texas Appeals Court." *Texas Observer*, September 6, 2018. Accessed Sept. 6, 2018. https://www.texasobserver.org/landmark-wage-theft-conviction-overturned-by-texas-appeals-court/

Bova, Gus. "Wage Wars." *Texas Observer*, June 13, 2018. https://www.texasobserver.org/wage-wars/ Accessed June 14, 2018.

Boyte, Harry, and Nancy Karl. *Building America: The Democratic Promise of Public Work*. Philadelphia: Temple University Press, 2005.

Bozell, Maureen R., and Melissa Goldberg. *Employers, Low-Income Young Adults, and Postsecondary Credentials: A Practical Typology for Business, Education, and Community Leaders*. Workforce Strategy Center, October 2009. http://collegeforamerica.org/employers-low-income-young-adults-and-postsecondary-credentials/ Accessed Oct. 16, 2018.

Brown, W.A., S. Jo, and F. Andersson. *Texas Nonprofit Sector: Describing the Size and Scope*. College Station: Bush School of Government and Public Service, Texas A&M University, 2013.

Browning, Rufus, Dale Rogers Marshall, and David H. Tabb. *Protest Is Not Enough: The Struggle of Blacks and Hispanics for Equality in Urban Politics*. Berkeley: University of California Press, 1984.

Chambers, Edward. *Roots for Radicals: Organizing for Power, Action, and Justice*. New York: Continuum Press, 2003.

Champagne, Anthony, and Edward Harpham. *Governing Texas*. 2nd. ed. New York: W. W. Norton, 2015.

Champagne, Anthony, Edward Harpham, and Jason Casellas. *Governing Texas*. 3rd. ed. New York: W.W. Norton, 2017.

Clarke, Susan E., Rodney E. Hero, Mara S. Sidney, Luis R. Fraga, Bari A. Erlichson. *Multi-Ethnic Moments: The Politics of Urban Education Reform*. Philadelphia: Temple University Press, 2006.

Corchado, Alfredo. "Common Ground: Poll Finds US-Mexico Border Residents Overwhelmingly Value Mobility, Oppose Wall." *Dallas Morning News*, July 18, 2016. http://interactives.dallasnews.com/2016/border-poll/. Accessed July 19, 2016.

Cortés Jr., Ernesto. "Making the Public the Leaders in Education Reform." *Education Week* 15 , no. 12 (November 22, 1995).

Crowder, David. "Improving Education Is Summit's Aim." *El Paso Times*, February 13, 2000, B1–B2.

———. "Set High Goals, Summit Told." *El Paso Times*, February 19, 2000, 1A–2A.

———. "Summit Sets Top Priorities." *El Paso Times*, February 20, 2000, 1A–2A.

———. "Summit to Examine Skills Taught in Schools." *El Paso Times*, February 13, 2000, 1A–2A.

———. "Summit to Tackle Education." *El Paso Times*. January 20, 2000, 1A–2A.

———. "Teaching Training Wins UTEP Kudos." *El Paso Times*, February 16, 2000, 1A–2A.

———. "Religious Leaders Quietly Hire Troublemaker to Better City." *El Paso Times*, June 20, 1982.

Cuban, Larry. *As Good as It Gets: What School Reform Brought to Austin*. Cambridge, MA: Harvard University Press, 2010.

Dallas-Area Interfaith. *Annual Reports*. Dallas: DAI, 2017, 2016, 2015.

De León, Arnoldo. *Ethnicity in the Sunbelt: Mexican Americans in Houston*. College Station: Texas A&M University Press, 2001.

Del Bosque, Melissa. "Checkpoint Nation." *Texas Observer*, October 8, 2018. https://www.texasobserver.org/checkpoint-nation/ Accessed Oct. 15, 2018.

Dow, Pauline, and Kathleen Staudt, "Education Policies: Standardized Testing, English-Language Learners, and Border Futures." In *Social Justice in the U.S.-Mexico Border Region*, edited by Mark Lusk, Kathleen Staudt, and Eva Moya, 217–229. Netherlands and New York: Springer, 2012.

Downs, Anthony. *Inside Bureaucracy*. Boston: Little Brown, 1967.

Dreier, Peter. 2007. "Community Organizing for What? Progressive Politics and Movement Building in America." In *Transforming the City: Community Organizing and the Challenge of Political Change*, edited by Marion Orr, 218–252. Lawrence: University Press of Kansas, 2007.

Edelman, Murray. *The Symbolic Uses of Politics*. Champaign-Urbana: University of Illinois Press, 1964.

El Paso Collaborative for Academic Excellence. Binder for Education Summit. El Paso: EPCAE, 2000.

El Paso Times, Opinion Editorial. "A Reason to Unite: Education Affects the Entire Community." February 13, 2000, 12A.

El Paso Times, Opinion Editorial. "Success at the Summit: Education Focus Is Only the Beginning." February 23, 2000, 6A.

Elazar, Daniel. *American Federalism: A View from the States*. New York: Harper & Row, 1984.

Ellis, Carolyn, Tony E. Adams and Arthur P. Bochner. "Autoethnography: An Overview." *Forum: Qualitative Social Research*. 2011. http://www.qualitative-research.net/index.php/fqs/article/view/1589/3095. Accessed April 24, 2017

Fanty, Carol Hardy. *Latino Politics, Latina Politics*. Philadelphia: Temple University Press, 1993.

Fausset, Richard. "Daring to Say No to Big Oil," *New York Times*, February 5, 2019, B1. https://www.nytimes.com/2019/02/05/us/louisiana-itep-exxon-mobil.html Accessed March 1, 2019.

Freeman, Jo. *The Politics of Women's Liberation: A Case Study of an Emerging Social Movement and Its Relation to the Policy Process*. New York: McKay, 1975.

García, Sonia, Valerie Martínez-Ebers, Irasema Coronado, Sharon Navarro, and Patricia Jamarillo. *Políticas: Latina Public Officials in Texas*. Austin: University of Texas Press, 2008.

Gecan, Michael. *Going Public: An Organizer's Guide to Citizen Action*. New York: Anchor Books, 2002.

Gecan, Michael. *People's Institutions in Decline: Causes * Consequences * Cures*. Chicago: ACTA Publications, 2018.

Gilligan, Carol. *In a Different Voice: Psychological Theory and Women's Development*. Cambridge: Harvard University Press, 1982.

Gonzales, Richard J. *Raza Rising: Chicanos in North Texas*. Denton: University of North Texas Press, 2016.

Goodlad, John. *A Place Called School*. 1984. repr., New York: McGraw Hill, 2004.

Graff, Harvey J. *The Dallas Myth: The Making and Unmaking of an American City*. Minneapolis: University of Minnesota Press, 2008.

Granovetter, Mark. "The Strength of Weak Ties." *American Journal of Sociology* 78 (1974): 1360–80.

Gutiérrez, José Angel. *Albert A. Peña Jr: Dean of Chicano Politics*. East Lansing: Michigan State University Press, 2017.

Haycock, Kati. "School-College Partnerships." In *Higher Education and School Reform*, edited by P. Michael Timpane and Lori S. White, 57–82. San Francisco: Jossey-Bass, 1998.

Heller, Nathan. "Is There Any Point to Protesting?" *New Yorker*, August 21, 2017. Published as "Out of Action." https://www.newyorker.com/magazine/2017/08/21/is-there-any-point-to-protesting accessed June 1, 2018.

Henson, James, and Joshua Blank. "The Demise of Local Control," *Texas Monthly*, March 30, 2017. https://www.texasmonthly.com/burka-blog/demise-local-control/. Accessed October 10, 2018.

Hero, Rodney. *Latinos and the U.S. Political System: Two-Tiered Pluralism*. Philadelphia: Temple University Press, 1992.

Hess, Frederick. *Spinning Wheels: The Politics of Urban School Reform*. Washington, D.C.: Brookings Institution, 1999.

Heyman, Josiah. "An Academic in an Activist Coalition: Recognizing and Bridging Role Conflicts." *Annals of Anthropological Practice* 35, no. 2 (2011): 136–153.

Hochschild, Arlie Russell. *Strangers in Their Own Land: Anger and Mourning on the American Right*. New York: The New Press, 2016.

Hunt III, Harry. "Houston Is Better than Dallas." *Texas Monthly,* Feb. 1978. https://www.texasmonthly.com/issue/february-1978/ Accessed Aug. 15, 2018.

Hunter, James Davison. *To Change the World: The Irony, Tragedy and Possibility of Christianity in the Late Modern World*. New York: Oxford University Press, 2010.

Ibarra, Leticia. "Microsociety: Civic Education, Academic Achievement, and Higher Education Aspirations through Experiential Learning." M.A. Thesis, Political Science, University of Texas at El Paso, 2001.

Industrial Areas Foundation, Network of Texas IAF Organizations. "A Post-2016 Texas IAF Organizing Strategy." Unpublished, 2016.

Ivins, Molly. *Who Let the Dogs In? Incredible Political Animals I have Known*. New York: Random House, 2004.

Jennings, Jay, and Emily Einsohn Bhandari. *Texas Civic Health Index*. Austin: Annette Strauss Institute for Civic Life, Moody College of Communication, University of Texas, 2018. https://moody.utexas.edu/sites/default/files/2018-Texas_Civic_Health_Index.pdf Accessed May 15, 2018.

Jillson, Cal. *Lone Star Tarnished: A Critical Look at Texas Politics and Public Policy*. New York: Routledge, 2014.

Kanter, Rosabeth. *Men and Women of the Corporation*. 2nd. ed. 1977. repr., New York: Basic Books, 1992.

King, Michael. "Point Austin: Welcome to Hard Times," *Austin Chronicle*, February 13, 2009. https://www.austinchronicle.com/news/2009-02-13/740124/ Accessed Feb. 9, 2019.

Korten, David C. "Community Organization and Rural Development: A Learning Process Approach." *Public Administration Review* 40, no. 5 (1980): 480–511.

Krochmal, Max. *Blue Texas: The Making of a Multiracial Coalition in the Civil Rights Era*. Chapel Hill: University of North Carolina Press, 2016.

Lind, Michael. *Made in Texas: George W. Bush and the Southern Takeover of American Politics*. New York: New America, 2003.

Lipsky, Michael. *Street-Level Bureaucracy: Dilemmas of the Individual in Public Service*. New York: Russell Sage Foundation, 1980.

Long, Norton. "The Local Community as an Ecology of Games." *American Journal of Sociology* 64, no. 3 (1958): 251–61.

Longoria Jr, Thomas. "School Politics in Houston: The Impact of Business Involvement." In *Changing Urban Education*, edited by Clarence N. Stone, 184–98. Lawrence: University Press of Kansas, 1998.

Lorentzen, Lois Ann, ed. *Hidden Lives and Human Rights in the United States: Understanding the Controversies and Tragedies of Undocumented Immigration*. Vols. 1–3. Santa Barbara, CA: Praeger, 2014.

Madrigal-González, Lizely. "Still 'Unfinished Education': Latino Students Forty Years after the Mexican American Education Study." EdD Dissertation. University of Texas at El Paso, 2012.

Maharidge, Dale. "The ACLU Reborn." *The Nation*, May 21, 2018, pp. 12–17.

Malesic, Jonathan. "Why Dallas Republicans Skipped an Interfaith Forum." October 16, 2018. https://rewire.news/religion-dispatches/2018/10/16/why-dallas-republicans-skipped-an-interfaith-forum/. Accessed Nov. 10, 2018.

Martin, Greg. *Understanding Social Movements*. New York and London: Routledge, 2015.

Márquez, Benjamin. *Democratizing Texas Politics: Race, Identity, and Mexican American Politics, 1945–2002*. Austin: University of Texas Press, 2014.

———. *LULAC: The Evolution of a Mexican American Political Organization*. Austin: University of Texas Press, 1993.

———. "Mexican-American Political Organizations and Philanthropy: Bankrolling a Social Movement." *Social Science Review* 77, no. 3 (September 2003): 329–46.

———. "Organizing Mexican-American Women in the Garment Industry: La Mujer Obrera," *Women & Politics* 15, no. 1 (1995): 65–87.

———. "Trial by Fire: The Ford Foundation and MALDEF in the 1960s." *Politics, Groups, and Identities* 2018 (online)

Martínez, Oscar. *Border People: Life and Society in the U.S.-Mexico Borderlands*. Tucson: University of Arizona Press, 1994.

Mediratta, Kavitha, Seema Shah, and Sara McAlister. *Building Partnerships to Reinvent School Culture*: Austin Interfaith, Annenberg Institute for School Reform at Brown University, May, 2009. http://www.annenberginstitute.org/sites/default/files/product/845/files/Mott_Austin.pdf Accessed May 15.

———. *Community Organizing for Stronger Schools: Strategies and Successes*. Cambridge: Harvard Education Press, 2009.

Michels, Robert. *Political Parties: A Sociological Study of the Oligarchical Tendencies of Modern Democracy*. 1911. repr., New York: Free Press, 1962, 1968.

Mizrahi, Terry and Jessica Greenwalt. "Women's Ways of Organizing: Strengths and Struggles of Women Activists over Time." *Affilia* 22, no. 1 (2007): 39–55.

Molotch, Harry. "The City as a Growth Machine: Toward a Political Economy of Place." *American Journal of Sociology* 82, no. 4 (1976): 309–332.

Montoya, Lisa J. "Gender and Citizenship in Latino Political Participation." In *Latinos Remaking America*, edited by Marcelo M. Suárez-Orozco and Mariela M. Páez, 410–429. Berkeley: University of California Press, 2008.

Mullen, Lincoln. "The Fight to Define Romans 13." *The Atlantic*, June 15, 2018 https://www.theatlantic.com/ideas/archive/2018/06/romans-13/562916/ Accessed July 1, 2018.

Muller, Jerry Z. *The Tyranny of Metrics*. Princeton: Princeton University Press, 2018.

National Assessment of Educational Progress (NAEP). *U.S. History, Geography, and Civics Assessments*. 2014. https://www.nationsreportcard.gov/hgc_2014/ Accessed Oct. 22, 2018.

Navarro, Sharon, and Rodolfo Rosales, eds. *The Roots of Latino Urban Agency*. Denton: University of North Texas Press, 2013.

Oakes, Jeannie, and John Rogers. *Learning Power: Organizing for Education and Justice*. New York: Teachers College Press, Columbia University, 2006.

O'Loughlin, Michael J. "Bishop Stowe: Why the MAGA Hats at the March for Life?" *America: The Jesuit Review*. 2019. https://www.americamagazine.org/politics-society/2019/01/24/bishop-stowe-why-maga-hats-march-life. Accessed Feb. 1, 2019.

Olson, Mancur. *The Logic of Collective Action: Public Goods and the Theory of Groups*. Cambridge: Harvard University Press, 1965.

Orr, Marion. "The Changing Ecology of Civic Engagement." In *Transforming the City: Community Organizing and the Challenge of Political Change*, edited by Marion Orr, 1–27. Lawrence: University Press of Kansas, 2007.

Orr, Marion, ed. *Transforming the City: Community Organizing and the Challenge of Political Change*. Lawrence: University Press of Kansas, 2007.

Osterman, Paul. *Gathering Power: The Future of Progressive Politics in America*. Boston: Beacon Press, 2003.

Pardo, Mary. *Mexican American Women Activists: Identity and Resistance in Two Los Angeles Communities*. Philadelphia: Temple University Press, 1998.

Parpart, Jane, Shirin Rai, and Kathleen Staudt, eds. *Rethinking Empowerment: Gender and Development in the Global/Local World*. New York: Routledge, 2002.

Parra, Mary Alicia. "A Case Study of Leadership in Systemic Education Reform." EdD dissertation, University of Texas at El Paso, 2002.

Pastor, Manuel. *State of Resistance: What California's Dizzying Descent and Remarkable Resurgence Mean for America's Future*. New York: The Free Press, 2018.

Pendall, Rolf with Carl Hedman. *Worlds Apart: Inequality between America's Most and Least Affluent Neighborhoods*. Washington, D.C.: Urban Institute, 2015.

Pew Research Center Religion & Public Life. "Attendance at Religious Services," (2014 data) Pew: Washington, DC. http://www.pewforum. org/religious-landscape-study/attendance-at-religious-services/ Accessed July 1, 2018.

Phillips, Michael. *White Metropolis: Race, Ethnicity, and Religion in Dallas, 1841–2001*. Austin: University of Texas Press, 2006.

Pollock, Cassandra, Carlos Anchondo, and Allyson Walker. "Democratic Women lead Biggest Shift in Texas House since 2010 Midterms," November 6, 2018. Accessed Nov. 15, 2018 https://www.texastribune. org/2018/11/06/texas-midterm-election-results-texas-house-races/

Pressman, Jeffrey, and Aaron Wildavsky. Implementation. 3rd ed. Berkeley: University of California Press, 1984.

Putnam, Robert, and David Campbell. *American Grace: How Religion Unites and Divides Us*. New York: Simon & Schuster, 2010.

Rippberger, Susan, and Kathleen Staudt. *Pledging Allegiance: Learning Nationalism in El Paso-Juárez*. New York: RoutledgeFalmer, 2003.

Risher, Robert, and Eric Shragge. "Contextualizing Community Organizing: Lessons from the Past, Tensions in the Present, Opportunities for the Future." In *Transforming the City: Community Organizing and the Challenge of Political Change*, edited by Marion Orr, 193–217. Lawrence: University Press of Kansas, 2007.

Ripps, Geoff. "Alliances in Public Schools." *Texas Observer*, October 11, 1996, pp. 13–14.

Rocha, Gregory, and Robert Webking. *Politics and Public Education: Edgewood v. Kirby and the Reform of Public School Financing in Texas*. 2nd ed. Minneapolis: West, 1993.

Rogers, Mary Beth. *Cold Anger: A Story of Faith and Power Politics*. Denton: University of North Texas Press, 1990.

———. *Turning Texas Blue: What It Will Take to Break the GOP Grip on America's Reddest State*. New York: St. Martin's Press, 2016.

Romero, Manuela, and Tracy Yellen. *El Paso Portraits: Women's Lives, Potential and Opportunities. A Report on the State of Women in El Paso, Texas*. El Paso: UTEP Center for Civic Engagement and YWCA Paso del Norte Region, 2004.

Rosales, Rodolfo. *The Illusion of Inclusion: The Untold Political Story of San Antonio*. Austin: University of Texas Press, 2000.

Schladen, Marty. "Mark Success, Shape Future: Religious Organizations Gather on 40th Anniversary," *El Paso Times*, April 30, 2016, pp. 1–2B.

Schutze, Jim. *The Accommodation: The Politics of Race in an American City*. Seacaucus, NJ: Citadel Press, 1986.

Schwartz, Mimi. "Troubled Waters: A Year after Harvey, has Houston Learned Anything?" *Texas Monthly*, August 22, 2018, Accessed Sept. 1, 2018. https://www.texasmonthly.com/news/harvey-anniversary-houston-preparing-next-big-storm/

Selznick, Philip. *TVA and the Grass Roots: A Study in the Sociology of Formal Organizations*. 1949. repr., New Orleans: Quid Pro Books, 2011.

Sharp, John. *Bordering the Future: Challenge and Opportunity in the Texas Border Region*. Austin: Texas State Comptroller, 1998.

Shirley, Dennis. *Community Organizing for Urban School Reform*. Austin: University of Texas Press, 1997.

———. *Valley Interfaith and School Reform: Organizing for Power in South Texas*. Austin: University of Texas Press, 2002.

Silverman, Lauren. "How the Death of a 12-year Old Changed the City of Dallas," https://www.npr.org/sections/codeswitch/2013/07/24/205121429/How-The-Death-Of-A-12-Year-Old-Changed-The-City-Of-Dallas, July 24, 2013. Accessed Nov. 2, 2018.

Skopcol, Theda and Vanessa Williamson. *The Tea Party and the Remaking of Republican Conservatism*. New York: Oxford University Press, 2013.

Slattery, James. *High School Voter Registration: How Texas Still Fails to Engage the Next Generation of Voters*. Austin: Texas Civil Rights Project, July 2018. https://texascivilrightsproject.org/wp-content/uploads/2018/07/2018-HSVR-Compliance-Report.pdf. Accessed Aug. 1, 2018.

Smarsh, Sarah. "How the American Left Is Rediscovering Morality." *The Guardian*, August 4, 2018. https://www.theguardian.com/us-news/2018/aug/04/american-left-morality-alexandria-ocasio-cortez-bernie-sanders Accessed Aug. 4, 2018.

Smith, Morgan. "A Possible Deal on Testing, Charter School Bills," *Texas Tribune*, May 23, 2013. https://www.texastribune.org/2013/05/23/governor-playing-role-in-testing-bill-talks/ Accessed Aug. 1, 2018.

Stall, Susan, and Randy Stoecker. "Community Organizing or Organizing Community? Gender and the Crafts of Empowerment." *Gender and Society* 12, no. 6 (1998): 729–756.

Stall, Susan, and Randy Stoecker. "Toward a Gender Analysis of Community Organizing Models: Liminality and the Intersection of Spheres." In *Community Organizing and Community Building for Health*, edited by Meredith Minkler, 196–217. New Brunswick, NJ: Rutgers University Press, 2004. http://homepages.neiu.edu/~sociolgy/facSStall.html

Staudt, Kathleen. *Border Politics in a Global Era: Comparative Perspectives*. Lanham, MD: Rowman & Littlefield, 2017.

———. "Democracy Education for More than the Few." In *Developing Democratic Character in the Young*, edited by Roger Soder, 45–68. San Francisco: Jossey Bass, 2001.

———. "Listening Sessions: TAKS and the Accountability System." Presentation to the Texas Select Committee on Public School Accountability. August 4, 2008.

———. *Managing Development: State, Society, and International Contexts*. Newbury Park, CA: Sage Publications, 1991.

———. "Neoliberal Regimes, Research Methods, Local Activism: Border Steel, Environmental Injustice, and Health in a Texas-Mexico Border *Colonia*." In *The Mexico-U.S. Transborder Region: Cultural Dynamics and Historical Interactions*, edited by Carlos Vélez-Ibáñez and Josiah Heyman, 305–21. University of Arizona Press, 2017.

———. *Violence and Activism at the Border: Gender, Fear, and Everyday Life in Ciudad Juárez*. Austin: University of Texas Press, 2008.

Staudt, Kathleen, and Jack Bristol. "Educational Renewal Across College Borders: El Paso Strategies Toward Change." *Making a Place for Change in Higher Education*. Washington, DC: American Association for Higher Education, 1999.

Staudt, Kathleen, and Irasema Coronado. *Fronteras no Más: Toward Social Justice at the U.S.-Mexico Border*. New York: Palgrave, 2002.

Staudt, Kathleen, Mosi Dane'el, and Guadalupe Márquez-Velarde. "In the Shadow of a Steel Recycling Plant in these Global Neoliberal Times: The Political Economy of Health Disparities among Hispanics in a Border *Colonia*," *Local Environment* 21, no. 5 (March, 2016): 636–52.

Staudt, Kathleen, César Fuentes, and Julia Monárrez Fragoso. *Cities and Citizenship at the U.S.-Mexico Border: The Paso del Norte Metropolitan Region*. New York: Palgrave Macmillan, 2010.

Staudt, Kathleen, Guadalupe Márquez-Velarde, and Mosi Dane'el. "Stories, Science and Power in Policy Change: Environmental Health, Community-Based Research, and Community Organizing in a U.S.-Mexico Border *Colonia*," *Environmental Justice* 6, no. 6 (2013): 191–99.

Staudt, Kathleen, and Josiah Heyman. "Immigrants Organize Against Every-day Life Victimization." In *The Immigrant Other: Lived Experiences in a Transnational World*, edited by Rich Furman, Greg Lamphear, and Douglas Epps, 75–89. New York: Columbia University Press, 2016.

Staudt, Kathleen, and Zulma Méndez. "Schooling for Global Competitive-ness in the Border Metropolitan Region," with Zulma Méndez. In *Cities and Citizenship at the U.S.-Mexico Border: The Paso del Norte Metro-politan Region*, edited by Kathleen Staudt, César Fuentes, and Julia Monárrez Fragoso, 173–194. New York: Palgrave Macmillan, 2010.

Staudt, Kathleen, and Clarence N. Stone. "Division and Fragmentation: The El Paso Experience in Global-Local Perspective," In *Transform-ing the City: Community Organizing and the Challenge of Political Change*, edited by Marion Orr, 84–108. Lawrence: University Press of Kansas, 2007.

Stiehm, Judith. *Bring Me Men and Women: Mandated Change at the U.S. Air Force Academy*. Berkeley: University of California Press, 1981.

Stoecker, Randy, and Elizabeth Tryon. *The Unheard Voices: Community Organizations and Service Learning*. Philadelphia: Temple Univer-sity Press, 2009.

Stone, Clarence N., Jeffrey R. Henig, Bryan D. Jones, Carol Pierannunzi. *Building Civic Capacity: The Politics of Reforming Urban Schools*. Lawrence: University Press of Kansas, 2001.

Stone, Clarence N., ed. *Changing Urban Education*. Lawrence: Univer-sity Press of Kansas, 1998.

Stone, Deborah. *Policy Paradox: The Art of Political Decision Making*. 3rd. ed. New York: W. W. Norton, 2012.

Storrar, William, and Katie Day, eds. "Special Issue—Faith-Based Organizing in the USA." *International Journal of Public Theology* 6, no. 4 (2012).

Stout, Jeffrey. *Blessed Are the Organized: Grassroots Democracy in America*. Princeton: Princeton University Press, 2010.

Swartz, Mimi. "Troubled Waters: A Year after Harvey, Has Houston Learned Anything?" *Texas Monthly,* September, 2018. https://www.texasmonthly.com/news/harvey-anniversary-houston-preparing-next-big-storm/ Accessed Sept. 15, 2018.

Swearingen, Jr. William Scott. *Environmental City: People, Place, Poli-tics, and the Meaning of Modern Austin*. Austin: University of Texas Press, 2010.

Tarrow, Sidney. *Power in Movement: Social Movements and Contentious Politics*. 2nd ed. New York: Cambridge University Press, 1998.

Texas Legislative Study Group. "Texas on the Brink." March 2013. http://www.austincc.edu/kseago/spring2013/2306/TexasOnTheBrink2013.pdf Accessed Nov. 24, 2018.

Texas State Historical Association, *Texas Almanac, 2018–19*. Austin: TSHA, 2018.

Tyack, David, and Larry Cuban. *Tinkering toward Utopia: A Century of Public School Change*. Cambridge: Harvard University Press, 1995.

U.S. Commission on Civil Rights. *Mexican American Education Study*, Volumes I–VI. Washington, D.C.: USCCR, 1969–74.

U.S. Conference of Catholic Bishops. *Forming Consciences for Faithful Citizenship*. Washington, D.C.: USCCB, 2015.

U.S. Conference of Catholic Bishops. *Strangers No Longer: Together on the Journey of Hope*. Washington, D.C.: USCCB, 2003.

University of Texas at San Antonio (UTSA) Archives, Library Special Collections, John Peace Library, "A Guide to C.O.P.S./Metro Alliance 1954–2009," MS 346 (multiple boxes, cited in footnotes).

Ura, Alexa and Jolie McCullough. "Meet your 84th Legislative Session: White. Male. Middle-Aged. Christian. *Texas Tribune* January 14, 2015. Accessed July 1, 2018.

Ura, Alexa, and Elbert Wang. "Poverty in Texas Drops to Lowest Levels in More than a Decade." September 13, 2018. https://www.texastribune.org/2018/09/13/texas-poverty-census-2017-lowest-levels-decade/?utm_source=Texas+Tribune+Master&utm_campaign=08cf60527c-trib-newsletters-the-brief&utm_medium=email&utm_term=0_d9a68d8efc-08cf60527c-101202457&mc_cid=08cf60527c&mc_eid=3b3e7d7416. Accessed Oct. 1, 2018.

Valenzuela, Angela. *Subtractive Schooling: U.S.-Mexican Youth and the Politics of Caring*. Albany: SUNY Albany Press, 1999.

Valenzuela, Angela. *Leaving Children Behind: How Texas-Style Accountability Fails Latino Youth*. Albany: SUNY Albany Press, 2005.

Vock, Daniel. "The End of Local Laws? War on Cities Intensifies," *Governing*, April 5, 2017.

Walsh, Sean Collins. "Faith Group: Bastrop Sheriff Maurice Cook Targeted Latino Neighborhood," *Austin American Statesman*, 2018. https://www.statesman.com/news/20180703/faith-group-bastrop-sheriff-maurice-cook-targeted-latino-neighborhood Accessed Aug. 1, 2018.

Warren, Mark R. "Communities and Schools: A New View of Urban Education Reform." *Harvard Educational Review* 75, no. 2 (2005): 133–73.

Warren, Mark R. *Dry Bones Rattling: Community Building to Revitalize American Democracy*. Princeton: Princeton University Press, 2001.

Wilson, James Q. *Bureaucracy: What Government Agencies Do and Why They Do It*. New York: Basic Books, 1989.

Wilson, James Q. *Political Organizations*. 1973, 2nd ed. New York: Basic Books, 1995.

Wilson, Robert H., ed. *Public Policy and Community: Activism and Governance in Texas*. Austin: University of Texas Press, 1997.

Wilson, Robert H., and Peter Menzies, 1997. "The Colonias Water Bill." In *Public Policy and Community: Activism and Governance in Texas*, edited by Robert H. Wilson, 229–274. Austin: University of Texas Press, 1997.

Wood, Richard L. "Higher Power: Strategic Capacity for State and National Organizing," In *Transforming the City: Community Organizing and the Challenge of Political Change*, edited by Marion Orr, 162–192. Lawrence: University Press of Kansas, 2007.

Wood, Richard, and Brad Fulton. *A Shared Future: Faith-based Organizing for Racial Equity and Ethical Democracy*. Chicago: University of Chicago Press, 2015.

Wong, Pat. 1997. "The Indigent Health Care Package." In *Public Policy and Community: Activism and Governance in Texas*, edited by Robert H. Wilson, 95–118. Austin: University of Texas Press, 1997.

Worth, Michael. *Nonprofit Management: Principles and Practices*. 4th ed. Thousand Oaks: Sage Publications, 2017.

Wright, Lawrence. "The Future Is Texas." *The New Yorker*, July 10, 17, 2017, pp. 40–63.

Wright, Lawrence. *God Save Texas: A Journey into the Soul of the Lone Star State*. New York: Alfred A. Knopf, 2018.

Young, Stephen. "Dallas Area Had Highest Number of ICE Arrests in the Country in 2017, New Study Says," *Dallas Observer*, February 14, 2018. https://www.dallasobserver.com/news/ice-arrested-more-people-in-dallas-than-anywhere-else-in-2017-10367404 Accessed February 5, 2019.

Zdun, Matt. "State Appeals Court says Austin's Paid Sick Leave Ordinance is Unconstitutional," *Texas Tribune*, 2018 https://www.texastribune.org/2018/11/16/appeals-court-blocks-austins-paid-sick-leave-ordinance/?utm_source=Texas+Tribune+Master&utm_campaign=db341b85cd-trib-newsletters-the-brief&utm_medium=email&utm_term=0_d9a68d8efc-db341b85cd-101202457&mc_cid=db341b85cd&mc_eid=3b3e7d7416 Accessed Nov. 19, 2018.

Zeig, Susan. *A Community Concern: A Documentary about Communities Who Refuse to Accept the System's Failure and Are Working for Change*. New York: Women Make Movies, 2009. www.acommunityconcern.org

Index